Who Am I in the Lives of Children?

Who Am I in the Lives of Children?

An Introduction to Teaching Young Children

Third Edition

Stephanie Feeney
University of Hawaii

Doris Christensen
Parent-Child Center of Hawaii

Eva Moravcik
Honolulu Community College

Photographs by Hella Hammid

Merrill Publishing Company
A Bell & Howell Information Company
Columbus Toronto London Melbourne

Cover Photo: Hella Hammid

Published by Merrill Publishing Company
A Bell & Howell Information Company
Columbus, Ohio 43216

This book was set in Usherwood

Administrative Editor: Jeff Johnston
Production Coordinator: Linda Hillis Bayma
Cover Designer: Cathy Watterson
Text Designer: Cynthia Brunk

Library of Congress Catalog Card Number: 86-62350
International Standard Book Number: 0-675-20567-0
Printed in the United States of America
    2   3   4   5   6   7   8   9 — 91   90   89   88   87

For Zachary

Foreword

We have all probably heard it said that good teachers are born, not made. This expression has been around for a long time which is too bad because there's only a grain of truth in it and a lot of error. While it certainly helps teachers of young children to have been born with a strong body, good eyes, keen hearing, quick reflexes, a generous share of brains, a strong back, and healthy arches, the expression is completely wrong in denying that good teachers are *made*. As teachers move about the classroom—dealing with behavior, providing instruction, coping with problems, and, most of all, preventing problems—they continuously call on skills and techniques that have become second nature to them. There is no end to their tricks of the trade. The notion that there is nothing made about the good teacher is an absurdity. No one is born with a skilled teacher's know-how. You have to learn it, both in your training and on the job.

One important strength of *Who Am I in the Lives of Children?* is its multiplicity of these practical, down-to-earth approaches in early childhood education. Interspersed throughout the text are pages of guidelines, strategies, and suggestions for coping with the many troublesome parts of teaching. Over and over the reader comes upon the statement: "We have found in our experience . . . " and then realistic, sound ideas follow.

The material on this and the next page appeared as the foreword to the second edition.

But much as I admire this flow of valuable, concrete specifics, I admire even more the underlying concepts behind the practical approach. The authors see that teachers are made, but they also see that a teacher is more than a bundle of tricks. While a teacher is made through good professional training, a teacher is also a whole human, a product of inheritance (that grain of truth mentioned earlier), a product of professional training, *and* a product of all kinds of day-by-day experiences: as a child, as an adolescent, and as an adult. The authors respect the fact that the whole life we lead helps to make us good teachers. We teach out of all that we are: everything that has happened and happens to us, all the joys, all the sorrows. This book respects that human in you, the reader, as you are getting ready to teach or are already out on a job.

As the authors present their myriad of good ideas, they do it in such a way that the reader becomes a part of the process. The ideas stand a better chance of ending up incorporated as part of the reader's perceptions, rather than remaining the authors'. This is particularly remarkable because the authors do not hide their own points of view. Time and again they use words like: "We are convinced . . ." or "We find we are no longer able to support educational approaches that . . ."

But the authors know that if teachers are to respect children, they themselves must be respected. Convinced of this, they are primarily concerned with the development of thoughtful teachers. They want people in the classroom who go through a never-ending process of questioning about themselves, about children, about the world children live in. Over and over they ask such questions as: "What are your values?" "What are you after?" "What is worth knowing when you are age two, three, four, and five?" "What are the ethical implications of this or that practice?" In its whole design the book says to the reader: "Think, don't memorize; question, don't simply accept." The book presents a chart and says: "This is designed to help you choose . . . " It makes statements like "both self-contained and open-design classrooms can be effective, and both have draw-backs" and invites the reader to be the judge.

Studying a book like this is not the easy way to become a teacher, but it *is* the way to become a good teacher. Young children need teachers who are not machines, not simply memories. They need people with searching hearts and seeking minds, people who are always trying better to understand themselves, their job, their young charges, and the world around them.

Many changes affecting young children have taken place since I wrote my earlier Foreword. The pressures on family life have steadily mounted: continuing increases in divorce and separation; steady rises in the number of mothers in the labor force and the number of single parents; the persistence of poverty for too many of us; the danger of war for all. . . . These have gone hand-in-hand with school changes. The need for top-quality child care, as far down the age-range as infancy, has become increasingly clear. The number of kindergartens for fives has vastly increased. There are strong movements to make kindergarten attendance compulsory, to lengthen the school day, to lower the entrance age to public school to four. These have not been times that easily, automatically build stability into children's lives.

This new edition makes a worthy contribution in this situation. The earlier strengths are all here: the clarity of the authors' stands; their down-to-earth specificity meshed with wide-ranging concerns for values and ethics; the richness of their own experiences; their honesty; their concern for the reader as a human . . . plus new content.

The adage warns, "If it's not broke, don't fix it." The earlier edition wasn't "broke" but it is even better now. And very welcome at a time when more and more children, more vulnerable, are apt to be in groups at younger and younger ages for longer and longer hours. The need for sensitive, skilled teachers is especially keen. Those who read this book, puzzling and thinking as they do it, are sure to join that number.

Carmel, California   James L. Hymes, Jr.

Preface

This book is about being a teacher of young children. We wrote it because of the need for a text that reflected the view that the personal development of teachers and their ability to work effectively with young children are inextricably linked. *Who Am I in the Lives of Children?* is an introduction to teaching which has been used in two- and four-year college programs of early childhood teacher education for courses in foundations and curriculum. We have also used it for Child Development Associate (CDA) training and the continuing education of teachers already working in the field.

Since the publication of the second edition, we have continued to work with children, parents, and teachers and have gained new knowledge. The third edition of *Who Am I in the Lives of Children?* has been expanded to include some clarification and rethinking of old ideas and to reflect some of our new knowledge and awareness. It is designed to provide information and activities that will help our readers to become competent and nurturing teachers of young children.

Our basic values and our concern with the total development of the child remain the same. We continue to choose from current approaches those which support the development of children and adults in both thought and feeling. We retain our commitment to individual choices, clarification of values, and diversity of program approaches. We encourage teachers to make their own decisions, develop self-knowledge, and acquire an individual philosophy and style of teaching.

Each chapter is constructed to help teachers and prospective teachers to gain awareness, gain essential knowledge, and develop needed skills in one area of early childhood education. Some material is presented graphically for easier understanding. Chapters conclude with questions and topics for further thought and discussion, projects designed to encourage application of the concepts presented, and a list of books and articles that will help students to extend their learning on each topic.

In this new edition we have done substantial revision and rewriting; we have combined the chapters on the field of early childhood education and historical roots, and teaching and surviving in the classroom, and present areas of the curriculum as four separate chapters instead of one large chapter as in the previous edition. We have added new sections on play and learning, and on the most current research on the development of literacy in young children, and look at the use of computers in early childhood education programs and the prevention of sexual abuse. We have also highlighted the CDA competencies addressed in the introduction to each chapter.

We had hoped for a miraculous change in English language usage that would save us from choosing between sexist language (calling the teacher *she* and the child *he* as we did in our first edition) and the sometimes awkward use of plurals that we used in the second edition. No such change has occurred, so we will continue the convention from the last edition and speak of teachers and children in the plural whenever possible and use *he* and *she* only when we mean a particular individual.

Acknowledgments

We wish to thank the many special people who have helped us to shape our ideas about young children and how to work with them, and who have provided us with invaluable assistance in writing this book. First and most important, we thank the children we have worked with and who have taught us so much. Much of our insight and thinking has been inspired by and shared with the people who have taught with us in programs for children and in programs for college students. We wish to acknowledge and thank them for their vital contribution. We also acknowledge our gratitude to students in the early childhood programs at the University of Hawaii and Honolulu Community College. We continue to learn and grow from our association with the Early School in Honolulu, a truly caring community; we especially appreciate their attention to relationships and to the quality of the experiences they provide for children and families.

Once again we want to express our gratitude for the contributions of our dear friend and colleague, Jean Fargo. She's a splendid model for us of an inquiring mind and the combination of caring and rigorous thought. We have learned a great deal from her about respecting people's best efforts and basing choices on clarification of values. This book would never have been created without her contributions to our understanding of the teaching/learning process.

Graduate students in early childhood at the University of Hawaii, both past and present, have been a tremendous source of intellectual stimulation, feedback, and assistance in the thinking and writing process. Our special thanks to Robyn Chun, Indira Fenkell, Mary Goya, Christine Jackson, Mary Ann Lester, Carol Phelps, Kathleen Reinhardt, Joan Senda, and LaVerna Westfall. Thanks also to Cyndi Uyehara and Linda Sysko for their support and assistance.

Chapter 14, "Children with Special Needs," was originally researched and written by Christine Jackson with support from a Dean's Grant for Mainstreaming from the Bureau of Education for the Handicapped of the U.S. Office of Education. Revisions for this edition were made by Linda Buck. The discussion of the development of literacy in Chapter 12 was researched and drafted by Kathleen Reinhardt, a graduate student at the University of Hawaii specializing in early language development. Some of the new material on children's play in this edition was abstracted from LaVerna Westfall's master's project at the University of Hawaii, "Helping Parents Understand the Difference Between Play and Learning." We thank her for letting us use her work. Much of the section on the music curriculum for young children was drawn from Anita Trubitt's module on music written for the University of Hawaii early childhood program.

Work on professional ethics in early childhood education, presented in Chapter 3, was developed by Stephanie Feeney and philosophers Kenneth Kipnis and Fred Elliston under a grant to develop workshops on ethics in early childhood education from the Wallace Alexander Gerbode Foundation. Ken Kipnis also offered invaluable assistance in helping us clarify our understanding of values and ethics and in writing the section of the chapter on ethics. We appreciate his willingness to share his expertise with us.

We are also indebted to many friends and colleagues who have shared their ideas and experiences and helped us to shape our thinking over the years. We would especially like to acknowledge the contributions of Hannah Lou Bennett, Carole Darcy, Jackie Dudock, Richard Feldman, Elizabeth Gilkeson, Kay Goines, Vivian Halverson, Elizabeth Jones, Marion Magarick, Anthony J. Picard, Anita Trubitt, and William T. Wright Jr., M.D.

We continue to be grateful to Roger Whitlock for raising our consciousness about writing and for introducing us to Peter Elbow's approach to criticism and editing. We offer special thanks to Jeffrey Reese for taking on the arduous task of entering previous text material into the computer. We have enjoyed working with Bev Kolz, the very supportive executive editor at Merrill Publishing, and also wish to acknowledge copy editor Carol Noel, production coordinator Linda Bayma, and the fine work of text designer Cindy Brunk.

Hella Hammid is an extraordinary photographer of children, and we are delighted to be able to feature her work in this book. We are also pleased that she was able to take some new photographs especially for this edition. Hella's photographs communicate the experience of childhood with power and sensitivity that we are sure will add to your enjoyment of *Who Am I in the Lives of Children*.

Photographs for this book were taken in California and Hawaii at Pacific Oaks Children's School, The Harold E. Jones Child Study Center, Maggie Haves School, John Adams Child Development Center, Beverly Hills Montessori School, the Clay Street Center, The Early School, Rainbow School, St. Timothy's Children's Center, Hanahauoli School, Parent Infant Child Care Services, Inc., St. Thomas Parish Preschool, Hill n' Dale Family Learning Center, Early Years School, and The Children's Place. We appreciate cooperation from the children, staff, and parents at these schools. Our thanks to Anna Belle Kaufman and Linda Gordon for their assistance in setting up sites for photographs and to Anne Barlin for allowing us to use photographs taken for her book, *Teaching Your Wings to Fly*. Thanks, too, to Marcia Berman, a talented children's song writer and performer, for setting up a special session with children for us to photograph.

No book is written without affecting the lives of the authors' friends and families. We thank, appreciate, and offer apologies to those closest to us who supported our efforts with patience and good humor, especially Dylan Stanfield and Jeffrey Reese.

S.F.
D.C.
E.M.

Contents

5 Observation and Evaluation 105

6 The Child in School 129

7 The Learning Environment   151

8 Relationships and Classroom Management   179

Who Am I in the Lives of Children?

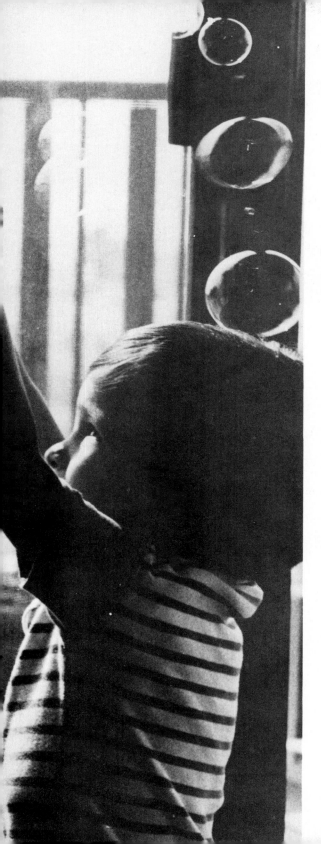

Introduction

When we wrote the first edition of *Who Am I in the Lives of Children?,* our primary purpose was to provide an overview of early childhood education. We also wished to help our readers understand themselves as people and as teachers and to assist them in choosing wisely from a variety of educational alternatives. Our intention was to speak to the needs of teachers and prospective teachers in a clear and personal way. We are pleased that so many of our readers have expressed their appreciation for the personal voice and direct style we use. Our goal for the third edition remains the same and continues to be reflected in a personal style of address.

When we read books we like to know who wrote them, why they wrote them, and about the authors' feelings and experiences with the subject. We want to include that kind of personal sharing in our book, so that you can know something about us, our beliefs, and how you want to respond to us. As we said in the first edition, this book grows out of our experience: as children, as adults, as learners, as teachers. Our childhood experiences in school included developmental nursery schools much like those we describe; large, dreary, anonymous public schools; a small multinational school in Europe; and a one-room country school with a teacher who truly cared about children.

Although our childhood experiences were very different, we have, as adults, many of the same feelings and ideas about education. We have visited and worked in schools that were happy, productive places and in schools that were mindless and destructive. We have met and worked with teachers who have been an inspiration to us in their ability to teach and relate to children, and we have known teachers who seemed to stifle the natural exuberance of childhood. We share a strong commitment to supporting those programs that nurture children and adults in caring and loving ways.

Although we believe that there are many ways to be a good teacher of young children and that there are many different kinds of programs that support children's growth and learning, we advocate a *developmental* approach to early childhood education. Developmental programs have their roots in a long tradition of education that goes back to Plato and in a more recent tradition of preschool education that originated in England at the beginning of this century. These programs are dedicated to the total development of the child—physical, social, emotional, and intellectual—and are characterized by a deep respect for the individual and the recognition that individual differences need to be responded to in educational settings. Teachers in these programs begin with children as they are and try to understand and help them grow in ways that are right for the individual child rather than according to a predetermined plan. They look at children in terms of potential to be "actualized" and not pathology to be corrected or an empty slate to be written upon.

Our ideas have been profoundly shaped by the field of early childhood education which has a unique history and philosophy. Within this field we have been directly and personally influenced by many fine educators including Barbara Biber, Barbara Bowman, Elizabeth Brady, Elizabeth Gilkeson, James L. Hymes, Lilian Katz, Elizabeth Jones, Daniel Jordan, and

2

Docia Zavitkovsky. We draw heavily on the work in psychology and human development of Margaret Donaldson, Erik Erikson, Thomas Gordon, Margaret Mahler, Abraham Maslow, Jean Piaget, Carl Rogers, and L.S. Vygotsky. We have also learned from child therapists and teachers who have shared their feelings and insights about children through their writing. These include among others Sylvia Ashton-Warner, Bruno Bettelheim, George Dennison, John Holt, Herb Kohl, and A. S. Neill.

There are many approaches to teaching others to teach. We believe that teachers cannot be taught to subscribe to a single viewpoint of education or approach to teaching. We feel strongly that *you* must create yourself as a teacher. Each college education instructor has a different idea of what is right or best for young children and what is desirable practice. Often, however, prospective teachers are not given the guidance they need to discover what they value and what they want for children or how to put the pieces together into a coherent whole. As a result, they have little chance to develop their own philosophy and teaching style. The traditional approach to preparing teachers to teach is comparable to making a clay figure by forming the pieces—head, arms, legs—and sticking them onto a central core. Students are given many pieces, but often are not shown how to make them hold together. Like clay figures which fall apart when subjected to stress, these teachers often find themselves inadequately prepared for a classroom filled with lively, unpredictable young children.

Our approach to teaching students to teach is more like creating a clay figure in which each part is shaped from the central piece of clay. Such an approach,

we have found, produces teachers whose work with children is an integral part of who they are. Thus, our approach is designed to assist in your personal, as well as your professional, development; in fact, we see the two as inextricably linked. Each person develops differently as a teacher because each has a different personality, different experiences, abilities, and values. We don't want every person who uses this book to come to the same conclusions or to teach the same way. We encourage you to develop your own teaching style and philosophy based on the best information now available in our field, and we hope to help you to do just that.

You will engage in several processes as you study to become a teacher of young children. You will develop an awareness of yourself as a person and as a potential teacher by examining your own values, experiences, and personal qualities. You will acquire knowledge about child development and early childhood education. And then you will put what you have learned about yourself and about children into practice and thus gain the basic skills that you need to work in an early childhood setting. Each chapter in this book is designed to increase your awareness, to give you information, and to help you develop skills in working with young children. We have divided each chapter into five parts:

Overview   The first paragraph of the chapter acquaints you with its purpose and the kinds of information that will be presented. In it we also tell you how the chapter relates to CDA, the Child Development Associate, a national competency-based child care credential.

Text of the Chapter   Each chapter contains an organizing framework and concepts and information needed to gain a basic understanding of the topic. In the chapter on the learning environment and in the curriculum chapters, we provide checklists to guide you in observing and evaluating classroom practice.

Questions for Further Thought and Discussion   These provide an opportunity to discover the meaning each chapter has for you and to share your insights, feelings, and experiences with others.

Projects   These activities (usually written) allow you to apply information from the chapter to your direct classroom experience with children and thus develop greater understanding and skill.

Recommended Reading   To enable you to find out more about subjects of interest or concern we have provided a list of reading materials which we have used, enjoyed, and found helpful.

Following the last chapter, we provide a list of references by chapter to let you know what materials we consulted as we did our research.

This book is organized so that each chapter lays the foundation for those that follow. The organization can be graphically represented in terms of a triangle (see Figure 1). A firm foundation is essential for strength and durability. The first four chapters, *The Field of Early Childhood Education, The Teacher of Young Children, Values and Ethics in Early Childhood Education,* and *Child Development,* present information and assumptions that form the base for all of our work with children.

Chapter 5, *Observation and Evaluation,* introduces basic and extremely valuable tools in your work in early childhood programs. You will use your observation skills to look not only at children, but also at programs, activities, relationships, environments, and yourself. This idea, found on the left of the triangle, intersects all of the levels.

Chapter 6, *The Child in School,* explores meeting the physical and emotional needs of children. Chapter 7, *The Learning Environment,* discusses the importance of the planned environment on children's learning and development. Chapter 8,

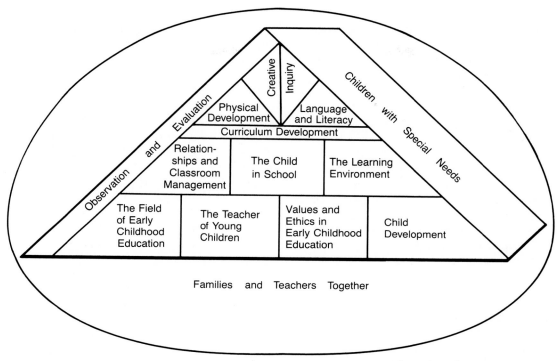

FIGURE 1

Relationships and Classroom Management, deals with the development of nurturing teacher-child relationships and how to support children's relationships and their ability to work in groups. These chapters describe how you can create and implement a good daily program for young children. They are closest to the base of the triangle because they provide the structure and raw materials for living and learning in school that need to be established before you can deal with curriculum effectively.

Chapters on curriculum are placed at the apex of the triangle, founded upon all of the rest. Chapter 9, *Curriculum Development,* deals with how teachers can plan meaningful learning experiences for young children. The next four chapters,

10–13, deal with four broad areas of early childhood curriculum: physical, creative, language and literacy, and inquiry.

In Chapter 14, *Working with Children with Special Needs,* we look at how all the previous information can be applied to provide learning experiences for children with special needs in the regular class-room. You will probably want to get an overview of the chapter first and later focus in more depth on sections regarding conditions that may be relevant to a particular child you are working with and about whom you might have concerns. Our triangle indicates that all of the areas considered in working with nonhandi-capped children also apply to meeting the special needs of these children.

Chapter 15, *Families and Teachers*

Together, examines the teacher's role in helping parents contribute to the growth and development of their children and introduces ways in which parents can be supported and involved in early childhood programs. We portray this graphically to suggest that the family provides the context for all that we do in early childhood programs.

We haven't included everything you might need to know about each topic. Rather we try to provide you with a lens through which to view the many choices *you* have to make in designing meaningful programs for young children.

Writing a book takes an enormous amount of time, effort, and energy. But there are some benefits as well: it motivates us to keep exploring and finding out about young children and how they learn; it enables us to keep thinking and working together; and it is gratifying to us that it may make a difference to people like you who are learning to work with young children.

You will play an important part in the lives of the many children you will teach, and we have designed this book to support you. We hope that it will help you to develop as a person, and as a professional who respects young children and who supports their growth in every possible way.

1

The Field of Early Childhood Education

"The past is prologue."

National Archives

This chapter examines the historical roots of early childhood education and how persons and events in the past have influenced current programs and practices. It is written to provide you with a perspective on the field, including major program approaches and policies. In it we also give an overview of the field today and its current prospects and future directions. It relates to the CDA area **Professionalism.**

What is the field of early childhood education like? What can you expect? What are the joys, the sorrows, the potentials for growth? Knowledge of the background of programs that have had a major impact on current practice lets you, the teacher or prospective teacher, know why we do many of the things we do today. While you read, identify the kinds of curriculum, teaching strategies, and teacher roles you feel most comfortable with and decide which you will want to adopt in your own teaching.

Early childhood education is a fairly new field, although it has old roots. For a long time, people believed that nothing important happened during the early years and that young children were not ready to learn until they entered formal schooling at the age of six. It was accepted that all children needed before they were of school age was a home in which their physical needs were met. Even after Freud revealed that important emotional development occurs in the early childhood, society persisted in the idea that anyone who worked with children under six was "only babysitting," a phrase that you will occasionally hear today.

American attitudes toward teachers of young children have been heavily influenced by the late nineteenth and early twentieth century origins of early childhood education in nursery schools, kindergar-

tens and day nurseries. This mixed heritage of the educationally-oriented nursery school and kindergarten, and the care-oriented nursery has lent early childhood education and early childhood educators a correspondingly mixed status, character, and reputation. This problem is reflected in the perception that preschool and kindergarten are a preparation for the serious learning of first grade rather than "real school." This attitude also influences pay scales; generally, the younger the children a teacher works with, the lower the status and salary.

Recent research on the importance of the early years has shown that early experience has a great impact on all areas of a child's development and has suggested that the first teacher is an extremely important person in the child's life. Yet there is a gap between research and practice. Today, programs for children under five are still not fully accepted or adequately funded. Most programs are privately supported (as opposed to programs for children five years and older which are fully state supported) though a few states sponsor preschool programs. Federal support for early childhood education is largely limited to programs for low-income families, and even these programs have been subject to recent budget cuts.

HISTORICAL ROOTS OF CURRENT PRACTICE

Early childhood education grows out of a long, distinguished historical tradition. Knowledge of this history contributes to our understanding of where we are and where we are going, as well as helping us to understand where we have come from. Historical perspective gives the teacher a sense of roots in the past, an idea of the sources of current philosophy and practice, and an awaresness that much of what is called *innovation* in current practice has been written about and experimented with before.

Early childhood education as a specialization did not begin until the early nineteenth century. However, many of the values and practices found in today's programs were created by philosophers, writers, and teachers of the past. Many of today's early childhood programs have their roots in what is referred to as the *humanistic tradition* in education. The theorists who contributed to this stream of thought were concerned with such issues as the education of the whole person, the interrelationships between mind and body, and the quality of the relationships between individuals and the role of play in learning. They supported education that fostered individual freedom. Many of them believed in universal education rather than educational opportunity only for the elite. Educators in this tradition tended to see childhood as a valuable time in its own right, rather than just as preparation for adulthood. The humanistic tradition was slow to be accepted, particularly during the lifetimes of its innovators. Although it was sometimes influential, it was more often

regarded as radical and treated with suspicion and hostility.

In order to put historical discussion into perspective, it helps to realize that childhood is a relatively new concept. During the Middle Ages, children were regarded as small adults and given no special consideration or treatment. This is evident in the portrayal of children as miniature adults in the art of this period (Aries, 1962). A specialized field of early childhood education could not arise until the concept of childhood as a unique developmental period emerged in the sixteenth and seventeenth centuries.

Some notable people in history have significantly shaped thought in today's early childhood education programs. The philosophers, religious leaders, and writers we discuss in this section had an influence on our field though they addressed themselves to a total philosophy of education rather than to the education of young children in particular.

Beginnings

Many educational historians trace the humanistic tradition in education back to **Plato** (428–348 B.C.) and **Aristotle** (384–322 B.C.). Plato was concerned with developing an ethical and reasonable ruling class. Both Plato and Aristotle recognized the importance of beginning education with young children, both saw human beings as essentially good, both emphasized the development of mind and body, and both sought to create a society in which good people followed good laws.

Martin Luther (1483–1546), the religious reformer of the Renaissance whose work led to the Reformation, was a strong advocate of universal education.

He believed that in order for people to take responsibility for their own salvation, they needed to read and understand the Bible for themselves.

Luther believed that schools should develop the intellectual, religious, physical, emotional, and social qualities of children. An extensive school system was developed in Germany in response to Luther's views, but his goals of universal education did not become reality until nineteenth century America.

John Amos Comenius (1592–1670) was a Czechoslovakian bishop, teacher, and educational theorist. Like Luther, he believed in universal education. He saw all people as being equal before God and believed, therefore, that all individuals, rich or poor, common or noble, male or female, were entitled to the same education.

Comenius stressed the importance of educating children while they are young and can easily be molded. He also advocated learning by doing and may have been the first to advocate learning through play. He saw education as beginning at birth in the "school of the mother's knee" and extending throughout a lifetime of learning.

Jean Jacques Rousseau (1712–1778), French philosopher, writer, and social theorist, was an early proponent of a developmental view of learning. Rousseau's ideas about proper child rearing and education were a reaction to a corrupt government and society. Rousseau did not believe that people were born with original sin, but rather that their inherent good was spoiled by civilization. In the novel *Émile*, Rousseau presents his view that innate goodness will flower when people are raised out of contact with corrupt society and are free to learn, not from books, but from direct contact with nature.

The Field of Early Childhood Education Emerges

Another group of educational theorists and reformers were directly involved in the education of young children. Their work has had a lasting impact and formed the basis for many modern educational practices. There are some common threads in the work of these educators; they were idealists, they were deeply humanitarian in their viewpoint, and they were often concerned with social reform as it affected the children of the poor.

Early childhood education as a distinct discipline had its beginning with **Johann Pestalozzi** (1746–1827), a Swiss educator who was influenced by the romantic philosophers, including Rousseau. Like Luther and Comenius before him, he believed in universal education.

Pestalozzi devoted his life to education, particularly for the orphaned and poor. He believed that education should be based on the natural development of children and that every child was capable of learning. He rejected the practice of memorization and advocated sensory exploration and observation as the basis of learning. He believed that children learned through self-discovery and could pace their own learning. Pestalozzi was also concerned with teaching human relationships: "My one aim was to . . . awaken a feeling of brotherhood . . . make them affectionate, just and considerate" (Braun, 1972, p 52).

Robert Owen (1771–1858), English social philosopher and controversial reformer, was a disciple of Pestalozzi. Owen became concerned with the poor conditions of families who worked in the cotton mills during the Industrial Revolution. He worked for reforms in their communities and established schools to improve the lives of their children, who from the age of six worked long hours in the mills alongside their parents.

Owen believed that education, starting with the very young, combined with an environment that allowed people to live by the principle of mutual consideration, could transform the nature of people and society. His infant school, the first in England for children three to ten years of age, had a warm, friendly atmosphere. Owen did not believe in pressuring children to learn or in punishing them; rather, he showed children the negative consequences of their actions. Sensory learning, stories, and visitors from the community were included in the school program in an attempt to make school relevant and interesting.

Owen's ideas were considered radical in his time, and his schools did not have lasting success in England. However, many of the practices originated in Owen's schools can still be found in today's early childhood programs. These include periods of time during which children choose their activities; emphasis on a warm, nurturing, and nonpunitive teacher; and the use of spontaneous play as a vehicle for learning.

MAJOR INFLUENCES ON TODAY'S EARLY CHILDHOOD PROGRAMS

A number of specialized approaches to early childhood education that were developed around the turn of the century have had a great impact on the nature of early childhood education in the United States today. Although they originated in different places and in response to different concerns, the approaches have in common the caring and respectful stance toward children characteristic of the reformers we have just described. These approaches include the kindergarten, created in Germany by Friedrich Froebel; the Montessori method, developed by physician Maria Montessori in Italy; progressive education, originating in the United States, best known in the work of educator/philosopher John Dewey; and the nursery, school, founded by the McMillan sisters in England.

The Kindergarten

Friedrich Wilhelm Froebel (1782–1852) was a German who studied with Pestalozzi and was a teacher in one of his schools. He was also influenced by the ideas of Comenius and Rousseau. Froebel was concerned with the education of children three through six and also with the mother's relationship to the infant and to the very young child. Froebel believed that children were social beings, that activity was the basis for knowing, and that play was an essential part of the educational process. He wanted children, assisted by their teachers, to have the opportunity to develop the positive impulses that came from within.

Froebel is considered the father of the modern kindergarten. The curriculum of the kindergarten he created included a set of *gifts* and *occupations* designed to enhance sensory development and to symbolically portray humanity's unity with God. The gifts consisted of such objects as yarn balls, blocks, wooden tablets, natural objects, and geometric shapes that encouraged discovery and

manipulation. Occupations included activities like molding, cutting, folding, bead stringing, and embroidery, all of which were intended to foster inventiveness and skill development. These activities reflected Froebel's belief that education must begin with the concrete and move to greater abstraction, and that perceptual development precedes thinking skills. These views are very much accepted today and borne out by contemporary research. Besides establishing the kindergarten, Froebel established an institute to train young women to become kindergarten teachers.

Froebel's work in Germany set the stage for the introduction of the kindergarten in the United States; it developed independently from elementary education and the nursery school. Early kindergartens (the first founded in 1855) were started as private ventures. Many of these were taught in German by teachers who

studied with Froebel and were patterned after his program.

Elizabeth Peabody established the first English-speaking kindergarten in Boston in 1860 and later studied with Froebel's disciples in Germany. She was very influential in winning public support for kindergartens in the United States. The first publicly supported kindergarten was opened in St. Louis in 1873 and was followed by rapid expansion of the kindergarten movement.

Two aspects of the society of that time appear to have contributed to the growth of the kindergarten. The first was the belief that children were inherently good and required a nurturing and benevolent environment in their early years. The second was concern for the problems of the poor, which led to the rise of philanthropic social work. Mission kindergartens for underprivileged children were established by social workers with the hope that they would increase poor children's chances for future success.

Early kindergartens emphasized the development of cleanliness, manual skills, and courtesy, as well as preparation for later schooling. Froebel's gifts and occupations were used as a base for the curriculum. A period of ferment in the development of the kindergarten caused by conflicting philosophies began in the 1890s and lasted for twenty years. The conservative group in the debate held to Froebelian principles and practices. The challenging group, known as the *progressives,* were influenced by new work in child development and by the philosophy of Progressive Education. By 1920 the conservative camp yielded, and a new curriculum replaced the original Froebelian approach. The new curriculum reflected many of Froebel's ideas but added a new emphasis on free play, social interaction, art, music, nature study, and excursions.

The first professional association concerned with the education of young children in the United States was the American Froebel Union established by Elizabeth Peabody in 1878. In 1884 the National Education Association (NEA) established the department of kindergarten education and the following year recommended that kindergartens become part of the public schools. In 1892 the International Kindergarten Union (IKU) was formed to promote kindergarten education.

As kindergartens gradually moved into public schools, they met with grudging acceptance. The rigid atmosphere of the traditional primary schools with their emphasis on drill and the development of skills was sharply contrasted to the atmosphere of kindergartens, which valued the development of the whole child. However, the gap gradually narrowed. Many kindergarten activities found their way into the primary grades, as

primary activities filtered down into the kindergarten.

Beginning in the 1920s, kindergarten teachers in public schools were urged to prepare children for reading, hence the stress on "readiness." This emphasis has been found in kindergartens since that time. Workbooks and other techniques usually associated with teaching older children are often used to prepare five year olds for upper grades.

To this day the kindergarten curriculum remains an arena of educational ferment and conflict, caught between the demands of public school personnel and those of educators trained in early childhood education. The debate about appropriate school learning for five year olds focuses on whether the purpose of the kindergarten should be academic preparation or a more child-centered approach, including learning through play.

The Montessori Method

Maria Montessori (1870–1952) was the first woman in Italy to receive a medical degree, though she is best known for her contributions to education. Early in her medical career she found successful approaches for working with retarded children previously regarded as incapable of learning. She then founded the *Casa Dei Bambini* (Children's House) in Rome in 1907 to explore the applicability to normal children of the methods she had devised for special children. The school was also used as a laboratory for the development of Montessori's educational method. The program she designed was based on her observation of young children, which led her to the conclusion that intelligence was not fixed and could be stimulated or stifled by the child's experiences. She believed that children learned best through their own direct sensory experience of the world.

Montessori was influenced by the work of Pestalozzi, Froebel, Freud, and also French physicians Seguin and Itard, who had developed humane methods for working with retarded children. She was very interested in the first years of life and believed that children went through *sensitive periods* during which they had interest and capacity for the development of particular knowledge and/or skills.

Montessori believed that children have an inherent desire to explore and understand the world in which they live. She saw these young explorers as self-motivated and able to seek out the kinds of experiences and knowledge most appropriate for their stage of development. She was concerned with preserving the dignity of the child, and she valued the development of independence and productivity.

The physical environment in a Montessori classroom is attractive, child-sized, and equipped with movable furniture. Montessori stressed the importance of an orderly environment that could help children to focus on their learning and to develop the ability to concentrate.

The classroom is also equipped with didactic materials developed by Montessori to help children develop their senses and learn concepts. These beautifully crafted materials are the basis for much learning in a Montessori setting. They are treated with care and respect and are displayed so that children can use them independently. The materials are graded by ability, sequenced from known to unknown and from concrete to abstract. The concept to be taught by each material is isolated from other concepts that might be confusing or distracting. For example, if the child is learning the concept of shape, the materials will be of uniform size and color so that the attribute of shape will be isolated. Materials are also designed to have immediate self-correcting feedback so children can judge for themselves if they have successfully completed a task.

The basis for learning in a Montessori classroom is firsthand experience, and children learn by observing and by doing. Practical life experiences such as buttoning, zipping, cutting, polishing, and gardening enable children to care for themselves and the environment and help them to gain skills that will be useful in later life. The didactic materials help children develop the ability to concentrate and enhance their sense perceptions, as well as to differentiate concepts of size, shape, color, texture, sound, and temperature. Conceptual learning extends into other areas, including writing, reading, and mathematics.

All learning in a Montessori classroom is based on a foundation of what has gone before, so that each activity paves the way to future, more complex activities. Activities are organized primarily for individual work rather than group interaction, and children are allowed to move freely about the environment and choose their own activities. Though social-emotional development was not emphasized by Montessori, educators trained in her method believe that children develop a sense of self-esteem as they increase their competence.

Montessori's schools were very successful in Italy and eventually spread throughout the world. Early childhood programs in the United States adopted Montessori's ideas of creating a child-size environment and the use of sensory materials. There have been private Montessori schools in the United States for many years, and in the 1960s, the approach received attention again because of its applicability to work with low-income children.

There are many Montessori schools in the United States today. Some of these schools use Montessori materials in combination with other approaches, while others rely exclusively on the methods and materials developed by Montessori. Even among teachers trained in her methods, there is some debate about how strictly her prescriptions should be followed and how much variation is acceptable.

There are two major professional associations concerned today with implementing Montessori programs, training teachers, and accrediting schools and teachers. These are the original organization, *Association Montessori Internationale* (AMI) with headquarters in the Netherlands, and the *American Montessori Society* (AMS) founded in 1956 in order to adapt Montessori methods to an American style of working with children.

Progressive Education

Progressive Education was a reaction against the traditional forms of public schooling prevalent during the nineteenth and twentieth centuries in which children learned predetermined curriculum and skills by rote memorization under the strict discipline of the teacher. **John Dewey** (1859–1952) was one of the leaders of this movement for educational reform, and stands as a giant among modern educational philosophers and theorists. Dewey believed that education needed to be integrated with the life of the child in the present and not just be preparation for future life. He stressed the development of social responsibility for life in a democratic society. This "child-centered" approach to education emphasized respect for the individual, consideration of the child's interests and abilities in planning curriculum, self-directed activity, and learning through doing—through experiencing and experimenting. Subject areas were integrated, and the role of the teacher was to watch and guide, not to control, children.

Progressive Education, as shaped by Dewey and others, took many forms but was based on the principles just described. It came under fire from educators who felt that students were not learning the fundamental subjects well enough. It is now felt by many educational historians that Dewey was misinterpreted by many of his followers, who became overly permissive instead of challenging youngsters intellectually and helping them develop self-direction and responsibility. Dewey's influence in the United States waned after 1950 except in a few schools such as the Bank Street School in New York City, which continued to demonstrate the key concepts of Progressive Education.

The influence of Dewey's ideas has been so pervasive that all areas of education in the United States have felt their impact. Progressive Education as a guiding philosophy has been phased out of most American schools, but it has had a continued influence on kindergartens and nursery schools, which have always remained more closely allied with Dewey than with traditional public schools.

Many of the ideas of the progressive movement had a rebirth in England in the mid-1960s in state-supported schools for five to eight year olds, called *Infant Schools.* This direction in education for young children was influenced by experiences that teachers had with children in the countryside during World War II. They lived and worked with groups of children informally, out of school settings, and found that valuable relationships and learning resulted. These experiences, combined with the philosophy of Dewey imported from the U.S. and the theoretical contributions of Piaget, led to the new approach, which has been referred to by a number of terms including *informal education, the integrated day,* and *the open school.* It first came to public attention in the late 1960s through the publication of a government study, *Children and Their Primary Schools,* also known as the *Plowden Report.*

Informal education in the infant schools is part of the regular public school system in England and shares the public school goals for teaching basic educational skills. The methods differ a great deal from traditional, formal approaches. Educators who initiated this new direction believed that children had to make sense of the world around them in their own way and through their own exploration. They believed that play was an important part of learning and that children developed concepts and thinking skills through direct experiences in environments prepared for learning. This approach has been described as the **open school** both because the use of space is "open," allowing children to move freely between interest areas, and because the content is "open," derived from children's interests rather than a prescribed curriculum.

Integrated day is another term that has been used to describe the organization of

the program. Classrooms are divided into a number of interest areas: a reading corner, math center, art center, building area, dramatic play area, and areas for blocks, sand, and water. Children have the freedom to choose the areas in which they want to work. Activities are not divided into discrete subject areas to be taught at specified times each day; rather, learning is organized around tasks or projects chosen by the children, and curriculum content is integrated into the pursuit of these projects.

American educators began to visit the British Infant Schools in the late 1960s and 1970s to observe and write about this new approach, and its influence began to be felt in some American schools that introduced more informal and integrated curriculum. Hence, Dewey's ideas had come full circle back to their point of origin. More recently the emphasis on "basics" and interest in more rigorous academic training in schools has again diminished interest in child-centered approaches, though they can still be observed in a few public and private demonstration programs. A pendulum swing from emphasis on the learner to emphasis on what is learned seems to occur in regular cycles in American education. Although at this time the pendulum has swung away from the learner, it is certain that in time it will swing back. The insights of Dewey and Progressive Education are likely to be with us for a long time to come.

The Nursery School

Margaret McMillan (1860–1931) and her sister Rachel established the first nursery school in England in 1911. The school was created in response to the McMillans' concern with the health problems they witnessed in school-age children in poor communities. The nursery school was designed to contribute to the physical and mental development of children with a special emphasis on ameliorating health problems of the very young before they began formal schooling, a concern which still exists in early childhood education.

The McMillans' nursery school provided for children's physical needs and placed heavy emphasis on allowing them to work and play outdoors. Health and nutrition, perceptual-motor skills, and the development of imagination were stressed. The role of the teacher in the program was to nurture children and to provide informal teaching in a planned environment. Many antecedents of today's nursery schools were present in the first English nursery schools, including materials for sensory development, gardens, sand boxes, movement activities, nature study, play with creative materials like paint and blocks, and involvement of parents.

American nursery schools were directly influenced by the English nursery school, as well as by Freudian theory and later by Dewey's ideas. The first nursery school in the United States was established in New York City in 1919 by Harriet Johnson. In the 1920s, a number of other nursery schools were established in America. Some of these included the Laboratory Nursery School at Columbia Teachers College, organized by Patty Smith Hill, and the Ruggles Street Nursery School and Training Center in Boston, directed by Abigail Eliot, who had studied with Margaret McMillan in England. In 1916 the first parent cooperative nursery school was begun, and more appeared during the 1920s. During the 1920s and 1930s, nursery schools were established in Home Economics departments in many colleges to train future homemakers and as centers for child development research.

Patty Smith Hill at Columbia Teachers College formed the National Committee for the Nursery School. In 1929 the organization became the National Association for Nursery Education (NANE) and later the National Association for the Education of Young Children (NAEYC), which is still working actively to support quality programs for young children.

Nursery schools were multidisciplinary in orientation because the early leaders were trained in a number of fields including nursing, social work, medicine, psychology, and education—hence the whole child orientation we describe in this

book. The earliest nursery schools emphasized social, emotional, and physical growth, with much less emphasis on cognitive growth because at that time it was believed that children were not ready to do academic work until they entered school at the age of six. Today the term **preschool** is generally used to describe programs that grew out of the legacy of the nursery school.

In the nursery school the child learns through interactions with people and with the environment. Children are seen as always in transition: growing, changing, experiencing. The role of the school is to keep the paths of exploration open so that children can develop in their own ways. The daily schedule is characterized by large time blocks in which children are free to choose activities and engage in them for as long as they wish. The classroom is divided into activity areas usually including an area for blocks, dramatic play, art, water play, sand play, and reading.

The role of the teacher in the nursery school is to create an environment that facilitates learning. Teachers also support social and emotional development by encouraging children to verbalize their feelings. Child management is carried out by problem solving and by modifying the environment rather than by imposing adult power.

Nursery schools are similar to Montessori schools in that children are viewed as inquisitive, self-motivated learners capable of selecting activities appropriate for their current needs and developmental stage. They differ from the Montessori schools in their greater emphasis on social interaction, self-expression, and creativity. In a Montessori classroom most educational materials have one designated purpose, while in a nursery school most materials are intended to be used in a variety of ways.

In response to new information about cognitive development and to the needs of low-income children, the traditional nursery school has continued to change. What remains constant is the insistence that the child is a person in the process of development, who can be supported by a sensitive teacher in a carefully designed environment.

PUBLIC POLICY AND PROGRAMS FOR YOUNG CHILDREN

Who is responsible for meeting the needs of children in our society? This question has been and continues to be the subject of great debate. The needs of children are addressed by their families, as well as by many other groups including churches, voluntary associations, foundations, and local, state, and federal governments. There is no clear-cut policy guiding which needs should be met by public resources and which by private means. Historically, it has been assumed that, barring disaster, families will care for their own children. Government involvement has generally been limited to the most needy: care for orphans, protection for abused children, and food for the children of the poor.

Federal involvement in promoting the health, education, and welfare of children began with the creation of the Children's Bureau in 1912. Its charge was to investigate child health and labor, and its role was mainly to make investigations and report their findings. Since that time, the federal government established a Department of Health, Education, and

Welfare in 1959 and an Office of Child Development in 1969 (later called the Administration for Children, Youth, and Families). These agencies have been involved in provision of welfare to families unable to care for their own children, in health and nutrition programs, in child abuse prevention, in educational programs for economically deprived children, and in child care for children whose parents must work.

There is no overall policy regarding programs for children in the United Stated today. According to Gilbert Steiner,

> Child development policy is uncoordinated. Public involvement in the field is a federal agency by federal agency, congressional committee by congressional committee, state by state, or city by city assortment of unrelated decisions that are as likely to be contradictory as complementary. (1976, p. vii)

The debate regarding the role of government in serving children centers around the following question: Should intervention occur only when the family is unable to meet children's basic needs, or is there a greater responsibility "to insure the maximum development of every child according to his potential"? (Steiner, 1976, p.3)

In order to understand trends in education and policy affecting young children, it is helpful to remember that these things occur in a larger world context. Changes in society and major political events have a powerful influence on our views of the family and our attitudes toward children. There is a tendency for social and political attitudes and concomitant educational change to occur in pendulum swings of reaction and counterreaction. The time line in Table 1.1 portrays some important events and influences on early childhood education. It helps us to see some of the possible interconnections among historical events, social policy, and programs for children. In the following sections we will look at child care, compensatory programs for low-income children, and programs for handicapped children; in each of these areas changes in social attitudes have been reflected in public policy.

Child Care

A major policy issue, which has at times been of some historical consequence, is the provision of child care services for working parents. The day nursery movement, begun in the late nineteenth century, had as its clientele the most desperately needy of the immigrants to the United States. By providing care for children, it enabled families in which both parents needed to work to stay together. Personnel in the day nurseries were largely untrained, worked long hours with very high child-adult ratios, and provided minimal care for children. In the eyes of society, the great virtue of the day nursery was that the children in them were given a reprieve from even more harmful environments. These programs were primarily concerned with the health of children, the daily bath being a major event, rather than with more lofty educational goals. Day nurseries provided quite comprehensive service with long hours of operation, infant care, and some family counseling.

The social climate of the early twentieth century did not support the idea of child care. It was viewed as help for the poor, not as an important social welfare provision, and most programs were discontinued during this period. During the depression in the 1930s, child care centers were established by the federal government to provide relief work for teachers, custodians, cooks, nurses, and others who needed employment. These programs were phased out as the depression ended.

During World War II, the U.S. government again turned to the business of sponsoring child care. This time the purpose was to meet the needs of the large numbers of women employed in defense plants. Under the Lanham Act, which authorized child care, approximately 600,000 children were served in forty-one states. Private industry also sponsored child care for its workers at this time. Most notable were two outstanding centers run by Kaiser shipyards.

Wartime government and industry sponsorship, contingent on a state of emergency, soon faded away. Child care during those years was primarily intended

TABLE 1.1
Important events and influences on early childhood education.

	Societal Context	Family Context	Philosophical and Psychological Influences	European Programs	American Programs	Professional Associations	Federal Involvement
1800	Industrialization Private entrepreneurship	Extended nuclear family	Rousseau Pestalozzi Froebel	Kindergartens IKU (International Kindergarten Union (later Association for Childhood International))	Kindergartens	American Froebel Association	
1900	Urbanization Rise of the Corporation		Montessori Dewey	Montessori schools	Day nurseries		Children's Bureau
1910	World War I		Child study Behaviorism	Nursery schools	Nursery schools Progressive schools		
1930	Great Depression	Isolated nuclear family	Gesell		WPA nurseries	National Association for Nursery Education	Social Security Act
1940	World War II		Psychoanalytic (S. & A. Freud, Erikson)		Industry-sponsored day care	World Organization for Early Childhood Education (OMEP)	Lanham Act (day care for defense workers)
1950	Korean War Launch of Sputnik		Piaget	British Infant School			
1960	Viet Nam War Social protest	Diversity (single parent and communal homes; families where both parents work)	Bloom Hunt Rogers Maslow		Head Start Compensatory programs	National Association for the Education of Young Children (NAEYC)	War on Poverty Office of Child Development (now ACYF)
1970 1980	Women's Movement Economic Recession and Recovery More women in labor force		Vygotsky McDonald		Mainstreaming Increase in Child care programs		Public Law 94-142 Budget cuts Tax credits

H.O.

23

to aid in the effort to win the war and not to help children and their families. The return to peacetime was heralded by the return to the traditional family, mothers at home tending to their children. Child care facilities were brought back to prewar levels, and most child care centers were closed. The children's centers in California were among the few survivors of the era.

The postwar attitude toward women, combined with the belief that children of working mothers suffered from lack of essential maternal care, gave strength to fears that child care was unnecessary and possibly even harmful to children. Between 1945 and 1960 it received little attention or support.

The 1960s and early 1970s, a period of national concern with social reform, saw a resurgence of interest in child care as a public policy issue. New research in child development combined with concern for the plight of the poor led to the creation of a new federally funded program called *Head Start*, as well as other other compensatory programs for low-income children. Early childhood programs were now seen as contributing to the development of the child as well as providing a service for working parents.

Legislation to provide child care for all working families who desired it was introduced, and a comprehensive child care services bill was passed by the U.S. House and Senate in 1972. The bill was vetoed by President Richard Nixon who justified his action by stating that the bill threatened the stability of the American family. In recent years federal sponsorship of child care has been replaced with more passive forms of support like tax credits. In 1985 another package of child care bills was introduced into the House of Representatives by congressman

George Miller of California. Proposed legislation provides for several important supports: restoration of budget cuts; child care provisions that allowed low-income parents to receive job training and find employment; incentives for states to improve licensing and sponsor programs; and expansion and improvement in teacher training, especially for infant caregivers and family day care home providers.

Programs for Low-Income Children

The launch of the Russian Sputnik in 1957 generated a sense of national uneasiness and the fear that American children were not being adequately educated to compete in a scientific age. This concern led to greater emphasis on the quality of education and to innovations in curriculum in elementary and secondary schools, especially in the areas of science and math.

At about the same time research by Piaget, Bloom, Hunt, and others began to dispel old ideas about intelligence being fixed and static and pointed to the significance of the early years on later intellectual development. Researchers and educators suggested that planned intervention in the early years might enhance children's development, help them to succeed in later schooling, and perhaps help them to be more successful in their adult lives. Hence, the idea developed that early childhood programs should have a much more significant role.

The climate of concern with education and new ideas about child development combined with the political climate of the 1960s to pave the way for a whole new era in early childhood education. President

Kennedy's concern with the plight of the poor in America led to a renewed interest in the plight of children of the poor, and the "War Against Poverty," administered by the newly formed Office of Economic Opportunity, was begun.

Head Start   Under the auspices of the Office of Economic Opportunity, an interdisciplinary panel representing the fields of pediatrics, education, child development, and social services was formed and directed to develop a program that might ameliorate the effects of poverty on children. It was hoped that such a program would be effective in increasing achievement and opportunities, and that it would give poor children a "head start." The resulting program, called project **Head Start,** was unique in its

focus on the total development of the child, in its emphasis on strengthening the family, and in its provision of comprehensive services.

Head Start was begun in the summer of 1965 as a six-week demonstration project. By the fall of that year, however, it was clear that six weeks was not enough time to achieve its goals, and it was converted into a full year program. In 1969, under the Nixon administration, responsbility for Head Start was transferred from the Office of Economic Opportunity to the Office of Child Development.

Over the years a number of alternatives have been created to make Head Start more accessible and more effective. In 1969 *Parent Child Centers* were founded to work with children under the age of three and their families, and in 1972

Home Start was created as another demonstration project that provided Head Start's comprehensive services for preschool age children and parents in their homes. A number of variations in program delivery have also been tried.

In 1970 the widely publicized Westinghouse Report declared that the cognitive gains made by children in Head Start classes were lost in the early elementary years. Critics of the report felt that it had not taken into account the multifaceted goals of the program, many of which are difficult to measure. They claimed that the study focused on cognitive gains that represent only part of the total program and that the methodology used was questionable. Although the Westinghouse Report cast a shadow on Head Start's reputation for a number of years, it had no impact on continued support of the program, and subsequent research has been much more favorable.

A recent summary of longitudinal studies of low-income children who participated in Head Start and other preschool intervention programs has shown that these programs have had a significant and lasting impact (Lazar, 1979). Studies of program participants in late adolescence and early adulthood have shown that in comparison to their peers who did not attend preschool, they are more likely to meet school standards, are less likely to be classified as underachievers, score higher on academic measures, are less likely to be placed in special education classes, engage in less delinquent behavior, and are more likely to hold jobs.

Follow Through   One of the most interesting and important experiments in modern educational history began as another offshoot of the Head Start program. In 1968 the Office of Child Development authorized an experimental program called **Planned Variation** to investigate the effects of a variety of curricular approaches (models) in Head Start programs. Another new program, called **Follow Through,** was introduced the following year by the U.S. Office of Education in order to continue special programs for Head Start children when they entered elementary school. Follow Through was designed to explore the effects of continuity in programming from preschool through third grade, to explore the effects of well-defined program models on children's development, and to investigate the long range effects of various program approaches.

The study included a number of educational models that varied greatly in theory and practice and that represented a spectrum of approaches to early childhood education based on clearly defined learning theories. Each of the models was developed by a program sponsor, usually based at a university or educational research center. Models differed greatly in their values, in their assumptions about motivation, in preparation of the learning environment, in presentation of learning experiences, in teacher role, and in management strategies.

Follow Through programs can be organized into three categories that point to major program differences. *Preacademic programs* (for example, those developed by Englemann and Becker at University of Oregon and Don Bushell at University of Kansas) advocate high teacher direction and use behavior modification techniques. *Discovery models* (like those developed at Bank Street College in New York and the Open Education Model at the Education

Development Center in Massachusetts) require that the teacher create a rich and stimulating classroom environment and guide children in their interactions with people and materials. *Cognitive Discovery models* (for example, the Tuscon Early Education Model in Arizona, the Cognitively-Oriented Curriculum developed by Dave Weikart in Michigan, and the Responsive Environment Model from the Far West Educational Development Laboratory in California) fall somewhere between the other two (Klein, 1973).

Models were chosen by selected communities, and an effort was made to coordinate the programs so that children attended classes employing the same curricular model from preschool through third grade. The Head Start portion of the study was phased out in 1973, but the Office of Education continued to sponsor Follow Through in public schools in many of the original communities.

Although the research has not definitively proven one model or group of models to be superior, the program has

taught educators a great deal about program development and implementation as well as teacher training. It has also demonstrated the difficulty of doing large-scale educational research with a mobile population.

Today Follow Through is being phased out as a federally sponsored program, but communities that have had models in experimental classrooms may now choose to incorporate the model or selected aspects of the model into the regular school program.

An interesting sideline of Follow Through has been the attention it has drawn to the relationships between an educational model as it is conceived by its creators and how it is actually implemented in the classroom. In Follow Through, as in every other educational model, it is the teacher who makes the difference. As Jenny Klein, former education specialist with Head Start puts it, "It is my conviction that in the final analysis, it is the teacher who makes or breaks the model. Without the teacher, the curriculum is just a lifeless piece of paper" (Klein, 1979, p. 365).

The Current Status of Compensatory Programs Before Head Start, federal support for children's programs had been accomplished only when tied to a national emergency such as a wave of immigration, depression, or a war. The Head Start program represented a new view of child development as a valuable end in itself and an unprecedented mobilization of resources on behalf of children.

The Head Start program has been popular with the families it serves. It has also been regarded positively by educators, by legislators, and by the public. Whenever the program has been threatened, there has been a groundswell of support, and it has survived as one of the last legacies of the War Against Poverty. Moreover, the comprehensive design of the Head Start program has had an important influence on subsequent child care policy and legislative proposals.

Yet, in spite of its successes, the impact of Head Start has been limited. It has remained a demonstration program that has been able to serve only a small percentage of children who are eligible because of a low family income.

Recent research findings (Lazar, 1979; Schweinhart and Weikart, 1980) on the impact of preschool education are very encouraging. Longitudinal studies have shown that young adults who attended quality early childhood programs are more intelligent and have better academic records than their peers who did not attend. Early school experiences also had a positive effect on the health and social behavior of participants and benefitted their families. Programs were found to be cost effective in that participants needed fewer remedial services in school and as young adults had less of a tendency to use welfare and had lower arrest rates. The vision of changing children's achievement and attitudes has been realized for those who are able to attend preschool programs, but the greater goal of ameliorating the effects of poverty has yet to be achieved.

Programs for Children with Special Needs

The care and education of children with special needs is a field with its own history and traditions. Today's emphasis on bringing these children into the mainstream of society through placement in regular education classrooms has resulted in a merging of two distinct and different approaches to education: special education and early childhood education.

The challenge of providing education for all children, including the handicapped, was first confronted in the early 1900s when compulsory school attendance laws were enacted. Public and private residential schools were established for the severely handicapped. Special classes evolved in regular public schools when behavior problems arose as a result of educating special needs children in regular classrooms.

From the 1920s to the 1960s, most of these children were segregated in special classrooms in separate school buildings far from main activity areas. Usually only mildly disabled children who were considered "ready" for education were included in public school classes. The more severely handicapped were confined to institutions or residential schools.

In the mid 1960s, special classes in the public schools became an issue of controversy. Some saw them as dumping grounds for problem children, including those who were culturally different, without actually attempting to meet their educational needs. At this time, too, some educators began to question whether special education classes were best for handicapped children; they suggested that these children could learn better in regular classes. Adding to this ferment, parents who had banded together to lobby for special education legislation took their concerns to court. In the early 1970s, legislators began specifying how, where, when, and what special education services must be provided by public schools. These laws prompted many innovative programs.

In 1975, the Education for All Handicapped Children Act, Public Law 94–142, was enacted. It has significantly changed how public schools teach children with learning problems and handicaps. The law mandates a free, appropriate public education for handicapped persons 3–21 years of age; education within the least restrictive environment; procedures for due process; nondiscriminatory testing and evaluation procedures; a written plan for individualized instruction; and parent notification and consultation (in their native language) in all matters relating to their child. Public Law 94–142 also provides federal funds to assist state and local governments in following its provisions.

Compliance with PL 94–142 has presented some special problems in providing the least restrictive environment for eligible three and four year olds because most states do not have publicly funded preschool programs. Head Start classes, which must serve handicapped as well as nonhandicapped preschoolers, are available to some of these children. In order to serve young children with special needs, state education departments are having to explore options for providing services that include: payment either to families or private preschools so children with mild handicaps and developmental delays can be "mainstreamed"; separate preschool programs in public schools for these children (which will not provide integration with their peers); and public preschool programs for all children.

EARLY CHILDHOOD EDUCATION TODAY

A number of different kinds of programs for young children are available today.

These may be classified according to their purposes: (1) to enhance the development of and provide education for young children, (2) to provide child care for working parents, and/ or (3) to provide education for parents. Some programs combine two or even all three of these functions. Programs may also be classified according to sponsorship, which may be public (federal, state, or local) or private. Private programs may be nonprofit, basically intended to provide a service to children and their families, or profit, designed as a business.

Child Care Centers

Child care centers provide care for the children of working parents and are usually open from early morning until early evening. Some centers are open later hours or provide drop-in-care according to parental needs. Most centers in the United States today are privately sponsored. Some programs receive federal support through Social Services Block Grant Child Care administered through the states (formerly funded by Title XX of the 1937 Social Security Act).

These programs provide care for children with substantial developmental delays, children who are abused or neglected or at risk for abuse and neglect, and children whose parents are enrolled in job training programs or whose salaries are below current poverty guidelines. Two relatively new trends in day care are a movement toward more industry-sponsored centers to provide care for workers' children and the proliferation of large chains of franchised centers that are operated as large-scale businesses.

Child care programs today combine aspects of the custodial day nursery and the nursery school. Programs for children can range from those that support the total development of the child to those which simply provide a safe place with adult supervision. Many states license centers only to care for children between the ages of two-and-a-half and four years of age, though at present there is an increase in state licensing for centers to care for infants and toddlers as well.

Family Day Care Homes

Child care in private homes, called family day care, provides an alternative to center-based care and is the least visible, yet most prevalent, form of privately sponsored child care in the United States today. Caregivers are usually women who take small numbers of infants, toddlers, and preschoolers into their homes. Most states have provisions for licensing or registering these homes, though requirements are difficult to enforce since the homes may not be known to the authorities. Caregivers may be reluctant to apply for licensing because of concern with meeting zoning requirements and the burden of paying taxes on income earned. The care provided in these homes, like care in centers, can vary greatly from highly nurturing to minimal supervision.

Preschools

Preschools (sometimes still called nursery schools) have traditionally been half-day programs that focus on the social-emotional development of children and provide enrichment activities. Today most preschools also place emphasis on cognitive development in forms ranging from learning through structured play to programs that are designed as academic

preparation for later schooling. These programs are most often used by families who do not need full-day care and where there is an adult available to pick up the child at midday. A good, developmental preschool program provides valuable social and learning experiences for young children.

Sponsorship of preschools can be public or private. Public sponsors may include education and child development departments in colleges, universities, and some high schools that provide laboratory settings to train students in education and child development while serving the community. Privately sponsored programs can include parent cooperatives (called **co-ops**), in which parents hire a trained person to serve as teacher, director, and educational leader and participate themselves on a regular basis as teachers and administrators of the school.

Programs for Low-Income Children

As previously described, Head Start provides a comprehensive program for children; it offers developmentally appropriate educational experiences as well as health screening and treatment, good nutrition, access to social services, and parent education and involvement in policy decisions. Many of the provisions of the Head Start program have been included in the Social Services Block Grant Child Care programs.

Kindergarten and Other Public School Programs

The most prevalent kind of program for young children in our society is kinder-garten, which is available but not mandatory for five year olds in most public school systems. Kindergartens range from informal programs, which stress socialization and the foundations for later school learning, to programs that emphasize reading and other academic areas and are almost indistinguishable from first-grade classrooms.

In addition to kindergartens, some states have introduced public school programs for disadvantaged four year olds and for learning disabled and physically and emotionally handicapped preschoolers. In a few places preschool programs are being made available for all four year olds.

Parent Education

There are many kinds of programs available for parents of young children. These can take the form of parent classes and meetings dealing with topics such as child development, educational techniques and child management; they can involve parents in working with children in early childhood classrooms; or they can provide trained visitors to work with parents and children in their homes. Programs for infants and toddlers which combine parent education with activities for children are becoming increasingly popular. Parent education, especially in combination with a good program for children, has proven to be very successful in producing positive developmental gains for young children.

TRAINING AND CERTIFICATION

There are a number of routes that can be taken to enter the field of early childhood education and a variety of opportunities for training and professional development. Some people who wish to work with young children get their initial experience through volunteering or taking a position in a preschool as a substitute teacher or classroom aide, or they enroll in a high school or college course in child development or early childhood education. Others go directly into a teacher education program in a two- or four-year college. Some early childhood educators were introduced to the field through observing the benefits of a good preschool for themselves and their children.

Professional qualifications for work in early childhood programs vary from state to state and are based on the provisions of center licensing requirements (usually administered by social service departments) and/or certification for teachers (handled by state departments of education). The minimum requirements to work with young children are good health and a high school diploma. Most states require that teachers be qualified for their jobs either by having a college degree (in some places it must be in education, early childhood education, or child development) or the nationally awarded Child Development Associate (CDA) credential based on demonstrated competency in working with young children. Some positions that involve supervision of staff or curriculum development may require a Master's degree in education or child development.

States also differ in the ways in which they certify teachers for the public schools, and college programs are often designed to meet these certification requirements. Some states give a preschool-primary teaching credential, which covers preschool through the third grade, some give a kindergarten-sixth grade certificate, with no provision for preschool teaching, and still others offer a preschool or kindergarten endorsement in addition to standard elementary certification.

Early childhood teacher education programs can be found in many two- and four-year colleges and universities. These programs award Associate of Arts, Bachelor's, Master's, and Doctoral degrees in early childhood education, elementary education, or child development. The National Association for the Education of Young Children (NAEYC) has recently developed guidelines for two- and four-year college programs in early childhood education. Training that leads to the Child Development Associate credential is available through the Head Start program and through some community colleges for teachers already working in the field.

When early childhood programs were first introduced in colleges, they tended to be housed in home economics departments as part of the agricultural extension service. Today they are found in home economics departments as well as in human development departments and colleges of education. Some institutions still provide programs for preparation of preschool teachers in the home economics department and for kindergarten through twelfth grade teachers in the college of education.

Specialized professional training in early childhood education is essential for people to become competent teachers who can provide positive growth experiences for young children. We don't believe that experience alone or a degree in another field (even elementary education) provides the knowledge of young children and of early childhood curriculum needed to effectively teach young children. Prospective teachers need to decide

which would be the most appropriate match for their interests, abilities, and professional aspirations.

PROSPECTS

Most people who work in early childhood education feel strongly that the work they do is valuable, even essential, to the well-being of children and society. Yet it is hard to hold on to this belief when it is not reflected in the salaries that they receive or in the respect and prestige accorded them.

Because most programs for young children are paid for directly by parents and not by public funds, salaries for teachers in programs for children under five and in privately funded centers tend to be much lower than those paid teachers in public schools who do comparable work. Low salaries are also a reflection of the general lack of awareness of the importance of having well-trained and competent people working with young children. Because it is so difficult to make an adequate living as a teacher of young children and because caring for children has traditionally been viewed as women's work, very few men choose to enter the field, even though there are some who would find it rewarding. Low pay also results in high staff turnover, which is especially unfortunate because it undermines the stability of adult-child relationships.

Early childhood education affects an extremely large group of people, including children, parents, and educators. The percentage of working mothers of children under six is growing faster than that of any other group of working mothers. Since there is no tax base to support preschools, demands for improved wages and working conditions fall on parents who are already overburdened and who then tend to turn to inferior sources of child care if costs become prohibitive. An additional consequence of private versus public funding is that very few preschool teachers belong to unions and are consequently less able to exert pressure for better pay and working conditions.

Despite these problems, there are some bright spots. There has been a steady growth of publicly-supported kindergartens across the country, and many states have now begun to develop programs for four year olds. As more women enter the labor force, the demand for more and better child care as well as for new services such as infant care and child care referral services is increasing. The National Association for the Education of Young Children (NAEYC) has launched a new program called CAP (Center Accreditation Program) to accredit quality child care programs. This may also contribute to greater public awareness of the importance of good programs for young children. Child advocacy, parent education, and child care information and referral are all growing fields with new employment opportunies.

A major issue in early childhood education at this time is the movement toward greater professionalism and recognition of those who work with young children. There is currently a growing sense of conviction about both the uniqueness and importance of our field. Membership in NAEYC, the largest organization of early childhood educators, continues to grow indicating increased concern and awareness of the needs of children and of those who work with them.

Many of us in the field are becoming more committed to child advocacy. We are growing more sophisticated about the political process and are forming alliances with others with similar concerns in order to heighten community awareness and influence public attitudes and legislation on behalf of young children.

FOR FURTHER THOUGHT AND DISCUSSION

1 Discuss programs that you have observed in terms of the ways that they appear to incorporate aspects of the major influences described in this chapter (Kindergarten, Progressive Education, Montessori, the Nursery School).

2 Compare the purpose and sponsorship of different programs for young children that you have seen. How did these seem to influence the experience of children, parents, and teachers?

3 How do you think a teacher's job might differ in each of the different types of programs described in this chapter ? How do you think children and parents might be affected by each of the different programs?

4 What life experiences helped to interest you in a career in early childhood education? At this point in your career what

kind of program for children described in this chapter do you think would best suit your interests?

PROJECTS

1 Write a research paper (based on a number of sources) or a book review (based on a biography or autobiography) of one of the educators mentioned in the chapter who has had an impact on the field of early childhood education.

2 Choose one of the following areas for a survey, and write a report on the kinds of programs and program policies in your community:
   □ Children with special needs
   □ Child care
   □ Compensatory education
   □ Preschool/Nursery schools

3 In a written or oral report describe how preschools, day care centers, and public and private kindergartens are licensed in your community. Include discussion of requirements for teacher qualifications and training and the daily program for children. Based on your examination of state regulations, what appear to be the primary concerns regarding programs for children?

4 In a written or oral report describe how teachers of young children are certified in your state. What are the salaries for teachers in different kinds of programs? What are the implications of your findings?

5 In a written or oral report describe training programs (credit and noncredit) available in your community for teachers of young children. Gather your information from universities, colleges, community colleges, high schools, and associations like your local NAEYC Affiliate group.

6 In a written or oral report describe the kinds of support provided in your state and community for children under five. What are the sources and amounts of funds for these programs and services?

7 Visit a program for young children in your community. Find out about its history, philosophy, sponsorship, tuition, ratios, provisions for parent involvement, teacher qualifications, and salaries. Present your findings in a written or oral report.

RECOMMENDED READING

Auleta, Michael S. *Foundations of Early Childhood Education.* New York: Random House, 1969.

Braun, Samuel J., and Edwards, Esther P. *History and Theory of Early Childhood Education.* Belmont, Cal.: Wadsworth, 1972.

Cartwright, G. Phillip; Cartwright, Carol A.; and Ward, Marjorie E. *Educating Special Learners.* Belmont, Cal.: Wadsworth, 1981.

CDA Credential and You: Information for Child Care Workers. Washington D. C.: U.S. Department of Health and Human Services, Agency for Children, Youth, and Families: Head Start Bureau, 1981.

Dewey, John. *Experience and Education.* New York: Collier Books, 1972.

Hymes, James L., Jr. *Early Childhood Education: An Introduction to the Profession.* 2d ed. Washington, D.C.: National Assocation for the Education of Young Children, 1977.

————.*Teaching the Child Under Six.* 3d ed. Columbus, O.: Charles E. Merrill, 1981.

Maccoby, Eleanor E., and Zellner, Miriam. *Experiments in Primary Education: Aspects of Project Follow-Through.* New York: Harcourt Brace Jovanovich, 1970.

Montessori, Maria. *Dr. Montessori's Own Handbook.* New York: Schocken Books, 1965.

————. *The Absorbent Mind.* New York: Holt, Rinehart, and Winston, 1967.

Read, Katherine, and Patterson, June. *The Nursery School and Kindergarten: Human Relationships and Learning.* 7th ed. New York: Holt, Rinehart, and Winston, 1980.

Seaver, Judith W., Cartwright, Carol A.; Ward, Cecelia B.; and Heasley, C. Annette. *Careers with Young Children: Making Your Decision.* Washington D.C.: The National Association for the Education of Young Children, 1979.

Silberman, Charles E. *Crisis in the Classroom.* New York: Random House, 1970.

Steiner, Gilbert Y. *The Children's Cause.* Washington, D.C.: The Brookings Institute, 1976.

Steinfels, Margaret O. *Who's Minding the Children?* New York: Simon and Schuster, 1973.

Weber, Evelyn. *The Kindergarten: Its Encounter with Educational Thought in America.* New York: Teachers College Press, 1969.

Zigler, Edward, and Valentine, Jeanette. *Project Head Start: A Legacy of the War On Poverty.* New York: Free Press, 1979.

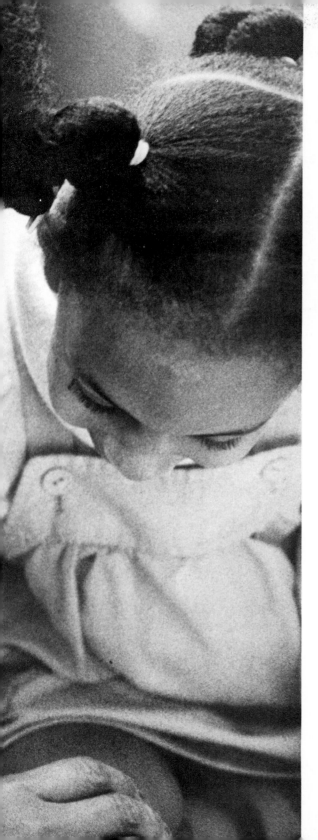

2

The Teacher of Young Children

"A teacher affects eternity: he can never
tell where his influence stops."

Henry Brooks Adams

*In this chapter we explore the nature of the teacher as a person and as a professional. We discuss the effect of teacher personality on young children and characteristics of effective teachers, examine the role of the teacher and the authority that comes with the role, and describe some things that teachers can do to feel good about themselves and about teaching. The content of this chapter relates to the CDA area **Professionalism.***

When teachers base what they do on respect for children and on sound knowledge of development and curriculum, children are likely to maintain the eagerness and curiosity that characterize the early years and make learning a meaningful process. While most children enter school lively and inquisitive, many soon become bored, passive, or even hostile students. Negative feelings about learning may well be a result of encounters with teachers who do not like teaching and who regard children as empty vessels to be filled with facts, rather than as intelligent people who come to school with many experiences.

Many of today's early childhood programs come from the developmental tradition of education that emphasizes children's natural inclination to grow and learn. It is the purpose of this book to help you become a teacher who nourishes the growth of children by helping them to develop their natural potential rather than teaching disembodied facts, drilling on skills or regimenting behavior. Your personality, attitudes, values and sense of professional identity will all play an important role in the kind of person you will be in children's lives.

UNDERSTANDING THE TEACHER AS A PERSON

The personal characteristics (personalities) of teachers have a powerful effect on how they relate to children and adults and how they behave in the classroom. Personality includes distinctive traits of mind, behavior and emotion. These derive from a complex interaction of inherited characteristics, sometimes called temperament; early experiences at home and at school; and personal values and choices. We have searched for a way to look at personality that would help us and our college students to understand the unique impact each teacher has on children. We have found a number of approaches that have been very useful including Chess and Thomas' work on child and adult temperament, the Myers-Briggs Type Indicator, and techniques for analyzing autobiographies of prospective teachers, developed by Jacqueline Rosen at Bank Street College.

Teacher Temperament and Decision-Making Style

The research of pediatricians Alexander Thomas and Stella Chess on the temperament of infants provides a valuable starting point for understanding the personalities of adults as well as children. Thomas and Chess refer to temperament as the observable manifestations; the "how" of behavior that explains a great deal about individual differences in style. They have found that, to some extent, these characteristics are inborn. Newborn babies show definite differences in certain traits. These persist over time, though they are often modified in adulthood because they have been influenced by life experiences. We have found the nine dimensions of temperament, described by Chess and Thomas and applied to adults by therapists Jayne Burks and Melvin Rubenstein (1979), to be helpful in explaining personality differences in teachers and to be a valuable source of self-knowledge. Each trait can be thought of on a continuum from a high to low incidence. (See page 40 for a brief summary of the nine traits as they apply to adults. These will be described as they pertain to children in Chapter 4, "Child Development.")

We have had our college students rate themselves on a questionnaire designed for adults based on these dimensions of temperament (Trubitt, 1981). This process has increased their self-awareness and has offered insight regarding their relationships with children. Students' with low activity levels or high levels or persistence have learned that these are not universally held, and that they cannot assume that the children they teach will respond the same ways that they do. This instrument offers a practical and useful way to acknowledge and respond to individual differences and needs among our students. Informal research on our

student responses to this questionnaire shows them consistently very high on the dimensions of positive mood and adaptability.

Another approach to helping teachers (and others) understand themselves is the Myers-Briggs Type Indicator (MBTI) based on Carl Jung's theory of psychological types. This instrument can help teachers learn more about the way that they characteristically look at the world and make decisions. The MBTI is scored on four dimensions with poles representing opposite tendencies. The first of these is **Extraversion-Introversion.** The poles of this dimension refer to the extent to which a person relates to the outer world of people and things (extraversion) versus the inner world of ideas (introversion). The second dimension, **Sensing-Intuition,** reflects either the tendency to work with known facts (sensing) or possibilities and relationships (intuition). The third dimension, **Thinking-Feeling,** has to do with whether a person bases judgments more on impersonal analysis (thinking) than personal values (feeling). The last dimension, **Judging-Perceiving,** deals with preference for a planned, orderly approach to life (judging) as opposed to a more spontaneous, flexible approach (perceiving). Each individual is assigned a four letter profile based on their responses to the questionnaire. Each profile is characterized by a unique pattern of interests and skills.

This instrument has been used to look at constellations of personality type that characterize people in different professions. Data from a number of studies using the MBTI (McCaulley and Natter, 1980; Keirsey and Bates, 1978) suggest that the majority of students entering

THOMAS AND CHESS' NINE DIMENSIONS OF TEMPERAMENT

1. **ACTIVITY LEVEL**—Level of physical and mental activity.

   Very active ——————————————— Inactive, quiet

2. **REGULARITY** (Rhythmicity)—Preference for predictable routines or spontaneity.

   Very regular/predictable ——————— Very unpredictable

3. **DISTRACTIBILITY**—Degree to which extraneous stimuli affects behavior; readiness to leave one activity for another.

   Easily distracted by outside ————— Very focused
   events/activities people   despite distractions

4. **APPROACH-WITHDRAWAL**—Ways of responding the first time to new situations.

   Enjoys new people ————————— Dislikes having to
   and experiences   face new people and
                                          experiences

5. **ADAPTABILITY**—Ease of adjustment to new ideas or situations (after the initial response.)

   Adapts easily to change ————— Has difficulty
                                      adapting to change

6. **PHYSICAL SENSITIVITY** (Threshold of responsiveness)—Sensitivity to changes in the environment including noise, taste, smell, and temperature.

   Very aware of changes ———— Not too attuned to
   in the environment   to changes in the environment

7. **INTENSITY OF REACTION**—Energy level that characterizes a response (either positive or negative).

   Very intense responses ————— Quite calm in responses

8. **PERSISTENCE/ATTENTION SPAN**—The amount of time devoted to an activity, even when it is difficult, and the ability to continue working when distracted.

   Stays with a task despite ————— Leaves a task if there
   distractions   are distractions

9. **QUALITY OF MOOD**—General optimism or pessimism; tendency to enjoy things uncritically or to be more selective about situations enjoyed.

   Happy, optimistic ————————— Sad, pessimistic

early childhood education tend to be more extraverted, sensing, feeling and judging. Individuals who are more oriented to ideas and possibilities (Intuitive) and who are flexible and creative (Perceiving) bring special qualities to teaching young children. Yet people of this type often move into research and teacher education positions.

Instruments like the MBTI and the Adult Temperament Questionnaire may help to explain some of a person's characteristic reactions, as well as differences in individual style; tendencies for people to be friendly or reflective, dramatic and exuberant or more subdued, active or quiet. Style, in this sense, is neither good nor bad; it is simply a part of us. It is not necessary to have a particular kind of style in order to be a good teacher of young children, although it appears that some temperamental characteristics, like a high activity level and high adaptability, might make it easier.

We have heard it said that teachers need to be exciting and dramatic, but we know excellent teachers of young children who are quiet and gentle. What *is* important is that you become aware of your characteristics, how they affect others, and how they fit or do not fit with the styles of the adults and children that you spend your days with. Awareness can help you to enhance or subdue aspects of your personality in the classroom when it is appropriate.

Personality Dynamics

While information about personal qualities helps us to understand differences in style, it does not explain the dynamics of behavior, those factors that grow out of a complex interaction of temperament and past experiences. Early experiences are very important in the formation of the ways that people feel about themselves and others and their ways of responding to situations. The ability to respond in positive and healthy ways appears to be related to a person learning to trust others in their early years and to see the world as a basically good and nurturing place.

Adults who have had their basic needs met in childhood and who have developed trust in themselves and in the world are likely to have the ability to support the growth and development of others. People who lack this basic trust may not have had their needs met in consistent ways in their early lives, and this may lead to unresolved problems and the need for a great deal of support and reassurance in

adulthood. They may have a difficult time being nurturing and supportive of others.

A series of studies addressing the question of teacher personality as related to teaching effectiveness was conducted by Jacqueline Rosen at Bank Street College in New York. Rosen's assumptions were that the quality of the teacher-child relationship is a key variable in children's learning and attitudes toward school and that adults vary in their capacity to develop positive relations with children. Studies (1968, 1972) based on analysis of college students' autobiographical essays found that prospective teachers' concepts of their childhood selves and their recalled relations with their parents can yield predictors of their ability to relate to children in general and also of their effectiveness with children of different ages, personalities and coping styles.

Rosen found that the autobiographical themes seemed to mirror developmental issues of the children that the students were rated as most successful in teaching. For example, the college students who were rated by college supervisors as best with preschool children often described the joy and sense of security they had as young children, and tended to have vivid and spontaneous recall of early experiences. Those judged most effective with the five- to eight-year-old age group frequently emphasized independence, the acquisition of grown up roles, and the early need to achieve basic skills. Those judged most effective with eight to eleven year olds tended to recall adults or older siblings who had stimulated in them a love of learning and ideas, and emphasized the importance of childhood peer relationships.

Rosen's 1975 study reports the development and field testing of *The Developmental Self and Child-Concept Scales* (DSCCS), a method for assessing adult personality that can be applied in the selection, training and guidance of adults who wish to work with children. This instrument was able to differentiate between the subjects who were judged as developing outstanding relationships and those who developed only fair or poor relations with children. The findings were consistent with those using autobiographical data. Rosen's work demonstrates that there is a relationship between how teachers view their childhoods and their effectiveness as teachers.

Sensitivity to others and a positive sense of self are essential requirements for becoming a person who can support the development of children. Skills in gaining trust and developing relationships are acquired as you come to know yourself better, accept yourself, and then learn more about children and how to work successfully with them. An important part of this process of development (and the major theme in this book) is to frequently ask yourself, "Who am I?" "What kind of person do I want to be?" and "What are my strengths, and in what areas do I need to grow and change?"

In order to become what Carl Rogers calls an *authentic person*, one who possesses awareness and empathy and who is willing to relate to others in nurturing ways, it is necessary to know and accept yourself, as well as to realistically appraise areas in which change may be needed, and to see yourself in a lifelong process of growth and change. It is important to be open to new experiences, to acknowledge and deal with feelings, and to experience relationships in ever-increasing depth and breadth. This self-knowledge is, to a great extent, dependent on developing the ability to observe oneself in the same honest and nonjudgmental way that one learns to observe children. It also involves learning to accept criticism from others as valuable feedback that can provide a source of growth, instead of as something to defend against or to use to berate or belittle oneself. The capacity for self-knowledge and acceptance is the corner-stone for the quality of compassion that is so important in a teacher. Arthur Jersild describes it like this:

> To be compassionate, one must be able to accept the impact of any emotion—love or hate, joy, fear, or grief—tolerate it and harbor it long enough and with sufficient

absorption to accept its meaning and to enter into a fellowship of feeling with the one who is moved by the emotion. This is the heroic feature of compassion in its fullest development: to be able to face the ravage of rage, the shattering impact of terror, the tenderest prompting of love, and then to embrace these in a larger context, which involves an acceptance of these feelings and an appreciation of what they mean to the one who experiences them. (Jersild, 1955, pp. 125–26)

We realize that no one of us is com-pletely self-aware, mature, wise, compas-sionate, and insightful all of the time. All of us have tendencies to be defensive. It is important to develop the capacity for

self-awareness and some vision of the kind of behavior and relationships toward which we aspire. It is also important to understand that while everyone experiences strong and unpleasant emotions like anger and fear at times, it is possible to learn to observe and choose how to respond to these feelings instead of acting upon them in ways that may be destructive.

Preference, Bias, and Prejudice

As you develop greater self-awareness, you can begin to observe your own personal preferences regarding the kinds of individuals (adults and children) that you prefer to interact with, and the kinds of activities and work settings that suit you best. Awareness of your preferences will help choose a setting that allows you to function most effectively as a teacher. If you are highly distractible and have a need for order, you might want to avoid large, open settings with lots of noise and confusion in favor of smaller, quieter self-contained classrooms. If you are an active person and not easily distracted, you might find a more informal and spontaneous environment more to your liking.

Your personality and past experiences also contribute to the development of *biases* and inclinations to favor or reject certain individuals or groups of people. Sometimes these inclinations are simply based on the human tendency to feel comfortable with people who are most like ourselves in their views of the world and the ways that they respond to it. Sometimes these biases are so strong that they become *prejudices,* opinions based on preconceptions (prejudgment) rather than on direct experience of the individual.

Leo Buscaglia in his popular book *Love* eloquently describes his distress as a child at being labelled as *dago, wop* and other derogatory terms used for Italians. He points out that the prejudice of those who called him names created distance and allowed them to think that they knew something about him when in fact they had no real knowledge.

Teachers are often unaware of their biases and prejudices and of the devastating effect that these can have. As a teacher or prospective teacher, your awareness of your own biases will be very important in monitoring your behavior so that it will not have negative effects on children. To learn something about your biases, begin by asking yourself the following questions and answering as honestly as you can.

- ☐ How do I feel about children who are dirty, ragged or smelly?
- ☐ How do I feel about children I find unattractive?
- ☐ How do I feel about children who do not conform to my expectations about good or acceptable behavior?
- ☐ Are there children I immediately dislike or with whom I feel uncomfortable? What are the characteristics of these children?
- ☐ Do I have strong feelings about children who are loud and aggressive?
- ☐ What are my feelings about children who are clingy and whiny?
- ☐ Do I generally tend to prefer children of one sex over children of the other?
- ☐ Do I have strong feelings about quiet, passive children or loud, verbal ones?
- ☐ Do I have strong feelings about children from certain economic backgrounds, races or cultures?

☐   Do I have feelings about working with children who are precocious, developmentally delayed, or even handicapped?

Remember that prejudice involves prejudgment and can be positive or negative. It can also be harmful to be prejudiced in favor of one group of children (these feelings may affect a whole group). When less favored children observe your preferences, they may perceive themselves as less worthy. If you discover that you do have some biases (and we all do), simple awareness may be enough to help you remember the special needs of a shy child or not to overreact to an aggressive, bossy, or whiny one. Self-observation and the resulting awareness may help you to know when you may be damaging children by rejecting them for things that they cannot control. If you become aware that you have strong prejudices that you cannot overcome, you should ask yourself if there are particular children or groups of children with whom you should not work. You may even need to consider seriously whether you should become a teacher.

UNDERSTANDING THE TEACHER AS A PROFESSIONAL

A profession is an occupation requiring advanced study and specialized training. The extent to which an occupation fulfills a set of criteria determines whether or not it will be considered a profession. Perhaps no single group completely meets all of the criteria though there is general agreement in society that doctors and lawyers are professionals and that day

laborers are not. Other groups, including early childhood educators, are somewhere in between in terms of their professional status. There are a number of ways to look at the nature of a profession. We find the following six criteria (adapted from Katz, 1985) most useful for looking at the field of early childhood education: (1) A profession involves *specialized knowledge and expertise* expressed in highly technical terms. This expertise involves unique abilities and accomplishments and abstract knowledge, based on systematic principles. It is used for socially useful and practical ends and is exclusive (can't be mastered easily by everyone); (2) A profession requires *prolonged training and has requirements for entry.* The training is specialized, difficult, offered by an accredited institution, and involves more learning than is used in daily practice. Entry requirements may involve passing an examination in addition to completing a prescribed course of study; (3) A profession requires conformity to a *code of ethics* to assure that services will be in accord with reasonably high standards and acceptable moral conduct; (4) A profession adopts *standards of practice* which are meant to ensure that practitioners apply standard procedures in exercising professional judgment; (5) A profession has *autonomy,* internal control over quality, and it regulates itself; and (6) A profession is characterized by a *commitment to a significant social value.* It is altruistic and service-oriented rather than profit-oriented and uses its knowledge and power for the good of society which accords it respect and high status.

When we examine our field in terms of these characteristics, we see that our status is mixed. At this time in our history, early childhood education is an occupation which is developing into a profession. We are becoming more knowledgeable about theories of development and learning, and more skillful in applying these in our daily work with children. We are working on professional issues including ethics and standards of practice. We are committed to serving society through providing the best possible alternatives in the care and education of young children. As anyone who has ever worked in a preschool knows, we are a long way from having autonomy and being accorded high status. Yet there are changes taking place.

Teacher Role

The first professional dimension of teaching young children that we will examine is the very important issue of the teacher's role. The term *role* refers to expectations that are made of people because they hold a particular position in society. The career of a teacher of young children is no small undertaking, in part because the expectations accompanying the role are many, varied, and sometimes contradictory. Most people agree that the job of the teacher of young children is to help them learn and grow. Yet the specific things that the teacher is expected to do to accomplish this goal is subject to a great deal of debate. Some of the disagreement has to do with differing views of what children should be learning and doing in school. Some people believe that teachers should be teaching facts and skills, others that thinking and problem solving are more important. Still others believe that intellectual development is not as important for very young children as learning to get along with others in groups and to

feel good about themselves as people and as learners.

While there is general agreement today that teachers of young children need to be involved in all areas of the child's development (social, emotional, intellectual and physical), there is tremendous variation in the ways that they do this. Concern with the development of all aspects of the child is especially important in early childhood programs because young children are less experienced and more vulnerable than older children. Programs differ in the values that underlie daily practice, in the organization of classrooms, and in the curriculum that they teach.

Because of the age and vulnerability of young children, the teacher needs to take on some of the nurturing role of the parent. Since early childhood programs often provide the first transition from home to the larger world, the teacher plays an important role in helping parents and children learn to separate from each other. In fact, the the teacher may be the second adult outside the home (the first is the pediatrician) who works with the family and has a close relationship with the parents and child. Therefore, your role involves working with parents, as well as children, and often includes helping parents deal with separation and understand and relate to their child in constructive ways.

There are many other roles that you will play as a teacher of young children. You will be called upon to provide children with a sense of psychological comfort and security; you will organize and maintain an environment in which children live and learn; you will plan for daily activities which are part of a broader curriculum design; and you will mediate

relationships between children. In a single day you may be friend, mother, colleague, nurse, janitor, counselor, and instructor. Teachers we know have pointed out to us that they have also functioned as entertainer, diplomat, interior designer, journalist, and on rare occasions as undertaker of small animals. You will have many roles and be called upon to perform many tasks.

Teachers of young children are in many ways like parents, more so than teachers of any other age group. Yet they are *not* parents, and it is sometimes difficult to walk the fine line between these roles. There are important similarities between parents and teachers, but there are also important differences. Lilian Katz (1980)

makes a number of interesting and valuable distinctions between the roles and responsibilities of mothers and teachers.

Katz points out that mothers and teachers need to be quite different in their level of attachment to the child. Mothers need to be favorably biased and think that their child is the most wonderful and special person in the world. The teacher needs to appreciate the child too, but in a more realistic way. Teachers need to keep more distance, to be more objective. Greater objectivity enables them to observe and assess children realistically and to work with them not just as individuals, but within the context of a group. Teachers need always to keep in mind the balance between the needs of the individual and the welfare of the whole group.

Teachers need to be more objective than mothers, and mothers need to be more spontaneous than teachers. It is a mother's role to respond warmly and intuitively to a child and not to worry too much about the effects of every action. Teachers need to be intentional and deliberate. They need to have clear goals and plan activities in systematic ways to enhance specific areas of children's development. Obviously, these are not absolute distinctions; parents also need to be thoughtful and teachers, spontaneous. What is clear is that the relative emphasis should be different if they are to provide what the child needs from each of them. Neither parents nor teachers should feel guilty because they are not doing the other's job. Yet we have seen teachers who feel badly that they cannot love and provide for every child as if it were their own, and parents who worry that they aren't doing enough teaching to insure their child's success in school. Each of them needs to know that partnership between home and school is possible and that neither teacher nor parent can singlehandedly meet all of the child's emotional and educational needs.

Herbert Kohl in his book, *Growing Minds: On Becoming a Teacher,* makes a distinction that we have found very helpful in our thinking. He states that it is unrealistic for a teacher to love every child, that love is too demanding and consuming, and each of us has a limited amount of it to give: "I don't trust teachers who say they love all their students, because it isn't possible to love so many people you know so little about and will separate from in six months or a year" (p. 64). But he adds, "Yet a certain kind of love is essential to good teaching, and that is what I choose to call loving students as learners" (p. 64). Kohl says that this kind of love relates to the teaching challenge of what children are able to do as a result of their interactions with us.

The job of a teacher of young children is varying and challenging; it demands knowledge, skill, sensitivity, and creativity. It is not always easy, and the roles are not always distinct. If these challenges do not deter you, you are probably in the right field. Early childhood education is especially rewarding for those who enjoy finding spontaneous educational opportunities in daily life with children. It can be frustrating for people who think that teaching involves only academic subject matter or those who like everything predictable and clear-cut. Our college students who had glorious visions of shaping young minds have sometimes become discouraged when they discovered how much of their time was spent mixing paint, changing pants, mopping floors, and wiping noses. Working with young children is demanding, difficult and tiring. It can also be challenging and gratifying. The more experience you can have in working in early childhood classrooms, the sooner it will become clear to you if teaching young children is the right choice for you.

Teacher Authority

By virtue of having the role of teacher, society confers a certain authority: the right to exercise power, give commands, expect obedience, make decisions, and take action. The most obvious source of the teacher's authority is adulthood.

Because teachers are larger, stronger, and older, children acknowledge their right to direct. Teacher's authority is reinforced by experience in teaching, by skill and knowledge, and by dedication and commitment.

Learning to deal with authority is one of the first important issues that faces a prospective teacher. We have watched our college students struggle with their notions of authority as they have sought to define their relationships with children in ways that felt natural and comfortable to them. Some of them tried to deny the authority that accompanies the role of teacher. They behaved as if they were one of the kids and have treated the children as "pals." They became confused and frustrated when the children did not respect them and treated them exactly the same way that they did their young peers. Other students expected children to respect them simply because they were a teacher. They felt that children had to learn "that the teacher is boss" and to accept authority just because it was there. They tried to exercise authority without earning it and were often surprised at the amount of rebellion and resistance they encountered.

We have found the concept of *natural authority,* described by George Dennison in his book, *The Lives of Children,* helpful in defining and exercising teacher authority in ways that feel natural and that have positive effects on children.

> Natural authority is a far cry from authority that is merely arbitrary. Its attributes are obvious; adults are larger, more experienced, possess more words, have entered into prior agreements among themselves. When all this takes on a positive instead of merely negative character, the children see adults as protectors and as sources of certitude, approval, novelty, skills. (Dennison, 1969, p. 124)

There are a number of issues in teaching that relate to the proper use of authority. Many of us have encountered teachers who were harsh, punitive, or unfair and who in other ways could be described as abusing their authority. We have also sometimes experienced teachers who were not clear and consistent and who did not give us enough direction. These teachers abdicate their authority and leave children without a sense of what is acceptable and without necessary structure. Authority that is authentic and lasting is based on mutual respect and not on coercion or abandonment of responsibility. It is used wisely and with compassion.

CARING FOR YOURSELF

Your first responsibility as a teacher is to take care of the needs of children; yet you also have a responsibility to take care of your own needs. All you have to give is yourself—your caring, your energy, and your commitment. You cannot do this when you are not at your best. To accomplish the demanding task of teaching young children, you need to be in good physical and emotional health. You need to feel that you are appreciated, meaningfully connected to others, intellectually stimulated, and that your job is worth doing.

Making sure that your needs are met depends, in part, on knowing about yourself. We have learned about individual biological differences from the work of Roger Williams, a biochemist. He describes how much people vary physiologically, from the size of their stomachs, to their ability to metabolize food, to their need for rest and nutrients (1971). Understanding that there are great differences between people can help you to be attuned to your body's individual responses and to learn to pay attention to its rhythms and needs.

Individuals also vary in distractibility, adaptability and sensitivity to changes in the environment. Some of us function well amidst noise and confusion while others find the same stimulation unbearable. Similarly, some people find uncertainty uncomfortable and disorienting while others thrive on its challenge.

These kinds of differences have implications for whether you will survive and thrive in teaching. It is important for each of us to know what causes excessive stress for us so that we can learn to minimize it in our lives. Understanding that your requirements for nourishment, rest, exercise, and intellectual stimulation are unique can help you know yourself better and make sure that your needs are met.

Knowing that people are very different can help you to perceive differences positively. One teacher's need for order, for example, may contribute to a well-maintained, calm classroom while another's delight in spontaneity may bring a creative zest to children. Just as you attempt to find out about and appreciate the individual differences in children, observe yourself and your colleagues, and learn to accept and appreciate your unique qualities.

Physical Well-Being

Whether it is your first year of teaching or your thirtieth, there is little that is more important than your health. Without physical stamina, good health, and a good diet, a teacher is not adequately prepared to work with young children for long hours every day. Studies conducted by Buhler and Aspy point to the direct connection between teachers' physical fitness and the quality of their relationships with children. They have found that teachers who are physically fit tend to have more humane classrooms than teachers who are not (Buhler, 1975). Being well is more than not being sick. It includes the vitality and well-being that come with a good diet, adequate rest, and regular exercise.

Although good teachers pay attention to the nutrition of the children they teach, they often overlook their own nutritional needs. This reflects a national tendency (but one which we are increasingly aware of) toward being overfed but undernourished. Research about nutrition suggests that many widely used foods (smoked meats; foods containing large quantities of fat, salt, refined sugar and additives, caffeine, and refined flour) are actually detrimental to health, especially if consumed in large quantities. Whole grains, lean meats, fruits, and vegetables are foods that contribute to good health.

It is important for teachers who work with young children to eat well. The effects of poor nutrition are gradual, but the long-term effects are profound. A simple deficiency of B vitamins can lead to reduced ability to deal with stress and handle anxiety (Jordan, 1973). A good diet combined with regular exercise will give you energy, strength and stamina.

Breakfast is your most important meal of the day, because after a night's fast, your blood sugar is low, and a good breakfast elevates and stabilizes it, enabling you to function efficiently throughout the day; moreover, your body utilizes proteins better in the morning than at any other time of day. Breakfast does not have to be traditional eggs and toast, but coffee and a doughnut will not give you the fuel you need for your morning's work with children. Try to include fresh fruit, whole grains, and a source of protein. It may be difficult at first to change your eating patterns, but once you realize that it is necessary, you can approach it in increments. No change is easy or fast, but good eating habits are important and worth working to develop. If you wish to learn more, refer to some of the books suggested at the end of this chapter.

Regular exercise also plays an important part in maintaining health. When you come home exhausted after a long day of teaching, you may not feel like lacing up your running shoes and going out to jog. If you can get past your initial resistance, you may feel much better after you have spent some time in vigorous exercise. If running is not for you, there are many alternatives. You can walk, dance, swim, bicycle, or play games like volleyball. The exercise that

you enjoy most, and *do,* is the right exercise for you.

Adequate rest is also important to your ability to function well in the classroom. In addition to getting enough sleep at night, you may need to find ways to replenish your mental and physical energy. We know teachers whose intense involvement with children consistently spilled into their thoughts at home and even their dreams. This kind of preoccupation over time can lead to burn-out. Some form of relaxation such as yoga, meditation, or a quiet time listening to music and sipping a cup of herb tea may be helpful in renewing both body and mind. Finding a quiet time for yourself is not an indulgence, but an important part of preparing yourself for your daily interactions with children.

Your need for rest and good nutrition is increased when you are ill. Staying home from work and resting when you are sick is doubly important when you are a teacher. You need to protect your health and that of the children and your colleagues; no one benefits when you come to work sick.

Emotional Well-Being

The way you feel about yourself and the world affects the quality of your interactions with other people both at home and on the job. Likewise, your perceptions of your competence as a teacher will affect how you feel about yourself and your work. To continue teaching over time, you need to have positive feelings about yourself both as a person and a professional. To keep growing you need to have a realistic view of your own abilities, be willing to try new things and to learn from your failures.

When you start to feel worried or depressed, it helps to have a good friend

to talk to about your concerns. Sometimes problems are rooted in the past, and seeing a counselor or therapist can help. When these bad times come, try not to get angry at yourself for weakness or failure; rather see what you are going through as a developmental stage, just as you would observe a child going through a difficult period. Don't judge yourself harshly; some things take time to work through, and remember that it won't last forever.

Social Needs

Another essential for survival in the classroom is someone to talk to. Having someone with whom to share your joys, frustrations, insights and ideas can be very important in determining how you feel about yourself as a person and as a teacher. It is ideal if there is someone you work with to fulfill this role. If not, you may have a friend who is willing to listen and understand, or you may find someone with similar needs for sharing in a class or the local early childhood association. What is important is that you have someone readily available with whom you can exchange ideas, feelings, resources, and moral support.

Schools where teachers feel appreciated and connected to others are often characterized by a sense of community, which involves feelings of belonging, friendship, mutual respect, and a shared sense of purpose . A feeling of interdependence is shared by staff and sometimes includes the families of the children who attend the school. A sense of community does not happen by accident; it must be nurtured in order to grow. We have found that a number of our graduates chose to work in schools which have a strong sense of community because, even though the salaries were low, the sense of purpose and connectedness was important to them.

Intellectual Stimulation

We all need intellectual stimulation—a sense that we are growing and learning and being challenged by our jobs. If you are not interested or challenged by your work and do not see potential for the situation improving, then you are in a state of professional stagnation. You will probably remain bored until you find something that will stimulate you to continue to grow as a teacher. Like children, adults are ready for different kinds of learning at different times. There are a number of sources and kinds of information that might be helpful in providing you some intellectual challenge.

Observing children is like an ever-changing kaleidoscope; understanding them and their behavior is the first, and usually most lasting, intellectual challenge for teachers. In addition to fascination with children, adults need environments which are stimulating, challenging and responsive. Like children, adults need resources, time and encouragement to explore, experiment productively, and learn. When faced with a question or problem about a child's behavior or curriculum, it will help you if there are people who are interested and willing to help you explore your question, resources in which you can seek possible understanding and solutions, and an administration that will encourage you to try different alternatives to see which works best for you. Elizabeth Jones suggests that teachers can regard their intellectual interests and concerns as a form of play. You can pursue topics that are interesting

and fun and make decisions about what *you* want to learn and do.

As you consider your needs for intellectual stimulation, it may be helpful to know Lilian Katz' (1972) description of the four stages of teacher development and the different kinds of stimulation and training that are most appropriate at each stage. Knowing your developmental stage as a teacher may be helpful in choosing the most satisfying learning experiences.

Stage 1: Survival   The difficult first year of teaching is a time when teachers need to develop skill in applying their training to the real world of the classroom. Most teachers are sufficiently challenged by the task of teaching. Moderate inspiration, technical assistance, and support from someone who knows your teaching situation can be valuable during this time.

Stage 2: Consolidation   When basic "survival" in the classroom has been accomplished (after two to four years), teachers often begin to want to bring together what they know to create a more personal approach to teaching. During this time they may find on-site assistance, consultants, and the advice of colleagues helpful.

Stage 3: Renewal   After three to five years in the classroom, teachers may find themselves feeling somewhat bored or dissatisfied. At this stage conferences, workshops, films, membership in professional associations, like the National Association for the Education of Young Children (NAEYC) or the Association for Childhood Education International (ACEI), and visits to other schools may renew

enthusiasm and give ideas for improving classroom practice, as well as a greater sense of belonging and professionalism.

Stage 4: Maturity   After five or more years of working with children, teachers often find themselves less interested in the day-to-day practical details of teaching (which they will have effectively mastered) and more interested in consideration of the values, theories, issues and philosophy that underlie their work. Seminars, work on advanced degrees, and extensive reading in professional literature at this stage may renew their sense of excitement and provide new areas of professional interest and involvement.

Burn-out and How to Avoid It

When you come home at the end of the school day physically and psychologically tired and find that you are not refreshed after a good night's sleep and are unable to be revived by exercise or a weekend off, you might be suffering from *burn-out.*

The burn-out syndrome is characterized by exhaustion, tension, and anxiety, and causes teachers to withdraw from the intense interpersonal demands of their job. Eventually it affects all of their activities and relationships, including their effectiveness in working with children. Talk of burn-out has become common among educators in recent years, and it is all too familiar in people who work with young children (Whitebook, 1980).

The causes of burn-out lie both in the nature of the profession—the combination of intense involvement and long hours—and in the care that teachers receive from their employers and themselves. As we have said, teachers who are no longer able to nurture young children often have unmet needs in their own lives, while those who can sustain their nurturing role over time may be better at meeting their own needs. Part of avoiding burn-out is to make sure that your basic needs are cared for.

Good nutrition, rest, and exercise, discussed earlier in this chapter, are absolutely essential in preventing burn-out. Our discussion about the distinction between mothers and teachers is also important in this regard. Some teachers suffer burn-out because they let themselves become so involved in the lives of children and families that they don't leave themselves energy for anything else.

Teachers' needs must also be met within their working day if they are to accomplish their professional purposes, continue their own development, and avoid burn-out. A school that strives to serve the best interests of teachers (as well as children and families) must provide them with time to accomplish needed tasks each day. This includes opportunity for quiet breaks, away from the hub-bub of a busy, noisy classroom; time for staff meetings and conferences with parents; and time for planning and other nonteaching tasks. It may require extra funds or ingenious planning to arrange regular preparation time for teachers, but the effort will be well worth it. Breaks are essential in a full day program and need to be a planned part of the daily schedule (unplanned breaks often don't occur), covered by alternative staff, and acknowledged as the teacher's right, not privilege. Breaks are more relaxing if a quiet, comfortable space is set aside apart from children's play areas.

Morale is important in preventing burn-out; teachers work best when they know that they are valued and that their needs are being considered. Whether you are a new or continuing teacher, it helps to be aware of the causes of burn-out and of the necessity of working to prevent it. It is essential that you take care of your most important teaching tool—yourself—if you are to provide the very best for young children.

FOR FURTHER THOUGHT AND DISCUSSION

1 How do you remember yourself as a child entering school? What were your feelings about the teacher? What kind of relationship did you have with the teacher? Does this have implications for how you want to relate to children?

2 Think about a teacher you remember well in terms of roles, authority, personal qualities, impact on children, and your feelings.

3 Think about a teacher you have observed recently in terms of roles, authority, personal qualities, impact on children, and your feelings.

4 Reflect on the teachers you have liked best and least in your school experiences from early childhood to today. Relate these to the concepts about teachers presented in this chapter. What conclusions can you come to?

5 How do you think your personal qualities will be likely to affect your work with children? Has this chapter given you any new insights about yourself as a teacher?

PROJECTS

1   Observe a teacher in an early childhood program for at least one hour. Describe five incidents where the teacher demonstrates different roles. Comment on your reactions to this observation and how it might influence your teaching. For each incident describe:
   □ The roles the teacher assumed
   □ The authority that appeared to have been exercised
   □ The temperamental qualities the teacher demonstrated
   □ The feelings, preferences, or biases expressed
   □ The degree of openness and genuineness demonstrated

2   Choose a child, and for at least one hour, attempt to experience the classroom and child's relationship with the teacher from the child's perspective. Describe as thoughtfully as you can what happened during the period of your observation and how the child might have felt. Describe what you learned about children, about teachers and about yourself.

3   Write a thoughtful self-analysis in which you relate concepts from this chapter to your ability to be a competent, nurturing teacher of young children. Consider the following:
   □ your tempermental characteristics
   □ your personal style
   □ your preferences and biases
   □ your ways of perceiving the world and relating to others
   □ your feelings about authority and your leadership abilities
   □ your physical health and stamina and the ways you take care of yourself

RECOMMENDED READING

Almy, Millie. *The Early Childhood Educator at Work.* New York: McGraw-Hill, 1975.

Ashton-Warner, Sylvia. *Teacher.* London: Virago, 1980.

Jersild, Arthur. *When Teachers Face Themselves.* New York: Teachers College Press, 1955.

Katz, Lilian. "Mothering and Teaching—Some Significant Distinctions." *Current Topics in Early Childhood Education,* Vol. III. Norwood, N.J.: Ablex Publishing Co., 1980.

———, and Ward, Evangeline. *Ethical Behavior in Early Childhood Education.* Washington D.C.: National Association for the Education of Young Children, 1978.

Kohl, Herbert. *Growing Minds: On Becoming a Teacher.* New York, Harper and Row, 1984.

Maslow, Abraham. *Toward a Psychology of Being.* New York: Van Nostrand Reinhold, 1968.

Moustakas, Clark. *The Authentic Teacher.* New York: Irvington Publishers, 1982.

Rogers, Carl. *Freedom to Learn.* Columbus, O.: Charles E. Merrill, 1982.

Thomas, Alexander, and Chess, Stella. *Temperament and Development.* New York: Brunner/ Mazel, 1977.

3

Values and Ethics in Early Childhood Education

"Would you tell me, please, which way to go from here?" asked Alice. "That depends a good deal on where you want to get to," said the cat.

Lewis Carroll
Alice in Wonderland

*This chapter explores both the personal and core values and the ethics of early childhood education. We discuss value conflicts, the importance of congruence between values and actions in the classroom, and we encourage you to examine your own values and to use them as a basis for developing your personal philosophy of teaching. We also look at professional ethics in early childhood education. This chapter relates to the CDA area **Professionalism.***

VALUES

Alice's conversation with the Cheshire Cat has some important implications for teaching young children. For how can teachers decide what they are to do in their classrooms if they do not know where they are going? Their decisions about where they are going are, to a great extent, based on values, those that are held by the individual teacher and those of the profession.

Much of life is a process of sorting, examining, and acting upon what we value. Values are those things we believe to be intrinsically desirable or worthwhile, that are prized for themselves; for example, truth, beauty, love, honesty, wisdom, individuality, and integrity. A value can also be seen as the underlying reason for an action. For example, if you ask someone why they wear shoes, they may tell you that they are trying to avoid injury that might result from walking around barefoot. The answer to the next question, "Why don't you want to be injured?" is, "To avoid pain, of course." Avoidance of pain is the value underlying the action, the thing that is desirable in itself and needs no further explanation. A value may also be a means to further another value, like exercise, in order to achieve an ultimate value, in this case, good health.

The development of values is a complex process that grows out of an individual's family background, culture, and life experiences. We begin to learn values early in life; often they are assimilated without our realizing it; later when we reflect on our choices, we are able to infer our underlying values. Values do not change quickly, though changes do occur as people gain new information and experience. There is a difference between personal values, instilled as you grow up, and professional values, which are acquired in the course of professional education and experience.

Values underlie most of our important life decisions, both personal and professional. They determine the goals that a teacher sets and the actions that grow from those goals. Much of what goes on in the classroom is a reflection of the teacher's values, the philosophy of the particular program, and the core values of the field.

Value choices are not always clear-cut. They can involve conflicting demands that call for a weighing and balancing of the positive and negative aspects of a choice. Many arguments about educational practices and policies are based on value differences. For example, the extent to which basic academic skills should be emphasized versus the acquisition of social skills and the development of creativity are value issues that are often debated in early childhood education. It is possible to weigh value decisions in programs according to two criteria: (1) which value is most worth embracing in terms of the future of the society, and (2) what is known about the knowledge and skills children need to get along right now? When we ask these questions, we are working toward establishing a hierarchy of those values in our profession which are most worth embracing.

Thoughtful reflection combined with child development information may be helpful in resolving some value choices. Yet it is impossible to know what the future will hold or to predict with any certainty the long range effects of our educational practices. So there is a point at which value choices must be made based on personal and program preferences rather than professional judgment. Programs and individuals may differ greatly in those things that are emphasized in their work with children. They vary in the extent to which they stress problem solving, interpersonal skills, environmental concerns, spiritual development, factual knowledge, skills needed in the next school setting, and a myriad of other things.

Our values evolve and change as we evolve and change. Willingness to examine values is an important characteristic of a teacher who is learning and growing. Teachers who are not clear about their values or the values of their profession tend to jump from one teaching technique to another without knowing whether their actions are consistent or if they really represent what they want for children. When teachers examine their own values and those of their field, they can weigh their decisions more carefully and choose alternatives with more clarity and wisdom.

VALUES IN EARLY CHILDHOOD EDUCATION

In order to identify, clarify, and act upon our values for education we must first look at our values for society, our feelings about the kind of world we want to live in, and the way that people need to be to enable such a world to exist. These decisions obviously will be strongly influenced by the society in which we live. Early childhood education in the United States, China, Russia, Israel, and other countries will reflect those practices that are perceived as effective in the development of the kinds of citizens the society wants to have. As early childhood educators, we need to make our own personal and professional commitments to the kind of society we wish to live in, the kinds of educational programs we wish to work in, and the kinds of people we want to nurture. In this way our educational commitments become an extension of a broader philosophy.

Within each society, this expression of values in educational programs can take many different forms. For example, we—the authors of this book—believe that it is important to find ways to help children develop into people who are caring, creative, and able to deal with an everchanging world. We are convinced that education needs to address itself to developing individuals who have the ability to live together in peace, to nurture one another, to use new technology with responsibility for its consequences, to protect our environment, and to respond to new challenges.

There is a long tradition in early childhood education of emphasizing those practices that recognize and respect the humanness and dignity of people and that

support the development of children's potential while enhancing their sense of self-esteem. The field has also emphasized the role of the school in making people humane as well as literate. As Barbara Biber says,

> We face first the basic challenge of coming to terms with the problem of goals for the educative process and for the school as an institution in the service of educational goals. By coming to terms, I mean, first recognizing that the school is a mighty force in influencing not only the excellence of intellect but in shaping the feelings, the attitudes, the values, the sense of self and the dreaming of what is to be, the images of good and evil in the world about and the visions of what the life of man with man might be. (Biber, 1969, p.8)

We have recently been involved in a project on professional ethics in early childhood education. Through it we have had the opportunity to work with philosophers and leaders in early childhood education to make the core values of the field more explicit. The core values of a field are those deeply held commitments which are consciously embraced because practitioners believe that they contribute to society. This work on core values is a step in setting down and building consensus regarding the core values of early childhood education as a profession. The views of the project participants about the commitments that characterize the "good early childhood educator" are represented in the box on page 63.

These professional commitments imply education intended to free people to be socially responsible individuals. Teaching strategies that are humane, respectful, and that provide for individual choice will best enable early childhood educators to recognize their commitments to children, to families, and to themselves.

TEACHERS AND VALUE CHOICES

Often a person chooses a career because there is a congruence between the values of the field and those of the individual. When you identify with the values of the field of early childhood education, you move from what you individually think is important to a broader commitment to what early childhood educators in general think is important. There is a merging of your personal values with professional values that can be endorsed and shared. In the best of circumstances, a teacher experiences personal pleasure in nurturing the development of young children on a day-to-day basis and actively acknowledges and supports the core values of the field.

CORE VALUES IN EARLY CHILDHOOD EDUCATION

For Children and Adults

☐ To respect and recognize each individual as a unique human being

☐ To support children and adults in realizing their full potential

☐ To promote environments which foster well-being and positive self-esteem in children, staff and families

☐ To foster autonomy and self-reliance in children, staff and families

For Children

☐ To appreciate the special vulnerability of children and their need for safe and healthy environments

☐ To recognize that each child is an individual with unique needs and abilities

☐ To help children develop socially, emotionally, intellectually, and physically

☐ To help children learn in ways that are appropriate to their stage of development

☐ To appreciate childhood as a unique and valuable stage in the life cycle

☐ To base practice on the best current knowledge of child growth and development

For Families

☐ To recognize and support the interconnectedness of the child and family

☐ To support families in their task of nurturing children

For the Profession

☐ To protect children and advocate for their rights

Some teachers may embrace the core values but not enjoy daily contact with young children, or may work with children for reasons which have no relationship to the core values, such as receiving a regular paycheck or needing a flexible work schedule.

Although the list of core values of early childhood education is in very early stages of formal development, it grows out of the long tradition of the field described in Chapter 1. Because it is so broad in its scope, there is room for a wide range of personal commitments and alternative ways of translating the values into classroom practice. Teachers who support these core values vary in their views about how children learn, about what motivates learning, and about how children can be helped to develop skills, knowledge, and the ability to get along with others. Some believe that we must begin with feelings and relationships and move into more academic learning when children are ready and motivated . Others feel that we must begin by focusing on the development of academic skills and that self-esteem and social skills will follow. Individual commitments to specific areas of content can also be included under the core values, for example, reading and writing, cultural awareness and acceptance, religious education, and peace education.

We believe that there is room for teachers to make many value choices while still supporting the core values described above. In order to help teachers examine their values, we have developed a guide, *Early Childhood Program Dimensions,* for observing values and their implementation in classrooms. We have given the terms *informal* and *formal* education to the spectrum represented by the two extremes of the continuum.

On the informal side of the continuum, the emphasis is on the *learner*. Educators who design programs of this kind believe that the development of the whole child is the first priority and that children are capable of making many of their own choices about learning. They also feel that school experience should be rich and personally meaningful for children, that the process of learning is more important than the product, and that education *is* life and not just preparation for later schooling. Informal programs tend to

value the child's development of autonomy more than conformity to adult expectation and freedom more than order. Learning is seen as an ongoing process of exploration, based on the assumption that children are internally motivated and will choose the activities that they need from choices provided in a carefully designed learning environment.

The term formal refers to programs that are concerned primarily with *what is learned,* that place major emphasis on the acquisition of specific knowledge and skills that are believed to be important. In these programs, the content and not the process of learning is the primary emphasis. Advocates of this approach believe that without a good deal of teacher structure, valuable time is lost and children may not acquire skills needed for later school success. In general, these programs place emphasis on conformity to adult standards and behavior and prefer order to freedom. External rewards like gold stars, grades, and special treats are often seen as necessary to motivate children to learn.

Every program will balance these dimensions in different ways though the underlying values, philosophy and view of the learner will influence on which side of the spectrum the majority of choices fall. When child development knowledge is not adequately considered, programs may emphasize content without regard to children's needs, or they may fail to provide adequate support for children's learning. These programs are not developmentally appropriate. On the extreme end of the informal side of the continuum are *laissez-faire* programs that do not give the structure, stimulation, content and guidance that children need to grow and learn. On the extreme of the formal side of the continuum are *rigid* programs that stress mastery of specific tasks to the exclusion of other goals and that tend to regard children as machines to be programmed rather than thinking and feeling human beings. Between the two extremes lie a range of alternatives that can contribute to children's learning and development. These extremes are graphically portrayed in Figure 3.1.

The value choices in the *Dimensions* include general assumptions, such as beliefs about human nature and motivation, broad program goals, as well as practical program considerations. Whether curriculum is emerging or predetermined, how learning experiences are initiated, and who makes decisions regarding the use of time, space, and equipment are based on educators' values in combination with their underlying assumptions about growth and learning. Each of the choices on the dimensions is presented on a continuum. The *Early Childhood Program Dimensions* (see page 66) illustrates basic value choices teachers make in designing and implementing educational programs for children.

FIGURE 3.1
The range of appropriate program goals

EARLY CHILDHOOD PROGRAM DIMENSIONS

INFORMAL	FORMAL
Focus on the Learner	**Focus on What Is Learned**

Assumptions about Children

Children are growth seeking ————	Children are shaped by their environment
Motivation comes from within ———	Motivation is based on external reward
Here and now is important ————	Preparation for future schooling is important

Goals

Autonomy ————————————	Conformity
Freedom ————————————	Order

The Teaching Process

Curriculum emerging ————— (based on needs and interests of the learner)	Curriculum predetermined
Learner-initiated —————	Teacher-initiated
Learner-chosen use of time ———	Teacher-initiated use of time
Learner-chosen use of space ———	Teacher-chosen use of space
Learner chosen use of equipment —— and materials	Teacher-chosen use of equipment and materials

The decisions you make regarding how to structure choices on each continuum will be influenced by your personal values, the values of your school and community, and by the age and abilities of the children you teach. Obviously, most of the choices you make for a group of two year olds will be closer to the informal side of the continuum than the choices you will make for kindergarteners who have interest in and the ability to handle more demanding instructional tasks.

We believe that it is important for teachers to be clear on their basic values and educational goals for children and to behave as much as possible in ways consistent with these values. Teachers are sometimes not aware of their values or when their actual behavior may be in contradiction to their purported values.

We worked with teachers in a school, for example, where the values of independence and child-directed learning were clearly articulated, but they did not allow children to choose their own materials from the open shelves. In order to avoid discrepancies between belief and action, you can examine your choices and how these relate to your goals for children. If you find that your values and classroom behavior are contradictory, it is time to think about whether the values or the behaviors need to be reconsidered. It is only through self-observation that values are clarified and made consistent with actual behavior.

Our college students have used the *Dimensions* to help them focus their observations of classrooms and to compare the different programs that they observe. It helps them to see that all programs have some underlying assumptions about learning and learners and that its structure grows out of these assumptions. Practicing teachers can use the *Dimensions* as a guide for self-observation and as a basis for reflecting on the relationship between values and classroom organization and teaching strategies.

Congruence Between Values and Actions

Children tend to do what adults *do,* regardless of what they say. Consequently, a teacher's behavior in the classroom is very important. Research in schools has shown that children often learn to be aggressive or cooperative by observing adults, that children who observe adults in problem-solving tasks are able to solve problems more readily than those who have not had that experience, and that the level of thinking demonstrated by teachers

sets the level for student thinking (Good and Brophy, 1973; Saiwin, 1969). It is apparent from these and other studies that children's behavior will be substantially influenced by the teacher's behavior in the classroom. Not only do children imitate the teacher's behavior, but they also observe and internalize values based on the teacher's example. The quality of the educational experience you provide for children is greatly influenced by your values. Only when your behavior is consistent with your values, however, do your actions have a positive impact. Sue Spayth Riley's book *How to Generate Values in Young Children* (1984) very sensitively describes the impact of adult behavior on the development of values in children.

There is room for a range of individual values in early childhood programs, but this does not mean that anything that is done as a reflection of a value is alright. Classroom practice must also rest on the core values of the field and a firm base knowledge of child development. Teachers who know how children learn and grow would not, for example, use harsh punishments, insist that young children sit quietly for long periods of time working at abstract tasks like workbooks, or allow them to run wild in a messy and disorganized classroom that did not provide enough order and stimulation for them to learn.

As we described in the previous chapter, the personal characteristics of the teacher are also an important determinant of the quality and effectiveness of the early childhood program. The extent to which the teacher has the capacity to be authentic—open, self-aware, caring, and genuinely respectful of others—is one of the most essential aspects of the ability

to nurture children and support their development.

There is an important relationship between program dimensions and teacher qualities. Any program can be enhanced or diminished by the personal qualities of the teacher. Clarity in values and philosophy is an important first step, but in order for children to gain the greatest possible benefit, teachers also need to be growing, open, and able to bring natural authority, rather than laxness or rigidity to their teaching.

To enhance your own professional development as a teacher look inward to discover what you value. Consider the kind of society you want to live in, the kind of people needed to make that society work, and the evolving core values of the field of early childhood education. Then examine whether your actions in working with children are congruent with what you believe. You will also want to ask yourself if what you do is based on the best possible information about how children grow and learn and whether you communicate respect and caring to the children.

Value Conflicts

Dealing with values in early childhood education is, unfortunately, more complex than simply becoming clear on your own values and those of the field and then developing daily practices to reflect them. We live in a society that is characterized by diversity in every area of life, including values. There are many different and often contradictory points of view regarding what is best for children and how they should be educated. These differences cannot be ignored.

It is either blind or false or a little of both to think that we all have fundamentally the same goals—as teachers, as parents, as citizens—and that our differences concern only how to best accomplish these purposes.

It seems of major importance to me that we discard superficial, albeit friendly neutrality and work at clarifying and stating our goals and the priorities within them. (Biber, 1969, p.8)

Value conflicts can occur in a number of different areas, and dealing with these can be one of the most difficult aspects of being a teacher of young children. Differences with others need to be acknowledged and discussed rather than avoided and denied if solutions are to be found.

Value conflicts can occur between you and teachers and/or administrators in your program. Differences with co-teachers may not cause overt problems if you teach in a self-contained classroom, but can be very difficult for the children and parents, as well as for you, if you team teach or work at different times during the day with the same group of children. Value differences based on administrative policy can be especially difficult for teachers when they are instructed to follow policies that violate their beliefs. These differences can also result in ethical issues which we will discuss in a later section of this chapter. Some of these conflicts can be minimized if school staffs spend time together clarifying their values and coming to agreements about how compromises can be made.

It would be easier and more pleasant to be a teacher of young children in a setting in which parents were in agreement with you on educational issues and gave you total and unconditional support. This doesn't often happen in the real world. Teachers often find themselves caught in a difficult dilemma between their beliefs and pressures from parents who want

them to teach and treat children in ways that violate these beliefs. Teachers need to listen to parents and evaluate whether changes can be made that are consistent with their values and the core values of the field. Remember that parents *do* want what is best for their children, though their vision of this can be colored by expectations about education based on their own school experiences. It may help a great deal if you are able to clearly articulate the rationale for what you are doing in the classroom and spend some time explaining this to parents. It is also important to remember that while parent and community concerns need to be heard and carefully weighed, you have the training and expertise in child development and should not compromise your most deeply held beliefs and values about what is good for children.

There will also be times when your own values are in conflict, for example, children's spontaneous expression and creativity (a loud and enthusiastic rhythm band during morning activity time) versus your need for a reasonably tranquil classroom. In these situations, it will be helpful to be able to analyze the nature of the conflict and try to establish which value is most important for you to act on at a given time.

Occasionally value differences between you and co-teachers, administrators, or parents may be so severe that you will find that you cannot, in good faith, continue to work in the setting. Coming to this conclusion can be difficult and painful, but it may be your only alternative if differences cannot be reconciled. It may be easier to make this decision if you realize that you are choosing based on your knowledge, experience, and commitment to children. Sometimes the issue may have to do with the way program values are balanced. You may find that you are happier and more comfortable teaching in a setting that more closely reflects your values, like a former student of ours who decided to leave a program because it did not adequately address her belief in the importance of nurturing creativity. Or you may choose to leave a program when you realize that it does not adequately serve the needs of young children and that no good early childhood educator would want to work there. If you have serious concerns that the well-being of young children is compromised you face an ethical issue regarding your responsibilities.

ETHICAL ISSUES IN EARLY CHILDHOOD EDUCATION

Some value issues in early childhood education, as we suggested earlier in this chapter, are not personal issues but those faced by all teachers of young children. These are problems of professional ethics in early childhood education, and they have to do with what the profession's standards should be. Professional ethics is a shared process of critical, systematic reflection upon our obligations as professionals; they answer the question, "What should responsible early childhood educators try to do and what should they refuse to do?" (Feeney and Kipnis, 1985). Ethical guidelines help us do what we believe is right and good, and not what is easiest, or will bring us the most personal benefit, or will make others like us the most. Ethics is of particular concern in our field because young children are so vulnerable;

they have very little control over their lives or power to defend themselves. It is therefore extremely important that we behave fairly and responsibly in their behalf.

Working out standards for behavior is part of the developmental process of an occupation becoming a profession. The field of early childhood education is at present addressing this task. A profession that takes seriously the ethical dimension of its practice will identify the most important dilemmas and provide the best advice and assistance to practitioners who find themselves dealing with these issues. This will involve a process of analyzing problems and deciding how they can best be reconciled in terms of the core values of the field.

The project on ethics and early childhood education that we are currently working on is designed to identify some of the most critical ethical issues facing early childhood educators and to help them learn to address these in professionally responsible ways. Through a nationwide survey in *Young Children,* we have identified some areas of ethical concern that seem to be most troubling to early childhood practitioners in their everyday work. These include:

☐ Dealing with and reporting child abuse and neglect

Example: Should you report suspected abuse even if you feel that there will be retaliation against the child or the child will be withdrawn from your program?

☐ Managing and sharing information

Example: Should you give a parent who requests it the name of a child who injured their child? Should you give a volunteer or another staff member information about a family which is confidential but might help them to better understand the behavior of a disruptive child?

☐ Dealing with administrative policy that is not in best interests of children

Example: Should you report program practices that are in violation of state licensing requirements if you have not been able to effect a change in any other way?

☐ Handling conflicts arising from parental separation and divorce

Example: Under what conditions should you testify in a custody hearing?

☐ Balancing the needs of the individual child and family with the needs of the group

Example: What should you do about an extremely disruptive child who requires so much of your time and energy that you are not able to meet the needs of the rest of the children in the group?

☐ Dealing with situations in which the best interest of the child and the parents' needs or wishes are in conflict. (These can be referred to as "complex client" cases because the professional has responsbility to more than one party.)

Example: How do you handle a parent who requests that her child not be allowed to nap in school because if he does he will not go to sleep until late at night? How do you deal with parental requests that you employ curriculum or management tech-

niques that you do not think are good for children?

☐ Dealing with situations in which children's best interests and child development information do not guide classroom practice.

Example: What should you do when you are required to use reading workbooks with a group of three year olds when you know that this is not appropriate?

These are difficult issues, and at present there are no ready answers. They are usually addressed by individual teachers and administrators on a case-by-case basis, which is a time-consuming

process and does not benefit from a shared vision of what the good early childhood educator should do. Guidelines for responding to these issues need to be worked out through a process of critical reflection by practitioners in early childhood education.

The task of working through these kinds of issues can culminate in the development of a *Code of Ethics,* a statement of standards for guiding practice in a field. A Code of Ethics in early childhood education will help teachers to make well reasoned choices based on the core values of the field. Lilian Katz and Evangeline Ward's book, *Ethical Behavior in Early Childhood Education* (1978), has made clear the need for such a code. Our present work on identifying critical issues and developing a statement of core values is another

step in the development of a Code of Ethics for early childhood education.

A Code of Ethics will help us to define and unify ourselves as early childhood educators. It will move decision making from an individual enterprise to a process based on consensus, providing the basis for an argument or an action. Such a code will make it easier for teachers and administrators to behave ethically because they will be acting not as individuals but as professionals governed by the principles and requirements of their field. And finally, our growing professional clarity, culminating in the development of a code, will serve to assure the public that we base practice on sound and agreed upon standards which are in the best interests of children, their families, and the community.

FOR FURTHER THOUGHT AND DISCUSSION

1   Think of three values that are of great importance to you. What do you believe to be the sources of these values in your life? What are the implications of these for you as a teacher of young children?

2   What kind of world would you like to live in, and what would schools have to be like to prepare people to live in that kind of world?

3   What can you infer about the values for education and society of early childhood programs you have observed? What specific practices suggest these values? How were the programs similar and different? How are they consistent/ insconsistent with your values, and what were your feelings about them?

4   Talk with someone who has also observed a program that you have recently visited. Explore and discuss differences in your perceptions and evaluation of the program. What experiences and values might account for these differences?

5 Are you aware of any ethical issues in your own work or in the programs that you have observed? What were the issues? How were they resolved, and what do you think would have been the most professional response? Would a Code of Ethics have been helpful in the resolution?

6 Review the list of core values of early childhood education. What changes and/or additions would you like to see made to the list? Could your most important personal values for children be realized within the broad framework of the core values?

PROJECTS

1 Make a list of at least ten incidents you have observed in an early childhood program in which the teacher seemed to express a value or make a value choice. Infer the teacher's values based on what you have observed, and describe your feelings and reactions.

2 Describe ten of the most important values in your life. Discuss the influences and experiences that you think contributed to this choice of values. Describe ten values that you think should be implemented in programs for young children. In what ways are your personal values and your values for children the same or different? What are the implications of these value choices for you as a teacher of young children?

3 Choose at least three early childhood programs that you have observed and plot them on the *Early Childhood Program Dimensions*. Explain why you placed each program where you did on each continuum. Describe your feelings and reactions to each of the programs and how each relates to your own values for early childhood education.

4 Make a collage representing three values that are very important in your life. Share it in class.

RECOMMENDED READING

Berman, Louise M., and Roderick, Jessie A., eds. *Feeling, Valuing, and the Art of Growing*. Washington D.C.: Association for Supervision and Curriculum Development, 1977.

Biber, Barbara. *Challenges Ahead for Early Childhood Education.* Washington, D.C.: National Association for the Education of Young Children, 1969.

Katz, Lilian G., and Ward, Evangeline. *Ethical Behavior in Early Childhood Education.* Washington, D.C.: National Association for the Education of Young Children, 1978.

Keliher, Alice. *Talks with Teachers.* Darien, Conn.: Educational Publishing Corp., 1958.

Moustakas, Clark. *Personal Growth.* Cambridge, Mass.: Howard A. Doyle, 1969.

Raths, Louis, and Simon, Sidney. *Values and Teaching.* Columbus, O.: Charles E. Merrill, 1966.

Riley, Sue Spayth. *How to Generate Values in Young Children.* Washington, D.C.: National Association for the Education of Young Children, 1984.

Toffler, Alvin, ed. *Learning for Tomorrow.* New York: Random House, 1974.

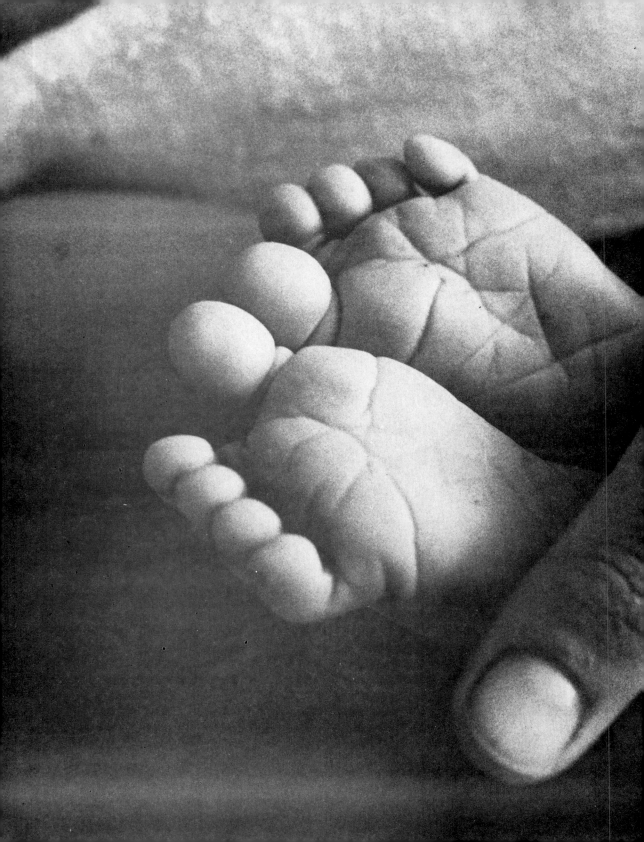

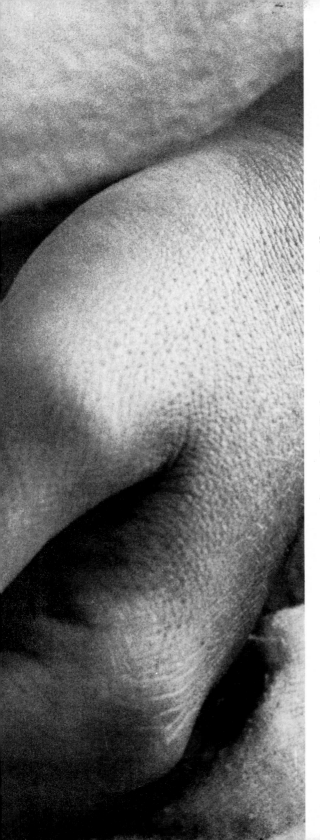

4

Child Development

"In all of the world there is no other child exactly like you. In the millions of years that have passed, there has never been a child like you. "

Pablo Casals

"Civilization arises and unfolds in play."

Johan Huizinga

In this chapter we focus on how knowledge of development can contribute to your understanding of children and your ability to support their growth and learning. We present some basic concepts and information, including the foundations of development laid down in infancy; biological and environmental factors in development; basic developmental processes; and a brief overview of brain physiology. We also review four major theoretical approaches to understanding children and summarize some of the research on the role of play in children's development. This chapter relates to all thirteen of the CDA areas.

Childhood today is quite different than it was in the past; in fact, a number of contemporary writers are expressing their concern that it might even be disappearing as a special time in the life cycle (Elkind, Postman). Today's world is extremely complex. Television pervades almost all of our lives, and instant replay of historical events makes the world seem much smaller than it once did. Family structures have changed; the extended family is disappearing, families move so frequently that there is a loss of community, and working mothers and single parent families are no longer the exception but the reality to a majority of children in our country. Violence is widespread, as are reports of sexual and physical abuse against children. This is a very different context in which to grow up than we remember in our childhoods and one which implies new responsibilities for those who care for young children. Teachers need to take into account these new and often disturbing developments, but they must relate it to their sound knowledge of child development.

There is an enormous amount of information on the subject of child development available today in books, journals, and even in newspaper and magazine articles. In addition, most students of early childhood education are required to do some systematic study of this field. We have found, however, that much of this information is quite general, and it is not always clear to our college students how it may be relevant to work with young children. In this chapter we present some concepts that we have found useful to teachers. We do not attempt to touch on all of the information about child development that you will need to know, nor do we present one all-encompassing theory about children (one does not yet exist). Instead, we focus on some of the major ideas and concepts that have been helpful to us, and we point to the implications of these ideas for your work in the classroom. This knowledge of development in combination with direct experience in early childhood programs will give you a solid basis for understanding children and making informed choices in your teaching.

FOUNDATIONS OF HEALTHY DEVELOPMENT IN INFANCY

Research on early childhood development in the last several decades has fundamentally changed our understanding of infant development. Once viewed as passive organisms engaged primarily in reflex behavior during a relatively unimportant period, infants are described today as active beings who have the ability to react to sensory stimuli, to interact with others, and to be alert to and observant of the environment. Infancy is now seen as a crucial time for laying the foundation for later development. Understanding this foundation will help you to see the continuity between infancy and the preschool period. It is important to understand what children need to have experienced and achieved in the first few years of life in order to help them to function productively in the school setting.

Today's specialists in child development are deeply concerned with providing optimal conditions for development from conception through the early years. They are increasingly aware of the importance of prenatal conditions including the health, mental health, and nutrition of the parents. There has also been a growing interest in birth procedures that are less mechanistic and more nurturing for mother and child than the traditional hospital delivery. A nontraumatic environment and contact between mother and infant in the first few moments of life appear to have a positive effect on the mother-child relationship. In order for a child to develop normally and thrive, a number of conditions including good nutrition, nurturing relationships, and a stimulating environment must be present in infancy.

Nutrition

Infants must first have adequate nutrition, which is "the single most important factor affecting physical growth and development in the young child" (Horowitz, 1982, p.22). Most doctors and nutritionists today recommend breast-feeding because of the bond it establishes between mother and child, because a mother's milk is the most nourishing food for an infant, and because factors in the mother's milk can have a positive effect on the child's resistance to disease and allergy. Malnutrition in the infant and toddler has been shown to be associated with retarded mental and physical development and may be related to attentional deficits. Brain development, particularly *myelination* (the laying down of myelin sheaths, the nerve insulation essential in sensory integration) is impaired in malnourished children. Children with good nutrition in infancy and early childhood tend to function better in all areas of development.

Nurturing Relationships

The second prerequisite for healthy development in infants is the development of a warm, intimate, continuous relationship with the mother or other primary caregiver referred to as **bonding**. Tender, loving care given in the context of this relationship is essential to normal physical and emotional development and helps the child to achieve basic trust, the first developmental task described by Erik Erikson (elaborated later in this chapter).

Research has established the significance of comforting tactile experiences such as caressing, cuddling, and rhythmic movement in the early development of all species of mammals. Harry and Margaret Harlow's well-known research showed that baby monkeys had a marked preference for contact with a terry cloth surrogate mother, who provided contact comfort but no food, to a wire mother, who had the advantage of providing milk but who had little else to recommend her in the eyes of the baby monkeys. The impetus for this research came from observations of the high mortality rates of unhandled research animals (Berger, 1980; Papalia & Olds, 1982).

A similar effect was observed among institutionalized human infants. A large percentage of these infants did not survive the first year of life when there was no opportunity for bonding to occur and where only the basic needs for nourishment and cleaniness were met. In institutions where caregivers provided frequent comforting physical contact, the mortality rate decreased sharply and infants developed normally. Other research on institutionalized and neglected children has demonstrated that those who suffer maternal deprivation in infancy often have many problems in later development. Research and clinical observation reinforce our awareness of the importance of the bond between the primary caregiver and the infant, and how this bond (or failure to bond) influences all aspects of later development.

A Stimulating Environment

The third important condition required for infants to develop normally is an environment that provides them with novelty and stimulation and includes opportunities to hear, see, reach, touch, and explore.

Interaction with people and objects in a stimulating environment in the course of play—the important work of infancy and childhood—has positive effects on subsequent intellectual development. This correlates to experimentation with animals as well. Researchers have found that rats exposed to enriched environments perform better on mazes and other measures of intelligence.

Good nutrition, nurturing relationships, and stimulating environments lay the essential foundation for later relationships and learning to proceed positively. They continue to be important throughout the early childhood years and the rest of childhood.

THE ROLE OF BIOLOGY AND ENVIRONMENT ON DEVELOPMENT

The history of thought about human development has been characterized by shifts in our beliefs about the relative impact of biological versus environmental forces on personality and behavior. Biological forces on development (sometimes referred to as *nature*) are genetic traits or inherited capacities and are expressed in the process of growth and maturation. Environmental forces (referred to as *nurture*) have to do with the kinds of interactions and experiences that enhance or restrict the development of biological potential. In the past, there was a heated debate (sometimes called the *nature-nurture controversy*) between people who felt that either the biological endowment or the environment was the primary force in shaping human nature. Views on the subject shifted from the belief that all development was biologically determined to the opposite view that children were infinitely malleable and that environment was all-important in shaping later behavior and achievement. Theorists today still debate the relative importance of biological and environmental influences on development, but there is general agreement that heredity and environment interact in complex ways and that each plays an important role.

Biological Factors in Development

Today most child development specialists regard biological development as being much more important than believed in the last two decades when the emphasis was on the powerful impact of the environment. Research on inherited temperamental characteristics conducted by physicians Alexander Thomas and Stella Chess (1977) and discussed in Chapter 2 with regard to teachers' characteristics, has influenced current views of the importance of biological inheritance. They have shown that newborn babies are not all alike at birth (something that parents have always known) and that there are distinct and observable differences in temperament among newborn infants that are fairly

persistent over time. Thomas and Chess' work has given us valuable insight into the importance of the temperament the child brings into the world at birth and how it interacts with the child's experiences.

According to Chess and Thomas, babies in their first days and weeks of life can be seen to differ in nine personality characteristics:

1 *Activity level:* the proportion of inactive periods to active ones.
2 *Rhythmicity:* the regularity of cycles of hunger, excretion, sleep, and wakefulness.
3 *Distractibility:* the degree to which extraneous stimuli alter behavior.
4 *Approach/Withdrawal:* the response to a new object or person.
5 *Adaptability:* the ease with which a child adapts to the environment.
6 *Attention span and persistence:* the amount of time devoted to an activity and the effect of distraction.
7 *Intensity of reaction:* the energy of response regardless of its quality or direction.
8 *Threshold of responsiveness:* the intensity of stimulation required to evoke a response.
9 *Quality of mood:* the amount of friendly, pleasant, joyful behavior as contrasted with unpleasant, unfriendly behavior.

These characteristics tend to persist over time but can change with experience. For example, babies who tend to be fearful of novelty may adapt more easily if their behavior is understood and accepted by their parents and they are given support in developing new patterns. Temperamental characteristics are partially explained by heredity and prenatal influences, but environment also plays an important role in shaping later behavior.

We have found Chess and Thomas' work valuable in helping us to understand the wide range of personalities in the young children we have taught and in understanding the importance of the "fit" between children's characteristics and those of the adults who relate to them.

Environmental Factors in Development

The first five or six years of life are critical in laying the foundation for all areas of the child's later development. Research has demonstrated that the experiences of these early years have a critical impact though, as we have just pointed out, we tend to view them today as interactive with biological traits. Until the 1950s and 1960s, the prevalent view was that people matured in predictable ways according to a biologically predetermined plan. The more recent view, greatly influenced by J. McVicker Hunt's book *Intelligence and Experience* (1961), suggests that functioning later in childhood and adulthood are greatly influenced by early experience.

Studies conducted by Benjamin Bloom (1964) indicate that fifty percent of the characteristics associated with mature intelligence develop by the age of four and approximately eighty percent by the age of eight. Other research has shown that in humans, as in animals, there are sensitive periods, certain times during which an important developmental

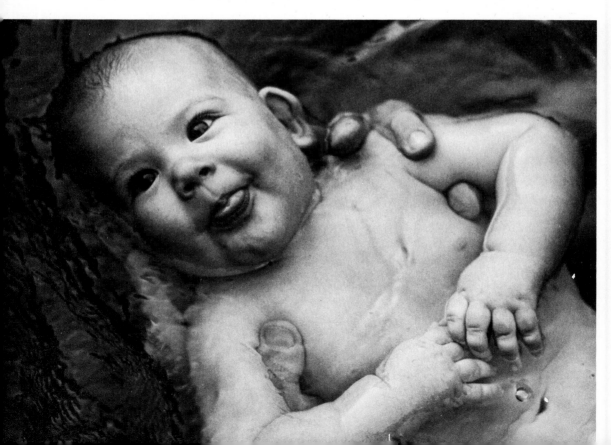

milestone is most likely to occur. Some kinds of development either cannot occur if this period is missed or they come about with much greater difficulty. These include sensitive periods for development of physiological structures like vision, as well as for language development in human beings.

Research on the importance of early experience led to the idea that preschool programs might be an antidote for the deprivation associated with extreme poverty in young children, and hence compensatory education programs developed. Research by Lazar (1979) and others reported in Chapter 1 has presented a persuasive argument for the positive impact that quality early childhood programs can have on the the lives of participating children.

A study conducted by Jerome Kagan (1973) suggests that inadequate nurture and stimulation in the early years does not necessarily cause irreversible deficiencies later in life. Kagan found that Guatemalan Indian children who were traditionally reared in ways that deprived them of daylight, adequate nutrition, and stimulation during the first two years of life, appeared to be functioning within normal ranges in all areas of development by the age of eleven. It must be pointed out, however, that the children in this study did have regular and loving contact with their mothers, and this may be what enabled later normal development. While repeated experiences of extreme and early deprivation may cause serious damage to the developing child, Kagan's study reminds us that human beings are remarkably resilient and early deprivation, when countered soon enough, may be ameliorated.

NEW DIRECTIONS IN RESEARCH ON THE BRAIN

In the last few years there has been a good deal of research that may, in time, revolutionize our understanding of the relationship between brain structure and learning. This research presents several ways to view the development and function of the brain that may have implications for early childhood education. This work may eventually result in important contributions to our understanding of learning and teaching, but it appears to us that some of the conclusions for education that have been drawn from this work may be somewhat premature. It is certainly an educational frontier of which teachers should be aware.

One of the approaches to looking at brain physiology is called the vertical model. When viewed vertically, the brain has three parts, and for this reason is sometimes called the **triune brain** (see Figure 4.1). Each of the parts has a different structure, serves a different function, and is increasingly more complex. The parts of the triune brain have been compared to the brains of different orders of animals. The simplest part, the **brain stem**, is compared to the brain of a reptile and hence is called the **reptilian brain**. It handles survival instincts. The **limbic system**, **mid-brain**, or **old mammalian brain** controls physical responses to emotions. The upper and largest portion of the brain is the **new mammalian brain** or the **neocortex**. The neocortex is the part of the brain that mediates thinking, planning, decision making, language, and consciousness. Leslie Hart (1981) suggests that brain structures serve different functions

The Triune Brain

The Split Brain Model
The Left and Right Hemispheres

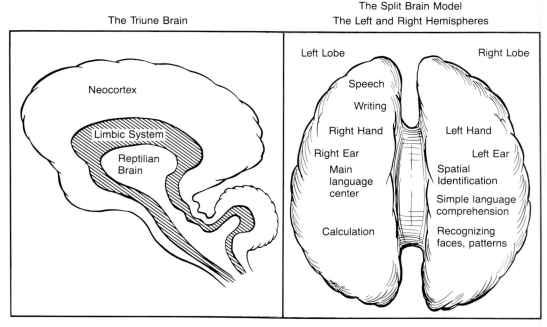

FIGURE 4.1

in different situations and that this may have implications for educators. In times of threat, the new mammalian brain's slow consideration of alternatives is not effective, and the quick survival instincts of the reptilian brain take over. Threats cause a downshifting of brain function. People think, consider, and plan less when threatened. Based on this information, Hart suggests that a sense of physical and psychological safety in school may be a prerequisite for helping children to use the higher level functions of the neocortex.

The **split-brain, horizontal, side-by-side**, or **hemispheric** model also reflects a structural aspect of the brain (see Figure 4.1). The brain is bilaterally symmetrical: it has two hemispheres. Pierre Paul Broca first discovered that there were functional differences in the two hemi-

spheres in 1846. Broca noticed language deficits in individuals who had damage to the left side of the brain.

Since Broca's time, dramatic experiments have demonstrated more about the function and connectedness of the brain's hemispheres. Each hemisphere has been shown to control and receive stimulus from the opposite side of the body. Information received by the right hemisphere was understood but could not be verbalized when brain hemispheres were separated by operations. Recent work has drawn a portrait of the general cognitive styles and functions of each hemisphere. The left side of the brain appears to function primarily to control the abstract, verbal, and symbolic; it is largely responsible for analysis and logic. The right hemisphere seems to involve more that is perceptual, spatial, creative, and intuitive. While each hemisphere has strengths and processes information differently, they are complementary and part of a whole. Many implications have been drawn from this work suggesting that schools have traditionally taught to the left side of the brain and urging educators to do more to include right brain functions in equal measure in school programs. If the implications of split-brain research are borne out in future investigations, it may provide a physiological justification for the whole child approach of early childhood education.

A third view has to do with brain growth. Using data from reports of autopsies on children, Herman Epstein has concluded that postnatal brain growth is not smooth and continuous but is discontinuous and occurs in spurts of five periods of rapid brain growth interspersed with plateau periods where little growth occurs.

The five periods of brain growth that Epstein identifies occur from three through ten months, two through four years, six through eight years, ten through twelve years, and fourteen through sixteen years. Girls tend to experience a growth spurt toward the beginning of the phase and boys toward the end, though, needless to say, individual children differ in precisely when they go through the period of rapid growth. The spurts seem to be the biological correlates of Piaget's psychological stages of cognitive development, discussed in the following section of this chapter, and suggest a strong correlation between intellectual development and brain maturation.

While much is yet to be learned about brain growth spurts and their implications for teaching, Epstein does draw some educational implications. His work

reinforces the Piagetian view that children cannot be hurried through intellectual stages but must be given experience and time to mature. Epstein also suggests that times of rapid brain growth may be the best times for the introduction of new concepts while plateau periods may be best for the reinforcement of concepts already learned.

PROCESSES OF DEVELOPMENT

Development results from changes in the child that are based on the interplay of growth, maturation, and experience. *Growth* is primarily an increase in size. *Maturation* is an increase in the complexity of organization, both physically and psychologically. *Experience* is all of a person's interactions with the environment. During the preschool years, the body of a child grows; that is, it greatly increases in size and mass. At the same time, maturation occurs; the child gradually develops control of the muscle system. Maturation cannot be sped up through special training, though it can be retarded by environmental factors such as poor nutrition or serious illness.

The same processes occur in psychological development. For example, infants lack the concept of object permanence: the awareness that even when an object is not in sight it still exists. As the child matures, the concept develops, but no amount of training seems to be able to significantly accelerate its acquisition. A lack of experience with objects that can be seen, handled, and then removed will, however, retard its acquisition.

There are two basic characteristics common to all human development. First, development proceeds in a direction toward greater size and more complex organization. Second, it proceeds in an orderly and predictable manner. Growth and maturation interact to produce physical development. This process proceeds from the top downward (the *cephalocaudal principle*), and is seen most clearly in the development of the fetus. In the early stages of development, the head is half the length of the body, whereas at birth the head is one quarter the body length. The same tendency is seen in motor development. The infant develops head control and reaching and grasping skill before sitting and walking. Growth and maturation also proceed from near to far (the *proximodistal law*). The large muscles closest to the center of the body grow and develop coordinated functions before the small muscles of the hands and fingers.

Since prior levels of size and complexity must precede later ones, development is sequential and cumulative. For example, before children can learn to write, they must have mastered the small muscle coordination required to grasp objects; have learned to use implements like brushes, pencils, and scissors; have had experiences forming shapes and letters; and have seen and used written language.

Chronological age and stage of development are only approximately related. The direction and sequence of development are similar for every child, but each individual moves through stages at his or her own rate and personal style. Each infant enters the world with a unique biological endowment, and since the interplay of physical and environmental forces are different for every person, no two children (even from the same family) are exactly alike.

Arnold Gessell (1940), who pioneered the scientific study of child development, collected data on large numbers of children and developed norms, levels of achievement that could be expected of children at various ages and stages of development. Gessell and his associates believed that maturation was the crucial factor in reaching new developmental levels. Their work led to the concept of *readiness,* a period of development in which a specific skill or response is most likely to occur. Gessell's work has been criticized because of its heavy emphasis on the role of maturation, its lack of emphasis on environmental stimulation, and because his data on ages and stages has sometimes been misused. Gessell's descriptions of stages of development can be very helpful for giving general guidelines for expectations regarding children's development. The developmental charts in the curriculum chapters of this book are derived from this kind of normative study.

The knowledge that growth is a process that follows a definite sequential order, combined with information about the characteristics of each stage, lets teachers know what can generally be expected of children and helps them plan developmentally appropriate experiences for them. Awareness of the cumulative nature of development helps teachers recognize that children cannot be expected to have understanding or skill for which their level of development has not prepared them.

New experiences that do not build from previous experiences can be meaningless or overwhelming to a child, while experiences that are not challenging or interesting may provoke boredom and restlessness. J. McVicker Hunt (1961) describes the concept of an *optimal match* between children's present level of understanding or skill and the acquisition of a new knowledge or skill. New experience needs to provide just the right amount of novelty or challenge in order to interest the child in engaging with something unfamiliar. Teachers can stimulate children's growth by planning experiences that provide challenge and by avoiding experiences that children find frustrating, because they are too difficult, or boring, because they are too easy.

MAJOR THEORETICAL APPROACHES TO UNDERSTANDING DEVELOPMENT

In the first sections of this chapter we introduced some basic information and concepts concerning child development. Most of this work is based on research of observable phenomenon. In the following section we will discuss some ideas about development that are more theoretical and which are less widely agreed upon. We will describe the work of number of researchers and clinicians who have created models or theories for understanding human development.

Human beings are naturally curious and try to organize and make sense out of their experience. One way to organize experience into comprehensible and useful form is to create a theory, a mental model of how things are and of the relationship between facts. We construct theories by generating *hypotheses*, tentative explanations (guesses) that can be explored and tested by observation and experimentation. When a hypothesis is proven to be true in a number of situations, it becomes a theory, and we can then generalize from it—relate the

things we have found to be true in one situation to other situations. While theories aid us in understanding the world, they do not represent a truth which is static and unchanging. As we gain new knowledge, a theory may be replaced by another theory that is simpler, more accurate, more comprehensive, or more useful.

The four theories of development described below are widely used in the field of early childhood education. They differ greatly in the aspects of human development on which they focus, in their underlying assumptions, and in the subjects and methodology used as a basis for their conclusions. No single approach illuminates all aspects of children's development. Each is like a lens that focuses on some unique aspect. Adherence to a single one of these views can be constricting, and some of the ideas are contradictory. It is important to keep in mind that there is no single theory today that is "right" and that ties up everything we know about children into one neat package, and while knowledge of developmental theory is useful in helping to understand children and their behavior, it provides no ready answers. Existing information about development tends to be fragmented, incomplete, and sometimes biased by the viewpoint of the theorist. Moreover, influences on your own development will affect the theories you feel most comfortable with and choose to use in your work with children.

So what are you to do when trying to make sense out of the information available? If theory does not provide all of the answers, what do you use as a basis for decision making? When it becomes confusing, it may be helpful to look again at your values for society and education.

These can form a basis for examining information about child development and choosing the approaches that most closely fit with your values and goals for children.

Psychodynamic Theory

This approach to human development focuses on inner processes and on emotional development. The basic concepts were formulated by Sigmund Freud, a nineteenth century neurologist and neuroanatomist. Freud worked with emotionally troubled patients and conceptualized his therapeutic discoveries into a framework that followed the scientific thought of the turn of the century. Freud was among the first to describe and categorize the stages of emotional development in childhood. Later these stages were adapted and elaborated by Freud's daughter Anna and by Erik Erikson.

Freud introduced the idea that behavior is influenced by unconscious factors—many of which are sexually motivated—that originate in early experiences. Awareness of these is often lost to conscious memory through the mechanism of **repression**. Although many of the researchers who later expanded the psychodynamic model de-emphasized Freud's discovery of childhood sexuality (despite the exciting stir it caused in nineteenth century Vienna), the recognition that unconscious processes frequently play an important determining role in our thought and behavior has been tremendously influential and remains a hallmark of those who have used this approach to understanding human development.

Freud's work has served as the basis for a number of other contributions to our thinking about children. Alfred Adler's revisions of Freudian theory came to be called **individual psychology**. His theory proposes that human beings are primarily motivated by social, and not sexual, urges and that normal development leads to the awakening of social responsibility. Rudolf Dreikurs has used Adlerian theory as the basis for the development of contemporary classroom management techniques that emphasize individual responsibility (see Chapter 8).

Erik Erikson, whose work is very influential in the thought of early childhood educators today, has described a series of stages of social and emotional development that expand Freud's original psychosexual stages to include social influences. Erikson believes that basic attitudes are formed as individuals pass through the stages and that serious problems at any stage lead to difficulty in reaching the next stage. Each stage is characterized by a major task or challenge. In infancy, the major task is the development of basic trust; for the toddler, it is the development of autonomy; for the preschooler, the development of initiative; and for the school-age child, industriousness.

For each stage, Erikson describes the potential for healthy development at one end of a continuum and the potential for development of negative and self-defeating attitudes at the other. He sees development as a product of the tension between the two extremes, with more positive than negative experiences necessary for healthy progress.

ERIKSON'S STAGES OF CHILDHOOD PSYCHOSOCIAL DEVELOPMENT

Trust vs. Mistrust (Infant)   During the first stage of development infants learn, or fail to learn, that people can be depended on and that they can depend on themselves to elicit nurturing responses from others. The quality of care an infant receives, especially in the first year of life, is essential to the development of basic trust. Through the love, nurture, and acceptance received, the infant learns that the world is a good and safe place.

Autonomy vs. Shame and Doubt (Toddler)   During the second stage of life, which begins at twelve to fifteen months, children develop a basic sense of autonomy: self-control and independent action. During this period they are growing rapidly. They are learning to coordinate many new patterns of action and to assert themselves as human beings. Children at this stage tend to vigorously oppose adult direction, and their favorite word is "no!" If caregivers are accepting and easygoing and if they recognize the child's developing need to assert independence, the child will move successfully through this stage. If adults are harsh and punitive and if the child is punished for assertive behavior, then shame and doubt may become stronger forces in the child's life.

Initiative vs. Guilt (Preschooler)   This is a period of interest, active exploration, and readiness for learning. Children need to express their natural curiosity and creativity during this stage through opportunities to act on the environment. If explorations are regarded as naughtiness and if parents or teachers are overly concerned with preventing children from getting dirty or destroying things, a sense of initiative may not be developed, and guilt may be the more prevalent attitude.

Industry vs. Inferiority (School Age Child)   During this period, children are ready for the challenge of new and exciting ideas and of constructing things. They need opportunities for physical, intellectual, and social accomplishment. They need many and varied interactions with materials. Success and a feeling of "I can do it!" result in a sense of industry. (Erikson, 1950)

While Freud's ideas were based upon his treatment of troubled adults, psychoanalyst Margaret Mahler (1975) used a laboratory setting to study behavioral, social, and emotional aspects of infants and toddlers as they moved from the security of infancy to the relative independence of the preschool years. Mahler believes that children are born first when they enter the world and a second time, psychologically, at about eighteen months when they begin to be aware of an identity separate from their mother or mother-figure. Mahler sees the major developmental task of infancy as the process of slowly differentiating the self from another: the acquisition of the sense of self. This process is called **separation-individuation**. The period around eighteen months is very important developmentally, for while children begin to move away from their principal caregivers and gain a feeling of pleasure in mastery, there is a continued need to maintain connectedness and to have the caregiver appreciate their developing skills and provide continuing reassurance. Some child development specialists urge parents not to place children in care situations out of the home before they reach this important developmental landmark.

Psychodynamic theory has contributed many important insights that have implications for teachers of young children. The development of the child is seen as progressing through a series of stages that are predictable, continuous throughout life, and influenced by many forces. Because crucial aspects of the child's development occur in the first five years when there is a very great dependency on adults, the relationships between children and significant adults in their lives is seen as very important. Teachers who understand that the young child is in the process of becoming a separate person can support the conflicting needs for connectedness and independence.

Psychodynamic theory has influenced educational programs through its emphasis on early emotional development and its encouragement of creative expression

as an outlet for children's feelings. By calling attention to unconscious forces that influence behavior, educators have become aware that children cannot consciously control their thoughts, feelings, and responses and are therefore less harsh in their judgments. It has also made educators increasingly aware of the impact of adult-child relationships and the importance of the psychological health of the adults who work with young children. This approach also provides insights into causes of psychological disturbance in children and techniques for treatment.

Recent psychoanalytic thought emphasizes the construction of the self as a central task of psychic development (Cooper, 1982, p. 490). The ideas of Heinz Kohut concerning the developmental importance of the child's interaction with the primary caregiver are becoming increasingly influential. Kohut believed that for healthy development to occur the

caregiver must respond empathically to the child's needs, affirm the child's positive sense of self, and provide a sense of identification with a strong and idealized presence. He stressed the importance of the parent's ability to stay attuned to the child and to changing developmental needs in terms of these issues from infancy through childhood. Preschool teachers also need to understand the importance of responding empathically to young children's needs for approval and confirmation of their autonomous sense of self while balancing this with the need for strong idealized figures to give a sense of security.

Cognitive Development Theory

In contrast to psychodynamic approaches, which focus on emotional development, the theory described in this section has to do with intellectual (cognitive) aspects of development. The best known approach

✗ method

to cognitive development comes from the work of Jean Piaget, who devoted many years of his life to the study of children's thinking. He began his career as a biologist and later became a philosopher as well. In his youth he studied how organisms adapt to their environment. His fascination with the biological adaptation of animal species evolved into an interest in how human beings adapt to their environments through their ability to use reason. Piaget's theory focuses primarily on the nature and development of logical thought. One of Piaget's important contributions was the innovative methodology that he devised for the study of children's thinking. His systematic, in-depth approach was based on interview techniques and case studies of individual children.

Cognitive development theory stresses adaptation as a result of the interaction (referred to by Piaget as the *transaction*) between the individual and the social and physical environment. Children are seen as active agents who construct their own

PIAGET'S STAGES OF COGNITIVE DEVELOPMENT

Sensorimotor Stage   During the sensorimotor period (from birth to approximately two years of age), the child changes from a reflex organism to one capable of thought and language. Behavior is primarily motor, and the child is dependent on physical manipulation to gain information about the world. The ability to form mental images for events that cannot be readily heard, felt, seen, smelled, or tasted does not occur until age two. During this period infants learn to differentiate themselves from others, to seek stimulation, and to develop the concept of causality.

The important developmental task of infancy that represents a shift in development and signals progress into the next stage is called **object permanence**. Children learn that objects exist in the world apart from their relationship to them, that an object may still exist even after it is out of sight.

Preoperational Stage   The preoperational period (between the ages of two and seven) is characterized by language acquisition and by rapid conceptual development. During this time, the child evolves from one who relies on actions for understanding to one who is able to internally represent events (think conceptually). Children learn labels for experience and develop the ability to substitute a symbol (word, gesture, or object) for an object or an event that is not present. Thought is based on how things appear to the child rather than on logical reasoning.

The early phase of this period is called **preconceptual**. Between the ages of two and four, children are **egocentric**; that is, they knowledge of the world through their direct experience and who have the capacity to adapt and change.

> Piaget is interested in mental activity, in what the individual does with his interaction with the world. Piaget believes that knowledge is not given to a passive observer; rather knowledge of reality must be discovered and constructed by the activity of the child. (Ginsberg and Opper, 1969, p.14)

Through his observations of children, Piaget identified *processes* of cognitive development. As a result of interaction with the environment, the child develops organizing structures or concepts that Piaget calls **schemes**. Early schemes become the basis for more complex future mental structures. Piaget identifies three complementary processes that children use to organize their experience into structures for thinking and problem solving.

The first process is **assimilation**, by which a person integrates new information or experience into existing schemes or

are unable to take the viewpoint of others. They tend to classify by a single salient feature. For example, they might classify all adult females as mommies. During the second, **intuitive**, phase of the preoperational period, between four and seven years, children are capable of more complex thought. They are less egocentric and more capable of social relationships. Moral feelings and moral reasoning begin during this stage.

The developmental hallmark of the early childhood period is **conservation**, the child's realization that the amount or quantity of a substance stays the same even when its shape or location changes. It is dependent on the child's growing ability to look at things from more than one point of view at a time.

Concrete Operations Period   During this period (between ages seven and eleven), children develop the ability to apply logical thought to concrete problems. Formal thought processes become more stable and reasonable even though children still have to think things out in advance and try them out through direct manipulation.

Formal Operations Period   During this final stage of cognitive development (between the ages of eleven and fifteen), children's cognitive structures reach their highest level of development, and they become able to apply logic to all classes of problems. Children develop basic principles of cause and effect and of scientific experimentation. They can weigh a situation mentally to deduce the relationships without having to try it out.

patterns of behavior. Through this process the child fits new information into his own framework for understanding the world. For example, the child who sees a goat for the first time and calls it a dog is trying to assimilate, or use a structure he or she already has. Assimilation does not result in a change of schemes, but it does create growth in them and therefore contributes to development.

If it is not possible to fit new information or experience into existing schemes, the child engages in the second process, **accommodation**, the changing of existing schemes to fit external reality more accurately or the creation of new schemes. Through this process cognitive structures change and develop to reflect the child's understanding of the world. The child has accommodated when she or he acquires the new scheme: goat.

The third process, **equilibration**, is based on the tendency for individuals to seek a dynamic balance between assimilation and accommodation. When there is such a balance, the child is in a state of *equilibrium*. Imbalance between the two creates a state of *disequilibrium*. Equilibration, then, is the process of moving from disequilibrium to equilibrium. It is through the tension of imbalanced assimilation and accommodation that intellectual growth occurs.

Through the processes just described, the child progesses through a series of very distinct developmental *stages* that build from the interaction among three elements: existing mental structures, maturation, and experience. Stages occur in the same predictable sequence for everyone, although the exact age at which a child enters the next stage varies with the individual and the culture.

The children you work with in early childhood programs will be in the preoperational stage of cognitive development. They are beginning to use symbols to represent experiences (words) in their thought processes. According to Piaget, they are still bound to their perceptions and see things only from their viewpoint **(egocentrism)**. The primary way that they learn is through direct experiences that involve sensory exploration and manipulation. During this period children are likely to focus on only one characteristic of an object or experience at a time, so they are easily deceived by appearances. One of our favorite stories that illustrates this concerns a child on his first plane ride who turned to his mother after the plane had completed its ascent and asked, "When do we start getting smaller?"

Piaget's work has been extremely influential in early childhood education in the United States since the late 1960s. One of his most important contributions has been to help parents and teachers become aware that children's thinking is fundamentally different from that of adults and to help them focus on understanding the nature of the individual child's thought. It is important that teachers realize that the thinking processes of children are affected by their stage of cognitive development and their prior experiences at home and school. Another important lesson that educators have gained from Piaget's work is that what is important in assessing children's intellectual development is not only the answer to a question, but also the line of reasoning that led to that particular response.

Piaget's insistence that young children are always trying to construct a more coherent understanding of their world through their direct experience of it has led many educators to believe that educational practices should allow ample opportunity for children to explore, experiment, and manipulate materials. Piaget was adamant that we cannot directly instruct children in the concepts that they need to know to move on to the next developmental stage. These concepts are acquired as a result of a complex interaction between experience, maturation, and adult mediation. He was critical of what he saw as an American tendency to hurry development rather than to let it follow its own course.

Piaget created a whole new focus and methodology for the study of children's cognitive development. Like any pioneering work it was neither complete nor fully formulated; the heavy emphasis was on

logical and mathematical thought. Jerome Kagan (1984, p. 192–93) suggests three areas of vulnerability in Piaget's work: (1) inadequate explanation for the transition from one stage of development to the next, (2) omission of important areas of cognitive functioning such as language development, and (3) recognition that children's development is more uneven and that some competences occur earlier than Piaget's findings indicated.

Margaret Donaldson in her book *Children's Minds* (1978) demonstrates that young children may show advanced thinking in situations that are familiar and have specific meaning for their own lives. She calls these *imbedded* tasks because they occur in the context of supportive meaningful events. She found that children were not so limited in their abilily to *decenter,* take on the point of view of another person as Piaget maintained, when they had a sense of the meaning of the task. Children are less able to deal with disimbedded tasks and ideas where the meaning is not clearly connected with direct experiences and context. Donaldson concludes that the extent to which children's tasks are meaningful to them has an important impact on what they will be able to do in a situation. Children can, in fact, accomplish certain developmental tasks earlier than has been thought in the past.

In the preschool years children need opportunities to use their thinking to do tasks that are meaningful to them. The transition to disimbedded tasks in later schooling should occur gradually with adult collaboration to help children establish connections between what they already understand and more specific and less relevant activities.

A number of researchers today are refining and extending Piaget's work.

Some are taking a *social interactionist* perspective, which focuses on the role played by adults in facilitating the young child's development. The ideas of L.S. Vygotsky, a Russian psychologist whose work has only recently been published in English though he wrote during the 1930s, have contributed to a new emphasis on the social origins of language and thought. Vygotsky believed, like Piaget, that children are active in their own development. However, Vygotsky's emphasis is on the relationship with other people as the major process contributing to development. In his view, young children develop in a specific social and cultural context, with early communicative interactions with adults becoming inter-nalized to form the basis for speech and thinking. Vygotsky describes develop-ment as proceeding from the *inter-psychic* (between the child and other people) to the *intra-psychic* (within the child) plane. Social experiences therefore form the foundation for human develop-ment. In Vygotsky's view the development of language is the primary task of childhood.

Because knowledge is created through interaction with other people, it is important not only to look at the child, as Piaget did, but also to focus on the interaction of the adult and child. Vygotsky suggested that it is important not only to understand what children can do by themselves but also to see what they can do in the **zone for proximal development**, the situation where the child is able to comprehend and do a task which could not be managed without adult assistance. He writes in *Thought and Language,* "What the child can do in cooperation today he can do alone tomorrow" (1962, p. 104). Current research in child development,

particularly in the areas of language and literacy development, has begun to reflect this social interactionist focus.

From the perspective of Vygotsky and many modern cognitive development theorists, teachers play a vitally important role in young children's learning and development because they are actually helping them to construct meaning in their lives. They accomplish this through conversation which is relevant to the particular child and through helping each child find a personal relevance in the activities offered at school. Knowing that children have different social and cultural backgrounds is important for teachers who can use this knowledge to help them find appropriate ways to communicate with each child.

Behaviorist Theory

The behaviorist approach to child devel-opment is based on the work of B. F. Skinner and his predecessors Thorndike, Watson, and Hull. The primary focus is on learning that involves change in behavior that can be observed and measured. Behaviorists do not deal with concepts like thought or emotion because they are not observable. They regard the mind as a mysterious black box whose nature can be inferred only from its actions (Baldwin, 1967, p.392).

These psychologists do not present a complete theory including developmental stages; rather, they regard learning as a *continuous* process governed by the same principles at all ages; that is, the same mechanisms of learning operate inde-pendently of the maturity of the learner. This differs substantially from ideas of Freud and Piaget that postulate develop-ment as *discontinuous,* marked by distinctly different stages that are dependent on changes in physiological structure and on environment.

A great deal of the research upon which behaviorist principles have been based was conducted in carefully controlled laboratory experiments with animals. Some of the results have been tested on humans, usually in laboratory settings as well, and similar results have been found. Behaviorist theory is the most scientific of the approaches to child development in terms of the careful and controlled experimental approach that it employs. Its critics feel that though the research may be good, it is limited in its scope, focusing on one small aspect of human experience.

Behaviorist theory emphasizes the action of the environment on the individual; external stimulation is seen as the source of growth and change. Langer has described it as a "mechanical mirror" theory.

> Like a mirror, the child comes to reflect his environment; like an empty slate, he is written upon by external stimuli; like a wax table, he stores the impressions left by these stimuli; and like a machine, he may be made to react in response to stimulating agents. (Langer, 1970, p.51)

Behaviorists regard the drive to satisfy physical needs as the fundamental force underlying human behavior. A drive spurs the person to be active for as long as the drive remains unsatisfied. Initial activity in response to a drive may be more or less random. When, however, a behavior helps a person achieve satisfaction, that behavior tends to be repeated when the same drive is felt again. Learning, according to behaviorists, consists of the build-up of associations between drives (the **stimulus**) and the behavior (**response**) that satisfies the drive. According to this view, all that is required to predict behavior and to shape it is a knowledge of present conditions of stimulation and past responses and the build-up of associations between the two. It is therefore often referred to as **stimulus-response (S-R) theory**.

The work of behaviorists helps us to understand mechanisms of learning and to appreciate how people are shaped by environmental forces. It also helps us to recognize the effects of rewards on molding learning and behavior. If a behavior is rewarded, it is likely to be repeated; if ignored or negatively reinforced, the likelihood of its being repeated is less.

Behaviorist programs for young children are designed so that the adult defines program goals and shapes children's behavior through the systematic use of reinforcements. These programs address themselves both to academic content and behavior management. They have been found to be very effective for children who have difficulties learning and for dealing with behavior management problems that result from faulty learning.

Many early childhood educators are uncomfortable with these programs because they feel that normal children will learn when provided with materials and experiences that stimulate their interest and curiosity. They do not believe that children require external reinforcers such as candy, tokens, or toys to encourage them. In fact, they see such external motivators as detrimental to the development of self-directed learning. These educators also believe that if a child's behavior problem is based on deep-rooted psychological causes, these need to be understood, and clinical intervention

needs to be made rather than an attempt to change the overt behavior without regard to the underlying problem.

Behaviorist techniques do work. Reinforcement principles are applied in classrooms all the time, either with or without the teacher's conscious intent. It is important that as a teacher of young children you understand these principles of learning and incorporate this knowledge into your repertoire of behavior. You need to become aware of the behaviors that you are reinforcing, and you need to know if your responses are consistent with what you really want to accomplish. With attention and careful thought, behaviorist principles can be selectively applied in the service of your goals for children.

Human Potential Theory

This view of development comes from the work of psychologists who saw existing approaches as inadequate in explaining the nature of human beings. They felt that Freudian and behaviorist theories based on the reduction of drives did not take into account what they saw as the unique qualities of human beings. These theories did not address human potential for consciousness, love, creativity, and the desire to understand the unknown. Psychologists concerned with human potential see people as having within them the ability to take charge of their lives and to further their own development in healthy and positive ways.

These theorists come primarily from the relatively new field of humanistic psychology. They are referred to as humanists, self-psychologists, phenomenologists, and existential psychologists. The movement is sometimes called the third force in psychology (Freudian theory and behaviorism being the first two). Some of the people who have contributed their ideas to this school of thought are Carl Rogers, Abraham Maslow, and Arthur Combs.

Human potential theories use normal people as their subject of study, and their concern is with how to support healthy and positive development instead of focusing on pathology. Sources of data include self-observation and the study of people who have developed their potential to a high level. These people are what Maslow has referred to as **self-actualized**. Their personal qualities have been identified, and they serve as a model of what people are capable of becoming.

Like behaviorism, human potential theory is not a fully conceptualized theory of development. There is no emphasis on childhood, and the stages of the life span are not described. The major feature of human potential theory is that it attempts to describe and validate human characteristics that other theories have regarded as too elusive to be the subject of scientific study. These are the unique qualities of humanity: thought, feeling, consciousness, choice, and the capacity to find meaning in existence.

Third force psychologists attempt to understand behavior from the point of view of the person who is behaving. This means that the feelings, thoughts, and values of the individual are as important as observable behavior in trying to make sense of human life. Deductions about inner life are made based on what a person says and does, and not on laboratory data.

This school of psychology has influenced programs for children by focusing attention on the development of the whole child, on what the individual can become. It offers a positive and optimistic view that affirms human dignity. The focus is an actualization of potential in all areas: intellectual, social, emotional, artistic, spiritual, and physical. It promotes programs that are characterized by positive relationships between teachers and learners and supports relationships based on mutual respect. It has influenced the development of curricula that focus on children's feelings and relationships (**affective education**).

Human potential theory is most useful in helping teachers to support children's impulses toward healthy development and in preventing problems that grow out of authoritarian and restrictive educational practices. This approach encourages adults to recognize that children are constantly striving to realize their potential and to organize experiences in meaningful ways.

THEORIES REGARDING THE ROLE OF PLAY IN DEVELOPMENT

Over the centuries a number of writers including Plato, Rousseau, Pestalozzi, Froebel, and Dewey have addressed the role of play as a special and important aspect of children's lives. In this section we will briefly survey some theories regarding the role of play in human development and touch briefly on some research findings.

A number of writers during the nineteenth and early twentieth centuries formulated explanations for the role of play in human development. Johan Huizanga (1872), a Dutch historian and educator, believed that ritual, poetry, music, and dancing are all forms of play and are essential components of man's civilized life. Herbert Spencer (1873), British philosopher and psychologist, introduced what has been called the *surplus energy theory,* which suggested that the purpose of play was to help man use energy that he no longer needed because of his "higher" animal status. The *recapitulation theory* of play, is credited to G.S. Hall (1920) who believed that during childhood the history of evolution is progressively relived. He saw play as an opportunity to rid the human race of primitive and unnecessary instinctual traits carried over by heredity from past generations (Levy, 1978). Another theory on play is called *instinct theory*. It was originated by German philosopher and writer Karl Groos (1861), who believed that play was a natural instinct and was necessary for children's growth and development. Although they both agreed that play was important, Hall saw its role as weakening and modifying past skills that were no longer needed, whereas Groos believed that it served an important role in allowing children to practice activities which would be useful when they became adults. Groos's ideas are still being cited by psychologists who are doing play research today.

Another group of theories concerning play grows out of Freudian theory. Freud and his followers felt that play helped children to feel more grown-up and powerful, to exert some control over their environments, and to relieve anxiety created by real life conflicts. Erikson, who placed heavy emphasis on the human social environment, saw play as instrumental in developing the ability to deal with experience through planning and experimentation and creating model situations. Play therapy, which evolved from the psychoanalytic tradition, uses play as a therapeutic mode for working through children's conflicts and problems.

Much of the current research on play derives from the work of Piaget, who believed that play contributed to and was a manifestation of cognitive development (Athey, 1984). He also offered a set of stages for looking at the development of children's play. The first stage of play he described is *practice games,* like peek-a-boo, which occur during the sensorimotor period, as the infant learns about the world through engaging in motor activities. The second stage he describes, *symbolic games,* like taking on and acting out adult roles, grows from the previous stage and occurs during the preoperational period when thinking is still limited to what can be experienced directly. The third stage, the period of *games with rules,* such as racing and chasing, hiding and guessing games (Kamii and DeVries, 1980), develops during the period of concrete operations when children become able to think logically.

Contemporary thinkers about play have attempted to explore it more scientifically. They are interested in definitions, descriptions, and characteristics of play and how it effects all aspects of development. There are many definitions, but this one by Garvey (1977) includes the essential elements. She writes, "Play is pleasurable, enjoyable. Play has no extrinsic goals and is unproductive. Play is spontaneous and voluntary and involves some active engagement on the part of the player" (p. 4).

According to Brian Sutton-Smith (1984) more than twenty books and two hundred articles have been written on children's play in the last fifteen years. Research by Lieberman (1977), Bruner, Genova, and Sylva (1976), and many others shows that play increases children's divergent thinking and problem-solving abilities. Other studies (Smilansky, 1968) investigate the play of economically deprived children and explore the possible contributions of "play training."

We do not have space in this chapter to do a comprehensive review of the research on play, but we are struck by the consistency of the findings regarding the very positive contributions of play to early development. Caplan and Caplan (1973) summarize it like this:

We believe the power of play to be extraordinary and supremely serious. Play time aids growth. Play is a voluntary activity. Play offers a child freedom of action. Play provides an imaginary world a child can master. Play has elements of adventure in it. Play provides a base for language building. Play has unique opportunities for mastery of the physical self. Play furthers interest and concentration. Play is the way children investigate the material world. Play is a way of learning adult roles. Play is always a dynamic way of learning. Play refines a child's judgments. Academics can be structured into play. Play is vitalizing. (p. xiii)

FOR FURTHER THOUGHT AND DISCUSSION

1   What is your view of the role of nature and nurture in children's development? Has it changed since reading this chapter? How?

2   Given the importance of early development, should the public school system in your community provide programs for infants, toddlers, and preschoolers? Why or why not? What might they do that would best meet children's needs?

3   In what ways are the four developmental theories discussed in this chapter visible in the early childhood programs that you have visited and worked in?

4   How do you think that your knowledge of child development will influence you in the classroom?

5   If play is important in children's development, why do you think it is not more prevalent in kindergarten and primary grade classrooms?

6   Consider your own school experience and the experience of the children in the classrooms that you have observed in terms of educating the right and left sides of the brain. What conclusions can you make about what you would like to provide in programs for children?

PROJECTS

1 Write an imaginary dialogue between a teacher trained in behaviorist theory and a teacher trained in cognitive development theory that concerns what they think children are like and how they should be taught.

2 Observe a young child and interpret his or her behavior in terms of Erikson's stages of child development.

3 Write a reflection about your own development. What forces seem to have been most significant (people, events, institutions, etc.)? How might these forces in your development influence your work with children?

4 Write a letter as if to parents who have been questioning you about why their child plays so much in your classroom. Explain your rationale for making play an important part of your program in terms of developmental theory and brain research.

5 Write a review of a book dealing with one of the topics in this chapter you want to learn more about. Describe the implications of what you learned for you as a teacher or future teacher of young children.

RECOMMENDED READING

Bruner, Jerome. *Child's Talk: Learning to Use Language.* New York: W.W. Norton, 1983.

Caplan, F., and Caplan, T. *The Power of Play.* New York. Anchor Press/Doubleday, 1973.

Donaldson, Margaret C. *Children's Minds.* New York: W.W. Norton, 1978.
———; Grieve, Robert; and Pratt, Chris, eds. *Early Childhood Development and Education: Readings in Psychology.* New York: The Guilford Press, 1983.

Elkind, David. *The Hurried Child: Growing Up Too Fast Too Soon.* Reading, Mass.: Addison-Wesley, 1981.

Erikson, Erik. *Childhood and Society.* 2d ed. New York: W.W. Norton, 1963.

Flavell, John H. *Cognitive Development.* 2d ed. Englewood Cliffs, N.J.: Prentice-Hall, 1985.

Garvey, Catherine. *Play.* Cambridge, Mass.: Harvard University Press, 1977.

Ginsburg, Herbert, and Opper, Sylvia. *Piaget's Theory of Intellectual Development.* 2d ed. Englewood Cliffs, N.J.: Prentice-Hall, 1979.

Kagan, Jerome. *The Nature of the Child.* New York: Basic Books, 1984.

Kamii, Constance, and DeVries, Rheta. *Group Games in Early Education: Implications of Piaget's Theory.* Washington D.C.: National Association for the Education of Young Children, 1980.

Languis, Marlin; Sanders, Tobie; and Tibbs, Steven. *Brain and Learning.* Washington D.C.: National Association for the Education of Young Children, 1980.

Maslow, Abraham H. *Toward A Psychology of Being.* 2d ed. New York: Van Nostrand Reinhold, 1968.

Nye, Robert D. *Three Psychologies: Perspectives from Freud, Skinner and Rogers.* 2d ed. Monterey, Cal.: Brooks/Cole, 1981.

Papalia, Diane E., and Wendkos Olds, Sally. *A Child's World.* 3d. ed. New York: McGraw-Hill, 1982.

Piaget, Jean. *The Origins of Intelligence in Children.* 2d ed. New York: International Universities Press, 1966.

Rogers, Carl R. *Freedom to Learn.* Columbus, O.: Charles E. Merrill, 1969.

Thomas, Alexander, and Chess, Stella. *Temperament and Development.* New York: Brunner/Mazel, 1977.

Tough, Joan. *The Development of Meaning: A Study of Children's Use of Language.* Boston, Mass.: George Allen and Unwin, 1977.

Vygotsky, L.S. *Thought and Language.* Cambridge, Mass.: MIT Press, 1962.

Wadsworth, Barry J. *Piaget's Theory of Cognitive and Affective Development.* 3d ed. New York: Longman, 1984.

5

Observation
and
Evaluation

"You see, but you do not observe."

Arthur Conan Doyle

"Bring with you a heart that watches and
  receives."

Wordsworth

*This chapter focuses on observation as a way of learning about young children and the use of evaluation techniques and instruments for appraising the developmental progress of children. Guidelines are given for learning to write useful observations and for using observational data in your work with children. Guidelines are given for selection of assessment instruments that can help you in program planning and in identifying children who may have delays in development. This chapter can be applied to all thirteen of the CDA areas but is particularly relevant to **Program Management.***

OBSERVATION

To observe is to take notice, to watch attentively, to focus on one particular aspect of all of the massive stimulus in the environment. The ability to observe is one of the most important skills that a teacher of young children can develop. Learning to observe involves more than casual looking, and it is not nearly as easy as you might think. To make useful observations of children and classrooms requires training and practice. You must be clear about the purpose of the observation and willing to gather information and impressions with a receptive eye and mind.

Observation in early childhood settings can take a variety of forms, but its basic components include selecting a focus and watching attentively. The data that such observation provides increase your understanding and give you insight into the meaning of children's behavior and the impact of classroom practice. Systematic recorded observations reveal trends and patterns in behavior. They enable you to increase your effectiveness since conclusions based on recorded observation correct misperceptions and biases that can occur when conclusions are based on recall and memory alone.

Observation is the basis for much of the work teachers do with children, and it is used in some form in every area discussed in this book. Teachers observe children, curriculum, and classroom environment. In a less structured, but no less important way, they also observe themselves, their values, their relationships with children and adults, and their feelings and reactions.

The first and most important subject for your observations is, of course, children. The primary focus of this chapter is to help you to develop skills in observing children so that you can use the information gathered to improve your teaching. Careful observation will help you to know children better, to plan and make decisions about your program, and to know when a child may have a problem that needs to be studied further. Information from observation will help you to communicate about the child's development to parents, teachers, administrators, and other professionals who might be involved in working with the child and family.

We have also learned from our college teaching experience that observation can stimulate a relationship of caring and concern. We first realized this when two of the four goldfish our students had been observing died over a weekend. Every student in the class was worried that *their*

USES OF OBSERVATION

Through observation teachers develop:
- [ ] Increased sensitivity to children and a heightened awareness of the unique qualities of childhood and the world of children.
- [ ] Greater knowledge of individual children: how they think, feel, view the world, and how this compares to developmental norms.
- [ ] A composite picture of each child, based on many situations that changes as new information is added over time.
- [ ] An overall impression of each child's interests, skills, characteristic responses, and areas of strength and weakness.
- [ ] Understanding of the kinds of social relationships among children and among children and adults and how these can be facilitated in school.
- [ ] Awareness of the class environment, schedule and program, how well these are meeting the needs of children and staff, and how they might be improved.
- [ ] Greater insight into their own ways of responding to children and situations.

fish was one of the casualties. We have since realized from our own observations of children and from our students' subsequent experiences in conducting in-depth case studies of individual children that observing another person in a detached but caring way creates greater understanding and hence greater empathy.

The consistent practice of observation in the classroom helps teachers develop *child-sense*: a feeling for children, their groups, and how they are functioning. This deep understanding is based on a great deal of experience in observing individuals and groups of children over time.

It is very difficult to be objective about yourself. As you watch your own behavior and interactions, however, you develop greater awareness of how you feel and

respond in various situations and of the impact of your behavior on others. Self-observation helps you to make choices about how to respond in any situation.

The Observation Process

In order to observe more objectively and separate out feelings and reactions from what was actually seen, we have found that is useful to divide the observation process into three components:

1 Data Gathering: what you see and hear.
2 Interpretation: what you think it means.
3 Acknowledgment of feelings and reactions: how it makes you feel.

Data Gathering The first and most essential step in observation is to look and listen carefully. Objective observation depends on experiencing as completely as possible while attempting to suspend interpretation and evaluation. To see what is actually taking place you must avoid value judgments and try to reduce the distortions that are the result of biases, defenses, or preconceptions (Read, 1976, pp. 124–125). Objectivity is difficult because you are a participant in the life of the classroom that you observe, and you both influence and are influenced by the people in it. If you are aware of your impact on the situation and its impact on you, you can work toward becoming an unbiased observer. This involves consciously focusing while quieting the inner voice that explains and evaluates situations. An effective teacher of young children has the ability to wait and see what is really happening instead of drawing conclusions based on hurriedly gathered impressions. Such "intensive waiting" (Nyberg, 1971, p. 168) requires that expectations be suspended and that you simply be receptive to what *is*: behaviors, feelings, and patterns. This doesn't mean that you must become an impersonal, robot-like machine, but it does require you to carefully separate what you see from what you might have wanted to see or from what you feared you would see.

It is also necessary to be aware of your characteristics as an observer. When you realize on what you tend to focus, you also have a better idea of what you characteristically ignore. You can train yourself to compensate and observe the situation more fully. We bring a bowl of goldfish to our classes and ask each student to write a description of one of the fish . Some describe the minute details of the fish's anatomy, some look at the fish in the context of its environment (bowl, sand, water, and other fish), and some describe the interactions among the fish. Not only do students learn something about the features they tend to observe from this exercise, but they are surprised to find how much they attribute motivations and feelings to these relatively inexpressive creatures.

Millie Almy says, of keen observers:

> They study facial expression, note the steady and the shifting look, the tightly or loosely held jaw and lips, the grimaces and the smiles. They hear not only words but tones, pitch, strain, hesitation, and pauses. They note body posture, slumping shoulders and puppet-on-a-string gestures, as contrasted with flowing, graceful movements and accurate, efficient coordination. They see all the details in relation to the settings where the behavior takes place. The clenched hands and intent frown seen in the reading period are different from the freedom and *joie de vivre* of the playground. These finer details, this attention to its quality, provide clues to the meaning of behavior. (Almy and Genishi, 1979, pp 39–40)

As Almy suggests, a good observer goes far beyond the obvious. Part of developing this keen observation sense is learning to read body language. Children communicate a great deal through their bodies, perhaps as much as through their spoken words and obvious actions. Suzanne Szasz's lovely book, *The Unspoken Language of Children* (1978), may help you to develop a sensitivity to body language, including indicators of body tension, the meaning of body and head position, as well as facial expression; the language of hands, fingers, and eyebrows; and the importance of a tilt of a shoulder and the ways children position themselves and respond to objects and people.

Interpretation   The second basic step in the classroom observation process is to make interpretations based on what you have seen and heard. While behavior is observable and can be described more or less objectively, the sources of behavior are not visible and may only be inferred. You need to observe closely and then seek the relationship between the observed behavior and its unobservable cause. While you can never truly know why a child behaves as he or she does, you will make decisions based on your assumptions about children's behavior every day. It is important that you develop skill in making the most accurate interpretations possible based on *what was actually observed.*

Interpreting a child's behavior is difficult because so many factors—stage of development, health, cultural influences, and individual experience—combine in complex ways to determine how an individual acts in a given situation. The same behavior can mean very different things in different children. Individual observers may interpret the same behavior or incident in dissimilar ways. For example, several of our college students noticed a little girl who was lying in a large cement pipe in the yard of a preschool they were visiting. One student thought that she was withdrawn and antisocial, another was convinced that she was lonely, unhappy, and in need of comfort, and the third felt that she was just taking a few moments for quiet contemplation. Obviously the students were drawing hasty conclusions based on minimal information, perhaps influenced by their childhood experiences or their feelings at the moment. They needed

more information about the child and the events that preceded their observation in order to make accurate and meaningful interpretations.

While it is useful to make interpretations based on your observations, it is important to be cautious. Watching even after you have come to a conclusion is never amiss: the extra information may change your mind. Since two people observing the same incident will often have different perceptions, it is useful to discuss your interpretations with someone else. Becoming aware of different perspectives can help you to realize how difficult it is to interpret accurately.

Acknowledgment of Feelings and Reactions   The third step in the observation process is to notice and acknowledge your feelings and reactions apart from more objective data and interpretation. You then have the opportunity to reflect on your responses without distorting the observation. These feelings and reactions don't belong in a file on the child or in the written information that you share with the child's family or other professionals. They are a useful part of your training in learning to observe. In the beginning, deliberately take time to note your feelings and reactions. Later, in many cases, it will be enough to notice them and correct any biases they might create.

Figure 5.1 illustrates the interrelationship of the components of observation and how the history and personality of the observer influence this process.

Written Observations

Learning to observe children and classrooms and to develop skill in writing clear, concise observations takes time,

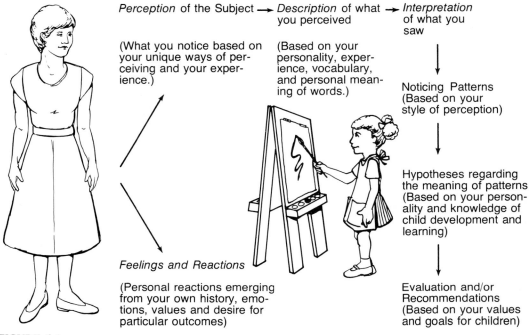

FIGURE 5.1
The observation process

commitment, and practice. Written observations should clearly separate objective data (description) and interpretation.

Description   Good descriptions use clear language and give enough information to convey the uniqueness of the subject under observation. To retain the clarity of your impressions, you may find it useful to take notes inconspicuously while you are in the classroom observing or to write soon after the observation is made. Some teachers we know carry a small notebook and pencil in a big pocket of an apron so that these are always handy to record observations.

If you are writing for someone who is unfamiliar with the child and the setting (for example your college instructor), the first thing you will note is the context for the observation: where you are (the school, location, indoors or outdoors, area of the classroom) and who you are observing (an individual child, a group of children, or a specific interaction). You will also want to describe the child, or children to help the reader to envision the situation. If you are writing for yourself or colleagues who are familiar with the child and the setting, you will simply note where and who you are observing and any special qualities of the child or the setting at the date and time of your observation. Then you describe what happened.

Though readers may agree that an observation should vividly portray a child or interaction, it is difficult to do more than give some general guidelines about how to write a description in a lively, yet relatively unbiased way. At first your writing may be awkward, and you may have difficulty deciding how much to record. You may include more or less than is necessary, perhaps attending to unimportant details while missing those that are more vital. This is part of the process of developing the skill. Later you will learn to focus on the essentials. The following suggestions have helped our college students develop skill in writing and in critically appraising their descriptions of children. These are intended to help you learn a technique, but they are not the sort of observations that, as a busy teacher, you will write regularly in the course of a day.

The first thing to do in writing a description of a child is to note physical attributes and manner: age, sex, size, build, facial features, coloring, body stance, gesture, way of moving, and so forth. The description that follows is so telegraphic that it conveys little useful information.

> She is an Oriental girl, approximately four years of age, shorter than her peers. She has a slight build, oval face, and brown hair and eyes.

When this description of physical attributes is elaborated with some of the child's unique personal qualities: way of moving, facial expression, gestures, tone of voice, etc., it conveys a better picture of the child as a unique individual. The following addition conveys a much more vivid sense of the child whose physical attributes were described above:

> She has black eyebrows and lashes, brown hair, almond-shaped eyes, a fair, smooth complexion, pouting lips and a small up-turned nose. She is slim and almost fragile looking, and strolls from activity to activity with small light steps, her eyes alert and her head turning occasionally from side to side. Her arms hang slightly away from her body and swing with the rhythm of her stroll.

The next step is to describe the child's activities and interactions. The addition of expressive detail, including body language, also enhances this description:

> When she was busy doing something, she was very intent and concentrating. She didn't actively seek out interactions with other children but responded with a smile when interactions were initiated by someone else. She spoke little, but when she did, it was without hesitation.

The language used in recording should capture the subtleties and complexities of children's behavior. Careful choice of words conveys the essence of the person and situation and is an important part of writing vivid descriptions. Colorful adverbs and adjectives enhance our ability to visualize the subject of the observation: "He had a brisk, fast pace—always rushing to the next place" instead of "He walked faster than most children." In choosing modifiers avoid words such as *pretty*, *sloppy*, and *dirty* that have a strong emotional impact or bias built into them. Avoid words that are interpretations or that describe your feelings: *cute*, *bright*, *attractive*. Value judgments about children should be omitted in both the description and the interpretation. Describing a child as *good*, *bad*, *bright*, *slow*, or *naughty* tells more about the values of the observer than the reality of the child. As a guideline, we suggest that you describe what a child *does*, instead of saying what he or she *is*. Since the observations you write may be shared with others, you have the responsibility to convey useful information that is as free as possible from personal bias or unsubstantiated evaluations.

A good description is specific, but does not give so much detail that the point is lost. Broad general statements do not convey much information and are not very effective in capturing important qualities of the child or interaction. For example, the statement "John worked at stringing beads today," does not tell the reader very much. We have a better picture of the child and situation when the observer tells us, "He had an intent look on his face, his tongue protruded slightly from between his teeth, and it appeared that all of his concentration was focused on stringing the beads." Additional details such as when John worked with the beads, how long he worked, how he worked, who he worked with, and the feelings he projected as he worked might also increase the reader's ability to understand the child and the situation.

Through experience you can enhance your awareness and develop greater ability to communicate in writing. Knowing about the nature of observation, studying your writing, and seeking feedback from others will help you to develop this skill.

Writing Interpretations Based on Description   Interpretations based on careful and complete descriptions make it possible for others to read what you have written and decide whether or not they agree with you. For this reason, it is essential that your interpretations be based on description. Others can then offer their insight, and you can benefit from the collective experience of all who

review your observation. Descriptions of the same child or incident written by different observers can be helpful since each of us tends to notice different things. It is also eye opening to have several individuals interpret the same written description of a situation. We encourage our students to make liberal use of the words *might* and *seems to* in their written interpretations to underscore the tentative nature of conclusions about children's needs, feelings, and motivation.

To assist students as they learn to write substantiated interpretations, we use a format for writing observations that has parallel columns for writing descriptions and noting feelings, reactions, and tentative interpretations. Figure 5.2 provides an example.

With such a format you are able to go back, add other possible interpretations of behaviors, and decide if you have enough

Description	Interpretations/Feelings
*Joshua enters the classroom well ahead of his father and makes a beeline for the block corner where John and Thomas have a large unit block structure well in progress. J. drops his lunch pail in the middle of the rug and begins issuing directions--"Make it go this way" as he takes a block from Thomas and begins a second wall at a right angle to the first. "Get more of the big kind." J. says to John.	poor impulse control--or loves blocks/ friends Bossy
*The two quickly join in and proceed with J's plan as J's father approaches, observes a few moments and then interrupts to tell J. to take his lunch pail to his cubby.	Leader
*J. acknowledges the request with an impatient glance and says "Just a minute Dad," and continues to direct the building with even more vigor and hurriedness.	
*Father says, "You can come back to the blocks after you've...." J. grimaces and scrambles over the wall, grabs the pail, runs to his cubby and deposits the pail inside. It falls to the floor as he turns to rush back to the blocks.	poor impulse control--or Loves to build/ create
*Father intercepts him half-way and points him back to his cubby and pushes him gently from behind. J. stops, looks up at Father and laughs as if sharing a joke.	sense of humor

FIGURE 5.2
Format for writing observations

descriptive data to substantiate your conclusions. If not, you can observe the child in other settings to see if the behaviors are characteristic or simply the outcome of a particular situation.

This format helps you assess whether your description is complete and extensive enough to support your conclusions or whether you should observe and take more notes before writing a narrative intepretation . The written interpretation should state your conclusions concisely and cite the descriptive data on which they are based. For example:

> Joshua appears to be a leader, John and Thomas accept his directives and do not seem upset by, or resistant to, his joining in their work.

Structured Observation

You can organize your observations of children to pay special attention to those things you want to learn more about. You may wish to observe aspects of development, potential problem areas, the strengths and weaknesses of individual children, or their interaction or learning styles. As you structure your observations, it is important to get the whole picture, to focus on strengths as well as weaknesses.

The observation technique you use will depend on your purpose. Observations can differ in the degree to which the process of observation and recording is systematized and standardized. If your intention is to develop awareness of self or of the situation, then simply taking

time to stop and observe and then mentally note what is going on may be sufficient. If you are gathering information about a specific child or for a particular purpose, then some form of systematic record-keeping will be helpful.

There are a number of techniques to help teachers use observation to objectively assess children and classroom incidents. Their purpose is to gain information about the behavior of a child or group of children. A structured observation can help to confirm hypotheses or raise further questions about something you have noticed. For example, you may use a structured observation to determine what percentage of time a seemingly withdrawn child is actually spending in passive activity and how much time the child is more actively involved.

Structured observation techniques have some common characteristics. They begin with a focus for the observation (a particular child, behavior, interaction, classroom practice, material) and a specific attribute that is being observed (how often a behavior occurs, what precipitates it). Many are conducted within a set time frame, which may be very short (every minute for fifteen minute periods) or which may be longer (any time a behavior occurs during a week). In order to choose an appropriate system for a structured observation, you will need to decide what your purpose is and what information you need to achieve your purpose.

Techniques for structured observation include anecdotal records, time samples, event samples, and checklists that organize observations of children and classrooms. Data from parent interviews and questionnaires can be added to your observations to create case studies. Day-to-day observations and knowledge of child growth and development, combined with structured techniques provide you with more pieces for understanding the fascinating puzzle of each child you teach.

Anecdotal Records   The most frequently used structured observation is the anecdotal record, a written, narrative description of a child's behavior and interactions in a natural setting (some

114

area of the classroom or play yard). Be selective in what behavior or event to record, and include details and information that will add to your understanding of the child. For example:

☐ Behavior or interactions that seem typical for the child.
☐ Behavior or interactions that seem atypical for the child.
☐ The achievement of a developmental milestone, the first time the child masters a new skill or engages in a new activity.
☐ Behavior or interactions relating to an area of special concern you have about the child.

Anecdotal records can be made with special emphasis on children about whom you have current questions or concerns.

You may find that there are "invisible children" in your group, children you tend to forget about because there is nothing notable about them. You may then decide to make regular notations about these children for a period of time so that you can learn more about them. You will need to make provisions to write while the impressions are still fresh. You may want to jot down key words or fragments of information and fill in more details later. Some teachers keep a small observation notebook and pencil handy, and in some classrooms, a notebook or filebox with a section for each child is left in an easily accessible place. These records become part of your collection of information about each child and should be kept with all other confidential records.

Event Samples In an event sample, the observer watches for a particular behavior or interaction and then records exactly

what preceded the event, what happened during the event, and what the consequences of the event were. Like an anecdotal record, this type of observation relies on the skill of the observer in making detailed descriptions. For example, if you think a child has been engaging in a lot a aggressive behavior, you may want to write a description of what precedes every aggressive act, exactly what happens, and what follows the behavior. You may discover that the aggressive behavior is only happening before lunch or nap, at the end of the day, or is triggered by interaction with one child or group of children. This type of observation can help you to better understand the antecedents and the nature of a behavior from the child's viewpoint.

Teacher-Developed Checklists Informal checklists can also give teachers information about the things that they want to learn more about: which children have acquired a particular skill or concept, how often a child engages in a particular behavior, children's play preferences, or how materials and equipment in the classroom are being used. They are a useful, relatively simple way to find out what children are doing or not doing and what is working in the classroom.

To create a checklist you first decide what you want to know (e.g., which children can recognize their printed names). You then decide on an *operational definition* (what you mean by the words you have used) of the behavior or activity so that anyone else will be able to understand it (e.g., children can "recognize their names " when they can select their name card from among a group of names printed on cards). Similarly you can use a

TIME SAMPLE 1

A fifteen-minute record sampled once every minute during choice time indoors

Time: 9:30–9:45   Date: 10/12/85
Child: Mary Ann

Activity	solitary observation	solitary play	cooperative play	fighting/arguing
	√√√√ √	√√√√√√	√√	√√

TIME SAMPLE 2

A fifteen-minute record sampled once every minute during choice time indoors

Code: I = initiates S = solitary R = rejects A = accepts C = child
      T = teacher x = continues

Time: 9:30–9:45   Date: 10/12/85
Child: Michael

9:30 S	9:35 x	9:40 x
9:31 x	9:36 S	9:41 AT
9:32 x	9:37 IC	9:42 AC
9:33 RC	9:38 RC	9:43 x
9:34 S	9:39 S	9:44 x

checklist to note other behaviors that more than one adult will be recording. The operational definition ensures that all the adults are recording the same thing.

Time Samples A time sample is used to track a child's behavior at regular intervals. It is not a record of everything that is happening. A teacher using a time sampling technique attempts to ascertain systematically how often a particular behavior (hitting, fantasy play, thumb sucking) is actually occurring. A total amount of time is divided into smaller segments. A simple checklist or a code may be used to help the observer record quickly what type of behavior is going on at each interval in the sample. (For example, *R* may stand for rejects interaction and *I* may stand for initiates interaction.) More elaborate codes provide detailed information about how the child is actually spending time.

During a time sample, the observer notes what behavior is occurring at precise intervals. The behavior is recorded, and the results are analyzed. This information can be used as a basis for drawing conclusions about the importance of particular behaviors.

We once designed a time sample to test our belief that a child named Mickey was initiating an excessive number of conflicts with others. Several staff members felt that they spent a great deal of time each day intervening in the conflicts that he provoked. Another teacher had difficulty understanding this because she perceived him as a very positive and cooperative person. The time sample was very simple. We agreed to track how frequently Mickey and the two friends with whom he was often in conflict actually initiated interaction and whether it was positive or negative. The outcome of three fifteen-minute time samples on each child uncovered that this child had many more positive than negative interactions and that this was also true of his friends. We discovered, however, that he initiated interactions three times more frequently than his two playmates. This helped explain our different perceptions of the child and helped us to understand why we felt taxed by our frequent interventions. Our increased understanding helped us to allow him the opportunity to handle interpersonal problems on his own.

Case Studies   There are times when you will want to pull together all of your information about a child because you have concerns you want to explore with others. This is called a case study. You may present this in a staff meeting or to a

specialist who can offer additional insights, or use it when you refer a child for a formal evaluation. Under these circumstances, it is advisable to document all that you know about the child and the problem. A case study will include all observations made by the teacher and other staff members, as well as information that may contribute to greater understanding of the child, including health records, assessment data (described in the next section), information about the family situation, and samples of the child's work. It might also include your conclusions and recommendations.

EVALUATING CHILDREN'S DEVELOPMENTAL PROGRESS

Evaluation involves gathering information systematically with the purpose of making some kind of appraisal of a child's development. Teachers use evaluation techniques to identify children with possible developmental problems and to evaluate the developmental status of children in order to plan appropriate programs and activities. Early childhood educators have generally evaluated children's progress through informal observation. In many programs today this is still the primary evaluation method. In other programs teachers combine observations with more formal techniques.

Screening

Screening is a relatively fast and efficient way to initially evaluate children. Every child is screened, in some way, beginning at birth. The new baby is observed for obvious defects. Simple screening such as observation and testing of heart rate,

muscle tone, and respiration occur in the first few minutes after birth. As children grow and develop, they encounter other forms of screening in the course of their regular medical care. Families may notice when a child appears to be different from others, and this too is an informal method of screening.

The primary purpose of screening is to attempt to identify, as early as possible, children who have health problems or developmental delays in order to reduce the time that elapses before beginning treatment. It identifies children who need further evaluation. Screening instruments are **norm-referenced**, that is, the individual child is compared with the norm for a large group of children of similar age. A child should *never* be labeled on the basis of the results of a screening since screening *cannot* predict future success or failure, prescribe specific treatment or curriculum, or diagnose handicapping conditions. Screening is simply a tool to let us know which children we need to look at more carefully.

Instruments designed for screening are relatively short, have few items, look at several developmental areas, and can be administered and interpreted by trained professionals or volunteers. Even if no children with handicaps or delays are identified, information from screening can help you to understand the relative strengths and weaknesses of the children in your care, give you a starting place for further observation, and provide some ideas for planning.

A screening instrument should identify children who have significant delays when compared to others of their age. It is important to remember that no method of screening is foolproof. With screening some children with developmental delays may still remain undetected (this is called a *false negative*). Others may be identified as needing further evaluation who have no disabling condition (this is called a *false positive*). Screening results are influenced by a child's cultural and experiential background. Traits that are related to culture or experience may seem to indicate a handicap where none exists (for example, a screening test used in Hawaii asked children to make judgments based on drawings of children in snowsuits, wearing mittens, and using sleds and snow shovels: their "incorrect" responses were not due to developmental delay but to different experience).

The screening services that are available to families vary from community to community and from state to state. Many have *Childfind* programs that attempt to make parents and other adults aware of the importance of early identification. Some communities provide screening just prior to or shortly after school entrance. You may be required to choose and/or administer a screening instrument and act on the results of screening. If screening is not provided where you work, you will observe to note children who may need further evaluation.

Choosing a Screening Instrument
Screening instruments have an effect on children and their families. If they fail, children may not get the special help that they need. False identification may label children and worry families unnecessarily.

Screening instruments are standardized on a group of children. They reflect the culture and experience of this group. Items that are routinely missed are rejected, and items that have a high success rate are retained as indicators of normal development. Items reflect the values of the people who create the instruments: what they believe is worthwhile for a child of a particular age to know, to do, or to have experienced. They are designed with a particular viewpoint and type of school or agency in mind.

QUESTIONS TO ASK IN CHOOSING A SCREENING INSTRUMENT

- ☐ Does the instrument address all major developmental areas?
- ☐ Does the instrument reflect the language or dialect of the population being tested? If not, can it be adapted? (If children are not tested in their first language, they may not perform in a way that reflects their true abilities.)
- ☐ Does the instrument reflect the experience and cultural background of the children to be screened?
- ☐ Does the instrument involve information from parents? (They know the child best and have important information to contribute.)
- ☐ Does the instrument reflect your program's values and goals for children?

When you evaluate an instrument, there are some questions you will want to ask to determine if they are a good fit for your school and your population.

In-Depth Evaluation

When observation and screening suggest that a developmental problem may exist, more information must be gathered. A diagnostic team that may include a physician, psychologist, other therapists, and teachers can help to evaluate whether or not a handicap exists, what it seems to be (diagnosis), and the kind of placement and services that would be most appropriate for the child (treatment). Diagnosis of this kind requires a referral to professionals who have training and skill in evaluating children in this way. Chapter 14, Children with Special Needs, provides more information on the referral process.

When you wish to find out more specifically the educational needs of an individual child, you may make a more in-depth assessment of ability. Comprehensive assessments are designed to help teachers learn more about children's actual functioning as a basis for planning. These assessments are made with commercially prepared and packaged instruments that give a profile of a child's abilities in a number of different areas. They are usually administered, interpreted, and used by teachers and other personnel in the classroom. Classroom assessment instruments are **criterion-referenced**; they reflect a child's degree of mastery over a skill or sequence of skills, but do not compare that child with others . These instruments may take quite a long time to administer—sometimes weeks or even months—and assess a number of skill areas. Using a classroom assessment may be a process that continues throughout the school year. You may do some testing early in the year to identify what skills the child already has and possible problem areas, and then may design experiences and activities to help the child to move to the next step. You can then reassess and repeat the process.

Classrooom assessments are often packaged with guidelines for lessons and materials that are appropriate in the development of specific skills. This process should address the whole child and not just areas of weakness or comparison to a norm. Assessment instruments are not meant to label children, nor should they become the entire basis for your curriculum. They are intended to give you information about the children you teach so that you can design appropriate experiences for individuals and groups.

Classroom assessment may also serve a screening purpose, especially if no other

120

TABLE 5.1

Screening and assessment instruments.

Instrument Name	Publisher	Date	Primary Purpose	For Ages	Areas**	No. Items	Time Required
Denver Developmental Screening Test*	LADOCA Project Publishing Foundation, Inc.	1973	Developmental Screening	2 weeks–6 years	FM, GM, L, S, SH	23	15–30 minutes
Developmental Indicators for the Assessment of Learning (DIAL)	Childcraft Educational Corporation	1975	Developmental Screening	2½–5½ years	FM, GM, L, C	28	20–30 minutes
Developmental Profile (Alpern-Bell)	Psychological Development Publications	1972	Developmental Screening	Birth to 11 years	FM, GM, L, C, S, SH	36	20–40 minutes
Rapid Examination for Early Referral	Charles E. Merrill Co.	1980	Developmental Screening	3–6 years	FM, L, C	4	5–10 minutes
Brigance Diagnostic Inventory of Early Development	Curriculum Associates	1978	Developmental Assessment	Birth to 7 years	FM, GM, L, C, SH	98	Variable, depending on skill sequence selected
Learning Accomplishment Profile (LAP)	Kaplan School Supply	1975	Developmental Assessment	2–6 years	FM, GM, L, C, S, SH	183	Variable, no restricted time period
Portage Guide to Early Education	Portage Project Portage, Wisc.	1976	Developmental Assessment	Birth to 6 years	FM, GM, L, C, S	166	Variable, depending on starting point and extent of completion
Illinois Test of Psycholinguistic Ability (ITPA)	University of Illinois Press	1968	Assessment and Diagnosis	2–10 years	C, L	Approx. 173, varies with subtests	45–60 minutes
Peabody Picture Vocabulary Test (PPVT)	American Guidance Service	1965	Assessment of Receptive Language	2–8 years	L	10–15	10–15 minutes
Child Development Assessment Form	Humanics, Ltd.	1979	Educational Assessment	3–6 years	FM, GM, C, S, SH	64	Variable, uses observation within program setting
Cognitive Skills Assessment Battery	Teachers College Press	1977	Educational Assessment	4–5 years	FM, GM, C, S	84	25 minutes
Pre-Academic Learning Inventory	Educational Dimensions, Ltd.	1975	Educational Assessment	5–6 years	FM, GM, L, C	37	30–35 minutes

SCREENING

ASSESSMENT

* All of the instruments listed may be administered by teachers. Some require special training.
** Code: FM = fine motor, GM = gross motor, L = language, C = Cognitive, S = social, SH = self help.

screening has been done. Results can indicate that a child may have a problem. A very general guideline is that, if there is a six month lag in language or a one year delay in any other area, the child should be carefully watched and receive special attention in the area of the deficit. If the delay is greater, the child may need a complete diagnostic evaluation.

Table 5.1 lists a number of commercial assessment instruments that are widely used and easily accessible. We have included some basic information about each one and indicated those used for screening and those primarily used for classroom assessment.

Choosing an Assessment Instrument

Commercial instruments can only test what can be observed, and they only test what their authors believe to be important. They may not assess what you or your colleagues value. There is debate among early childhood educators concerning whether or not it is possible to test for the complex range of skills that we attempt to develop in early childhood programs and when it is appropriate to use assessment tools that are inevitably limited . This debate will certainly continue, and the instruments will be refined and improved as time passes. In the meantime, you must choose carefully, be aware of

QUESTIONS TO ASK IN CHOOSING A CLASSROOM ASSESSMENT INSTRUMENT

☐ Does the instrument have goals for children that are similar to, or compatible with, the goals of your program? (If not, you may be assessing skills you do not necessarily value.)
☐ Are guidelines for use given? Are they adequate?
☐ Can the instrument be administered and interpreted by school personnel?
☐ Can you use the instrument with the language or dialect of the school's population?
☐ Does the instrument reflect the culture and typical experience of the school's population? If not, can it be easily adapted to make it appropriate?
☐ Does the instrument involve age-appropriate types of responses and timing (manipulative and verbal rather than written responses and short testing periods followed by rest intervals)?
☐ Are criteria for success clearly spelled out, or is there a danger of results being dependent on the opinion of the examiner?
☐ Does the instrument give information that will be helpful to you in planning for children?
☐ Does the assessment include the type and amount of parent input desired?

the limitations of these instruments, and realize that you should continue to use your own informal observations to create a more complete picture.

When you choose an assessment instrument, it is important to consider what use you wish to make of the results. With your purpose in mind, you can more easily look at what instrument will best suit your needs and the needs of the children in your classroom. If you use information from an assessment instrument in the design of your program, then the day-to-day reality of life in your classroom will be tied to that assessment. Used well, this helps you to create a program that is developmentally appropriate and responsive to the needs of individual children.

Some schools, after examining commercial assessment packages, decide to design their own. The assessment can then be designed around the goals of the program and the characteristics of the specific group of children. "Home-made" assessment devices also have drawbacks; they are very time consuming to create, are not based on a norm, and do not reflect the skills of specialists in test design. If you choose to design or modify an assessment instrument, it is important to have a person skilled in the area of assessment help you with the process.

Conducting an Evaluation with Children

It is important to remember that test reliability varies. Young children are affected by the immediate events in their lives and environments. Performance in a test situation is affected by the events of the day, the immediate surroundings, the child's state of health, feelings, and willingness to engage with the person administering the assessment. No one instrument or occasion will disclose everything that you need to know about a child. It will help a great deal if you plan carefully and think through potential problems before you administer an assessment instrument.

SUGGESTIONS FOR CONDUCTING ASSESSMENTS WITH CHILDREN

- ☐ Read the manual accompanying the assessment instrument with special attention to the directions for administration.
- ☐ If a child experiences anxiety about separating from the group or from parents, screen a quiet corner of the classroom, or invite a parent to sit in on the session (not in the child's line of vision).
- ☐ Remove stimulating pictures from the wall to help the child focus on the task.
- ☐ Establish rapport with the child through play during a warm-up session.
- ☐ Introduce the tasks as soon as you feel the child is comfortable in the testing situation.

☐ Choose materials that are large, easy to see, and colorful.

☐ Have all materials ready and easily accessible to keep transitions short.

☐ Keep verbal directions short, simple, and clear.

☐ Give directions first, demonstrate if appropriate, then present materials.

☐ Use a game format (for example, "Your turn," "My turn") to maintain the relationship during the testing.

☐ Allow the child to take the lead and play with the materials in a nondirected way. When the child is attentive, you can structure the activity to get the information required.

☐ With a shy or nonverbal child, start with active tasks that do not require verbal responses. Let a nonverbal child be actively involved in a task. (A puppet may help a shy child to warm-up and speak.)

☐ Sit close to the child to control behavior if necessary. Keeping one hand on the child's arm or back may help an impulsive child.

☐ Use attention-getting phrases like, "Watch me" and "Are you ready?" before the child begins the task.

☐ Break up the sitting and attending time by alternating active and sit-down tasks. If possible, change physical space (move from table to floor).

☐ Be prepared to reschedule the assessment for another time if the child refuses to participate after an adequate warm-up period.

(Adapted from Bailie et al., *A Manual to Identify and Serve Children with Specific Learning Disabilities: Age 3–5,* 1980, pp. 48–57.)

FOR FURTHER THOUGHT AND DISCUSSION

1 In a small group, share a description you have written of a child. Have each person respond by telling you the words in the description that seemed strong and that communicated a sense of the child to them and the words that seemed weak or inappropriate.

2 In your small group, examine a photograph of a child. Have everyone write an interpretation of what the child might have been thinking, feeling, and doing. Compare to see how your

interpretations were different. Check the extent to which your interpretations were based on what was actually in the picture.

3 Observe another person in your small group for five minutes without speaking, and find out all you can about the other person. For the next five minutes find out everything you can about each other by talking. Share your feelings about the experience with each other. In the group, discuss what you learned by looking and by talking.

4 Why is it important for teachers of young children to know about screening and classroom assessment procedures? What experiences did you have as a child or teacher with these forms of assessment ? What are your feelings about them?

PROJECTS

1 Observe a child engaged in an activity or an interaction with another child and describe:
   □ The physical attributes of the child
   □ Some of the child's unique qualities
   □ Your interpretation of what the child might have been thinking, feeling, and doing
   □ Your feelings and reactions to the child

2 Observe an adult and a child interacting and describe:
   □ The child
   □ The adult
   □ The interaction
   □ Your interpretation of what the child might have been thinking, feeling, and doing
   □ Your interpretation of what the adult might have been thinking, feeling, and doing
   □ Your feelings and reactions

3 Observe a child's physical development and describe:
   □ The child
   □ The way the child uses his body, including coordination and balance, use of large muscles of the arms, legs, and body, use of the small muscles of the fingers and hands, and coordination between eyes and hands

   Make some inferences about the child's physical development and how physical development seems to influence the child's total functioning. Describe what you learned from doing the observation.

4 Observe a child's social and emotional development and describe:
   □ The child
   □ The child's relationship to other children and adults
   □ The extent to which the child demonstrates self-control or lack of self-control
   □ The child's ability to cooperate
   □ The primary emotion the child projects

   Make some inferences about the child's social-emotional development and how it seems to influence the child's total functioning. Describe what you learned from doing the observation.

5 Observe a child's intellectual development and describe:
   □ The child
   □ What knowledge and understanding about the world the child seems to have
   □ The child's ability to solve problems and his or her approach to problem solving

   Make some inferences about the child's intellectual development and how it seems to influence the child's total functioning. Describe what you learned from doing the observation.

6 Using a commercially prepared assessment instrument, assess a child from your class or observation setting in one developmental area. Describe the experience and answer the following questions: What does the assessment tell you about the child? What doesn't it tell you that you might want or need to know? What does this experience suggest to you about the possible advantages and/or disadvantages of using commercial instruments?

7 Using the questions suggested in this chapter, review one screening and assessment instrument in depth, or compare two from one category. Consider the merits and shortcomings of each, and describe why you would or would not choose to use the instrument with children in your setting.

8 Write a case study, a "portrait of a child," based on extensive observation over time of one child. Include:
   □ A profile of the child's physical, social-emotional, and intellectual development (this can be abstracted from Projects 1-5)
   □ The child's development in terms of norms for his/her age group (you may use data from Project 6) and in comparison to his or her peers in the classroom

☐ How you see the child progressing developmentally (strengths and weaknesses)

☐ Your feelings and reactions to the child, to writing the case study, and what you learned about yourself and about children

RECOMMENDED READING

Almy, Millie, and Genishi, Celia. *Ways of Studying Children: An Observational Manual for Early Childhood Teachers.* rev. ed. New York: Teachers College Press, 1979.

Boehm, Ann E., and Weinberg, Richard A. *The Classroom Observer: A Guide for Developing Observation Skills.* New York: Teachers College Press, 1977.

Cartwright, C., and Cartwright, P. *Developing Observation Skills.* New York: McGraw-Hill, 1984.

Cohen, Dorothy H., and Stern, Virginia. *Observing and Recording the Behavior of Young Children.* New York: Teachers College Press, 1983.

Lindberg, Lucile, and Swerdlow, Rita. *Early Childhood Education: A Guide for Observation and Participation.* Boston: Allyn and Bacon, 1980.

Medinnus, Gene R. *Child Study and Observation Guide.* New York: John Wiley and Sons, 1976.

Meisels, Samuel. *Developmental Screening in Early Childhood: A Guide.* Washington, D. C.: National Association for the Education of Young Children, 1985.

Read, Katherine, and Patterson, June. *The Nursery School and Kindergarten: Human Relationships and Learning.* 7th ed. New York: Holt, Rinehart and Winston, 1980.

Rowen, Betty. *The Children We See: An Observational Approach to Child Study.* New York: Holt, Rinehart and Winston, 1973.

Szasz, Suzanne, *The Unspoken Language of Children.* New York: W.W. Norton and Co., 1980.

6

The Child
in School

"We must have . . . a place where children
can have a whole group of adults they
can trust."

Margaret Mead

*This chapter explores factors to be considered in meeting the physical and emotional needs of children in early childhood programs. We look at ways you can help children with the first separation from their parents when they enter your program. Guidelines are provided for how you can design and handle routines and transitions each day and throughout the year. We also look at endings, what you can do to help children adjust to a new class or program, to the transition to their next school, or to the departure of their teacher. This chapter relates to the CDA areas **Learning Environment, Self, Social, Families,** and **Program Management.***

BEGINNINGS

Beginnings are times of change, excitement, and hope. They are also times of stress, fear, and anxiety. They are a time to say farewell to the security of the familiar and to go forward to meet new challenges. Life is composed of many beginnings; some are large and stressful, while others are small and easy to deal with. Teachers can help guide children over the sometimes rocky paths of the transitions between home and classroom and the transitions within the early childhood program.

The Transition from Home

During the preschool years (primarily between the ages of eighteen and thirty-six months), children forge a sense of themselves as individuals who are separate from their parents. Achieving this sense of separateness can be an anxiety-fraught experience filled with frightening realizations ("I can exist separately from my parents; they can exist without me"), unnamed fears ("Am I a bad child who deserves to be abandoned?"), and sometimes intense anger ("I hate my

parents who refuse to perfectly understand and meet my needs"). Although there are individual differences, generally, by the time children are three years old, their initial sense of separateness and identity is formed. They begin to understand that neither their parents, the world, nor they themselves are either all good or all bad.

All of us can recall the anxious, sometimes stomach-clutching feelings that we had in relation to separating from the familiar: leaving our childhood homes, moving to a new city, starting a new job, becoming a parent. When young children enter your program, they face an unfamiliar world. They are assaulted by sensations: new people, noises, objects, smells, and activities. They may have had little experience with being parted from their parents, with being among many children, or with making choices. This strangeness is made less traumatic when teachers and parents work together.

Teachers help children and their parents to realize that the bonds that exist between them are strong enough to thrive despite separation. At the same time they need to help children to build relationships in the new setting. When

130

children trust their teachers and feel assured of their own competence, they become comfortable enough to benefit from their school experiences. They adapt more easily when they know that their parents have confidence in the school and in the teachers.

Children can best make the transition from home when the introduction is gradual and when they have an opportunity to integrate familiar aspects of their homes into their new lives in the class- room. One way to accomplish this is for the teacher to present some aspect of the program on a home visit before the child's first day in school. Such a visit gives the child the opportunity to experience this new important person, their teacher, in the security of their own environment. During visits, teachers build the base of later relationships with children and learn about their homes and families. Such visits are also opportunities for parents to get to know and to develop confidence in the teacher.

Classroom visits by parents and children are another way to provide the information needed for children to feel comfortable and competent in the new setting. It is essential that all children experience their classroom in the company of a familiar adult. A visit orients the child to the teacher and the classroom. In some programs, initial visits occur during the course of a regular day: the child and parent sit in on an hour or two of the program. In other places, a special orientation for several new children or individual parent-child visits may precede the child's first day. Whatever its form, the initial visit helps prepare both child and parent for the new experience.

First Days and First Weeks

Your goal for the first day is to begin to know children and to help them to get to know you, each other, and the routines of the program. Because adjustment on the first day can be a difficult, parents are sometimes asked to spend part or all of the day with their child.

Individual children react differently on their first day; some want to touch and try everything, some are cautious observers, and others want to stay close to their parents. All children carefully observe the behavior of the teacher and the arrange- ment of the environment to understand what is expected of them and to find out how the teacher will react. It is especially important to be aware of what you say and do those first days of school. You will want to be calm, and caring, letting children know that you will help and protect them in this new, and possibly scary, place. Since so much is unknown, the environment, the activities, and the schedule of the first day should be simple

SUGGESTIONS FOR THE FIRST DAY

☐ If possible have the child begin with a short first day. Children who have had little experience with school may have absorbed all they can in an hour.

☐ Encourage a parent, other relative, or familiar caregiver to spend all or part of the first day at school with the child.

☐ Greet children and their parents by name as they arrive and say goodbye as they depart.

☐ Show the children the location of the toilet and the water fountain. Show them how they work and accompany them when they seem uncertain.

☐ Show clearly what you expect of children but do not try to teach everything they will need to know on the first day. Avoid being overly concerned if children cannot meet seemingly simple expectations.

☐ Allow children to bring a special toy or comfort object to help provide a tangible bridge between home and school.

☐ Allow children to borrow a book or toy from the classroom to provide the same bridge when they return to their homes.

☐ Provide an interesting but limited number of materials in the environment. These could include blocks, books, simple puzzles and manipulative toys, dolls, and crayons.

☐ Provide soothing open-ended materials like water, sand, and dough.

☐ Provide time for independent exploration of materials.

☐ Provide an activity like a song or story that helps children to feel that they are a part of a group.

to allow children to focus on a few new experiences at a time. This will allow them to understand what is happening without being fearful of doing the wrong thing.

Eventually, parents must go and the child will be left in your classroom. Almost all children experience anxiety at this time. Although some children overcome this easily, others express their anxiety through tears, tantrums, or angry words, and still others become despondent and quietly wait while sucking thumbs or holding comfort objects. Some, not as visibly upset, may have toilet accidents, nightmares, or angrily reject their parents when it's time to go home. A few will appear fine for a few days or a week and then will react very strongly as if it were the first day. Our interpretation of this delayed response is that, as the novelty of the new experience wears off, the child realizes that going to school will henceforth be a perpetual part of life, one that involves little personal choice. If a reaction persists or is extreme, it may mean that the child needs a more gradual or a delayed entrance into the program.

Since many children need the reassurance of physical contact with an adult during the first days and weeks, you may sometimes feel like a mother opossum moving about the classroom with the small bodies of young children clinging to you. As they become comfortable, most children will find more interesting things to do. For many children a treasured blanket, stuffed animal, or piece of clothing is important in the separation process. These personal possessions are comforting reminders of home that help some children to feel secure. It is important that children be allowed to keep them near. With time, comfort objects become less evident and may only

SUGGESTIONS FOR THE FIRST WEEKS

☐ Hold children who need extra reassurance.
☐ Avoid abrupt or major changes and excitement (fire drills, films, trips, room rearrangement).
☐ Continue to greet children and parents by name each day as they arrive and as they depart. Keep parents informed of how their child is adjusting.
☐ Help children to know their school by taking small excursions to important places in it: the parent room, the play yard, other classes, the library, the office, the kitchen, and so on.
☐ Make sure that familiar, home-like materials are available in the classroom: pillows, stuffed toys, and personal comfort objects.
☐ Have play materials available that encourage children to role play familiar home situations.
☐ Sing name songs to help children to get to know one another and to acknowledge each child during group meetings.

be needed when a child is under stress or having a nap.

During the first weeks, children become accustomed to the daily rhythm of activities linked by transitions, learn that they can care for many of their own needs, and discover that you will be there to help when needed. The most important tasks of the first weeks are to develop trust, to build relationships, and to establish routines. It is not nearly as important to create exciting curriculum. You will want to ensure that children's successes outnumber their failures and that your expectations of them are realistic. This is a time when you learn what children can and cannot do. These observations will help you to plan.

By understanding and supporting children as they go through the separation process during first days and weeks, you help prepare them to be active and competent learners. As children become more comfortable, you can begin enriching the environment with materials, activities, and trips that might have been overwhelming at first.

THE CHILD'S DAY

Your program is influenced by your values, your observations of children, and by the values and concerns of your community, the school administration, and parents. Program structure is influenced by staff and administrative decisions regarding what is important for children during the school day.

Both spontaneous and teacher-planned activities occur in the daily program for young children. In informal programs curriculum is often emergent; it evolves from the interests and experiences of the children. Teachers lead a few key activities

each day, observe children's interests and responses, and work to support these in spontaneous play and planned activities. In more formal programs there are more teacher-directed activities. In these settings, there tends to be less emphasis on "free play."

The typical day in any program for young children must be an artful blend of routines and learning experiences linked by smooth transitions. We think of the daily ebb and flow of teaching-learning activities and routines as being part of a larger experience of day-to-day life with children.

The Daily Schedule

Time in early childhood programs may be structured in many different ways. As you design your schedule, you may be confronted with the rationale of tradition: *this is the way that we have always run our program.* The schedule may be appropriate, but such a rationale is insufficient. It is important to consider the reasons for any given practice and to reconsider and possibly redesign schedule based on the many factors that influence the day.

Children's Needs and Developmental Stage   Early childhood programs must include provisions for children's needs and take into account developmental differences. All children need time for rest, personal hygiene, and nourishment. It is important that there are periods of vigorous activity and quiet and times daily when choice is permitted to allow for individual interest and attention. In programs for younger children large blocks of time for each of these activity periods must be provided. Teachers must remain flexible since younger children's needs vary greatly. At ten o'clock in a group of young two year olds that we recently visited, Aimee was lying down and drinking a bottle, Ian was having a nap, Walden was rocking on the rocking horse, Nadine was cuddling on a teacher's lap, and Jonathan needed to use the bathroom. A rigid schedule could not meet such diverse needs and would inevitably lead to frustration for teacher and children. The range of appropriate schedules runs the gamut according to the developmental needs of the children. Typical schedules for different age groups might have the following characteristics:

Infants: Each child regulates him- or herself: meals, rests, active/quiet times

Toddlers: Regular meals, snacks, and rest with active/quiet times occurring in response to children's needs and interests

Younger Preschoolers: Scheduled eating and rest times and flexibly scheduled group and outdoor times

Older Preschoolers and Kindergarten Children: Routines scheduled as above with closer adherence to plans for group and activity times

Values and Goals   Your values and goals are among your most important considerations in planning your schedule. If you value creativity and the development of responsibility, you will allow fairly large blocks of time (one to two hours) during which children choose their own activities and teachers work with individuals and small groups. If you place more emphasis on the acquisition of knowledge and skills, larger portions of the day may be directly guided by the teacher leaving less time for free choice. In such programs, time will be divided into smaller units to

enable you to better hold and direct the attention of children. Without a consideration of your values and the implications of your scheduling decisions, you may inadvertently fail to foster the very things you most care about.

The Physical Setting   The building in which you teach will influence the arrangement of the learning environment and how you use time. If you teach in a building that houses only your program and has sufficient space for younger children to be separated from older ones, it is relatively easy to arrange the day so that it meets the needs of all age groups. Where space is limited or facilities are shared with other programs, it may be more difficult to meet the needs of various groups. You may need to work out ways to accommodate different eating and resting schedules, separation of rest and activity areas, and use of bathrooms and playgrounds. If the bathroom or playground is located at a great distance from the classroom, you will have to take this into account in your planning. Young children are not ready to use the toilet on a schedule, so you may have to plan frequent trips to make sure that children have adequate access to toilets. Even if children are capable of traversing the distance between classroom and yard or toilet on their own, you may need to schedule supervision to ensure their safety and security.

Length of the Program Day   If you teach in a morning-only program, some routines may be unnecessary. If children come to you at 9:00 A.M. after a good night's sleep and a hearty breakfast and depart in time to eat lunch and take an afternoon nap at home, scheduled rest time is unnecessary, and a light snack is usually sufficient. The practice of having an enforced rest period with children on mats or seated at tables with heads on folded arms will probably meet with resistance. Since preschoolers rarely need this morning rest, it is a waste of your limited time together. If children appear overstimulated or tired, a quiet period of reading books is generally adequate for preschoolers. In a short program, a good blend of vigorous outdoor activities and indoor activities with a short snack break will provide for a pleasant, productive half-day experience.

A program ending in the late afternoon must provide lunch, a midday rest, and snack periods in order to avoid overstimulated, hungry children. Children who receive full-day child care may spend fifty to sixty percent of their weekday waking hours in a center. Eight to ten hour days are a significant portion of a young child's life. For these children, the program becomes a second home, and staff and other children become extended family. Because of this, it is especially important to pay close attention to the quality of relationships, to the design of the environment, and to scheduling. You must create a program that is flexible enough to be responsive to children's needs while stable enough to provide security over many hours.

While children in full-day programs may stay eight to ten hours, the staff in such programs generally remain for only six to eight hours. Children are often cared for by a separate morning and afternoon staff. The coordination of the staff transition must help children to maintain their sense of trust in the setting if they are to benefit from the experiences offered in the latter part of the day. Since "school" traditionally takes place in

the morning hours, there is often a misperception that those who care for young children in the hours following the midday rest are somehow less important than those who perform the same tasks in the morning. Involving afternoon staff in training and program planning is one way to overcome this. Recognizing the vital tasks accomplished by afternoon staff, especially in the realm of interacting with families, also helps in maintaining program quality throughout the day.

Time of Year A program day may differ greatly from the beginning of the year to the end. During the first days, weeks, and even months, your program day must allow time to help children become accustomed to routines and new activities. As the year progresses, children will have mastered routines, become accustomed to working independently, and will be more able to cooperate in group activities. Your schedule can then be adjusted accordingly. Group times can be planned for longer periods as children gain group skills. Scheduled routines, like toileting, may be omitted as children become independent and no longer require support and supervision.

Staff-Child Ratio and Group Size The number of staff members in relation to the number of children is an important factor in how you structure the day . In a program with an adult-to-child ratio of one to seven, events, routines, and activities can be scheduled with a great deal more flexibility than if you work in a program with one adult for every fifteen children. With lower ratios you are free to be more spontaneous and to plan for activities that have an unpredictable time frame or that require more intense teacher-child interaction.

The size of the group will also influence the day. With smaller groups you have more flexibility in planning because you can make spontaneous changes without disrupting others. You are able to give your full attention to individuals because there are fewer people to attend to. Larger groups require more advance planning for the use of facilities (like playgrounds, vans, and lunchrooms), and you must stick more closely to the schedule to meet the needs of other groups. Groups of more than twenty children, no matter how low the ratio of adults to children, tend to be noisy, overstimulating, and can be stressful to young children. Table 6.1 shows staff-child ratios and group size as recommended for quality programs by the NAEYC Center Accreditation Program.

Routines

Regardless of whether your program lasts for three hours or ten, there are some recurring events in the basic structure of a day for young children. Arrival must provide a smooth transition from home. There need to be opportunities for nourishment, rest, toileting, play, and learning. The end of each child's day should provide a sense of closure.

Teachers of young children have long accepted the routine parts of daily living as legitimate and important aspects of the child's school experience. They recognize that children must have their basic needs met, that they must feel safe, secure, and accepted before they can begin to learn, and that a primary task of young children is to develop competence in independently meeting their physical and social needs. As a teacher of young children, you will want to give the routines, of classroom life attention and thoughtful planning, just as you do the other aspects of the program. When daily routines are predictable, children know what to expect and have the resources

TABLE 6.1
Staff-child ratios and group size.

Age of Children	Group Size									
	6	8	10	12	14	16	18	20	22	24
Infants (birth–12 mos.)	1 : 3	1 : 4								
Toddlers (12–24 mos.)	1 : 3	1 : 4	1 : 5	1 : 4						
Two year olds (24–36 mos.)		1 : 4	1 : 5	1 : 6**						
Two and three year olds			1 : 5	1 : 6	1 : 7**					
Three year olds					1 : 7	1 : 8	1 : 9	1 : 10**		
Four year olds						1 : 8	1 : 9	1 : 10**		
Four and five year olds						1 : 8	1 : 9	1 : 10**		
Five year olds						1 : 8	1 : 9	1 : 10**		
Six to eight year olds (school age)								1 : 10	1 : 11	1 : 12

Source: Accreditation and Criteria Procedures of the National Academy of Early Childhood Programs, 1984.

**Smaller group sizes and lower staff-child ratios are optimal; larger group sizes and higher staff-child ratios are acceptable only in cases where staff are highly qualified.

they need for ordering and understanding their experiences. When you communicate your good reasons for establishing a routine and your commitment to having it work, children will usually cooperate and participate willingly.

Arrival Arrival each day should be a friendly, predictable event. It is important to establish a routine that allows every parent and child to be greeted. An arrival period during which you are free to personally greet and talk briefly with every parent and child sets a relaxed tone. At this time, you can notice if each child is in good health and appears ready to participate in the daily program. Arrival time may be one of the few regular contacts you will have with parents, and it can be a good time for exchanging information. In some programs, the staff

member who opens the center is available to greet the family and help each child make the transition into the classroom. When all the children arrive at the same time, the whole staff may gather to greet families.

Toileting Children can become self-reliant in toileting when bathrooms are clean and well-lit with child-sized fixtures and when their clothing is manageable. They may be anxious and reluctant about using unfamiliar or unpleasant bathrooms. Teachers should accompany young, fearful, or inexperienced children to the toilet to reassure them and to help them overcome their fears. They become comfortable if you are patient and help them learn how to manage the plumbing and if some attention is paid to making the bathroom pleasant. Encourage families to provide clothing that is easy for children to handle such as loose dresses, or pants and shorts with elastic waistbands. Discourage the use of coveralls and pants with belts since these present problems in coordination for young children. If the environment has only adult-sized fixtures, stable step stools to enable children to reach toilet and washbasin are essential.

Toilet accidents are a normal aspect of a child's life and a regular feature of a preschool teacher's day. Your handling of these situations is of critical importance. A child who is genuinely upset may need to be sheltered from public awareness and given help with clean-up. Other

children may only need a small amount of direction and encouragement to take care of their own change of clothes. Always have spare clothing on hand as well as a good supply of plastic bags for soiled garments, stored safely out of children's reach.

Mealtimes and Snacks   Some of the nicest moments of the day occur when teachers and children have a chance to converse over food. This is best accomplished when teachers sit with children at meals and snack times, rather than standing over them or sitting separately. Snacks and meals are pleasant when they are orderly enough to focus

on eating and casual enough to be a social experience.

Resistance and fears about eating are common. You should let children know that you will neither force them to eat nor deny them the opportunity to eat. Young children become restless and irritable when they are expected to wait until everyone is served or while others finish. They may become anxious and unable to eat if they are hurried. Many problems can be avoided if you have a set routine for children who have finished eating before the rest of the group, for example, allowing them to leave the table to read a book or to play quietly with a game or toy.

Not all families are able to feed their children a good breakfast before their early arrival. Because of this, it is important that a nutritious snack or breakfast be served in the morning, and that snacks and meals are planned to meet children's daily nutritional needs. Independence can be fostered as children participate in meal preparation and serving. For example, children can spread their own peanut butter on a cracker or pour their own juice. Children can gain self-help skills if meals are served family style with bowls of food and small pitchers passed so that children can serve themselves.

Clean-up   Clean-up prepares the classroom for the next activity and is a natural and necessary part of living with others. Children can begin to understand that they are members of a community and that they need to share in the responsibility for maintaining cleanliness and order. Although clean-up is seldom a favorite routine, it need not be hard or unpleasant. Much of the drudgery that often surrounds clean-up comes from the attitude that is projected by adults. When you participate in clean-up with an attitude of expectant good-will ("I feel good about doing this and I expect that you share my feeling"), children are generally also cheerful and cooperative. Often clean-up is made the punishment that one must endure for the pleasure of play; such an attitude discourages not only clean-up but play itself. Children frequently resist clean-up when they are forced to straighten large messes without assistance; to a young child, such a mess may appear large and impossible to clean. Although it is often actually easier to "do it yourself" than to insist on children's participation, your expectation and firm but gentle follow through will help children become able and responsible members of their group.

Rest Time   Rest time can be a positive experience for children and adults if children are tired, if the environment is made restful, and if children understand the importance of relaxing their minds and bodies. As with other routines, it is essential that children feel secure. If they are fearful of the school setting, they will be unable to relax. Most children will sleep if the environment is soothing and comfortable. Every child needs a mat or cot for sleeping. To create an atmosphere conducive to rest and sleep, dim the lights, play quiet music, and allow children to cuddle favorite stuffed toys or blankets.

When you are helping children to fall asleep, it is important to be calming. Focus on children as they begin to rest, gently rub their backs, avoid speaking to others, and whisper when you must speak. Wait until most of the children are sleeping before you begin any other tasks. Children who nap will generally do so for

SUGGESTIONS FOR ROUTINES

☐ Offer help when children request it or show unusual frustration, even if the task is one you know they can ordinarily do by themselves.

☐ Be flexible about time while maintaining the usual sequence of events. (Activity Time might be lengthened if it doesn't mean skipping another important activity.)

☐ Acknowledge cooperation by commenting on individual and group efforts.

☐ Ignore noncooperation as much as possible, or give an alternative that is neither punishing nor rewarding. ("If you are not helping, you may wait at that table." "Please come stand by the door; I'm afraid someone will be hurt when you push in the bathroom.")

at least one hour. When they are finished resting, children should be free to put away their mats and play quietly.

Children who do not sleep will respond to rest time positively if, after an initial rest, they are allowed to look at books and play quietly. Children who regularly do not sleep can rest away from others so that their activity is not disturbing. The child who is unable to sleep can rest for at least half an hour. Rest for nonsleeping children should be based on the individual's tolerance for inactivity and their ability to relax.

Rest time may provide a quiet period for teachers to collect themselves and do some planning or preparation. However, the length of nap and rest periods should be based on children's needs for rest and not on the desire of teachers to accomplish their tasks.

Departure   The end of the school day should provide a smooth transition back into life at home. Departure time can

provide an opportunity to talk to parents about the child's experiences. Sharing this information helps parents to know what kind of a day their child has had and to anticipate the behavior and needs of their child at home. For example, a child who usually naps but does not do so on a particular day may be unusually irritable, and a parent who knows this may respond with an early bedtime.

If all the children leave at the same time, departure can be structured to provide closure. Teachers may read a story, go over the events of the day, and plan for the next day. If the children leave at different times throughout the afternoon, a staff member should be available to share information with parents as they say farewell to each parent and child.

Transition Times

Each time a scheduled activity or routine ends, there is a transition, a time of gathering children together or of move-

SUGGESTIONS FOR TRANSITION TIMES

☐ Give children several minutes warning before any transition begins.

☐ Maintain your communication style and tempo of movement during transitions. (It is disruptive if you suddenly start barking orders and rushing around.)

☐ Avoid having children wait in lines or large groups with nothing to do.

☐ Give clearly stated reasons for the transitions. ("We'll all clean up now so that we can sit down to lunch together.")

☐ Offer choices only when there really is a choice; avoid offering choices you are unwilling to allow. ("It's time to go inside now," *not* "Would you like to go in?")

☐ Acknowledge children who are helpful during transitions rather than using them to make negative comparisons. ("Thanks for the help Vernon!" *not* "I wish everyone cleaned tables as well as Vernon.")

ment into a new activity. Transition times can be smooth and relaxed if they are well planned and if children are prepared for them.

Teachers and children may perceive transitions very differently. Because of this, transitions can be times of frustration and conflict. As the teacher, you have the responsibility for moving children from one activity or routine to the next according to a preconceived plan based on the needs of the children and your program goals. Children who do not know the reasons for the changes may respond to transitions as interruptions of things they would prefer to continue doing.

In nearly all programs, transitions take up between twenty and thirty percent of the total time (Berk, 1978). Transitions in which many children are gathered together can often be avoided by having children go on to the next activity

independently, for example, by letting children go outside after they have finished cleaning up their area rather than waiting for the entire group to finish. Other transitions can be turned into productive time by using them as moments to share songs and fingerplays, games, or as times for listening to relaxing music or looking at books.

When children are leaving a group to go on to the next activity, you can use techniques that avoid a chaotic stampede or excessive regimentation. You may use chants and songs that include a child's name and what to do next, such as singing "This is the way JOHN washes his hands every day at lunchtime" (for older children the name can be spelled out), or "Everyone wearing red (or stripes) can hop like a bunny to the playground." Experienced teachers design many creative ways for making transitions smooth, interesting learning experiences.

You may wish to collect such ideas and invent your own.

THE PROGRAM YEAR

The character of any program year is influenced by a number of factors. These include people, events in the world, the structure of the program, geographic location, and special events, such as holidays and celebrations. The maturity, activity level, and social needs of children as individuals and as a group influence the way that you pace schooling experiences. For example, a group of especially mature children may speed through activities.

Some years children will be more concerned with their relationship with the teacher, while in other years, peer relationship will be more important. An active group of parents can also influence the character of the year. When parents volunteer in the classroom and support the activities of the school, they enrich the program and may make your job easier. If they are unable or unwilling to work with you, you will need to find other kinds of resources and may be less able to provide special activities.

The interest and energy level of teachers and the way that they work together will also influence what happens during the year. If you and your co-workers have time, energy, and creativity to give to your jobs, the program will be richer. When you know one another well and work together comfortably as a team, the year will flow more smoothly. If there are many new staff members, the energy and teamwork will be different. Should other aspects of your lives require more attention, you will have less to give.

The Flow of the Year

The flow of the year in a classroom has a rhythm that is influenced by young children's responses to their lives both within and outside of the program setting. To some extent this rhythm is predictable; it relates to the characteristics of the community, the structure of the program, and the season. In other ways, each year is unique, with a character that is influenced by the personalities of children, by families, and by experiences that families and children have during the year.

Events in the World   Classrooms are a part of, and not separate from, the rest of the world. Schools, children, families, and teachers are affected by social, political, and cultural events. A loss or decline in social services for families, and even television shows and movies affect classroom life because they affect children. You need to be attentive to these events in order to understand the experience of children and to plan wisely for them. A few hours spent reading the local newspaper, occasionally watching current children's television programming, and taking in the movie of the moment will enable you to communicate more easily with children and their families.

The Structure of the Program   The structure of the program will influence how the year progresses. Programs that follow a public school calendar have clearly marked beginning and ending times; most children start school at the same time and remain in a group throughout the year. Vacations are taken by teachers and children while school is out of session. In such programs, the rhythm of the year will be closely related to the calendar. Teachers can predict that children will enter and get adjusted in September, that there will be a flurry of activity around the December break, and that January and the months that follow will be calmer, since children will be well acquainted with routines.

In a twelve-month program, beginnings and endings are less clear-cut. Children enter the program at many different times in the year and may be moved into new classes at the discretion of teachers or administrators. School beginnings, endings, and vacations will inevitably interrupt classroom life. Since these changes are an integral part of life in a full-year program, it is necessary to plan for them in order to minimize disruptions and so that the year progresses more smoothly.

Geographic Location   Active play and experiences with the natural world are integral parts of good programs for young children. The location of the program will influence what you do in school. If you are in a rural location in a part of the country where the climate is generally warm and dry, children's access to outside play and exploration have few limits. If your program is located in an urban area, you will have to include specially planned opportunities for experiences with nature.

In winter months in cold or rainy climates, ensuring outside time requires more effort and active planning. When we taught in these situations, outside time was often limited to a few minutes of brisk walking and deep breathing preceded by twenty minutes of dressing and followed by twenty minutes of undressing. In locations where air pollution affects the quality of the air, outside play may be dangerous on heavily polluted days.

When outdoor time is limited, indoor environments and daily schedules must include both time and space for active play; and good days should be fully utilized and enjoyed, even at the expense of planned "academic" content.

Holidays and Celebrations   Holidays and celebrations are part of children's home and school lives. They are often celebrated in schools and act as markers in the year.

Although holidays and celebrations are often happy times and can generate positive school experiences, they are also times of excitement, unusual stimulation, and confusing disruptions of the usual routine. Celebrations can often be highly charged emotional events that influence life in the classroom. Holidays are less stressful when you accept children's enthusiasm for the holiday and make it part of what you do in the classroom without unusual fanfare, the way that you might integrate other events and interests.

Time seems much longer to young children, so weeks of holiday build-up add to children's stress. We believe that school preparation for celebrations should be limited to a few days before the event. The days that follow a holiday are also times when children feel the impact of the celebration. It is valuable to spend time afterwards recalling feelings and experiences to help children to make sense of them.

ENDINGS

In every classroom for young children, there are endings. Just as beginnings require special thought and planning, so endings require special care. The relationships that children build during their first school experiences can be very close, and it can be painful when they are over. For many children, this may be the first time that an important tie has ended.

Changing Classes and Teachers

When children remain in a program for more than a year, they will usually experience at least one change of class or teacher. In programs that follow a ten-month or public school calendar, this will occur in September after a long summer vacation. In full-year programs, this change may occur when the teacher feels that a child is ready for a new group or when space is needed in the group for younger children entering the program.

Although many children are ready and eager to move on to a new class, some are not. To make the transition to a new group requires the cooperation of both teachers and parents. The change to a new class can arouse feelings of anxiety similar to those experienced during the initial days of school, and similar techniques can help make a bridge between the old and new class. This transition is made easier when children know about their new class, when they can carry something familiar with them into the experience, and when the transition can be gradual. It also helps if children feel their parents and their first teacher have confidence in the new group and teacher.

Allow children in transition to make visits to their next class accompanied by their first teacher or special friend. Let them visit for an activity time that they especially enjoy, perhaps circle time one day, choice time another day so that they can discover new materials, activities and companions. On the official day of transition let the child take responsibility for transferring personal belongings and setting up a new cubby. Going back to the old room to share lunch or nap or simply to visit for a few minutes helps the child feel secure.

When Teachers Leave

Teachers, like children, take vacations, become sick, and eventually must end their association with a school. These events sometimes take place during the course of a year. Many programs for young children use team-teaching as one way of minimizing the upsets of staff absences and departures. When children relate closely to two or more adults in the school, it will be less traumatic when one of them must leave. When a teacher leaves either permanently or for an extended period of time, children experience feelings of loss. They may be sad that you are gone and angry with you when you return. They may be fearful of the change and feel less secure until they build a relationship with the new teacher.

When you know that you or a teacher you work with will leave, it is important to make adequate preparation for the transition. Leave-taking is a natural part of relationships. Most young children can accept this more easily if adults do. During this time of transition, minimize changes in the environment and routines. Most importantly, help children understand that teachers leave schools because of changes in their own lives and not in response to the behavior or actions of children or their families.

The Next School

Children in preschool go on to kindergarten and elementary schools. The "real world" of school can be a very different kind of place from an early childhood program. One of your jobs is to prepare the children in your class when they make the transition to the next school.

Children will anticipate starting their new schools with both interest and concern. You can aid in the transition by helping to strengthen children's sense of themselves as competent, successful individuals. Acknowledge the growth that

has taken place and mention how this will be useful in their new school ("You really know how to take care of your own lunch now, Mark; you're going to be able to handle it all by yourself in kindergarten").

Early childhood programs should not be boot camps or training grounds for elementary school! The time that children spend in preschool should be spent on experiences that are appropriate for the early years. It may be beneficial, however, to use the last few weeks of school before transition to an elementary school to help children learn skills that they will need. Like early childhood programs, elementary schools vary. The more that you know about the schools in your community, the better able you will be to prepare children for the transition. If children will be expected to know about responding to bells, standing in lines, getting their lunch from the cafeteria, doing work sheets, or raising hands, you can help them to learn these skills in a short time. At the end of the program year, when children are more mature, they will be more able to learn them. If you are in contact with the teachers in the next school, you may be able to get more specific information or even take the children to see their prospective school and teacher. Tell the children that they are practicing for their next school, and role play some of the routines that they will be expected to follow. When children know what to expect and feel comfortable and self-confident, they start school more positively. Parents and teachers can work together during this new transition to make it a beginning filled with enthusiasm and hope.

FOR FURTHER THOUGHT AND DISCUSSION

1   Recall your most recent anxious separation from familiar things (a move, change of jobs, return to school, etc.). How did you feel? How did you make the separation more comfortable for yourself? Compare notes with other adults. How could you use these insights for understanding and helping children in their first separations? How might your experiences be different and inapplicable?

2   Remember your first day of school or your first day in a new school or class. What stands out in your memory? What was most reassuring? What was most frightening? Why?

3   Remember everything that you can about your earliest school experience. How were your basic needs met? Did the physical setting influence the structure of the day? How? Do your memories reflect anything about the number of children in your class or the teacher-child ratio? Did it influence your experience? How?

4   What might a teacher of young children need to know about a child before the start of school? Why?

PROJECTS

1 Report on the way that time is scheduled in an early childhood program you have observed. Comment on the effectiveness of the routines and schedules in meeting the needs of children. Describe the advantages and disadvantages you see in the way the routines and schedules work. Suggest changes that might improve the program's functioning.

2 Plan a daily schedule for an early childhood program which you think would meet the needs and interests of children and in which you would enjoy working. Explain your choices in terms of your objectives for children.

3 Observe and keep a journal on a child during the first days and weeks of his or her school experience. Report on the child's responses to his school, the teacher's techniques for supporting the child, and the parents' reactions to the experience. Describe what you learned from your observation and what you might do in your own classroom.

4 Make a resource file of ways to create smooth and pleasant transition times. Use your observations of teachers and books, as well as your own creativity, as resources. Try out some of these ideas with children and report on what happened.

5 Interview two teachers concerning:
   □ Program differences in their classes between the beginning and ending of the school year, including time spent on routines and kinds of activities planned
   □ The ways they deal with separation
   □ Their ways of preparing children for the next class and the next school

   Report on the similarities and differences between the two.

6 Write your own recollections of your first separations from your parents. If possible, interview your parents about their perceptions of this experience and include these. Comment on what may have made the experience easy or difficult and what might have helped make it better. Report on the implications that this has for you as a teacher.

RECOMMENDED READINGS

Harms, Thelma, and Clifford, Richard. *Early Childhood Environment Rating Scale*. New York: Teachers College Press, 1980.

Hirsch, Elisabeth. *Transition Periods: Stumbling Blocks of Education*. New York: Early Childhood Education Council of New York, n.d.

Janis, Marjorie Graham. *A Two Year Old Goes to Nursery School: A Case Study of Separation Reaction*. Washington, D.C.: National Association for the Education of Young Children, 1965.

Jones, Elizabeth. *Dimensions of Teaching-Learning Environments: Handbook for Teachers*. Pasadena, Cal.: Pacific Oaks, 1977.

Kaplan, Louise J. *Oneness and Separation: From Infant to Individual*. New York: Simon and Schuster, 1978.

Katz, Lilian. "Education or Excitement?" In *Talks with Teachers*, edited by Lilian Katz. Washington, D.C.: National Association for the Education of Young Children, 1977.

Read, Katherine, and Patterson, June. *The Nursery School and Kindergarten: Human Relationships and Learning*. 7th ed. New York: Holt, Rinehart and Winston, 1980.

7

The Learning Environment

"There is no behavior apart from environment."

Robert Sommer

*In this chapter, we discuss the environment of the early childhood program and its influence on children's development. We explore how an environment communicates to children and offer guidelines to help you design spaces and choose equipment and materials. We introduce a number of dimensions and discuss how these can help in evaluating and modifying environments so that they better meet children's needs. This chapter relates to the CDA areas **Safe, Healthy,** and **Learning Environment.***

The physical environment speaks to people. When children enter the classroom you have created, they can tell if it is a place intended for them and how it is best used. A cozy corner with a rug, cushions, and books says, "Sit down here and look at books." A ladder supported by two sawhorses and connected to the ground by a plank suggests, "Climb up, go across any way you can think of, and jump down." An airy environment with light, color, warmth, and interesting materials to be explored sends a clear message: "We care; this is a place for children." In such settings, there is enough space to move comfortably, the furnishings are child-sized, and the arrangement suggests how materials can be used.

Learning environments can meet the needs of children and support teacher values and developmental goals. You make choices as you design the environment that directly influence the quality of the child's relationship to other people and to learning materials. In making these choices, you need to consider three very basic questions:

1   Is the environment safe, healthy, and appropriate for the developmental stage of the children?

2   How does the environment affect human relationships among children, among adults and children, and among adults?
3   How does the environment facilitate children's learning and development?

CREATING A SAFE AND HEALTHY SPACE

There are many important aspects of a teacher's role, but in the eyes of the world and the families served, maintaining safety and health comes first. It is fundamental that a program environment be both psychologically and physically safe and healthy for children if they are to grow and learn.

Psychological health and safety involve the child's perceptions. Children can tell when and where they are welcome. They know that they are in a safe place when their needs are cared for and when adults show respect in the ways they listen and talk to (and around) them. In psychologically safe and healthy environments children do not fear rejection or humiliation. They are comfortable and feel secure. This sense of safety is dependent on warm, consistent adults who are physically accessible to children. Teachers contribute to psychological health by being encouraging and by believing in children's competence. They support this belief by creating environments in which it is safe to experiment and acceptable to make mistakes. They accept children as unique people with their own pace and stage of development.

A good environment for children must be safe physically as well as psychologically. Such an environment has basically sound facilities, equipment, and materials. It is arranged to ensure that teachers can supervise children at all times. Dangerous substances are stored out of children's reach. Hazards (like electric cords in pathways) are avoided. Awareness of safety enables teachers to minimize potential hazards of the program setting; they can be taken care of before a problem exists. Use of a checklist can help you to oversee the safety of your program environment.

Preparedness involves anticipation of such situations as fires and accidents. In order for an environment to be safe, a plan for emergencies is necessary. Staff training in basic first aid and the availability of adequate first aid supplies are also a part of establishing a safe environment.

Additionally, safety involves making sure of the security of the program. Yards, gates, and doors must ensure that children do not leave without supervision and that the threshold of the program is broached only by those selected to enter. Sign-in and sign-out procedures and staff awareness must prevent a child leaving with strangers or noncustodial adults. Ratios must be low enough and group size small enough so that staff can always supervise children well.

Although there are many safety measures that are absolutely necessary

for the well-being of children, there are other concerns that are not as clear-cut. As we work with our students in the real and complex world of the classroom, we find that teachers must often make choices that contrast safety and learning. Individuals treat these differently according to the purpose and policies of their program, the characteristics of the children (age, experience, temperament, skills), the size of the group, the staff-child ratio, the particular situation, and the philosophy and beliefs of the staff and families. Some typical concerns include the use of functional but potentially hazardous materials (like sharp knives and scissors), children's ability to negotiate hazardous situations (like an inclined trikeway), and the availability of materials and equipment commonly found at home but usually restricted in programs (such as electric outlets and sticks). As you consider these gray areas, you must consciously make safety decisions and not simply react to an immediate concern or embrace an easy solution to a current problem.

Awareness of physical health is another essential aspect of teaching. In the first early childhood programs an emphasis on health was common. As more was learned about children's intellectual and social growth, less attention was paid to health. Recently health problems and epidemics have been traced to child care centers, and public health practitioners have pointed to the need for a return to looking at the fundamentals of health in early childhood environments.

Healthy environments provide children with the necessary facilities, materials, and routines for maintaining health: water, hand washing and toilet facilities, good light, ventilation and heat, nutritious

SAFETY CHECKLIST

☐ Building and furnishings are free of rust and splinters.

☐ The environment is arranged so that the teacher can easily supervise all activity centers.

☐ Electric outlets are covered.

☐ Hazardous substances (cleansers, detergents, medicines, insecticides) are out of children's reach.

☐ Entrances and yard are secure; a sign-out procedure is followed and well-known to staff.

☐ Hot water taps are turned off or are turned down so that hot water does not scald.

☐ Sharp tools are out of children's reach.

☐ Glass items are out of children's reach.

☐ Places where children use water have nonskid floors or coverings.

☐ Electric cords do not cross pathways.

☐ A first aid kit is adequately stocked, easily available, and marked for visibility.

☐ A first aid handbook is available.

☐ An emergency exit plan is in existence and is posted; the fire department has evaluated the plan.

☐ Emergency evacuation procedures are practiced monthly.

☐ A fire extinguisher is available and functional; the teacher knows how to use it.

☐ The teacher is trained in first aid; certificate is current.

☐ There is soft dirt, sand, grass, or other material beneath climbing, swinging, and sliding apparatus.

☐ A telephone is available and is easily accessible; the name of the closest physician and hospital and emergency numbers are posted nearby.

☐ A first aid kit (which includes supplies, emergency phone numbers, parental consent for treatment forms, change for the telephone, and an emergency plan) is carried on trips.

☐ Children are appropriately, legally, and safely restrained in cars.

food, and cleanliness. Teachers ensure health by attending to potential hazards (e.g., cleaning and garbage removal), keeping health records, and having plans and policies concerning health routines and emergencies.

Every teacher needs to have basic training for coping with minor health emergencies such as fevers and vomiting and for recognizing when a child needs to see a physician, dentist, or be isolated from the others for health reasons. After receiving such training ourselves, we were struck by the fact that adults who work with young children are at high risk of contracting disease and that the most effective and important preventative measure is conscientious and thorough handwashing. In some programs a nurse or health aide will look after health situations; in others you will be responsible.

It is helpful to periodically evaluate for health by using a checklist. The box on page 156 is a health checklist that we have devised for our students.

It is important to remain attentive to health and safety not only as you design the environment, but also in everyday practice. Children need information in new situations such as on trips and in the introduction of new equipment, materials, or experiences. You can help them to recognize hazards and activities that may be dangerous and teach them procedures for handling emergencies:

> This is a knife. One side is sharp and the other side isn't. When you cut with a knife, it's important to have the sharp side down and to make sure that your fingers aren't under the cutting blade. It's a good idea to hold onto the blade with one hand and to use the other hand to push down; that way you won't accidentally get cut.

When children understand safety and health routines and precautions, they will be more willing to cooperate. As in other areas of classroom management, it is more effective to be positive. Tell children what to do and why rather than insisting that they stop something:

> Please climb on the jungle gym instead of the table. The table might tip from your weight and you could be hurt.

When children know that both you and the environment are trustworthy, they can direct their energy to exploring and experimenting in a setting designed to help them learn and grow. When you know that children are safe and healthy in the environment that you have designed, you are able to devote your energy to helping them use the environment fully.

ORGANIZING SPACE FOR LEARNING

The kind of facility that houses a program is the first aspect which influences the environment you create. In the design of facilities, early childhood programs have frequently been afterthoughts and were housed in buildings created for other purposes. Although these settings may not be ideal, they can be workable and even charming. We have known and loved programs in converted homes, church sanctuaries, basements, condominium apartments, offices, coffee houses, and storefronts.

The design of a building may suggest certain types of use. The way that you and children actually use the space may be different. Buildings with self-contained classrooms are designed so that single classes of children and their teachers work within four walls where most of the materials needed for learning will be found. Each class is intended to spend most of the time in "their" room. Teachers often use self-contained classrooms this way, but can also use them in teams, giving children access to more than one room and providing teachers with larger

HEALTH CHECKLIST

- ☐ Clean drinking water is available to children at all times.
- ☐ Tissue, soap, paper towels, and toilet paper are available where children can reach.
- ☐ Toilet facilities are clean and easily accessible to children at all times.
- ☐ If children in diapers are in the program, sanitary diapering procedures are known and practiced.
- ☐ Soiled clothes are stored in closed plastic bags away from children's play areas.
- ☐ Children and adults wash their hands after toileting and before handling food.
- ☐ Tables are cleaned prior to meals, snacks, and food preparation.
- ☐ Nutritious foods are chosen for meals, snacks, and cooking activities.
- ☐ Food is stored and prepared in a safe and sanitary fashion.
- ☐ Children brush their teeth after meals, and toothbrushes are stored hygenically.
- ☐ Records on children's health include: emergency phone numbers, allergy, and medication information.
- ☐ Health records are well-organized and accessible.
- ☐ A policy and procedure exist for isolating sick children within the setting or for removing them from the setting.
- ☐ A basic manual of childhood health and disease is available.
- ☐ Program has written health policies which are given to parents.
- ☐ There are clean, individual napping arrangements for each child.
- ☐ Garbage cans are lined, and liner is changed daily.
- ☐ Garbage is emptied daily, and garbage cans that contain food are covered.
- ☐ Animal cages are cleaned frequently and regularly as needed.
- ☐ There is a source of ventilation so that the air is clean and fresh.
- ☐ The temperature is regulated as necessary.
- ☐ There is adequate light for children to see easily as they work without areas of darkness or shadows falling on their work. As much as possible, this is from natural sources with incandescent or full-spectrum flourescent light used when necessary.

amounts of space within which to create a learning environment.

Open design buildings, whether created for classrooms or converted, are constructed so that many people (sometimes all of the children in the school) will be within one room most of the time. Teachers can work in teams and arrange large interest centers throughout the open room or they can try to create self-contained "classrooms" using dividers, furniture, and taped lines to suggest walls.

Both self-contained and open-design classrooms can be effective, and both have drawbacks. Self-contained classrooms offer children and teachers a home-like atmosphere, a pride of ownership in the classroom, and a feeling of security and belonging that is especially beneficial for very young children. Some self-contained classrooms are not large enough to provide the variety that teachers would like and that older or more experienced children may need. Large open-design classrooms offer more space, more variety, and more diversity. They can also be noisy, distracting, and confusing to children and frustrating to teachers who prefer to have greater control over the use of space. Extremes of either type of classroom are not optimal. We have seen teachers and children confined in classrooms that were little larger than closets, and rooms housing over a hundred children where noise and confusion precluded conversation or concentration.

Program environments vary in the degree to which they can be changed, but building structure is not flexible. Your first thoughts in accepting a job may not

be about the environment; however, since this is a place where you will spend many hours of your waking life, it is important to make sure that it is one in which you can work effectively and comfortably.

Informal classrooms in which arrangement allows activities to occur simultaneously with child direction tend to be natural, casual, relaxed, and spontaneous. In an informal environment, children work either individually or in small groups. Both quiet and noisy activities happen throughout much of the day. *Formal* early childhood programs are represented by classrooms where desks, tables, and teacher-directed tasks prevail and where outside time is often called recess and given little teacher attention. These settings tend to be marked by extreme regularity, and they lack the ease and freedom characteristic of more informal settings. The organization of the learning environment can be viewed on a continuum from *informal* to *formal.**

The extreme, and inappropriate, informal end of the continuum provides little organization of the classroom or materials and minimal teacher direction. The extreme, and also inappropriate, formal end of the continuum is represented by the now obsolete classroom where desks were bolted down in rows and teacher direction predominated. Classrooms for young children can fall in many places between these extremes but should be toward the informal end. Teachers who understand child development design space that gives children

*Our use of the words *formal* and *informal* came after considerable debate. We rejected *open-closed* since this often refers to architecture or the arrangement of space, and *structured-unstructured* since we feel that all programs have structure that may be more or less visible.

opportunities to move, interact, explore, and manipulate. The developmental needs of young children require that they move their bodies frequently. They learn through physical interaction, manipulation, and sensory experience, and not through paper and pencil tasks. An atmosphere of warmth and informality meets the social-emotional needs of young children.

The Arrangement of Indoor Space

To create an informal classroom environment, many preschools and kindergartens, and some primary schools organize space into interest centers. These may include areas for art, science, blocks, books, dramatic play, sensory materials, music, woodworking, and manipulative toys and games.

When you design a classroom with interest centers, it is a good idea to begin by defining areas for different types of activities: messy, active, quiet, large group, small group. Areas that have particular requirements can be located first. Quiet areas should be separated from noisy areas. The art area should be near water and will be easier to clean up if it has an uncarpeted floor. The block area should be set out of pathways between centers. It needs space to encourage complex building and low-pile carpeting to reduce noise . Other areas can be arranged in the remaining space, keeping in mind their purpose and requirements. The library area will require good lighting. You may need an electric outlet for an aquarium and a record player.

Aesthetics is another aspect to consider in arranging a classroom . We believe that children's classrooms should be among the most beautiful of places. Attention to the aesthetic quality of the environment

means looking for ways to make aspects of the classroom harmonious (for example, by paying attention to color and design and by grouping shelves or chairs of the same color or design in one area) and eliminating clutter. See page 160 for suggestions for the aesthetic enhancement of environments for young children.

The Arrangement of Outdoor Space

Every program for young children also needs an outdoor play area. Just as there is variety in the buildings which house the programs, there is also variety in the available outdoor space. Unfortunately,

large yards carefully designed for young children are the exception rather than the rule. Whether your outdoor space is a rooftop or a well kept garden, there are things you can do to enhance the space to meet children's needs. An empty asphalt parking lot is no longer considered adequate. Educator's ideas about the purpose and importance of outdoor environments have changed. Since we know that children are learning all the time, not just when they are in the classroom, outdoor space and equipment should support a range of developmental goals: physical, social, cognitive, and creative. It can also be used for an endless variety of learning activities. Animals, gardens, sandboxes, and water play areas located outdoors can be the

SUGGESTIONS FOR AESTHETIC ENHANCEMENT OF ENVIRONMENTS

☐ **Color**   Bright colors will dominate a room and may detract from art and natural beauty present. If you have a choice, select soft, light, neutral colors for walls and ceilings. Try to color coordinate learning centers so that children begin to see them as wholes rather than as parts. Avoid having many different kinds of patterns in any one place; they can be distracting and overstimulating.

☐ **Furnishings**   Group similar furniture together. Keep colors natural and neutral so as to focus children's attention on the learning materials on the shelves. When you are choosing furnishings, select wood rather than metal or plastic. If you must paint furniture, use one neutral color for everything so that you have greater flexibility in moving it from space to space. Have a cleaning activity periodically; give children brushes and warm soapy water and let them scrub the furniture on a sunny, warm day.

☐ **Storage**   Rotate materials on shelves rather than crowding them together. Crowded shelves look unattractive and are hard for children to maintain. Baskets make excellent attractive storage containers. If you use storage tubs, try to put all the same kind together on one shelf. If you use cardboard boxes for storage, cover them with plain-colored paper or paint them.

☐ **Decoration**   Mount and display children's artwork. Provide artwork by fine artists and avoid garish, stereotyped, faded, or tattered posters. Make sure that much artwork (both by children and adult artists) is displayed at children's eye level. Use shelf tops as places for displaying sculpture, plants, and items of natural beauty like shells, stones, and fish tanks. Avoid storing teacher's materials on the tops of shelves; if there is no other choice, create a teacher "cubby" using a covered box or storage tub.

☐ **Outdoors**   Design or arrange play structures to be an extension of nature rather than an intrusion upon it. If possible, use natural materials like wood and hemp rather than painted metal, plastic, or fiberglass. Provide adequate storage to help maintain materials. Involve children, parents, and other staff in keeping outdoor areas free of litter. Add small details like a garden or a rock arrangement to show that the outdoors is also a place that deserves attention and care.

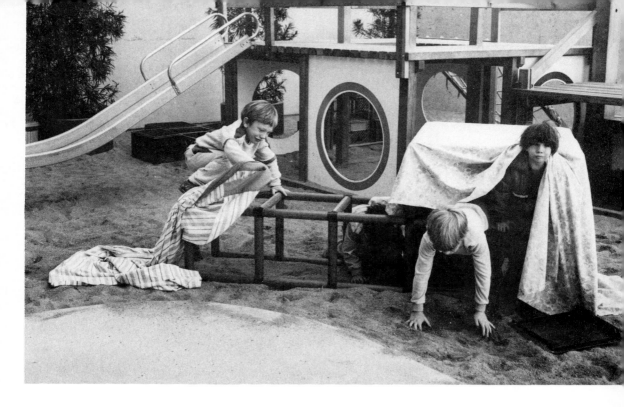

source of science, math, language development, and creative activities. Messy art materials like clay and finger-paint are especially well-suited to outdoor use. Many learning experiences take on new dimensions when they go on outdoors. A story about trees, for example, read in the shade of an oak provides concrete experience and carries new meaning.

The outdoor area is typically used as a site for physical development apparatus. Playground equipment and play structures are very important components of the outdoor environment and should be designed thoughtfully with safety and developmental goals in mind. In play yards that are used by children with a wide range of ages and different degrees of strength and ability, there should be equipment that provides challenge and success at a number of different levels. Toddlers and younger children require different challenges than older preschoolers or kindergarteners. If you work with younger children, you will want to make sure that play structures are lower and wider (to accommodate a child who needs time to climb up or down) and less steep. You will also want to minimize irreversible choices (e.g., tall slides from which you can't back down). Older children require greater variety and more challenge in ways to get up and down. As with indoor furnishings, we have found softer and more natural materials preferable for structures. Wood, hemp, and rubber are aesthetically pleasing and safe.

If there is not enough play equipment for the number of children or if there is insufficient variety or challenge, additional equipment can be improvised from tires, cable spools, ropes, and planks. Whether your yard's equipment is purchased or improvised, this part of your environment requires thoughtful planning and evaluation on a regular basis.

161

EQUIPPING AN EARLY CHILDHOOD PROGRAM

Equipment and materials suggest direction and provide raw materials for children's exploration, development, and learning. Generally, *equipment* refers to furniture and other large and expensive items such as easels and climbing structures. *Materials* usually refers to smaller, less expensive items such as puzzles, books, games, and toys. Consumables like paint, paper, glue, and tape are referred to as *supplies*. Through interaction with well-designed equipment and materials, children develop large and small muscle coordination, concepts about the world, creativity and self-expression, social skills, and self-awareness.

Both boys and girls need experiences with the same kind and variety of learning materials. Special care should be taken to provide materials and present activities without subtly suggesting that one sex will find the material more attractive.

Selecting Equipment and Materials

When you bring any item into a learning environment, it will influence children. Good equipment and materials are attractive. They have sensory appeal: they feel good to touch and hold. They are sturdy and not easily broken and are kept in good repair. Since they are the tools of learning, they must work properly and fit children's size, abilities, and interests. They must be nontoxic, adequately clean, and free of hazards like broken sharp parts.

Natural materials like sand and water, and supplies like paint and paper are important materials which we consider in a slightly different way; their durability is not an issue, and they suit a wide range of developmental stages and abilities. Primary concern must be given to their safety and to having a sufficient quantity for the number of children.

Basic Furnishings   Environments for young children require furnishings that support classroom activities and respond to the needs of children. Wood is a favored material because of its aesthetic appeal, sturdiness, and because it is easier to maintain than plastic or metal. Furnishings must be stable, portable, and have rounded corners and edges. Furniture should be proportioned to the size of the children. When seated in chairs at tables, children's feet should touch the floors and their elbows should rest comfortably on table tops. The easel surface should be at children's eye level, and they should be able to reach the top. Small tables where several children can sit provide greater flexibility than large tables. Every child needs space for the storage of clothing and personal belongings. Manufactured or improvised *cubby holes* meet this need. Low open shelves are essential for the storage of materials that children use independently. Storage of this kind allows children to make choices and encourages them to become responsible for clean-up. A shelf specially designed for books invites reading by displaying the books with their covers facing the children. Since it is relatively easy for young children to return the books to such a shelf, it helps to protect books.

Adequate storage must also be provided for the adults who work with children. Materials that must be closely supervised such as cleaning supplies, files, first aid equipment, and teachers' personal belongings need secure storage within the classroom or nearby areas.

Equipment and Materials for Learning

An environment that supports the development of young children will have many different materials which lend themselves to planning and organization. We have found it helpful to organize these materials into the following groups.

Natural Materials   Sand, clay, water, and other natural materials provide children with rich sensory experiences and an opportunity to learn about mathematical concepts like volume and measurement. Simple observation of almost any child will tell you that these are satisfying play materials. They are open-ended and can be used in many ways. Children learn about the properties of substances through pouring, feeling, and mixing. They may be soothed by the responsiveness of the materials and can safely vent strong emotions in their play with them. Cooperative and imaginative play is fostered as children work together with these materials. Sand and water play areas are often found outdoors, but can also be provided indoors with tubs and water tables.

Active Play Equipment   Equipment for active play offers opportunity for vigorous movement and exploration. Active play helps children develop and explore their physical limits, develop creativity, release energy, and learn many spatial concepts (up, down, under, over) by experiencing these with their bodies.

Simple inexpensive equipment such as sturdy wooden boxes, planks, tires, cardboard cartons, and natural structures such as logs, trees, and boulders can present appropriate challenges and encourage active play. Swings, slides, seesaws, rocking toys, tricycles, and wagons offer opportunities to use and develop the large muscles of the arms and legs and provide experience in balance and coordination. Rubber, wood, and hemp are more responsive than concrete and metal and are less likely to cause injuries. To ensure safety and appropriate challenge, all manufactured active play equipment should be scaled to fit the size of the children.

Construction Materials   Construction toys like blocks and Lego help develop fine motor coordination and strength, enhance imagination, and provide opportunities for children to work together. The use of these materials provides learning experiences in measurement, ratio, and problem solving.

A set of hardwood unit blocks is an essential part of a learning environment for young children. As well as providing the learning experiences of other construction materials, they also demonstrate mathematical relationships when children experience that blocks of one size are equivalent to larger blocks. Blocks provide a medium through which children can express their growing understanding of their world. You can enhance and extend block play by adding toy cars, trucks, human and animal figures, and other props. In order for blocks to be fully used, children need adequate space and sufficient time for block play. Clearly marked block storage shelves are important in helping children to find the appropriate blocks for their constructions and to enable them to take responsibility for clean-up.

Manipulative Materials   Manipulative materials like puzzles, beads, and pegboards are designed to give children practice in hand-eye coordination and to help develop the small muscles of their fingers and hands. These experiences are important preparation for writing, and they expose children to such concepts as color, size, and shape which help in the ability to recognize letters and words. Children also have opportunities to solve problems and be creative as they work with these materials.

Dramatic Play Materials   Dramatic play materials provide learning experiences and allow children to practice the skills of daily living. The manipulation of the physical environment, such as putting on clothes with buttons and zippers, and the management of relationships are learned skills. Children imitate the actions

of the very important grown-ups in their lives through dramatic play, and thus learn about how different roles might feel.

Dramatic play materials can be organized in an interest center that includes props and dress-up clothes for different kinds of work and play, from different cultures, for different ages, and for both men and women. To prevent clutter these can be stored in sturdy, attractive, lidded boxes, and can be organized by occupation or role types. Dolls representing a variety of racial backgrounds and common objects of daily life such as kitchenware, books, furnishings, and tools also form a part of the equipment of the dramatic play area.

Often dramatic play centers are organized into a "home" area emphasizing domestic activity. They can be changed to present other options: a post office, hospital, store, bus, farm, camp, or restaurant. The home theme relates to the most common and powerful experiences in children's lives, but children themselves find new ways to vary this theme. In one classroom we observed children become a lively family of spiders when they spread a crocheted shawl between chairs to become a giant web. You can respond to children's dramatic play by adding appropriate materials when you observe a new interest developing, for example by contributing fire hats, a rain slicker, boots, and a length of hose when the children are pretending to be firefighters rescuing the baby.

Art Materials   Art materials provide opportunities for creative expression, problem solving, and physical and sensory development. A good selection of art materials should include paint, crayons, dough, glue, clay, and collage materials.

Chapter 11 provides a more detailed explanation of art materials and their uses.

Books The best way to help children to learn the joy of reading and become motivated to read is to have good books available and to use them often. Children need many opportunities to look at books, to hear stories, and to see adults using and enjoying books. The use of books is encouraged when you provide a book area that is comfortable, quiet, well-lit, and stocked with a selection of good quality children's books. Well-cared-for, appropriate books, displayed at children's eye level on an uncrowded book shelf with the covers visible, invite children to use them. In Chapter 12 we describe criteria for selecting good books for children.

Cognitive Materials All of the types of materials and equipment that we have just described contribute to intellectual development. Activities such as wood-working, cooking, and block building are especially important in helping children develop concepts. In addition, materials such as scales, balances, lotto, and matching games are specifically designed to help children learn about the world through the processes of comparison, classification, and measurement. Teachers

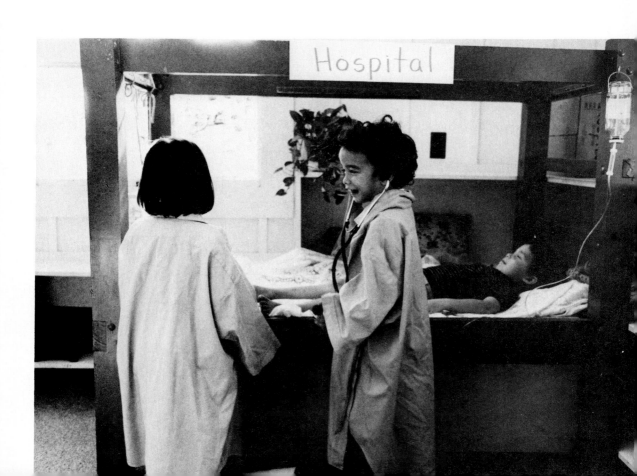

can make games to teach concepts about the world. Many of the materials based on the work of Maria Montessori are designed to teach young children very specific concepts through the manipulation of attractive materials. Chapter 13 provides information about the use of materials in the curriculum areas of math and science.

Computers are yet another type of equipment which can contribute to children's cognitive development. The way that they are used and the purposes to which they are put can vary enormously. Appropriate software (programs) for young children are just starting to be developed. The best software enables children to create and program for themselves. Unfortunately, while the technology of computers is innovative, many programs are simply electronic workbooks designed to teach concepts out of context. Truly innovative and appropriate programs for young children are emerging as educators become computer literate. These programs can help children to learn about computers and programming and, perhaps most important, help children to be confident members of the community of computer users. If your school has funds to purchase computers for educational use, it is important to remember that not all computers are equal and that you will need to do research to find the system that has software that meets your needs and is consistent with your values. Computers are no substitute for the traditional play materials of early childhood education, but they can be useful additions.

Arrangement and Storage

Attention to storage can contribute to the smooth functioning of a classroom as well

as to its aesthetic quality. Uncrowded materials that are stored in attractive containers make the room a pleasant

place in which to live and work. A thoughtfully organized classroom helps children to understand and maintain order.

Keep in mind that your classroom's primary function is to encourage children to engage with materials, a sometimes disorderly process. Avoid being excessively concerned with maintaining order while children are working because such concern can be disruptive. Instead, work on building an environment and routines that contribute to helping children restore order as a worthwhile phase of the activity.

It is important that all new materials be introduced to children. This can be accomplished in a small group where children can talk with you about safe and appropriate ways to use, store, and care for equipment. Although this may seem time-consuming, it saves both time and materials and gives children the information that they need to be full participants in the life of the classroom.

Materials that are reserved for special use by teachers need to be stored so that they are clearly out of children's reach or view. If materials are stored on low open shelves, they tell children that they are available for their use. When children look at the environment, they should be able to tell at a glance what materials are available to them. Low open storage encourages independence and responsibility by allowing children to choose and return materials on their own. You may wish to aid this independence by creating a system to help children to understand and participate in classroom organization. Materials can be stored in containers labeled with pictures of the contents. Shelves and materials can be coded with self-adhesive colored dots. Outlines of equipment can be drawn on

shelves to help children match the equipment to its proper place.

MAKING THE ENVIRONMENT WORK

When you are planning an environment, you need to consider what kinds of experiences you want children to have. Arrangement of learning environments influences what happens within them. Robert Sommer, a psychologist who has studied the effect of environment on behavior, has said that "There is no behavior apart from environment, even in utero" (Sommer, 1974, p. 19).

Look at the space and the equipment that are available and consider what you wish the environment to communicate to children. Keep in mind their age and experience. Create interest centers, and make the environment as safe, aesthetic, and as supportive as you can. If adults will spend time in the classroom, adapt the environment for their needs too. Create a corner where they can sit and relax on an adult-sized comfortable chair or couch.

Designing a learning environment is not a one-time event; it is an ongoing process. As you live and work with children, you will wish to remain sensitive to the ways their needs change as they grow and learn. Plan on regularly reevaluating and changing the environment. Any setting can be modified and improved.

Using a checklist (see pages 168–171) or the Harms-Clifford *Early Childhood Environment Rating Scale,* or reviewing environmental guidelines, such as those designed by NAEYC for the Center Accreditation Project, can help you to take a structured approach to this part of your work.

ENVIRONMENT CHECKLIST
Classroom Atmosphere and Arrangement

Arrangement
- [ ] Paths between centers that do not lead through work areas
- [ ] Noisy areas separate from quiet areas
- [ ] A private area for children
- [ ] An adult-sized chair/sofa
- [ ] Space for messy activities
- [ ] Space for active play
- [ ] Space for large group meetings
- [ ] Space for small group meetings
- [ ] Separate teacher storage

Aesthetics
- [ ] Walls painted in neutral coordinated colors
- [ ] Patterns, colors, and storage in centers coordinate
- [ ] Bulletin boards and other displays used for children's art, fine art, interesting photographs, educational, and parent displays
- [ ] Freedom from materials that promote commercial products or depict media characters
- [ ] Shelf tops uncluttered
- [ ] Items of beauty such as flowers, plants, or sculpture
- [ ] Many pictures and displays at child's eye level

Space is designated for:

A DRAMATIC PLAY CENTER

furniture:
- [ ] A child-sized table with at least two chairs
- [ ] A full-length mirror
- [ ] Open shelves for storage
- [ ] A "bed" sturdy enough to hold a child
- [ ] A small cupboard with closing doors

materials:
- [ ] Materials in good condition
- [ ] Small-sized adult men and women's clothes typical of daily life among children's families
- [ ] Props to encourage multi-age pretend play
- [ ] Two telephones
- [ ] Uniforms, costumes, and props representing different cultures and occupations (e.g., briefcase, kimono, hardhat, sarong, typewriter, cookware)
- [ ] Posters and photographs depicting family, fantasy, and careers

organization:
- [ ] Props and costumes organized into kits for easy storage and variation
- [ ] Shelves and hangers marked to help children in clean-up
- [ ] Materials rotated with children's interests and themes to minimize clutter

A WRITING CENTER (may be included in art)
- [ ] Proportioned table and chairs
- [ ] Storage baskets, jars, or cans for pens, crayons and pencils
- [ ] Large peeled crayons
- [ ] Wide and narrow non-toxic felt marking pens
- [ ] Sharpened primary pencils
- [ ] Low open marked shelves for storage
- [ ] Hole punch
- [ ] Yarn
- [ ] Clear paper cut in uniform sizes
- [ ] Rulers, protractors
- [ ] Recycled envelopes

168

A LIBRARY

books:
- [ ] In good condition
- [ ] Appropriate for children
- [ ] Fiction: realistic and fantasy
- [ ] Accurate information
- [ ] Mood and concept books
- [ ] Poetry
- [ ] New and classic books among which are Caldecott and other award winners
- [ ] Representing a variety of styles of illustration
- [ ] Excluding those based on commercial products
- [ ] Depicting multi-ethnic and multi-age characters in non-stereotyped roles
- [ ] Depicting females and males in a range of occupational and personal roles—both nurturing and adventuresome

decoration and furniture:
- [ ] A low shelf which is used to display books' front covers
- [ ] Is well lit
- [ ] Located away from noisy activities and traffic
- [ ] Comfortable clean pillows, chairs, and carpeting
- [ ] Decoration with art prints, book covers, and posters

AN ART CENTER

- [ ] An easel adjusted so that the smallest child can reach the top of one side
- [ ] A low sturdy table for woodworking unless this is contained in another part of the classroom
- [ ] Open low shelves for materials that child may have access to
- [ ] High or closed shelves for restricted materials

materials:
- [ ] A variety of brushes long and short handles, wide and narrow, and special brushes
- [ ] Cafeteria trays
- [ ] Plastic cups or containers
- [ ] Airtight storage containers
- [ ] Scissors that cut well in either hand
- [ ] Crewel needles
- [ ] Small functional hammers, saws, drills, vise
- [ ] Clay boards and clay tools and separate dough boards and tools
- [ ] Bowls and measuring tools for making dough and paste
- [ ] Spoons for stirring

supplies:
- [ ] Tempera paints in at least primary colors (red, blue, yellow), black and white
- [ ] Paint extender for fingerpainting (liquid laundry starch or bentonite)
- [ ] Watercolors
- [ ] Large peeled crayons
- [ ] Paper for drawing, painting, and cutting may be recycled
- [ ] Special papers (construction, tissue)
- [ ] Flour, salt, and oil to make dough and paste
- [ ] Potter's clay
- [ ] Food color
- [ ] White glue
- [ ] Yarn
- [ ] Wide weave fabric
- [ ] Wide headed nails
- [ ] Soft wood scraps
- [ ] Recycled materials for use in activities and storage (cardboard, styrofoam, wrapping paper, ribbons, fabric scraps, plastic jars, and jar lids)

A SCIENCE/MATH CENTER

furniture:
- ☐ Low open shelves for storage
- ☐ Water/sand table
- ☐ Low table or counter to stand or sit and work

materials:
- ☐ Trays
- ☐ Aquaria, insect and animal cages
- ☐ Measuring tools (rulers, cups/spoons)
- ☐ Sorting trays
- ☐ Magnifying glass
- ☐ Balance/scale
- ☐ Sorting collections (buttons, rocks, etc.)
- ☐ Probes
- ☐ Sensory exploration materials
- ☐ Plastic tubs and pitchers for transporting water and other things
- ☐ Living creatures kept as pets in clean cages, runs, or aquaria
- ☐ Airtight containers for storage
- ☐ Animals/birds/fish/reptiles fed, given water, and protected
- ☐ Machinery to investigate and dissemble
- ☐ Materials that illustrate sequence and proportion (e.g., Cuisenaire rods)
- ☐ Attribute beads or blocks
- ☐ Colored cubes
- ☐ Concept games
- ☐ Accurate appropriate information books
- ☐ Photographs or posters that illustrate concepts

A MANIPULATIVE TOY CENTER

- ☐ A low open shelf to store materials
- ☐ A comfortable carpet or low tables provided for work
- ☐ Toys appropriate to age/skill range of children (larger pieces for children who still put things in their mouths)
- ☐ A variety of materials that require different skills
- ☐ Located close to work space
- ☐ Materials arranged in an orderly and attractive manner
- ☐ Several choices for every child (e.g., if 4 children play in the area at a time, there are at least 8 different toys)
- ☐ Complete toys with pieces unbroken
- ☐ Complete puzzles

OUTSIDE ENVIRONMENT

space:
- ☐ Space for group to run and play
- ☐ Sand and dirt for digging
- ☐ Hard surface for vehicles away from other play
- ☐ Shelter from sun, wind, rain
- ☐ Comfortable surfaces for sitting and lying
- ☐ Naturally occurring plants and animals
- ☐ Access to water for drinking and play

equipment:
- ☐ For climbing, sliding, swinging
- ☐ Children can move
- ☐ Wheeled riding vehicles
- ☐ Storage for sand/water tools

materials:
- ☐ Access to quiet activities
- ☐ Water and sand table or tub
- ☐ Props to encourage active play: parachutes, rope
- ☐ Large playground balls that bounce
- ☐ Baskets and bags for ball storage
- ☐ Tools for digging and pouring

A BLOCK CENTER

furnishings:
- ☐ Low open shelves with adequate space for all blocks to be stored easily
- ☐ A low napped carpet to build on

materials:
- ☐ Hardwood unit blocks
- ☐ 12-25 shapes
- ☐ 100+ blocks available for every 4 children who use the area at a time
- ☐ Figures and vehicles
- ☐ Posters or photographs to stimulate building

organization:
- ☐ Blocks arranged in order on shelf
- ☐ Marked for clean-up

Dimensions of Teaching-Learning Environments

We have found it helpful to use specific dimensions or attributes described by Elizabeth Jones in *Dimensions of Teaching-Learning Environments* (1977) as another tool for planning and evaluating program settings for children. These five dimensions can be used as a kind of lens through which to observe adults and children's use of an environment, and then to evaluate the setting.

Hard-Soft The first dimension relates to responsiveness and physical comfort. Hard environments are not responsive and have been traditional in such institutions as hospitals, bus stations, prisons, and schools (Sommer, 1974). Typically they are characterized by indestructible materials like cement, unattractive colors of paint, and harsh lighting. Function precludes comfort and human interaction; for example, hard desks or chairs are set in immovable rows facing the same direction. Hard environments are created because the clients (children, prisoners, the general public) are expected to damage soft, vulnerable settings. Hard environments are viewed as serious and conducive to work.

Homes and the places that people choose to be (parks, restaurants, theaters, hotels) are very different. These more responsive places have soft, comfortable furnishings, carpets or soft grass, decorations, attractive colors, and soothing lighting. Studies suggest that soft environments are conducive to greater productivity, better craftsmanship, higher motivation and morale, and lower absenteeism in industry (Jones, 1977).

Softness changes the character and feeling of the environment, as well as what happens in it. Early childhood classrooms provide a bridge between home and school. The environments of young children's programs need to reflect the softness of homes (Prescott, 1978).

Teachers as well as materials can soften an environment when they provide warm, physical contact with children, when they hug, crouch at child eye level for conversation, when they allow children to sit in their laps, and when they rub backs during rests. Maintaining physical distance hardens the environment.

Open-Closed The second dimension describes the degree to which materials, storage, program, and teacher behavior restrict children. Open-closed can be viewed on a continuum. Closed mate-

MATERIALS THAT SOFTEN A LEARNING ENVIRONMENT

☐ Cozy furniture such as couches, stuffed chairs, and pillows
☐ Carpets and rugs
☐ Grass and sand
☐ Furry animals and soft toys
☐ Sling and tire swings
☐ Dough, fingerpaint, clay, mud, water, and other messy materials
☐ Adults who are physically available to children

rials—such as puzzles, which have only one right way of being used—are on one end. Open materials—where alternatives are virtually unlimited, such as sand and water—are on the other end.

Open-closed does not mean good-bad. Materials that are closed can be rewarding for children when the task provides both sufficient challenge and opportunities to succeed. Open materials inspire children to be innovative and to create their own challenges.

Younger or less experienced children require long and frequent access to open materials. These are their best and most important learning tools. Great care must be taken that closed materials provide the appropriate challenge since overly difficult materials cause frustration, and damage to the material is likely to follow. Older, more experienced children also need and enjoy open materials which they often use in innovative ways. They are able to cope with a wider range of closed tasks and especially enjoy the challenges of an optimally matched closed activity.

The balance between open and closed is not static or prescribed. It varies both with the space and with the changing needs of children over time. When

children appear bored or frustrated, you may want to observe the environment and see if the cause might be in the balance of open/closed experiences.

Simple-Complex   The third dimension describes the ways that equipment holds children's interest. Both equipment and learning areas can be described as units of increasing complexity (Kritchevsky and Prescott, 1969). *Simple units* have one obvious use; they do not allow children to manipulate or improvise. *Complex units* allow children to use two different play materials together. This makes the play less predictable and more interesting and holds children's attention for a longer period of time. A third type involves three or more different materials used together; these are called *super units.* They offer the largest number of possibilities and hold children's attention much longer since there is much more to do.

Classrooms for inexperienced or less mature children need to be simple to enable them to focus and make choices without being overwhelmed. As children become able to handle additional complexity, more materials can be added. Complexity can also be added by your behavior. When you enter the dramatic play area, put on a hat, pick up a doll, and say, "I think this baby is hungry," or when you enter the block area and comment, "I wonder what would happen if you added another layer of blocks" the environment is made more complex.

Intrusion-Seclusion The fourth dimension concerns who and what penetrates the boundaries of the program. Boundaries exist within the environment between the children in one classroom and the other rooms, people, sights, sounds, and events in the center. Boundaries also exist between the program and the people and things that come from outside. When boundaries are permeated by the outside coming in and by the children going out, novelty and stimulation enrich learning. The important stimulation that intrusion brings can come from trips and visitors to the setting.

Seclusion is also vital. It offers privacy and shelter from stimulation and provides children with the opportunity to concen-

trate on tasks, time to think, and space to be alone. When seclusion is not provided by design, it is often imposed through rigid rules. When opportunities for seclusion do not exist, children often create their own seclusion by hiding behind or beneath furniture, in closets or bathrooms, or by withdrawing physically and retreating emotionally.

Tables or easels set up against walls provide partial seclusion on one or two sides. This enables children to work with minimal visual distraction. Insulated spaces, small areas with protection on three sides, allow a small group to share privacy. Individual hiding spaces, cozy closed places in boxes, crates, curtained lofts, or a draped table, allow one or two children to escape the stimulus of the classroom.

Low Mobility-High Mobility The final dimension characterizes activities by the level of physical involvement and motion. High mobility involves large muscle activities and usually active motion. Low

EXAMPLES OF SIMPLE, COMPLEX, AND SUPER UNITS

Simple Units
- [ ] Trikes
- [ ] Puzzles
- [ ] Slides
- [ ] Concept games

Complex Units
- [ ] Sandbox with tools
- [ ] Collage with paint
- [ ] Blocks with props

Super Units
- [ ] Cimbing structures with the addition of hollow blocks
- [ ] Sand with tools and water
- [ ] Dramatic play area equipped with furnishings, dress-up clothes, props, and dolls

mobility involves small muscle, sedentary activities. Because children's energy levels vary, it is important to provide opportunities for both high mobility and low mobility throughout the day. Classrooms can be equipped with large motor equipment like miniature trampolines and access to outside yards. In the same way, quiet activities like painting, books, and table games can be provided outdoors where low mobility is often neglected.

Teachers influence this dimension through rules and activities. By providing space, materials, and encouragement and by modelling involvement, you demonstrate that both high and low mobility are acceptable and important. Since young girls often have large motor deficits, it is especially important that female teachers model high mobility activity.

FINAL THOUGHTS

Your home changes as you change. It reflects your needs, tastes, activities, and life. It grows with you and your family. Creating an environment for children and making it work is also a process of growth. It allows you to use your knowledge of children's development, your sensitivity in observation, and your creativity. As you gain greater skill and information and as you devote time, energy, and resources to the environment, it will better meet children's needs. This kind of creation is a challenging and very satisfying aspect of teaching young children.

FOR FURTHER THOUGHT AND DISCUSSION

1   Consider your earliest clearly remembered school experience, and remember the environment of the classroom:
    □ How was the space arranged? How did it affect your relationships with your peers and your teachers? How did it support or discourage those relationships? What kind of learning did the environment support? How was independent exploration supported or discouraged by the arrangement of space?
    □ What was in the classroom? How were materials stored and distributed? How did you feel about the materials you had to work with? What did you enjoy most? Why?

2   Think about a setting for children that you are familiar with and consider:
    □ Provisions for health and safety. Does the environment seem to meet children's needs for physical and psychological safety? Are there opportunities for rest and active play? What choices has the teacher made about safety?
    □ How is the space arranged? In what ways does it affect relationships and learning? Does the environmental arrangement support and contribute to program goals? How?
    □ What is in the classroom? How are materials stored and distributed? How do materials and storage contribute to children's learning?
    □ How does this classroom compare to your earliest remembered classroom? Which do you like better? Why?

3   Rate your college classroom on the dimensions of teaching-learning environments. Is it hard or soft? Are the activities open or closed? Are materials simple or complex? Does it allow high mobility and/or low mobility? Are there opportunities for seclusion? Intrusion? How might you change it?

PROJECTS

1   Observe an early childhood program. Use the Health and Safety Checklists in the chapter to observe the environment. Report on the extent to which the program seems to meet children's needs for psychological and physical health and safety.

2 Draw a diagram of the indoor and outdoor space in an early childhood program that you have observed. Report on how the areas are delineated, how the traffic flows, the ease of supervision, and the variety and suitability of equipment and materials. Use incidents that you observed to illustrate how effectively the environment is arranged.

3 Observe a classroom using the Learning Environment Checklist. Answer the following questions:
   □ Are the centers adequately equipped?
   □ Are the centers attractive?
   □ What kinds of development do the centers and areas support?
   Comment on what you have observed including your own feelings about the environment and how you might modify it for your own teaching.

4 Observe a classroom from a child's eye-view by kneeling or by sitting on a very low chair. Observe from this perspective and from the classroom entrance and the interest centers. Write down all that you can see in each location. Go back to each position and observe it again from your regular height. Describe your experience. Did you experience the environment differently when viewed from a child's perspective? What did you learn about this classroom? What did you learn about the design of environments?

5 Draw a floor plan of a program that you have observed or worked in. Think about your goals for children, and consider how the space meets or fails to meet your goals. Redesign the space to make it more effective or to help better meet your goals for children. Draw another diagram showing the changes. If you are working in the classroom, implement some of the changes. Describe what you did and why.

6 Plan your ideal environment for young children. Include a diagram of the indoor and outdoor spaces and a list of the equipment you would include. Describe your environment, and explain your decisions in terms of your objectives for children.

7 Observe an early childhood program and prepare a brief profile of the environment in terms of the *Dimensions of Teaching-Learning Environments*. What changes would you make based on your observations? Why?

RECOMMENDED READING

Child Health Alert. Newsletter concerning current issues in children's health. PO Box 338 Newton Highlands, MA 02161.

Gandini, Lella. "Not Just Anywhere: Making Child Care Centers into Particular Places." In *Beginnings*, Summer, 1984.

Green, Martin L. *A Sigh of Relief.* New York: Bantam Books, 1977.

Gross, Dorothy Weissman. "Equipping a Classroom for Young Children." In *Ideas that Work with Young Children,* edited by Katherine Read Baker. Washington D.C.: National Association for the Education of Young Children, 1972.

Harms, Thema. "Evaluating Settings for Learning." In *Ideas that Work with Young Children,* edited by Katherine Read Baker. Washington D.C.: National Association for the Education of Young Children, 1972.

————, and Clifford, Richard. *Early Childhood Environment Rating Scale.* New York: Teachers College Press, 1980.

Hill, Dorothy M. *Mud, Sand and Water.* Washington D.C.: National Association for the Education of Young Children, 1977.

Hirsch, Elizabeth. *The Block Book.* Washington D.C.: National Association for the Education of Young Children, 1984.

Jones, Elizabeth. *Dimensions of Teaching-Learning Environments: Handbook for Teachers.* Pasadena, Cal.: Pacific Oaks, 1977.

————, and Prescott, Elizabeth. *Dimensions of Teaching-Learning Environments II: Focus on Daycare.* Pasadena, Cal.: Pacific Oaks, 1978.

Kritchevsky, Sybil; and Prescott, Elizabeth; with Walling, Lee. *Physical Space: Planning Environments for Young Children.* Washington D.C.: National Association for the Education of Young Children, 1969.

National Academy of Early Childhood Programs. *Accreditation Criteria and Procedures.* Washington D.C.: National Association for the Education of Young Children, 1984.

Pantell, Robert H.; Fries, James F.; and Vickery, Donald M. *Taking Care of Your Child.* Reading, Mass.: Addison-Wesley Publishing Company, 1984.

Rausher, Shirley R., and Young, Teresa. *Sexism: Teachers and Young Children.* New York: Early Childhood Education Council of New York City, 1974.

Ross, Malcolm. *The Aesthetic Imperative: Relevance and Responsibility in Arts Education.* Oxford: Pergamon Press, 1981.

Stone, Jeanette Galambos. *Play and Playgrounds.* Washington D.C.: National Association for the Education of Young Children, 1970.

Sprung, Barbara. *Non-Sexist Education for Young Children: A Practical Guide.* New York: Citation Press, 1975.

8

Relationships and Classroom Management

"Nothing I have ever learned of value was taught to me by an ogre. Nothing do I regret more in my life than that my teachers were not my friends. Nothing ever heightened my being or deepened my learning more than being loved."

J. T. Dillon

*This chapter examines two vital aspects of living and working in a group setting with young children: developing nurturing teacher-child relationships and managing the classroom to support children's relationships and their ability to work in groups. In it we focus on self-concept and how it can be enhanced and on techniques and approaches for positive classroom management. The chapter relates to the CDA areas **Self, Social** and **Guidance.***

TEACHER-CHILD RELATIONSHIPS

The relationships children have with teachers are of great importance in determining the quality of their educational experiences. Based on these relationships children will decide if the classroom is a safe and trustworthy place in which they may live and work. Only when they feel safe, cared for, and secure will they have the confidence to explore and develop new skills and understandings. Children cannot be productive when they feel threatened, anxious, or uncertain. One of your roles as a teacher is to communicate with children in ways that help them function both competently and creatively. The relationships they experience with you will also influence how they learn to relate to others.

Research on teaching and learning supports the view that good interpersonal relationships are of primary importance in effective teaching (Gazda, 1975). Good interpersonal relationships between children and teachers like good relationships between adults are characterized by such qualities as honesty, empathy, respect, trust, and warmth. They are *authentic* and not forced or artificial. Needless to say, in such relationships children must be safe from fear of corporal punishment and humiliation. Relationships and children's feelings about schools, teachers, and learning can be irreparably damaged by these tactics.

The most effective teachers we know have relationships with children that are characterized by appreciation and respect for the individual. These teachers feel positive about their work and enjoy and often share children's playfulness. While they seem to gain children's willing compliance, they do not demand unquestioning obedience; in fact, they welcome questions as signs of growing independence.

Since children are unique individuals, your relationships with them will not all be the same. With capable and confident children, you too may be boisterous and join their play. With hesitant or awkward children, you may simply add an encouraging presence, a word of confidence, or a shared joy in success. Since teachers are also individuals, there is no one right way to have good relationships with children. Learning to create caring, growth-producing relationships with children is perhaps your most vital teaching task.

Self-Concept

As children grow and develop, they not only form concepts about the world and how it works, but they also form concepts about themselves. **Self-concept** is the total picture that children have of themselves based on their own perceptions and on what others tell them. Self-concept influences children's ability to develop meaningful relationships with people, ideas, and the physical world. It includes perceptions of the physical self and perceptions of social and cognitive qualities and competence. One of the goals of early childhood education is to help children to develop strong, positive, and realistic self-concepts.

The self-concept of young children is subject to change because it is greatly influenced by the opinions of significant people in their lives. The nature of children's self-concept is dependent on how family members, caregivers, and teachers relate to them.

Parents are usually children's first and most influential sources of information about who they are. It is from parents that children begin to establish their identities as individuals of a gender, race, and culture and to learn whether this identity is desirable or undesirable. In families, children first learn whether they are acceptable: attractive and competent or unattractive and incompetent. Their first appraisal of their intellectual potential and whether or not they are likely to succeed in the academic world also comes from their parents.

Self-esteem is one's internal appraisal of one's own worth. A child's self-esteem is profoundly affected by that of their parents. Indeed, low self-esteem seems to be "catching"; when parents judge themselves negatively, they tend to judge their children negatively, and eventually the children may judge themselves the same way (Samuels, 1977). Affectionate care and attention from adults who are secure and who feel good about them-

selves will help children to conclude that they are attractive, competent individuals.

Adults who are unable to provide such care or who have unrealistically high standards may cause children to fail to develop respect for themselves, to feel that they are unworthy of love, incapable of social interaction, and unable to achieve. Such low self-esteem seriously hinders children in their ability to relate to the people, activities, and ideas that help them learn and grow.

As a teacher, you are a significant person who has the power to influence self-concept and self-esteem. *What* you teach may not be nearly so important as *how* you teach and what kind of person you are as you teach. Young children need teachers who accept them as they are and who encourage them to value and positively evaluate themselves.

To be able to bolster the self-concept of children, you must yourself possess an adequate self-concept.

Affirmation of self precedes affirmation of others, and an authentic adult can do much to induce and bolster a child's affirmation of himself by displaying rich and open feelings toward him, by showing unyielding confidence in him, and by providing and sharing with him genuine human encounters. (Yamamoto, 1972, p. 17)

You need not view yourself as flawless in order to have a positive self-concept. Instead you must appreciate your strengths, acknowledge your weaknesses, and have an inner acceptance of who you are. If you are unable to accept yourself, you may have difficulty being truly accepting of children, however much you may think you like them.

Viewed broadly, this entire book is about how you provide experiences that enhance each child's self-concept. The many roles of a teacher can be carried out with this in mind. Environments can be designed and managed to provide positive experiences and to encourage independence and responsibility. Routines can be handled to ensure that each child feels safe, secure, and self-confident. Problems can be handled in ways that preserve children's good feelings about themselves. The curriculum can contribute to each child's positive sense of self.

Communication

Your relationships with children are largely dependent on your awareness and skill in communication. How you communicate and what you communicate affects how children feel about themselves and the degree of safety and trust they feel in your classroom. Respectful communication conveys to children that you value their feelings and thoughts and

that you trust their capacity to grow and learn.

Basic abilities that will help you to be effective in communicating with children include the ability to perceive accurately, the capacity to respond authentically, awareness of barriers to communication, and willingness to try to overcome these barriers. Development of these abilities requires thoughtful attention.

Listening The first skill that you will need to develop is the ability to **listen well.** By this we mean that you truly *understand* the message that a child is sending. Listening well requires that you pay very careful attention to words, gestures, body stance, movement, and tone of voice. Often we receive one message from a person's words while their body and expression convey something else. Young children's nonverbal messages are frequently your best source of information about their thoughts and feelings since their verbal skills are often not very well developed.

General knowledge of age and stage of development and of an individual's background and experiences helps you understand the young child's needs and interests. The combination of this knowledge with attention to the environment and experiences that a child is having will enable you to understand the meaning behind the words and behavior of that child at a particular time.

We recently observed a three year old who was having a hard time at the beginning of his first school year. The morning was punctuated by bouts of crying, "I want my Mommy!" As the children left circle time to play at different centers, the boy's crying started again, and the cry for Mommy took on a new and more desperate tone accompanied by a dance-like motion. His observant teacher approached him, spoke with him quietly, and then took him to the toilet. She had used her observations of this child, her awareness of his day at school, and her knowledge of three year olds to understand what the child was actually communicating.

Responding The responses you make to another person's communication can express your concern and demonstrate that you listened and understood both the words and the feelings that were conveyed. To respond effectively you need to consider your verbal and nonverbal messages. Your timing, the quality and register of your voice, your facial expression, gestures, and body posture often convey more to a child than the words you use.

An appropriate response to children's words about their ideas, actions, and feelings is often to simply **listen** quietly and **acknowledge** what you have heard with a nod, smile, or word of encouragement. Children then know that you are paying attention to them and care about their thoughts and feelings. These responses give more time to a child who is struggling to express ideas and feelings in words. They also give you time to try to piece together the words and body language of a very young child.

Words of encouragement invite further communication. They say, "I'd like to hear more about that and spend more time with you." You may want to think about what you will say to encourage children. Statements like, "I see," "Tell me more," "Yes," "Great," "O.K.," "Is there anything else you want to tell me?" and "Thank you for telling me" are encouraging responses.

Sometimes despite our best efforts at understanding children we make mistakes. To help avoid mistakes you can **restate** what you think a child has communicated to you or ask a **question** that is an interpretation of a child's message. This allows the child to confirm your interpretation or correct any misunderstandings. For example, we recently heard a child say, "I want pupu." Her teacher responded, "Are you looking for the purple pen?" which the child confirmed.

It is useful to look at communication as a code for a person's **feelings** as well as thoughts. How you interpret what the other person means may be accurate or inaccurate. **Active listening** is a term used by Thomas Gordon to describe a process in which you listen and respond to the feeling as well as the content of a message. You give the child the opportunity to clarify the message and express the feelings involved. Here are two examples of a situation where a child's words and actions had different meanings and the teacher used active listening.

Situation 1 A two-year-old child, during the first month of school, was absent-mindedly stacking several blocks. His teacher walked by and the child said, "When is my Mommy coming?" The child's voice, face, and body communicated sadness. The teacher responded, "You wish you could see your Mommy now?"

Situation 2 A four-year-old child, during her fifth month of school, was intently building an elaborate block structure. The teacher walked by and the child said, "When is my Mommy coming?" The child's face, voice, and body communicated intense concentration and concern.

The teacher responded, "You're worried you'll have to stop before you're finished?"

The teacher in both of these examples used what she knew about the children and their situations and observed nonverbal cues to make an educated guess about the strong feelings of each. She helped the children to feel free to talk further about their concerns and needs and gave them the opportunity to correct her perceptions. When you use active listening, you help the person feel free to think, discuss, question, and explore. It is especially valuable because it demonstrates to children that you really care and are a person who is worthy of trust.

Conversing   The teachers we know who love their work genuinely appreciate and respect young children and their interests. They show this when they **talk** with children to share ideas and feelings that each of them have. Conversation is a mutual endeavor in which both teacher and children must have interest.

Good conversations begin with genuine shared interest. The workings of the plumbing, the quality of the easel paint, the traits of a favorite character from a story, home, family, the world, play, and literally thousands of other shared experiences make up the the content of conversations between teachers and children. To have a conversation with a child or an adult you must be willing to invest your time and attention to finding these interests.

Too frequently teachers talk with children only to give directions, handle problems, pronounce truths, or teach skills and concepts. While these are parts of every teacher's day, they are not the materials of which relationships and communication are built.

Talking with a young child requires some special techniques. Since there is a size difference that interferes with adult-to-child conversations, get down to the child's eye-level and make eye-contact. There is also a vast difference in experience between you and young children. To minimize this, speak in a relaxed and natural voice using words and a style of speech that is not unlike the way you talk with your own friends, but talk about things that are within the experience of both you and the child. The emotional tone of your words need not be highly modified for children but should express your real feelings and intention. While you obviously cannot talk about all the adult aspects of your life, you can have many worthwhile and meaningful exchanges with children. We have found that, with the modifications suggested, many children prove to be very interesting, competent conversationalists.

Barriers to Communication

It is important to be aware of things that get in the way of communication so that you can consciously avoid them. Barriers include physical distractions, personal bias, and inappropriate or disrespectful ways of talking.

Distractions in the environment can create barriers. If it is too noisy, crowded, or uncomfortably hot or cold, it is difficult to focus on what another person is saying. Communication is facilitated when you make the environment as nondistracting as possible; for example, by sitting in a sheltered corner to talk.

Strong feelings about an individual's appearance, race, culture, or personality may also interfere. Everyone has some feelings of bias, but these are not inborn or permanent. It is not possible to change anyone else's attitudes, but you *can* be aware of, and thoughtful about, your own strong feelings with the goal of becoming more open to others. Your acceptance of an individual will help other staff and children to also be accepting.

Communication can be hindered when you are unaware of the effect of your words on others. A teacher we know took her three and four year olds on a tour of the local police station. The officer in charge was completely oblivious to the effect of his words as he showed the children a juvenile holding cell and said, "This is where we keep bad children." His inappropriate attempt at humor resulted in many of the children being very frightened of the police. Although this is an extreme example, we all occasionally make statements that have unintended negative effects. Observing yourself and children's responses to you can help you to avoid such thoughtless miscommunication.

Sometimes our responses to another person's ideas and feelings are well-meaning but detrimental to real communication and sometimes even to self-concept and the relationship. These tell children that their ideas are unacceptable or irrelevant. Thomas Gordon calls them **roadblocks.** It is often difficult to avoid using roadblocks since you may have been met with them in your childhood and in your adult relationships . Awareness can help you to be more sensitive in your responses.

There are three categories of roadblocks: advising, evaluating, and avoiding. Because of adult knowledge and experience, it is tempting to give children **advice** about their feelings, behavior, or problems. When you respond to children's ideas or concerns by telling them what to do or by warning them about the consequences of their actions rather than responding to their ideas and feelings, you are creating a barrier which may encourage children to challenge you or be angry and defensive. As you attempt to persuade them to your viewpoint, you may discourage exploration as well as communication.

Child: Teacher! Look at this big snail I found.
Teacher: Put that snail down; it carries germs that can make you sick.

Child: Teacher! Look at this big snail I found.
Teacher: I don't think you should carry that snail around. You should do unto others as you would have others do unto you. Wouldn't you like to put that snail down here? It will be so much happier.

Similarly, **evaluating** children effectively halts their attempts to share. Criticism or ridicule makes them feel foolish and unacceptable, and even praise is sometimes a roadblock because following praise, there is little left to say.

Child: Teacher! Look at this big snail I found.
Teacher: You are always being cruel to animals. Don't you know how to take care of pets?

Child: Teacher! Look at this big snail I found.
Teacher: What a wonderful little scientist you are!

When you **avoid** talking about a child's behavior, feelings, or problems by analyzing, questioning, distracting, or humoring the child, you are disregarding their ideas and concerns, and they will soon stop trying to talk to you.

> Child: Teacher! Look at this big snail I found.
> Teacher: You must be lonely being all alone with your snail; won't anyone be your friend?

> Child: Teacher! Look at this big snail I found.
> Teacher: Oh yes. Have you seen the new hats we have in the home area today? I bet you can run over there faster than a snail.

The same situation could, of course, have supported the relationship had the teacher simply listened, questioned, or commented on the child's feelings and interest.

> Child: Teacher! Look at this big snail I found.
> Teacher: You sure are excited about that snail. What would you like to do with it?

The manner in which teachers talk to children can be another barrier to communication. Some teachers talk to children in exaggerated, "cute," or condescending ways either because they feel this is appropriate or because they are attempting to communicate a generalized acceptance. This sends the message to children that they are not perceived as individuals worthy of sincerity and respect. Although these teachers talk to children, they do not seem to have a genuine interest in children's concerns and may cut a conversation off because the subject matter isn't "nice."

The degree to which a teacher's talking dominates conversations may also be a barrier. Teachers often talk a great deal and leave only a short amount of time for children's responses. They do this perhaps because they feel that it is part

of their teacher role or because they are uncomfortable with silence. They give little opportunity or encouragement for children to express ideas and feelings and often wonder why the children in their classes seem to have so little to say.

It is virtually impossible to eliminate all barriers to communication. You can, however, keep alive your own awareness. Notice the circumstances that surround children's active and eager communication, and contrast it with the times when conversation is difficult. Be aware of the times when you too feel threatened or "turned off" by other adults, and try to learn from these situations. Don't expect communicating with children to be effortless; it can, however, be one of the great rewards of teaching.

CLASSROOM MANAGEMENT

The central goal of classroom management is to help children learn to relate to people, experiences, and materials in positive ways. How you achieve this goal will depend on the values you have for children, your comfort level with children's behaviors, the demands and constraints of the school setting, and your ability to communicate effectively. Indeed, attention to communication is an integral part of classroom management. Many problems never begin when the teacher knows how to communicate with children.

It is important to keep in mind the fit between what you do and what you value. Without this awareness you can accumulate a "grab bag" of techniques that "work" (i.e., control immediate behavior problems) but that can have unintended consequences or that violate your underlying values. Your decisions about the success of management techniques should focus on whether the outcome was consistent with your goals for children's development, rather than on whether the technique was effective at a particular moment.

Theoretical Approaches to Classroom Management

A number of approaches have been designed to give guidance to teachers and parents in the theory and practice of child management. These approaches differ in underlying values, assumptions, and techniques. We will discuss three of these theoretical approaches as they have been applied to classroom management: the humanistic approach, based on the work of Carl Rogers; the democratic approach, based on the work of Alfred Adler; and the behaviorist approach, based on the work of B.F. Skinner.

In the humanistic approach, the values of positive self-regard and individual responsibility are emphasized. In the democratic approach, the individual's ability to function cooperatively in social settings is valued. The behaviorist approach stresses the shaping of children's behavior in desired directions through the creation of a purposeful and orderly learning environment. Though they reflect different values, all three approaches offer useful techniques for teachers when applied humanely and thoughtfully.

The Humanistic Approach   The humanistic philosophy and therapeutic practices of Carl Rogers have been applied to classroom management by a number of interpreters, including Haim Ginott and Thomas Gordon. In this approach to classroom management, your central task

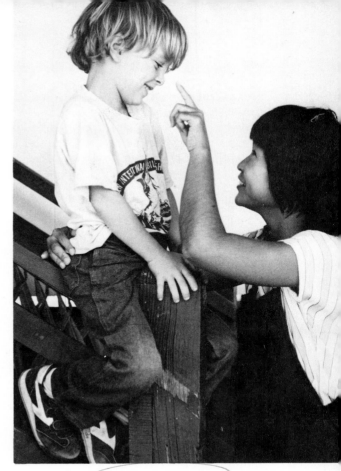

is to develop good relationships between individuals and within groups and to help children realize their unique potential and their capacity to see the world and themselves positively.

To accomplish these goals, you need the skills we have described for achieving open, honest, and authentic communication. You also need to be able to send nonjudgmental messages to children about the effects of behavior and engage in problem solving to find mutually acceptable solutions. In the section on *Interacting with Children When There Is a Problem,* we suggest the humanistic approach.

The humanistic approach to child management works well when children have few deep-seated problems and are used to dealing with adults verbally in relationships where they have been treated with respect. It is less immediately effective with children who are not used to this kind of relationship or with very young children who have limited verbal ability . Other strategies may, at least initially, need to be employed.

Insight and skill in the application of humanistic principles will be helpful to you as a teacher, as a parent, and as an adult relating to other adults. You can learn more from the writing of Faber and Mazlish in *How to Talk So Kids will Listen and Listen So Kids will Talk,* Gordon in *Teacher Effectiveness Training,* and Ginott in *Between Teacher and Child.* These give many practical suggestions for relating to children in educational settings. Participating in classes and workshops is another way to continue to grow and learn in this area.

The Democratic Approach   Rudolf Driekurs has interpreted and applied to classroom management many of the ideas of Alfred Adler's *individual psychology.* In Driekur's democratic approach to classroom management, children are viewed as social beings with a strong desire to be part of a group. Disruptive behavior is seen as a result of not knowing how to be part of the group in a positive and cooperative manner. When children feel unsuccessful in gaining acceptance within the group, they become discouraged and try to gain entrance in disruptive ways.

The central task in this approach is to help children discover appropriate ways to gain approval and to become respectful and responsible members of a group of peers. This is done by establishing a group in which the teacher functions as the leader and employs the democratic

concepts of respect, cooperation, and participation in decision making. The rules for group living and the consequences for breaking the rules are first established. If a child uses a toy to hurt someone else, the consequence might be to lose the opportunity to play with that toy. In following through on the consequence (not allowing the child to play with the toy), the teacher would be calm but not angry, and would simply say, "You may not play with that now. You used it to hurt; you may play with it another time." Children confront the direct consequences of their behavior and thus learn the laws of living as a member of society.

This approach to classroom management relies heavily on teacher control of the consequences and on children relating the consequences to their past behavior. Such a feat of memory is often beyond the ability of a young child unless the rules are few, the consequences very clear, and the follow through consistent, timely, and just. We have observed abuses of this system of management where young children thought that "consequence" was just a fancy word for "punishment," and in our observation, the teachers shared this misperception.

Psychology in the Classroom and other books by Dreikurs and *Systematic Training for Effective Parenting* by Dinkmeyer, McKay, and Dinkmeyer contain many suggestions for how teachers can use this management approach.

The Behaviorist Approach   Principles and techniques developed by B.F. Skinner have been interpreted and applied to classroom management by many theorists and educators who are commonly referred to as behaviorists. They see all behavior as a function of learning and believe that children misbehave because they have been unintentionally rewarded for the inappropriate actions. They also believe that external stimuli determine all learning so that procedures for evoking and changing behavior can be taught. Using the awareness that teacher behavior is sometimes reinforcing, behaviorists avoid reinforcing actions that are undesirable and reward desired actions. When used in classrooms, these procedures allow the teacher to control events so that the children behave according to the prescriptions of the adult. The adult does not engage in conflict, but rather decides which behavior is to be reinforced and which is to be extinguished. When children have severe behavior problems, they frequently respond well to this approach. All teachers use behaviorist principles at some time either knowingly or unknowingly. When you smile at a shy child who attempts a new activity for the first time, you are providing reinforcement. When you fail to respond to a child whose demands are disruptive, you are ignoring the behavior in an attempt to avoid reinforcing it. We find it most useful to become aware of what is rewarding to different children. If even negative attention from an adult is rewarding to certain children, you will want to avoid giving attention when they are disruptive or damaging and take special care to give them attention when they do something positive. We recently observed a teacher who took a child on her lap and gently stroked his back while she explained why he should not have hit another child; her actions were more powerful than her words, and the child was well-rewarded for his aggression. If she had recognized this child as one who used negative strategies to gain adult attention, she might have responded quite differently.

Behaviorist techniques do not actively involve children in making choices and becoming responsible for their own actions. While these techniques are effective for the moment, they may not contribute to your long-range goals for children. We have found Lilian Katz's paper, "Condition with Caution" (1971), a useful reminder that behaviorist techniques are only appropriate when negative behavior is an outcome of conditioning. Other approaches are called for when disruptive behavior is caused by a lack of information about what's appropriate or by emotional problems.

The Recommended Reading list at the end of this chapter gives suggestions for readings if you would like to find out more about the theory and application of behaviorist principles. Many classes and texts in special education can also help.

Selecting Management Strategies   All of these management approaches can be used in ways that take into account individual needs and that show respect and care for children. Techniques can be chosen that support developmental goals and your personal philosophy and that fit the particular situation and the child or children with whom you work.

The communication and problem-solving skills presented in humanistic approaches are helpful for building relationships and dealing with everyday upsets and problems. When conflicts arise, the democratic approach is helpful for understanding the mistaken strategies that children have adopted and for helping them to redirect their behavior more positively. When destructive patterns have developed and become habitual, the consistency and power of reinforcement techniques may be effective in changing or eliminating the behaviors.

Practical Aspects of Classroom Management

Young children are just beginning to develop the understandings, attitudes, and skills needed for living with groups of people and for dealing with their feelings. Classroom management can support such learning and can have the long-range effect of helping children gain competence and feel good about them-

selves. Any teacher of young children needs to develop skill in three areas of classroom management:

1 Anticipating and preventing problems.
2 Developing rules to guide children's behavior.
3 Interacting with children when there is a problem.

Anticipating and Preventing Problems
Before the first child steps through the door of your room on the first day of school, there are things that you can do to ensure that conflict will be minimized. Many management problems are avoided when children have enough attention

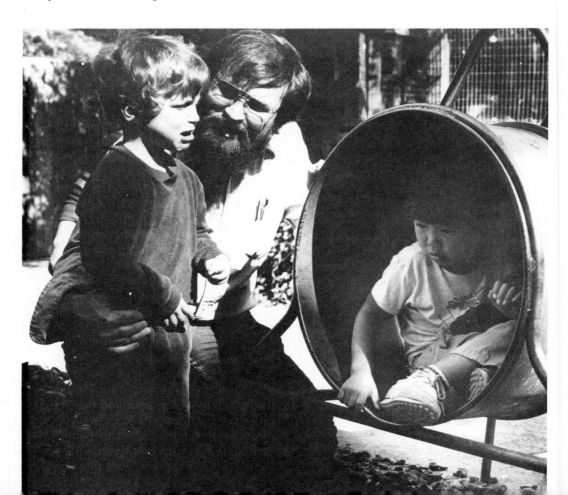

from adults, access to materials, and space to work and live comfortably. When they have opportunities to do interesting and worthwhile things and sufficient time to complete activities, your classroom will work better.

Adult attention for individual children may be inadequate for a number of reasons. Two teachers in a group of sixteen who spend the bulk of their time talking to one another, answering the phone, preparing materials, or talking to visitors have a ratio of about 1 to 16 rather than 1 to 8. Similarly, if adults rather than children take out materials, clean up, or tend to children's belongings, there is very little time left for them to interact with children. Children often behave badly simply because it is an effective way to gain teacher attention. You may be unable to change your program's ratios, but you can focus more on children while you are with them and create a classroom where they can take care of many of their own needs.

Problems also occur when children compete for access to a limited number of desirable materials and activities. If there are several appropriate and appealing choices for each child, conflict over a few particularly interesting items is avoided. When a new or appealing activity is presented to children, interest will be high and demand will be great. To avoid conflict make sure that there is enough time and materials available for all or most of the children or present several high interest activities simultaneously. As you gain experience, you will become more and more sensitive to the events that are preludes to problems.

The box on page 192 contains strategies and guidelines that can help you maintain a classroom where problems are less

likely to occur and where children's self-esteem is supported.

Developing Rules to Guide Children's Behavior   Children need to learn many things about life in school: what behaviors are acceptable, how to handle routines and materials, and how space is to be used. Frequently problems occur because children lack information. You will need to communicate your expectations with clarity and simplicity through a few easily understood rules. A rule is a simple statement of your expectations which enables people to work together in harmony.

Rules for young children need to be simple enough so that they can be easily understood. Care should be taken to establish only those rules that are necessary for making the setting function. A few general rules that address important principles of behavior are better than a laundry list that addresses every conceivable situation.

Rules should be stated so that they invite children to do something rather than deny them an activity. They must also be appropriate to the developmental level of the children. It is unreasonable, for example, to make a rule requiring young children to sit quietly for long periods of time.

Children respect rules when they understand the reasons for those rules and when the behavior required is within their ability. Following are some examples of rules and their reasons:

Rule: Walk and talk quietly where people are working.
Reason: Loud voices and activity make it hard for others to work. If there are lots of people working with lots of things,

SUGGESTIONS FOR CLASSROOM MANAGEMENT

☐ As the noise level during group time rises, talk more softly. Often children will listen out of curiosity, and the noise will diminish.

☐ To get children's attention, move close to them, crouch down to their level, and speak directly to them. Avoid shouting across the room or yard or addressing the group about a problem with a particular individual.

☐ Use children's names positively and frequently so that they don't fear something negative when you address them by name.

☐ Indicate what *to do* rather than what *not* to do when correcting behavior. People often feel rebellious and challenged when they are told what not to do.

For. . .	Substitute. . .
Don't run with the scissors.	*Please walk when you carry scissors so no one will get hurt.*
Don't get paint on your clothes.	*Wear a smock so you won't get paint on your clothes.*
Don't tear the book.	*Turn the pages carefully.*

☐ When a child doesn't respond appropriately to correction, as in the above examples, give the child two acceptable choices. Choices help people to feel powerful and in control.

Please walk when you carry scissors so no one will get hurt, or *Let me carry the scissors while you go outside to run.*

Wear a smock so you won't get paint on your clothes, or *You can use pens to make your picture.*

Turn the book's pages carefully, or *You can use newspaper if you'd like to tear.*

☐ Avoid phrases that compare and evaluate children. They can be damaging to self-esteem and may discourage children.

For example, if you say, "George is going to be the first one finished," the unspoken message is "The rest of you are really slow." "I like the way Susie is listening," implies "I don't like what the rest of you are doing."

☐ Avoid giving children choices that you are unwilling or unable to allow. "Would you give me the knife?" is not appropriate when you mean "Give me the knife right now; it is dangerous!"

children can be hurt when they move quickly and noise makes it hard for people to work.

Rule: Treat people gently.
Reason: School is a place where everyone works and plays. No one can work and play if they are scared of getting hurt.

Rule: Use toys and games carefully.
Reason: Toys and games can get lost or broken if they are not used carefully; then we would not have them to use anymore.

Rule: Put toys and games away when you are done.
Reason: When toys and games are left out it's difficult to find them again.

There tend to be two types of problems regarding rules in early childhood programs. The first problem involves the number of rules. There are often so many rules that it is difficult for children, and even for teachers, to remember them. Teachers then spend much of their time enforcing rules, or they can only enforce the rules sporadically without clarity as to which are most important.

Another problem occurs when rules are ambiguous and don't really guide children or teachers. Such a rule as *Blocks are for playing,* for example, fails to address the issue of using blocks as weapons or missles, and hence, it is frequently misunderstood and not followed as the teacher wished. A clearer rule would be *Use blocks for building not hurting.* Unclear rules jeopardize the safety and orderliness of the environment, and children and teachers are usually surprised at the resultant injuries, broken equipment, or chaos.

Rules are *mutual* guidelines for behavior that all of the members of a group must understand and agree with. Children abide by rules that are clearly stated and consistently enforced. In agreeing to a rule both teacher and child are making a commitment to the safety, happiness, and well-being of the individuals in the group. You can help children to understand the underlying principles of your shared rules by repeating the reasons for those rules and by helping them to understand that the rules are there to protect all of the children, including themselves.

Interacting with Children When There Is a Problem A child enters a classroom at at a particular stage of development with needs, established likes and dislikes, a communication style, behavior patterns, and unique perceptions of the world. These contribute to the quality of relationships and the problems that will occur in your classroom. When you meet children, you need to respect, accept, and deal with all of their characteristics, even those that contribute to conflict. You can help children understand the effects of their behavior on themselves, on others, and on the total functioning of the school environment.

You show respect for children by helping them to understand the possible consequences of undesirable behavior and by giving them the option of controlling behavior themselves. Such an approach indicates that you see children as mature and intelligent enough to control their own behavior. Acknowledging acceptable behavior and communicating clearly when and how a behavior is unacceptable are effective management strategies and consistent with the goals of helping children to develop self-control and a positive view of themselves. Punitive methods of control like corporal punishment, shame, and humiliation communicate to children that they are bad or inadequate people.

You demonstrate understanding of children's problems through your willingness to listen to them and hear their

feelings. But when you have a problem, your needs and rights are being violated, or a situation makes you uncomfortable or unhappy, listening does not help. Feelings, especially unpleasant ones, can be difficult to share, but collected negative feelings sometimes come out harshly and may damage relationships. If you don't maintain your own rights in the classroom or if you try so hard to be nice that your needs are not met and respected, you may soon find yourself disliking children.

Sending **I-messages** (Gordon, 1974) is a way to communicate your problems and feelings without telling children that they are wrong or that you don't respect or care for them. When you give an I-message, you maintain your rights, get your point across, and avoid hurting children or your relationship with them. An effective I-message has three elements:

1   A statement of the condition or behavior that is problematic.
2   A statement of the effect on you.

3   A statement of the feelings generated within you.

For example, "When you talk during story, it's hard for others to hear and I feel frustrated" is an effective I-message. It does not send a negative evaluation, and it leaves the development of a solution in the hands of the child. A more common response than the above example might be to respond with a roadblock: "Please be quiet! If you don't behave, you will have to leave the circle." Such a **you-message** focuses on the child's behavior in a blaming or evaluating manner, ignores the effect of the behavior on others, and imposes a solution on the child. It denies the child the opportunity to solve the problem.

I-messages communicate that, even if you don't like a particular behavior or situation, you trust that the child is caring enough and capable of helping to solve the problem. Often the behavior will stop once the child knows that it causes a problem. When an I-message does not end the problem, you must take other steps.

Interpersonal problems inevitably occur in the course of day-to-day classroom life. In order to maintain good relationships, they must be handled. You can help children learn to negotiate differences by using problem-solving techniques to deal with problems that arise in the classroom. In this way they experience how useful such techniques are in making relationships work.

You can involve children in finding creative and mutually acceptable solutions to interpersonal problems. In this problem-solving process you begin by defining the problem and then invite the child to join you in figuring out a solution.

> **Teacher:** When you run and holler in the room, it's dangerous and it makes it hard for people to work. What shall we do about that?
> **Child:** I could run behind the block shelf—no one is playing there.
> **Teacher:** That's one solution; can you think of any more?
> **Child:** I could run outside or I could climb on the inside climber instead.

Together you think about whether the solution will work.

> **Teacher:** Do you think it would work to run behind the block shelf?
> **Child:** No, there's not enough room.
> **Teacher:** There's no teacher outside right now, so that won't work either, but I think climbing on the inside climber would work.

When the solution has been implemented, you can give children feedback on their effectiveness.

> **Teacher:** I'm so glad your idea worked. The room is a much better place for all of us to work now.

In our own experience we find young children often interested in and able to go through this simple problem-solving process. When we have consistently involved children in handling problems with us, we have found that they also start to do this quite effectively in their own problems with peers.

In addition to helping children negotiate problems, you can provide alternatives to nonproductive or disruptive behavior. This is especially important if children are unwilling to engage in problem solving because it requires that they give up behaviors they have found useful in other settings or that they have used to fulfill basic emotional needs. Children may need time, courage, and your persistent encouragement to change from old reliable behaviors to new untested ones, even when the old behaviors no longer work. The time when children are in the process of changing can be the most frustrating to a teacher. You may want some support from a colleague during this time.

You can remain sensitive to the struggles, feelings, and situations that bring children into confrontation with one another. Many children lash out when they are tired or frustrated. Regardless of the circumstances, children need to learn that while they must not act in ways that hurt people or property, it is all right to have strong feelings and to express them. When conflict threatens to cause serious harm, you must act immediately. With practice children can learn to tell each other how they feel and what they want instead of striking out when a confrontation occurs. Your communcication and modelling can help children to learn constructive ways of dealing with the problem. Simply telling a child that hitting, biting, or yelling is not acceptable, or that they should "use their words," provides no alternatives. Instead, help children to think through to the next step by saying things like:

> I won't let you hurt Sherry. You can tell her, "It makes me mad when you take my truck. Please give it back to me."

> I can see you're angry about what happened. How can you let him know?

> Let's think of some other ways to handle this problem.

Despite the good advice and good examples that you may receive in your training, you are likely to find that your first practical experiences with children involve frustrations as they test your limits as a teacher. It's important to realize that children do not test you to be malicious but to find out what they can expect from you. They need to know this in order to be secure in their classroom. Any teacher, experienced or not, will be tested by children during the first days of teaching. Experienced teachers are usually clearer about their expectations of children and communicate these from the very beginning in words, body language, and behavior. Children quickly become "well-behaved" with them in a manner which may seem like magic to the new teacher. Less experienced teachers often hesitate and send mixed messages. Children respond with behavior the teacher may dislike. When children know what to expect, teaching becomes much easier.

Our students often ask us, "What do you do if I-messages and problem solving don't work?" There is never one prescriptive answer to a management problem since there are many things which may cause a problem in the first place. Used consistently with good will, the problem-solving techniques described above usually do work. However, if you are a new teacher, it may take a while for you to learn to use them effectively. In our example with a child who is disruptive at storytime,

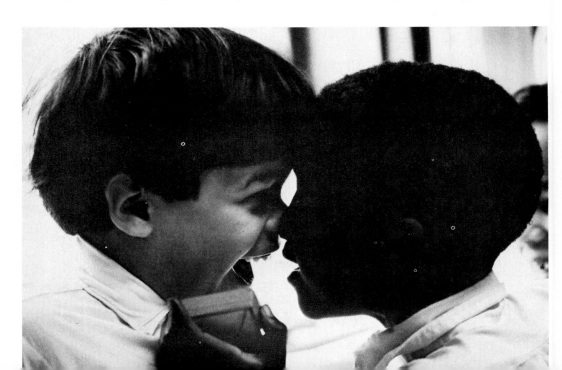

the teacher might follow this sequence of thinking and acting:

The Problem: Kyle, a four year old, talks during story.

The Teacher, Christine, thinks: *Kyle doesn't understand that his behavior is disturbing me and the other children.*

Christine gives an I-message: When you talk during the story it's hard for others to hear and I feel frustrated.

Once the child understands, this is often the end of the problem, but today Kyle continues to talk during the story.

Christine thinks: *Kyle is not clear about my expectations and his alternatives.*

Christine states: Storytime is a quiet time so we can all get to hear. If you would like to listen to the story, you may listen quietly; otherwise you may go and play with the Spider group on the playground.

Often the child chooses to modify his behavior or make the alternative acceptable choice, but again Kyle continues to talk during the story.

Christine thinks: *This is a problem; it's just too disruptive.*

Christine initiates a problem-solving process: Hey, we have a problem. Our storytime isn't working because it's too noisy. I can't go on reading. What shall we do?

This is often the beginning of a productive problem-solving process, but today Kyle refuses to engage in the problem solving and acts "silly" saying "goo-goo, boo-boo" and rolling around.

Christine thinks: *Kyle is not willing or able to be responsible right now, and it is spoiling the experience for everyone. He may need to get away; I sure know that I need him away from here!*

Christine identifies the behavior and talks to Kyle: Kyle that's just too noisy. It looks like you're choosing not to be with us. Please join the Spider group outside.

Usually a child will comply with such a request, but today Kyle refuses to leave the story area.

Christine thinks: *The rest of the group is going to start having a hard time. Kyle must really be upset at something today. I'll take Kyle out, but I'd better think of something for the other children to do or I'll lose them too.*

Christine tells Kyle and the group what she will do and what she would like them to do: I'm going to walk Kyle outside to Sarah (the Spider's teacher), and then I'll finish reading the story. See if the rest of you can sing the cow song while I'm gone. I'll sing with you.

Christine starts the group singing and sings with them while she steps outside the door and informs Sarah that Kyle will play outside for a few minutes until the group is ready to go out. She returns to the group singing the lively cow song and finishes up the story with few problems. Later on she talks with Kyle and engages him in a dialogue about the problem, reminding him that he has choices at storytime but that he may not spoil the time for others.

Sometimes one or more of the children in a classroom have problems that cause them to have frequent and severe outbursts. We have found Bruno Bettleheim's guidelines from his book *Love is Not Enough* (1950) effective for handling destructive behavior and for reassuring violent children who usually fear retaliation. Bettleheim suggests telling destructive children that you will not allow them to hurt themselves or other people, nor will you let anyone else hurt them. As children learn that their feelings will be respected, their needs met, and that others will not be allowed to hurt them, they often turn less and less to destructive behavior.

Sometimes you may have to put your words into action. A child who occasionally behaves in ways that seem out of control may need to have some time away from the group to become calm and able to return to acceptable group behavior. Providing a safe, pleasant space away from others for a child to regain composure is helpful and is often called *time out.* Time out is not an educator's way to describe the old practice of making a child stand in the corner with the dunce cap. Instead it is a small island for calm reflection that you too may wish to take advantage of on a stressful day. In many classrooms time out is administered in ways that are humiliating and ineffective in helping a child to become a responsibile member of the group. If you find yourself sending a child to time out every time you have group, you can be pretty sure that you are applying it ineffectively.

A child who is fiercely lashing out and hurting self or others must be physically restrained. This can be done gently, firmly, and with respect. Hold the child from behind in a seated embrace which firmly restrains flailing arms and legs. Although you may feel quite upset, speak calmly and let the child know that as soon as self-control has returned, you too will welcome the opportunity to release him or her. If your environment contains safe open space away from others, you might wish to take an out-of-control child to a space where the angry feelings can be worked out in vigorous physical activity that does not harm anyone. Such outbursts are usually short-lived, espe-

cially if you remind children that they are able to control and handle themselves with more control, and if you believe it.

One of the reasons that corporal punishment is never acceptable in an early childhood program is because it demonstrates that it is all right to hurt someone if you are big enough. Additionally, although children who have been physically punished may behave appropriately when there is an adult threatening them, at later times they tend to show increased aggressive behavior.

Conflict is a part of life and of all relationships both inside and outside of the classroom. Even in the most well-designed settings, children occasionally have conflicts with others. The way you deal with conflict is an important model for young children. They can experience that conflict while not pleasant, is a part of life that provides an opportunity for problem solving, rather than something that is violently disrupting and harshly controlled.

FINAL THOUGHTS

As a teacher of young children, you have a profound effect on every child you teach. No two children are alike and what you do, how you do it, and when you do it can be of great importance in their perceptions of you and of themselves. A management strategy that is appropriate and effective in helping an aggressive child to become more cooperative and thoughtful may be totally inappropriate for a shy child, even if the specific behavior is the same. It is essential that you strive to develop knowledge, skills, and sensitivity so that your efforts to guide behavior are appropriate for the individual and supportive of self-concept.

FOR FURTHER THOUGHT AND DISCUSSION

1 Recall a relationship you had with a teacher. What can you remember about the way this teacher listened to and spoke with you? What were your feelings about the teacher and the classroom? What implications does this have for you as a teacher?

2 Recall an incident in which you were punished or reprimanded in school. What happened? How did you feel? Did this have any long-term effects? What do you wish had happened? What implications does this have for you as a teacher?

3 Recall an experience at school or home that effected your self-concept. What happened? How did you feel? How did this effect how you are today? What implications does this have for you as a teacher?

4 What do you think were the major goals of the rules and management techniques you experienced in school? At home? Were they effective? Why or why not? Did they achieve their goals?

5 Think about a teacher you have recently observed and describe the kinds of communication and discipline you saw. Was it effective? What were your reactions to this style of communication? Did the guidance and discipline techniques clearly fit into one of the models described in this chapter? Were they effective? Why or why not? How do you think children felt in this classroom?

6 What other criteria might be used to evaluate a management strategy besides, . . . *It works?*

PROJECTS

1 Observe a teacher interacting with children for at least one hour. Attend to the way he or she listens and responds. Notice any roadblocks or barriers to communication. Describe what you think is being communicated. Comment on your own feelings and reactions and the possible implications for your own teaching.

2 Observe a classroom and teacher for at least one hour. Note the ways that the teacher expresses appreciation and respect for children, or fails to do so. Report what happened and the effect this seems to have had on individual children.

3 Observe a teacher handling a conflict in a classroom. Describe the conflict and the method of dealing with it. Evaluate the teacher's effectiveness. How do you think the children felt? What were your reactions and possible implications for your own teaching?

4 During a visit to a classroom try to deduce from people's behavior and the environment what the rules are. Are they developmentally appropriate; do you think children understand the reason for them? Are the teachers consistent in enforcing the rules? Report on what you discover including how you think it might feel to be a child in this classroom.

RECOMMENDED READING

Bettelheim, Bruno. *Love is Not Enough.* New York: Free Press, 1950.

Charles, C. M. *Building Classroom Discipline.* 2d ed. New York: Longman, 1985.

Dinkmeyer, Don; McKay, Gary; and Dinkmeyer, Don Jr. *Systematic Training for Effective Parenting.* Kit with leaders manual. Circle Pines, Minn.: American Guidance Service, 1980.

Dreikurs, Rudolf. *Psychology in the Classroom.* New York: Harper and Row, 1969.

Dreikurs, Rudolf, and Cassels, Pearl. *Discipline Without Tears.* New York: Hawthorn Books, 1972.

Evertson, C.; Emmer, E.; Sanford, J.; Clements, B.; and Worshaum, M. *Classroom Management for Elementary School Teachers.* Englewood Cliffs, N.J.: Prentice-Hall, 1984.

Faber, Adele, and Mazlish, Elaine. *How to Talk So Kids Will Listen & Listen So Kids Will Talk.* New York: Avon Books, 1980.

Gazda, George. *Human Relations Development.* Boston: Allyn and Bacon, 1975.

Ginott, Haim. *Teacher and Child.* New York: Macmillan, 1972.

Glasser, William. *Schools Without Failure.* New York: Harper and Row, 1961.

Gordon, Thomas. *Teacher Effectiveness Training.* New York: David McKay Co., 1974.

Krumboltz, John D., and Helen, B. *Changing Children's Behavior.* Englewood Cliffs, N.J.: Prentice-Hall, 1972.

Maslow, Abraham. *Toward a Psychology of Being.* New York: Van Nostrand Reinhold, 1968.

Patterson, Gerald D., and Gullian, Elizabeth M. *Living with Children: New Methods for Parents and Teachers.* rev. ed. Champaign, Ill.: Research Press Co., 1971.

Rogers, Carl. *Freedom to Learn.* Columbus, O.: Charles E. Merrill, 1969.

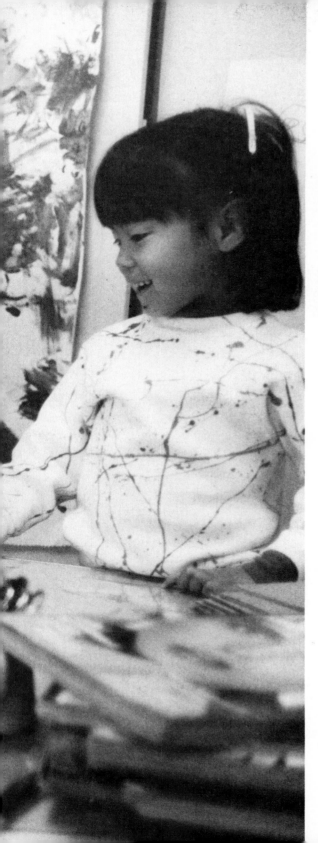

9

Curriculum Development

"Awareness of alternatives and the bases of choices distinguishes the competent teacher from the merely intuitive one."

Elizabeth Brady

In this chapter, we discuss ways to combine your knowledge of child development, curriculum content, and observation and assessment with your program's purpose and goals to plan a curriculum for children. We look at the ways that children learn in school from spontaneous play and teacher-directed activities and consider how you can use these modes of learning to design appropriate curriculum. We examine different levels of planning and frameworks for organizing curriculum that integrate experiences to enhance their meaning for children. This chapter relates to the CDA areas **Program Management** *and* **Professionalism.**

Young children are learning all the time and from all of their experiences, both in and out of school. The question that teachers need to ask themselves about children's learning is "How, when, and in what ways do I want to intervene in this natural process?" Understanding of the overall purpose and goals of your program, knowledge of child development and appropriate curriculum content, and skill in observation and assessment are vital tools for planning a good curriculum. Using them, you can thoughtfully design the kinds of experiences that children will have in your program.

Teaching in early childhood programs involves building upon children's existing interests and motivations. The teacher provides a wide range of experiences, and guides interactions to nurture curiosity and to help children develop understanding of the world and positive feelings toward learning.

WHAT'S WORTH KNOWING

What you teach makes a statement about your values and goals as well as about your knowledge of young children and understanding of curriculum. Choosing what to teach is one of your most vital tasks. As you work with children, your skills will become refined, and you will become a better teacher. Yet those skills will have little value if what you are teaching isn't worth knowing.

What is worth knowing when you are two, three, four, and five years old? This is a crucial question that you need to ask yourself. We asked ourselves this question and became increasingly concerned about the answers. We became aware of how often skills are taught as subject matter ("Our curriculum this month is shapes and colors"); how theory, intended to describe development, is used to prescribe curriculum ("We're teaching volume conservation"); how curriculum is handed down by administrators or school boards who are trying to please parents ("All our two year olds are studying the alphabet and the numbers up to 100"); and how curriculum is often dictated by a commercial product ("We use the DISTAR or PEEK program"). These sources of curriculum often replace thoughtful consideration of what is important for young children to know.

As we grappled with the question of what is valuable knowledge for young children, we came to some conclusions for ourselves. We believe it is important to know how to take care of yourself. This includes knowing how to dress yourself, how to deal with conflict, and how to find a friend when you're sad. It's worth knowing about yourself, about other people, and about other cultures and the world we live in. The better you know, appreciate, and understand our physical and social environment and yourself, the better you will be able to respect and care for our world and its people.

It seems to us that these are appropriate bases for curriculum since they are, ultimately, the learning tasks that all people take on at the moment of birth and deal with until the end of life: competence, knowledge, appreciation, and caring for ourselves, the world, and other people. What about teaching shapes, prepositions, and conservation of volume? These are isolated pieces of knowledge. They are the ways the world is classified and defined so that it can be better known and understood, but they are not valuable in isolation.

As you choose what you will teach, we urge you to look at what is worth knowing, what we all need to know to help us become more human and to help our world survive. We believe that to attempt to achieve less gives children less than they need and less than they deserve.

WAYS THAT CHILDREN LEARN

Young children learn through direct experience. They learn little of value when facts are separated from their real lives. Since the school experiences of most adults were dominated by teachers who communicated information by talking, this is often the way they try to teach children. If the word *teacher* brings

to mind a person lecturing in front of a blackboard, you may feel that you are *really teaching* only when the children sit and listen to you. Young children, however, learn in many different ways. Simply telling them facts is not an effective way to teach.

Throughout this chapter, we use **experiences** as the umbrella term to describe all forms of learning that occur in early childhood program settings, including spontaneous play. The term **activities** refers to specific planned opportunities for learning. These include teacher-led lessons and games, informal play in planned interest centers, and group activities like singing, discussion, and stories. **Lessons** refer to activities with planned teacher involvement that are written and that specify learning objectives and procedures in detail.

Good learning experiences for young children are multi-faceted. They develop more than one skill or concept. Playing with blocks, for example, not only develops children's building skill but heightens spatial awareness, gives experience with size, ratio, and weight, and provides problem-solving practice. It builds strength and coordination in the hands and fingers and encourages children to symbolize what they know. As children play together with blocks, there are social opportunities that develop cooperation and turn-taking. A skillful teacher can build on this rich play by encouraging children to think about and solve new building problems, to cooperate with one another in projects, to attempt difficult tasks, and to use language to express ideas about their work. As another example, a teacher reading a book about spiders to children, not only teaches about spiders, but also develops concentration, demonstrates that information can be found in books, and shows that reading is a useful skill.

We have found Elizabeth Jones' (1977) four categories of activities that occur in school useful in helping us think about the experiences we offer young children. **Play**, an open-ended activity without preestablished rules, procedures, or predictable outcomes, should be the dominant learning mode in the preschool class. **Games**, the point between work and play, have a beginning and end and preset rules and procedures. They challenge children's skill and retain the joyful and free qualities of play. Older preschool children enjoy and benefit from games, and they are usually used informally by children on their own, one-to-one by a teacher and child, or in planned small groups. **Work** is a product-oriented activity that is experienced by children as personally important and significant. Teacher-led lessons, usually in small groups, are often examples of children's work. **Labor**, is different from work since it lacks a sense of joy, optimism, and self-challenge. While labor may yield useful results, the learning lacks personal relevance—because of this, reward or punishment is often required to keep children at their labor. The fatal flaw of many large group activities, especially paper and pencil tasks conducted in large groups without regard for the individuals, is that developmental inappropriateness makes these activities labor for many children. When schoolwork is unpleasant labor, children soon come to dislike school and learning. Children's behavior will very quickly tell you whether the tasks you have set have provided work or labor.

Learning Through Play

Play is such a significant mode of learning that it is considered the real work of young children. In the same way that early childhood teachers are not *just babysitting*, so young children are not *just playing*. Play is the most important way children have for clarifying and integrating all their experiences. It is an enjoyable activity performed for its own sake, and any final product is secondary. Play often involves fantasy. Children at play are highly motivated and focused. In our college classes, we like to combine the words play and work into the term **plerk**, to describe the intense concentration of young children's play-learning.

In play, children explore and learn about their world. It is a rich and varied activity through which many kinds of learning occur simultaneously. A child involved in dramatic play, for example, is developing physical and social skill, expressing ideas, learning concepts, and being creative, all without a teacher's intervention.

The essence of play is that it grows from within the child or group of children who are playing. It is a creative expression of their thoughts and feelings based on their own life experiences. Jerome Bruner writes,

> . . . in play, process is more important than the product. There is a lessening or elimination of the risk of failure. There is a temporary moratorium on frustration, and play is an invitation to the possibilities inherent in things and events. (1976, p. 244)

Awareness of the importance of children's play is critical to your role as a teacher in an early childhood program. Understanding and supporting children's play is an essential part of your work. While play is natural and occurs independent of adults, you have important contributions to make. You support and enhance play when you provide materials such as sand, water, blocks, paint, and dramatic play props and allow children to use them in an environment designed for play. A rich background of real experience is the foundation for play, and so you provide experiences with the world through trips, visitors, and hands-on activities like cooking.

Time is also of great importance. With adequate time, play and learning is rich and elaborate. Without sufficient time, play may fail to develop and evolve into experiences from which children learn. Instead, it becomes superficial and primarily expends pent-up energy. We have seen classrooms where children were allowed only ten or fifteen minutes for play; the children rushed to the shelves and quickly pulled toy after toy down attempting to do as much as possible without the care and focus that is necessary for play-learning.

Through careful observation of children's play, you can sensitively guide their interactions when it seems necessary or desirable. You may occasionally wish to extend children's understanding one step further by asking a question (when a child hands you a pretend muffin in the dramatic play corner you might say, "Did you make this yourself? How did you make it?"). But you must be careful to do so without imposing your adult purposes ("What color is the muffin? What shape is it?"). Another appropriate response is for you to assist in the elaboration of the play by adding props (in this case a jam jar, butter knife, or baking equipment).

Learning Through Interactions with Teachers

Children also learn through activities planned by teachers. We use three categories to organize our thinking about planned learning activities. These differ in the degree of direct teacher involvement and in the number of children who are involved at any one time.

One-to-One Experiences In one-to-one interactions with children, you concentrate on the child's learning process and feelings and participate in a learning dialogue. These special teacher-child experiences allow you to observe carefully and modify what you do based on the child's response. They are the most effective way to assess children's knowledge and skills.

When you are teaching a specific concept or skill, you may find it useful to formally plan an activity to present to one child at a time or to a child who has a specific need. You accommodate one-to-one interactions by allowing time for the other children to play independently while you work with one child. We find that in order to adequately focus on a one-to-one interaction, we usually need to be working with a team member or volunteer who

supervises and interacts with the rest of the class. Freedom to work with a single child and to work with children in small groups is created as you schedule time for independent play.

While planned one-to-one experiences provide an excellent teaching medium, spontaneous, informal one-to-one interactions are also very valuable. They emerge from the day-to-day interests and needs of children. As you talk with a child about play materials, read a story, or share your wonder at a snowfall or cricket, you are having some of the loveliest and most meaningful learning experiences. Although you cannot plan for them, you can be responsive to these opportunities by being attuned to children and your environment.

Small Group Experiences Activities involving eight or fewer children and a teacher provide an effective teaching mode. In small groups, you can present activities, teach concepts, and facilitate interactions between children. The group is small enough for you to have meaningful personal contact with each child and is especially appropriate for an exchange of ideas between children. Turn-taking and activities requiring teacher assistance become appropriate since the wait is not unbearably long for a young child. You are able to attend to the way children respond in a small group and can be flexible enough to evaluate and modify your teaching right away.

Small groups of children who meet together regularly develop some very important skills that they cannot acquire in a large group. These include the ability to listen and talk in a group, to solve problems and make decisions democratically, to take leader and follower roles, and to accept responsibility for the outcomes of their decisions. Small groups develop an identity of their own. In our classes, we have had groups name themselves to further cement the feelings of belonging and responsibility.

Like all other experiences you provide, small group activities need to be planned with some learning objective in mind. Often it is sufficient to prepare by thinking through the objectives and the sequence of activities which you will follow. At other times you will want to plan in greater detail using a lesson plan to guide you.

Large Group Experiences   Activities involving all or most of the children in one class allow them to share a common experience and hear the same information. Large groups are economical in terms of your time and energy but are not the most effective way to teach young children most things. The most appropriate and successful large groups happen when children are actively involved, doing the same thing (singing songs, for example), or when they observe a presentation that captures their interest such as hearing a story or seeing a puppet show.

Since young children vary in interest level as well as attention span, the length of a scheduled group session should depend on their activity level, mood, and developmental stage, as well as your personal style, skill, and educational objectives. Large group experiences work best when they have a wide appeal and are relatively short (ten to fifteen minutes for younger preschoolers). Young children may have a very difficult time concentrating in a large group because there are many people to distract them. As children grow older, their interest in and ability to participate meaningfully and for longer amounts of time increases (interesting,

participatory activities can hold the attention of older preschoolers for up to half an hour). Large groups are not an appropriate medium when you want to attend to individual needs and responses. When you want children to explore and discover or participate in activities, like cooking or sharing, you will choose a different approach.

In planning large group activities it is important to remember that children need to wiggle and move. Often this can be built in. Storytime can be broken up with exercises or fingerplays that let children stand and stretch. Movement songs can be a part of more sedentary music activities. Carefully thinking through the purpose and sequence of activities helps to ensure greater success. If you are a beginning teacher, it is essential to plan large group sessions in depth. Outlines of the major activities supported by a plan for introductions, transitions, and closure will help you have successful large group times. If you reach the end of the activity before you reach the limits of children's interests, be willing to say, "That's all for now; we'll do this again another time."

When you are leading a large group, you are the center of the learning experience. You act as a leader and an entertainer, and the children respond to your direction. Your sensitivity to the mood and energy of the group and your ability to respond to them will determine the quality of the experience. Like a performer, you must keep your audience interested, involved, and cooperative. A large group often fails if it requires too much waiting or if children lack interest in the activity. Despite careful planning, it is not always possible to hold the attention of a large group. We have

found it more effective to allow nonparticipating children to observe or choose a quiet activity than to expend our energy and waste the other children's time trying to gain their cooperation. Managing large groups is one of the skills that beginning teachers find most difficult to master. It is a different and taxing teaching role. Learning to read and respond to a group takes time, experience, and self-confidence. If you are not immediately successful, be reassured that you are not alone, and this is not the most important of your teaching tasks.

Selecting Types of Learning Experiences

Every type of learning experience has advantages and disadvantages and can be appropriate for some kinds of teaching, in some situations, with some children. Cooking, for example, works best as a carefully planned and structured small group activity and may invite chaos and frustration when attempted in a large

group. As you plan, your first job is to identify learning objectives and then select and plan the type of activities that best accomplish those objectives. Some subjects seem best suited to one or another type of activity. Table 9.1 is designed to help you choose the best ways to present the content of early childhood curriculum areas. It is quite possible to turn almost anything into pleasurable play or work and by the same token turn almost anything into hard labor. By selecting the most appropriate ways and by retaining a playful, good-humored attitude you will be able to retain the joy which characterizes good play, good work, and good learning.

CURRICULUM PLANNING

Planning in an early childhood program may take many forms. Teachers plan each day's activities, develop weekly plans to provide continuity from day to day, and plan in very general ways to provide

TABLE 9.1
Choosing learning activities.

	INQUIRY AREAS: Math, Science, Social Studies	CREATIVE AREAS: Art, Music, Movement	COMMUNICATION AREAS: Language, Literature	SENSORIMOTOR AREAS: Physical, Sensory, Nutrition
Play in a Planned Environment	The environment: interest centers (math, science, dramatic play, blocks), equipment for exploration, outdoor environment Books Pets and Plants Artifacts	The environment: interest centers (art and music), space for movement, art and music in the environment (records, spontaneous singing, children's and adults work displayed)	The environment: space to interact, writing and library centers Materials to generate conversation Games	The environment: equipment and materials for large and small motor, sensory development Self-help activities (tooth brushing, buttoning)
One to One	Planned and spontaneous interactions Guided exploration Guided research	Instruction in technique Teacher-child interaction	Conversation Shared reading Key words Child-authored books Language experience charts	Teacher-child interaction Guided instruction Discussion of experience
Small Group	Experiments Record-keeping (e.g. tracking the growth of a mouse) Discussion Games Guided observation and exploration Trips Books, both child and adult authored	Instruction in technique Group projects Guided exploration of material or technique Trips to experience creative work of others	Discussions Games Trips Storytelling Puppets	Active games Group exploration Trips Cooking activities
Large Group	Demonstrations Games Trips Resource people	Group singing Resource people Trips Productions for children	Stories Games Trips Resource people Drama productions for children	Games Directed movement and exercise Trips Resource people

a direction for the entire school year. Planning is essential in a smoothly functioning program, but teachers choose how much they will plan, in what detail, and how far in advance.

With an awareness of the established purposes and underlying assumptions of your program, you begin to plan curriculum. Careful attention to program goals and objectives and your knowledge and understanding of children will guide you.

Decisions Underlying Curriculum

Whether you teach in a program that has existed for a long time or in one that is just beginning, there are things you must understand before you can plan curriculum. You need to know the **purpose** of the program and the **assumptions** about the nature of learners and learning that underlie its structure.

A statement of purpose (often found in the bylaws of the program) explains the reason for the program's existence and implies the values or assumptions under which it operates. When a program has a well-thought-out written purpose, it can guide practice. It helps you make teaching decisions and serves as a basis for evaluating what you do. Many choices that you will make concerning the environment, management strategies, and the design and presentation of curriculum can grow out of your thoughtful consideration of the mission and beliefs that underlie the program.

Program purpose statements are often fairly brief and general. One program with which we've worked states its purpose as: "to support the development of resourceful and interdependent children and families

through the provision of educational and child care services within a caring community."

A program's underlying assumptions or beliefs about the learning and development process and the nature of learners should be acceptable to you. Few programs will have a written statement of their assumptions. You can, however, discover them through observation of activities, the environment, schedule, and the interactions that teachers have with children. If your beliefs strongly differ from the program assumptions, you will have difficulty. For example, if you assume that children are intrinsically motivated to learn and that the role of the teacher is to be a resource person, you may be uncomfortable in a program that is based on a system of structured rewards for task accomplishment.

Every program has overall goals (the end result towards which staff and board effort is directed) and objectives (what is done to accomplish the goals). These should be based on the program's purpose and underlying assumptions. Written goals and objectives provide valuable information. Like the statement of purpose they guide you in deciding what you should be doing and provide a way to evaluate your success. They are much more specific and so give you clearer criterion for evaluation. For example, if program goals included providing parent education and developing family social networks, and you offered only good classroom experience for children it would be obvious that some goals were not being met. The following is a program goal and supporting objectives that might be found in a program with the purpose stated earlier:

Program Goal:

To prevent physical, intellectual, social, and emotional deficits and to support the optimal development of preschool age children.

Program Objectives:

To identify and prevent health disabilities in children by providing dental, medical, and nutritional screening and treatment plans for each child within sixty days of enrollment.

To provide children with carefully designed classroom and learning experiences that support the development of physical, intellectual, social, and emotional competence.

In some programs, goals and objectives will exist in writing, but in others this will not be the case. If written goals do not exist, you and other staff may find it useful to give yourselves the task of writing goals to guide your planning. Creating purpose, goals, and objectives can be both useful and exhilarating. They are of little value, however, if they fail to take into account what is known about the development of children and the needs of families.

Creating a Curriculum Framework

What you teach *(content)* and how you teach it *(methods)* must support the purpose, goals and objectives of your program and relate directly to your assumptions about learning and learners. Your values, observations of children, and the values and concerns of your community, the school administration, and families influence the kind of curriculum you plan. Parent and community concerns often reflect educational trends that vary with time and locale. At this time, for example, concern with the development of basic academic skills is prevalent. At

another time, trends may be very different. Regardless of current demand, it is important that you create curriculum based on what is known about children's learning.

Children's development and integrated themes are two different but complementary approaches that can guide you in the development of a curriculum framework. When used appropriately, they provide a good basis for long-term, as well as weekly and daily plans.

Development as Framework Curriculum can consist of activities that support physical, social, emotional, and intellectual development. The relationship between developmental goals for children and the various types of curriculum content is portrayed in Figure 9.1. While each subject contributes to total child development, each can be seen as particularly emphasizing one area of development. Curriculum areas need not be seen as distinct subject matter but as natural parts of the life of the child.

When you focus on children's development and integrated themes you look at curriculum as a way to enhance what children do—communicate, think, move, perceive, and create—rather than as subject matter unrelated to the tasks of development. Curriculum content areas are separated for the purposes of helping you understand their role in development and for presenting a balanced variety of learning experiences. The danger inherent in this division is that you might forget that these divisions are arbitrary and are not separate in the child's life or perception.

With development as the framework, you can plan daily and weekly activities

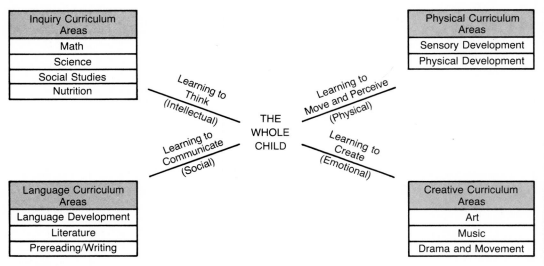

FIGURE 9.1
Curriculum and developmental goals.

that specifically meet children's needs in different areas. As a curriculum framework, it is particularly useful when you plan activities based on the observation and assessment of individual children. The framework then enables you to evaluate the environment and the activities available in terms of each child's particular needs.

A team of teachers we observed used this framework to structure their planning to help children with similar needs accomplish developmental tasks. Classroom observation was used as the basis for planning teacher-guided activities to meet individual needs. Three or four children who were observed to be behind the norm in fine motor skills were asked to the manipulative table where a teacher would present a new activity designed to develop their skill. Others, who seldom chose creative activities, were invited to begin at the easels. This strategy gave

some children a gentle nudge into activities they otherwise seldom selected. This same staff regularly brainstormed ideas to create activities that met similar developmental needs in a variety of different ways. They used observations of the groups of children and their interests and social relationships to design activities that would entice children and balance and expand their skills and learning. In order to attract new children to the hollow block area, for example, dramatic play props, books, labelled objects, and musical instruments were added.

Themes as Framework Themes (sometimes called *units*) can also be used to organize and integrate teaching. A particular idea or field of study becomes the hub around which appropriate activities are planned. Curriculum content areas all relate back to the central idea. Integrated themes have helped us to think in new and creative ways and have taken us on learning adventures with children.

Any theme must be developmentally appropriate. Young children must be able to understand the underlying concepts, and the required skills must be within their grasp. It is important that a theme help children to gain meaning from their life experience, that the central concepts are *worth knowing*. A unit on pumpkins, which can be seen and experienced and which play a significant role in a common childhood celebration, might be appropriate. A unit on Christopher Columbus would not since it could not be meaningfully experienced and is not relevant to a young child's life. Meaningful themes help children make connections. They reflect life and are not separate from it.

Children's lives—their families, cultures, community, or environment—make good organizing themes because they can integrate many curriculum areas. Every ethnic and cultural group, for example, uses special language, words, or phrases, has literature, folklore, arts, songs,

foods, dances, ways of dress, and special ways of taking care of people's needs. Cultural artifacts (household objects, toys, tools, clothes, arts, and so on) provide materials for exploration. Children's families can share knowledge of their heritage. The theme contributes to children's awareness and understanding of the world and themselves. It heightens their sense of uniqueness and builds pride and a sense of community. Through activities designed to support these larger goals, children are also developing other skills such as fine motor coordination and the ability to discriminate by size, shape, and color.

Themes can also evolve from carefully planned trips. For example, if children take a trip to the tide pools, you might begin by discussing what may happen or by sharing a relevant story or film. On the trip, you would pay careful attention to the children's interests and their questions. When you return to class, you would spend several days or weeks on follow-up activities. These might include drawing

pictures and dictating stories about the trip, classifying and counting shells or seaweed, reading books about shore life, dissecting a fish, cooking with fish and seaweed, building a plaster of paris tide pool, or doing creative movement about the sea.

Integrating themes can arise from children's interests. Teachers we know used food, a highly motivating subject, as a theme. Trips were taken to a dairy, a commercial fishing boat, a farmer's market, a chicken farm, and the supermarket. The children planted a garden, painted and drew pictures about their experiences, and dictated stories to accompany the pictures. The library was filled with food-related books like *Stone Soup* and *The Carrot Seed*. Many of the children shared fruit grown in their yards and joined in preparing a school snack of fruit salad. As a culminating experience, they planned, shopped for, cooked, and shared a huge pot of stew. The children

learned many things about where the foods they ate came from. They had many social and language experiences and learned how foods would help their bodies to grow.

Holidays are frequently used as the basis for curriculum. Some such as Christmas, New Year's, Thanksgiving, and Passover have an impact on children's lives and are used as appropriate themes for school activities. These holidays can be dealt with in terms of their deep, personal meaning. Instead, they are often made trivial and inappropriate, and look-alike crafts dominate the planning. Some holidays that are celebrated with children can be used to integrate worthwhile content. Halloween, for example, can introduce a focus on coping with fears or on distinguishing between fantasy and reality. Other holidays have so little appropriate content for young children that they can't be used to create meaningful learning activities. Presidents'

216

Day, for example, is difficult for children to understand and usually has no real impact on their lives. Although holidays are times of excitement, they are not necessarily appropriate curriculum content for children. Your desire to celebrate holidays may stem from the welcome relief they brought to the hard, colorless institutions of your elementary school days. In a beautiful and ever-changing classroom designed for young children, such relief may be unnecessary.

Theme possibilities are rich and varied. Well used, they help children to understand that learning is connected to life. They make planning easier and more fun. When themes are not appropriate or meaningful, or if purpose is lost in a flurry of activity, a theme may distract from real learning. Themes can give the surface appearance of connecting ideas but not really enhance children's understanding of the world. We observed a group of three year olds "studying" the letter *M* by making *m*agazine collages and

*m*uffins and by coloring a large picture of a *m*onkey. When we asked the children what they had been doing, they responded that they had been cooking, gluing pictures, and coloring. Their teacher quickly corrected them saying that they had been studying *M*. This approach failed to integrate children's learning because the central concept was not relevant to this lively group of three year olds.

The Planning Process

Regardless of your guiding framework, it is important to be aware of your starting point for planning. We have found it useful to think of the planning process as having three possible beginnings. You can base your planning on previously identified learning objectives, on your observation and assessment of children's developmental needs, or on an activity that seems appropriate and relevant to the children you teach. These are diagrammed in Figure 9.2. Each is an integral part of

FIGURE 9.2
The planning process.

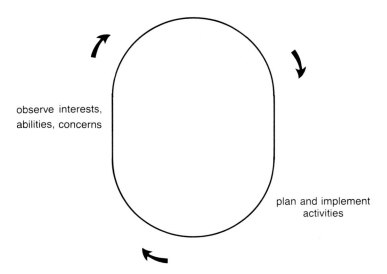

formulate learning objectives

observe interests, abilities, concerns

plan and implement activities

the planning process and relates to the others, and all must ultimately be considered in the development and final evaluation of your plans.

To begin with the observation and assessment of an individual child or group of children, you can make observations of children's skills and knowledge or use a commercial assessment instrument. After observing and assessing children, you formulate learning objectives and design activities to achieve them.

Planning may also begin with learning objectives, either developed by the staff or administration of your school or selected from an early childhood curriculum. You can then design activities that will achieve those goals or use the suggested activities from the published curriculum. Through observation and assessment, you determine if the objectives have been achieved and when it is time to move on.

Finally, planning may begin with the interests and concerns of the children (what we call an *emerging curriculum*). Children may be interested and concerned about such things as the birth of a baby in a child or teacher's family or a shared experience like a trip or play. You observe children's reactions to these events, formulate new objectives, and plan experiences that extend the learning. This process is useful whether you are planning for the year, semester, a month, week, or day.

Writing and Using Plans

Written plans organize and guide teaching. Almost all teachers write some kind of plans, but there is enormous variation in the amount and detail. It is important to know the purpose for every activity you

provide for children, but it is not necessary to write a plan every time you do something. Most teachers write flexible plans, roughly outlining the forthcoming week or two of activities. Less frequently they write detailed plans for specific activities. Such detailed plans are useful where clarity and sequence are crucial (a creative movement activity, for example) or where procedure or content is complex or unfamiliar (for instance, teaching about another culture).

Writing Long-Range Plans   Long-term plans are useful for preplanning, for making decisions about ordering materials, and for providing direction for short-term plans. They can give parents information about your curriculum and provide them with advance notice so that they can participate in classroom events. Having the year or semester planned in advance may also give you a feeling of confidence.

There are also hazards in long-range planning. Made without knowledge of the specific needs and interests of children, plans may be inappropriate and even meaningless. It is best if your long-range plans are very general and tentative. If you then find out that your advance planning was inappropriate or if you discover unanticipated resources, you can change your plans with little regret. However well-organized you are, it is foolish to go on with plans that do not meet children's needs. We once planned a unit on "feelings" for a group of young three year olds and met with little success until we brought up the subject of parents. It quickly became clear that "family" and not "feelings" was the relevant curriculum for this group and we changed our plans accordingly.

Writing Weekly Plans   As a teacher of young children, you will almost certainly create weekly written plans that sketch out the major activities of each program day. The schedule and fixed activities during the day and week impose a structure around which you may plan. Weekly planning may revolve around regularly occurring activities such as storytime, music, group meeting, cooking, or outdoor time. Sometimes teachers plan for classroom areas that are used each day such as art, science, and dramatic play.

Writing weekly plans begins with a consideration of your purpose. Write down your objectives, and list the skills and concepts which you hope children will develop through the week's activities. If you are using a theme for planning, you will consider activities that develop skills and concepts that also relate to your theme, or you may choose a theme that relates to those skills and concepts. You will then tentatively organize the activities into your schedule using a planning format such as the ones in Figures 9.3 or 9.4. After you have looked at this week's plan and decided whether or not it is practical and appropriate as scheduled, you will commit your plans to paper in a final form that you can use and share with others (see Figure 9.5).

Writing Lesson Plans   As you begin to teach, you will find it tremendously valuable and reassuring to think through and write down the steps in presenting activities to children. These plans (sometimes referred to as **lesson plans**) are more than mere exercises. They are guidelines for thinking and acting and are useful tools for focusing your actions

and assessing the extent to which your objectives have been achieved. When your planning is good, you will feel more comfortable and will express yourself clearly to children. As you gain experience, you will be able to plan many activities with only minimal writing, keeping the organization in your head. Learning first to write clear activity plans helps you to be a more effective teacher.

Having a lesson plan format will help you to develop your plan. The lesson plan outline we use for ourselves and our students follows (see pages 223–224). You begin by deciding on your purpose; then you choose an activity that will achieve your purpose. You go on to write specific objectives for the activity, decide what materials you will need, and finally, what you will do and say and in what order. See pages 225–226 for an example.

In order for a plan to be useful, you need to know what to do before and during the activity. A written plan should include a list of materials and a description of the space needed. Think about whether the children are likely to understand the words and concepts that you will be using in the activity. The major steps in the plan should be simply described without so much detail that you get bogged down trying to follow it, but with enough information that you will be able to use it again a year later. We find it useful to plan both the introduction to the activity and its closure. Without adequate introduction, a good activity may never get off the ground. Without smooth transitions and a closure, the objectives may get lost in a trample of children.

Writing Objectives for Lesson Plans
Objectives are an important part of all

Activities	Monday	Tuesday	Wednesday	Thursday	Friday
Large Group 8:30–8:45	This week's songs:				
Small group 8:45–9:00					
Art, Cooking, Interest Centers 9:00–10:15					
Outside Play 10:15–11:15					

Activities available in interest centers all week	Blocks	Home Area	Library	Writing Center	Games
	Manipulative Toys	Science	Math	Sensory-Perceptual	Special Display

* Times are flexible based on children's interests, the weather, and unforseen circumstances!

FIGURE 9.3
Form for weekly planning.

lesson plans. They are statements of the desired outcomes of an activity or group of activities that help you to focus on what you really want children to learn. Written objectives serve as a gauge against which you assess whether you have been successful in your teaching.

Objectives can be written for each of the developmental areas: social,

emotional, physical, and intellectual. You can describe the **concepts, skills, awareness,** and **attitudes** which you want children to gain in each of these areas. Realistic objectives that are written for a single activity are few in number and limited in scope. Larger goals (such as learning to cooperate) are achieved over time as children achieve the more limited

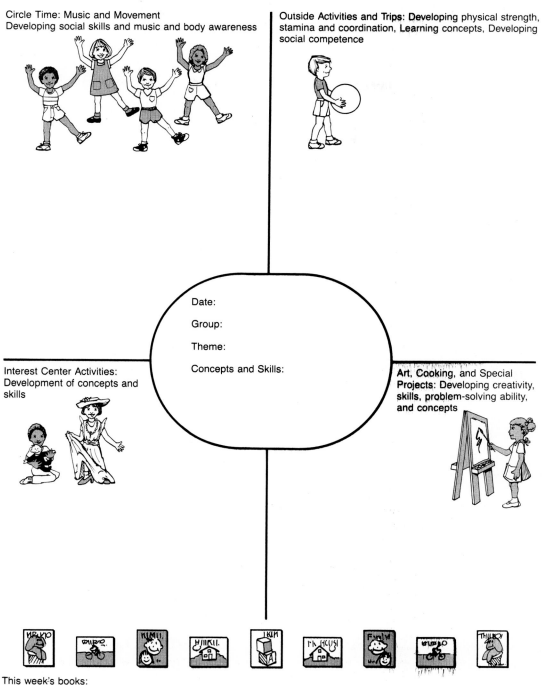

Circle Time: Music and Movement
Developing social skills and music and body awareness

Outside Activities and Trips: Developing physical strength, stamina and coordination, Learning concepts, Developing social competence

Date:

Group:

Theme:

Concepts and Skills:

Interest Center Activities: Development of concepts and skills

Art, Cooking, and Special Projects: Developing creativity, skills, problem-solving ability, and concepts

This week's books:

FIGURE 9.4
Flow chart for weekly planning.

Circle Time: Music and Movement
Developing social skills and music and body awareness

Songs and Music Activities:

You Are the One Your Mommy Loves
Name rhythms--clapping family names
My family fingerplays
Records: My Mommy is a Doctor

Movement Activities:

Daddy walks and baby walks
Family jobs and pet movement

Special!!!
Zach's mom and dad will
come and sing with us
on Tuesday at 9:00

Outside Activities and Trips: Developing physical strength, stamina and coordination, Learning concepts, Developing social competence

Balls--everyone is
invited to bring their
ball to school

Stroller--we will
push one another in
John's big stroller

Water Table--Washing dolls
and doll clothes

Friday we will walk to Spencer Street
to see Maria's, Stephen's, and Chanel's
houses

Weeding the class garden and
picking carrots

Date: *Nov. 5-10*

Group: *Rainbows*

Theme: *I am a member of a*
         Family

Concepts and Skills:

*a family is the people who
love you and take care of you and
who you love and take care of
*identifying family roles

Interest Center Activities:
Development of concepts and
skills

Home Area   *Family dress-up clothes and dolls*

Block Area   *Doll house and doll house family*

Science Area *Marcia's mouse family will visit*

Manipulative Area *New lego people*

Games Area   *Mothers/Fathers work job*

Writing Center *Family names to copy*

Art, Cooking, and Special
Projects: Developing creativity,
skills, problem-solving ability,
and concepts

Art:
Easel painting
Magazine collage with people
* and family picture*
Fresh dough--recipe goes home for kids to
* make with their families*
Painting using people cookie cutters

Cooking:
Sandwiches with different spreads--peanut
butter, cream cheese, tuna, egg salad
--what's your family's favorite?

This week's books:

Leo the Late Bloomer, Emily and the Klunky Baby and the Next-Door Dog,
All Kinds of Families, Talking without Words, Corduroy, Good Night Moon,
The Runaway Bunny, Blueberries for Sal, Tell Me a Mitzi

FIGURE 9.5
Flow chart example.

222

objectives of many activities (e.g., cooperating with others to complete a group mural). We ask our students to phrase their objectives as "At the end of or during this activity the children will . . ." to help them to keep in mind the limitations of a single activity. This has helped them to focus on achievable teaching tasks and to avoid vague and overambitious objectives such as *to develop a positive self-concept*.

Behavioral objectives precisely specify what children are to do in order to achieve success in a lesson. These objectives are useful when you are teaching skills or concepts that have a visible or measurable outcome. The behavior that indicates successful learning is called the *terminal* behavior, an observable action such as cutting along a straight line. In a behavioral objective the conditions under which the terminal behavior takes place are described and the criteria for success are specified (When the child is presented with five sheets of 8½" by 11" paper with lines drawn down the center and a pair of blunt-ended scissors and is asked to, "Cut the paper along the line," within two minutes the child will cut at least one sheet of paper along the line with less than a quarter inch deviation). While it is valuable to know how, writing behavioral objectives is very time consuming. Most teachers of young children rarely write them. Teachers may use the skill if they work with children with special needs for whom the teaching/learning process must be broken down into small increments.

Since inner states cannot be observed, objectives can be written in terms of the experiences and opportunities that might develop them. For example, when you want to foster the appreciation of poetry, your objective might read: "During

this activity children will have pleasurable experiences that foster poetry appreciation: hearing poetry read with enthusiasm, having the opportunity to reflect on poetic words, and a chance to share their response to a poem." This kind of objective is descriptive of a process that you can observe and evaluate. If you focus on behavior that may be only tangentially related to your goal, it trivializes the intent of your activity, such as sitting quietly while a poem is read and responding to the question, "What do you like about the rain?" with a complete sentence.

Using Written Plans   Your plans will provide you with useful guidelines to follow, but you should not be rigidly tied to them. If children are interested in different things or if you sense that the plan is not going as you had anticipated, redirecting or changing often helps. As you gain confidence and experience, you will find yourself able to adapt more easily to children's needs and interests. When you first begin to use written plans, you may want to follow them very closely. It is a good idea to know the plan thoroughly so that you can concentrate on the way children are responding. The plan itself should be easy to use, store, and retrieve. We like to write lesson plans on 5" x 8" cards and keep weekly plans on single sheets of 8½" x 11" paper.

Evaluating Plans

The last step in using a written plan is evaluating it. Evaluation does not mean simply labelling a plan a success or failure. It is more important to consider the degree to which the specific learning objectives were met and the overall program goals accomplished. You will

LESSON PLAN OUTLINE   Date_____

I. **Activity Information:**
    Name of activity and brief description
    Curriculum area(s)
    The children: group or individual's name, number of children,
    ages

II. **Assessment/Rationale:** Why you planned the activity
    Why did you choose to do this activity, with these children,
    at this time; what have you observed or learned that made
    you think this might be important?

III. **Objectives:** Concepts, skills, awareness, or attitudes you
    have designed the activity to teach or develop

    At the end of or during this activity the children will:

IV. **Space and Materials Needed:** Exactly what materials and
    space will be needed

V. **Procedure:** A step-by-step description of the activity
    Introduction What you will say or do to get children's interest
    and to let them know what they will be doing
    Teaching Sequence including questions to be sure to ask
    Closure How you will bring the activity to an end and help
    children to make a smooth transition to the next activity

VI. **Evaluation/Follow-up:** What was the children's response?
    What worked well? What didn't work? What might have
    made the activity more successful? Did you notice any
    potential for follow-up activities based on what children said
    or did?

LESSON PLAN EXAMPLE   Date <u>November, 1986</u>

I. **Activity Information:**
   A. *The Family Graph*
   B. A *math* and *social studies* activity to compare the number of members in a family using a bar graph
   C. For a small group of 8 four year olds

II. **Assessment/Rationale:**
   We have been talking about families. Children were confused when I said that I had a little family because they know that I have no "little" children. I think they will understand this concept better if they see it graphically represented.

III. **Objectives:**
   At the end of this activity the children will:
   A. Have worked together in a group and listened to each other.
   B. Have had an experience that contributes to positive self-concept and family pride.
   C. Be able to point to big families on a graph and small families, when requested to do so (quantity).
   D. Have experienced using a bar graph to compare quantities (comparison).
   E. Have developed greater understanding of differences between families and vocabulary to describe these.

IV. **Space and Materials Needed:**
   A. Space: A carpeted area large enough for the children to sit comfortably and a bulletin board to post the graph, near a table for drawing.
   B. Materials: 1 sheet butcher paper approximately 30" divided into 2½" squares, children's names written beneath columns, squares drawn to portray me and my family members, lots of 2½" square pieces of paper (50 or so), 7–8 paste pots with applicators, 2 sets narrow tip felt markers, yardstick.

V. **Procedure:**
   A. *Introduction*: "I drew pictures of my family to show what a little family I have. Here are the people in my family (discuss each). My picture takes up one square (paste on

graph); each of the other people in my family takes up one square too. We are a little family. I wonder how many squares your family will make and if you live in a little family or a big family."

    B. *Teaching Sequence*: Pass out squares and have children draw a picture of each family member (discuss with them). As they finish, write the child's name on each square and show them how to glue the picture in the column with their name on it. When all of the pictures are glued on, have the children find the columns that are biggest, littlest, the same (use yardstick). Have children tell who is in their family.

VI. **Evaluation/Follow-up:**

    A. The activity went very well; the children seemed to enjoy it and understand the concepts better.

    B. Next time have them discuss family members before they start drawing in order to focus.

    C. Make a separate graph or color code the squares for pets next time; Lani had 8 dogs!

---

want to consider what contributed to the plan's success or failure. Seeming disasters in planning are often simply the result of mistakes in timing, room arrangement, or activity sequencing—too many exciting activities planned for at once, too few activities planned for the number and developmental range of children, or insufficient opportunities for physical activity or rest when they were needed. Tried again with an appropriate modification the other elements of the plan may prove sound.

Keep your plans in an organized and retrievable form where you can jot down your thoughts concerning what worked and what didn't work and why. Include your ideas for next time while your memory of this time is still fresh. You will be glad to have them and will be able to make use of them in the future. We have our students make files of activities they've tried with children that include evaluation notes. They grumble that the assignment is time consuming but often thank us later when they find their work has provided them with a valuable resource.

In evaluating your planning, there is no better guide than sensitively observing the children you teach. You will develop the ability to judge what themes and activities meet their needs. No book or curriculum guide can tell you as much.

FOR FURTHER THOUGHT AND DISCUSSION

1 What were you curious about as a young child? What did you want to know? How did you go about finding out? How did school contribute to this?

2 What was your favorite kind of play as a young child? How might it have contributed to your development?

3 What are your feelings about the role of play in the lives of children and in your own life?

4 Think about the play, games, work, and labor in your early school experiences. What made it play? What made it labor? How did this affect your feelings about school?

5 Recall your earliest school experience and share your memories about the kinds of learning experiences your teachers provided and any evidence that you saw of the planning process.

6 How were the learning experiences planned and organized in the early childhood programs you have visited? What do you believe the goals and objectives might have been? Did the experiences seem successful? Discuss your reactions.

7 What do you believe were the goals in a program which you have observed? How did they effect the planning?

8 Recall an activity that you planned and implemented with children. How did the planning contribute to the experience that you and the children had? Compare this to an experience that was not planned.

9 To what extent has the planning that you have observed been related to the needs and interests of children? To what extent has it been related to predetermined objectives? What seem to be the advantages and disadvantages of each?

PROJECTS

1 Observe children at play in an early childhood program. Describe the way they interacted with materials and each other, the kinds of feelings they seemed to be having, the role of the teacher, and what they might have been learning. What did you learn about children and play?

2   Write an imaginary dialogue between a preschool teacher and a parent who is upset because children play at school all day, instead of learning something useful.

3   Observe a teacher-directed learning activity. What do you think the goals and objectives of the activity might be? How does the activity contribute to the accomplishment of the goals? Do you believe the activity was successful in accomplishing its purpose?

4   Interview a teacher about his or her program goals. Ask about how these are modified or influenced by the community, the interests of children, the concerns of parents, the school administration, and educational trends. How does this effect the experience of children?

5   Using the *Lesson Plan Outline* provided in this chapter, plan a lesson for children in any subject area you choose. Implement the plan with children and evaluate your success in achieving your objectives. To what extent could you keep to your plan? How and why did you modify it? What might you do differently next time?

6   Choose a social studies area as described in chapter 13. Use it as an integrating theme for a week's plan for a class of preschoolers. Decide on appropriate concepts and relate activities to the theme and concepts. Plan for daily large group and small group activities, relevant materials for interest centers, outside play, and integration of other subject areas. Try some of the activities with a class of children and report on what happened.

RECOMMENDED READING

Brown, Janet F., ed. *Curriculum Planning for Young Children*. Washington, D.C.: National Association for the Education of Young Children, 1982.

Dittmann, Laura L., ed. *Curriculum is What Happens: Planning is the Key*. Washington D.C.: National Association for the Education of Young Children, 1977.

Hartley, Ruth E. *Understanding Children's Play*. New York: Columbia University Press, 1952.

Holt, John. *How Children Fail*. New York: Pitman Publishing, 1964.

———. *How Children Learn*. New York: Pitman Publishing, 1967.

Joyce, Bruce R. *Selecting Learning Experiences: Linking Theory and Practice*. Washington D.C.: Association for Supervision and Curriculum Development, 1978.

Seefeldt, Carol. *The Early Childhood Curriculum: A Review of Current Research*. N.Y.: Teachers College Press, 1986.

Spodek, Bernard, ed. *Play: The Child Strives Toward Self-Actualization*. Washington, D.C.: National Association for the Education of Young Children, 1971.

Sponseller, Doris, ed. *Play as a Learning Medium*. Washington, D.C.: National Association for the Education of Young Children, 1974.

10

The Physical Development Curriculum

"And look at your body . . . what a
wonder it is!
Your legs, your arms, your cunning
fingers, the way they move."

Pablo Casals

*In this chapter we discuss the ways in which you can select and create worthwhile experiences to support the physical development of young children. Areas of physical development—sensory, and large and small muscle—are used as the organizing framework. Teacher role and teaching strategies are considered. A checklist to evaluate this aspect of programs is provided. This chapter relates to the CDA areas **Physical** and **Self**.*

We begin our discussion of curriculum with physical development because the body is the child's connection to the world. Physical well-being is essential to all other aspects of development. A sensitive, strong, flexible, coordinated, healthy body allows a child to function competently in the world. The senses are the primary mode for gathering information. In early childhood programs three integrated components constitute the physical development curriculum. The **sensory, small muscle** (sometimes referred to as fine motor), and **large muscle** (sometimes referred to as gross motor) curricula are part of daily life in every early childhood program. Although *large* and *small muscle* is the term that is generally used to refer to these areas of curriculum, more than muscle is involved. *Neuromuscular* is another term that is used to describe these aspects of development and curriculum.

Curriculum designed to promote sensory and physical development enhances learning in other areas as well. With a few shovels, a group of children may be challenged to channel water downward from a water source at the top of a hill. In the process, they may learn to use tools, to solve a physical science problem (how to use gravity to make the water go where they wish), to exercise, and to develop communication skills as they cooperate to accomplish the job. A group of five year olds playing "Red Rover" test their strength and stamina and at the same time learn about turn-taking, following rules, fair play, and other aspects of social interaction.

To translate ideas and feelings into words or art we must first have many experiences in the physical world. To understand many words and concepts children need to experience them; imagine trying to explain what *push* means to someone who has never felt or done it, or *color* to a person who lives in a black and white world. To read, visual and auditory discrimination are required. Writing uses fine motor skill in addition to this. To appreciate beauty we must first see, hear, feel, or smell it.

A DEVELOPMENTAL PERSPECTIVE

Completely helpless at birth, unlike other animals, human beings spend years gaining facility in the use of their bodies. A major developmental task of the preschool years is to become physically competent. Physical skill enables children to care for themselves and move beyond the limits that are imposed by their dependency on others. As they gain the ability to control and use their bodies, they become self-confident and learn to feel independent.

The work of Arnold Gesell and his associates, begun in the 1930s, provides much of the information about physical development currently used by early childhood educators. Subsequent observational data, research, and practice have served to substantiate these findings. More recently Ashley Montague and others have brought to the forefront the critical nature of early sensory experience.

Genetic inheritance plays the biggest part in how the body will develop. Skin, hair, and eye color are with us for life. Height and weight tendencies are given, but may be altered by environmental factors. For normal growth and maturation to proceed children must have nutritious food, affectionate human contact, and adequate opportunities to exercise. Montague (1972) reports on the critical nature of tactile experience in normal physical and psychological development. Human touch is essential to human growth. Children need protection from disease, injury, and environmental hazards. Day-to-day care needs to be supplemented by periodic medical examinations to make sure that a child's growth patterns are normal and un-impeded by illness.

Children need opportunities to move, explore, and manipulate materials, to help them develop their fullest potential for physical sensitivity and competence. As a teacher, you will make use of information about physical development to design and plan appropriate curriculum experiences and activities.

Because physical development follows a predictable sequence, you will be able to plan activities that help children move on to the appropriate next steps. A child who has learned to skillfully jump in place on two feet and who has the confidence and ability to balance momentarily on one foot, for example, can then learn to hop on one foot. Knowing this, you can plan activities where children see and experience hopping and encourage them to try the activity if they are *ready*. Growth (increase in size and mass) and maturation (increase in complexity of organization) interact to produce physical development. All development proceeds toward greater size and complexity. A child cannot learn to read until fine perceptual discriminations can be made; cutting cannot occur until coordination and strength of the hands is well developed; the arms, legs, and trunk must learn to work in concert before a child can pump on a swing.

Growth and maturation proceed from the top downward. The infant develops head control and reaching and grasping skill before sitting and walking. The large muscles closest to the center of the body grow and develop coordinated functions before the small muscles of the hands and fingers. Because mastery of the muscles of legs, arms, and torso must be accomplished first, good early childhood teachers provide many opportunities for active movement. Growing mastery makes large muscle activity very enjoyable to young children, and it is a feature of much of their play. They first develop strength, coordination, and skill in these large muscles and gradually go on to develop small muscle control. An overview of the physical capabilities typical of young children is presented in Table 10.1.

TABLE 10.1
The development of motor ability.

Activity	Age: 2	2½	3	3½	4	4½	5
LARGE MOTOR							
Walking	Heel-toe pattern		On tiptoe	On a line			Backwards
Running	Just able to run	True running appears	Runs with little stumbling		Runs with good leg-arm coordination		Runs faster
Jumping	Jumps down from object with both feet	Jumps off floor with both feet	Jumps in place with two feet together		Jumps skillfully		Broad jumps 2–3 feet; jumps forward 10 times without falling
Climbing	Walks up and down stairs with some assistance		Climbs stairs with alternating feet holding onto handrail		Climbs jungle gym		
Balancing	Picks up objects from floor without falling		Climbs up slide and comes down		Balances on one foot; walks on balance beam		Turns somersaults
Skipping				Hops on one foot	Basic gallop	Skipping	Skillful skipping
Ball throwing		Responds to thrown ball with delayed arm movements	Catches; throws with some accuracy; kicks ball forward		Throws, catches and bounces large balls		Catches small ball using hands only; mature ball-kicking patterns: kicks through ball
SMALL MOTOR							
Drawing	Scribbles		Holds crayon with thumb and fingers; makes dots, lines, circular strokes		Copies circle; imitates cross	Prints a few capital letters	
Painting	Paints with whole arm movement		Paints with wrist action				
Cutting			Cuts with scissors				Cuts on line continuously
Other skills	Turns knobs	Uses one hand consistently	Rolls, pounds, squeezes, and pulls clay		Holds cup in one hand	Buttons, zips, ties shoes with practice	

TEACHER ROLE

Teachers have a vital role to play in the physical development of children. Physical skill and sensitivity are developed through play and are a side benefit of many other activities. Given an appropriate environment and freedom to choose, children create many opportunities for their own physical development. It is unnecessary and inappropriate to plan elaborate physical education experiences, like gymnastics classes and many organized games, for young children. It is important, however, to be attentive to the balance and scope of the physical experiences that children have in your classroom.

The quality of the physical development curriculum is largely determined by the equipment and space available. The space required, and the size and expense of much of the equipment needed for motor and sensory development can seem prohibitive. Tricycles, blocks, sand and water tables, climbing structures, rocking boats, and good quality balls may require substantial financial investment. Programs without adequate resources are often underequipped, and physical development experiences are limited. In such a situation an important part of your role is to improvise. Regular trips to nearby parks or gyms can sometimes substitute for a spacious play yard. Recycled materials can be used to build equipment and to substitute for more costly pieces of equipment; for example, baby bathtubs make adequate water and sand tables; cable spools, planks, sawhorse, and ladders or a length of heavy marine rope wrapped around a tree serve for climbing structures; a log or telephone pole are challenging balance beams. In one program we observed,

sand was unavailable; a pile of dirt was used as a satisfying, if messy, digging substitute.

Despite the vital importance of physical development, teachers often overlook the sensory and large muscle curriculum areas in their thinking and program planning. Sensory and large muscle activities are so clearly "play" that planning for them may seem frivolous. Teachers, themselves, may not enjoy this part of the curriculum. As adults, they do not have the pressing need for activity that children do and use outdoor time as a much

needed respite. A certain amount of mess and hazard is involved in the sensory and large muscle curriculum, which disturbs many adults.

Small muscle development opportunities are more frequently planned for as part of the curriculum. They are usually not messy, disruptive, or noisy. Activities which develop coordination and control of the hands and fingers rarely cause adults concern. Indeed, because of the obvious link to adult tasks like writing, computer skills, and assembling materials, small muscle activities are generally looked on with favor by parents and teachers.

Part of your role is to pay attention to the range of skills so that you can provide children with opportunities and encouragement for physical development. To support children you must understand and accept the importance of all physical development experiences. You need to be able to clearly articulate to parents, administrators, and other staff the rationale for a total physical development curriculum.

THE SENSORY CURRICULUM

Sensory experience is at the core of the curriculum for very young children. Learning depends on sensory input: hearing, smelling, seeing, touching, moving, tasting. We are not born with the ability to fully discriminate between different sensations but must become aware of them. Each child must have opportunities to learn to perceive using all of the senses: to taste, to smell, to hear, to see, to touch, and to gain awareness of the body in space.

One part of growing and developing competence in the world is becoming sensitive. By the time children come to you in the preschool setting, they may have already been taught to avoid many of the sensory avenues to learning. Touching, smelling, and tasting are often particularly restricted even in children as young as two. They have been given messages like: "Don't taste; it's dirty." "Don't touch; it's dangerous." "It smells bad." "It may be poisonous." "Don't touch; you may break it." Looking and listening are generally considered acceptable ways to find out about the world, but while they are valuable for young children, they should not be encouraged to the exclusion of taste, touch, smell, and physical manipulation. If children are to gather and use the information that is available to them in the world, they need opportunities to fully develop each of their senses. The obvious joy which a child takes in rolling down a hill, playing with water, smelling a rose, or rubbing fingers along a soft piece of velvet are the observable evidence of how important sensory experience is to young children.

Young preschoolers are in a transition stage between sensorimotor and preoperational modes of learning. In the sensorimotor period (from birth to two years) children learn about the world through direct sensory experience. Only later do they start using and manipulating symbols, like language, in their learning. In the preschool years children continue to learn best through experience. If the child's ability to receive and use sensory input is severely impeded, normal development will be retarded. For these reasons, all preschool curriculum should include a strong sensory component.

A Framework for Sensory Development

The senses give you a natural framework for planning and organizing the sensory component of your program. While this is useful, it is important to realize that each sense is not isolated. Children involved in a cooking activity touch and compare the flour and salt, smell the banana as it is mashed, experience resistance when the thick batter is stirred, see the bubbles that form as air is beaten in, hear the sizzle as batter is poured in the pan, and taste the finished pancake. To separate these would be difficult and unnecessary: children learn from the combined sensory experience.

The **kinesthetic** sense is an internal awareness of movement, touch, and gravity. It is probably the first sensation that human beings experience. Before birth we feel movement and rhythm within our mothers' bodies; afterwards we are held and rocked. Children have kinesthetic experiences in play and when they are touched and held. To remain upright, to make judgments on how we move, we need to have the ability to discriminate and control using the kinesthetic sense.

The **auditory** sense, **hearing**, also begins before a child is born. Differentiating between sounds is a major developmental task. Learning to screen the auditory environment—to exclude irrelevant sounds and to attend to what is meaningful—is an important part of language development. In a typical noisy preschool class it is easy to become insensitive to subtleties of sound. Children are often admonished to "listen" without being helped to develop the ability to

accomplish this difficult task. We can help children to attend to and differentiate between sounds in music, language, and the world around them.

The sense of **touch**, or **tactile** sense, is a primary mode of learning. The organ of touch is the skin which by its sheer size and all-encompassing nature makes touch a dominant aspect of our lives. Touch gives us information about the world and allows us to make decisions for comfort and safety. Indeed, the survival of an infant has been demonstrated to be dependent on tactile and kinesthetic stimulation, including holding, hugging, and other nurturing experiences (Berger, 1980; Papalia and Olds, 1982). Early childhood experiences help children learn to identify and discriminate between tactile sensations to make judgments

237

about the world based on texture, temperature, and pressure.

We make many decisions based on our sense of **smell**—the **olfactory** sense. We smell bread baking and decide to eat; we smell a rose and put our faces closer to bask in the sensation; we smell a dirty diaper and know that it is time to change it. Very young children have limited olfactory experience and may not be able to make clear judgments based on smell. This is one of the reasons that they sometimes drink poisonous liquids like ammonia. Older preschoolers make many choices based on the smell of things and often reject experiences, settings, foods, and people because of an odor which is unfamiliar or which they judge unpleasant.

The sense of **taste** is sometimes called the **gustatory** sense. There are actually only a few taste characteristics—sweet, sour, salty, and bitter. Eating is a multisensory experience: taste characteristics, together with the aromas of food, create the multitude of flavors that we experience. Texture and temperature (elements of the

sense of touch) also influence how we experience food. The mouth is of primary importance in the exploration and learning of an infant. Very young children do not confine their gustatory exploration to things that we consider edible. Not only food, but also playdough, sand, thumbs, blankets, and toys are experienced with the tongue and mouth. In the preschool classroom children can be provided with a range of safe and satisfying taste experiences and can be helped to develop an understanding of which things are unsafe or unhealthy to put in their mouths.

The sensory mode which we most commonly associate with learning is **sight**. Learning to make visual discriminations begins early in life. From infancy we use visual information to make judgments, but the ability to make fine discriminations takes many years to develop. **Vision,** like other senses, requires opportunities for practice. Because it is so critical in deciphering written language, visual discrimination tasks are often given a disproportionately larger share of teacher attention than

the other senses. This is rarely necessary. Children normally develop visual discrimination ability in their day-to-day activities at home and in the classroom. As they work with toys, books, games and materials, they make decisions based on what they see. A child working with a puzzle, for example, evaluates the empty space and the remaining pieces, chooses one, tries it, and experiences the results of the visual judgment; no further teacher intervention is necessary at that time. Children sorting buttons do so based on what they see: color, shape, size, number of holes, etc.

Supporting Children in Sensory Development

Your classroom setting can open avenues for sensory learning. You must first recognize the importance of sensory experiences, create an environment which includes them, and then plan for them to be an integral part of your program. Comparing and contrasting are the ways that children learn to differentiate sensory experience.

Most early childhood classrooms have materials that clearly contribute to sensory development: water, sand, mud, dough, and clay. Although much other learning is accomplished with these materials, children's sensory and playful involvement proves that the sensory qualities are most important. You can add other planned activities using the senses as a framework as we have suggested. Consider each sensory avenue and evaluate what you could provide to stimulate it. Include classroom activities that require matching, sorting, or arranging materials, such as sound cans, sorting boxes, texture boards, pegboards, puzzles, collage materials, color chips, and blocks.

In our own teaching we have enjoyed tasting and smelling days when children brought their favorite items to savor, listening walks when we went to hear what we could hear, and color days when we all wore the same color.

Raw materials for sensory exploration also exist in common everyday objects and activities. An orange at lunch, an interesting piece of driftwood, the texture of a carpet, and other ordinary things give children a chance to use all their senses. Collections of objects like rocks, shells, leaves, beans, and seeds give children opportunities to look, touch, and sort.

Many materials designed for other curriculum areas are sensory in nature. The colors in a beautifully illustrated children's book, the different weights and sizes in a set of unit blocks, the sound differences of rhythm instruments, the feel of moving through space on a swing set, the cool mush of finger paints or clay, the tastes and smells as children cook applesauce are all sensory highlights of activities that may have had other purposes. As you provide experiences for children, you can stay alert to the sensory qualities and encourage their sensory exploration and involvement.

When a small group of children and their teachers move beyond the classroom to take a walk or hike, they encounter many experiences that heighten sensory awareness. They can observe different places and people in the neighborhood. They can smell new smells—a flower, a bakery, or a roof being tarred. They can experience textures as they walk through grass, on asphalt, across a gravel road. Along the way a leaf, a friendly cat, or moss on a rock can be felt. Unfamiliar sounds may heighten awareness of hearing—a truck rushing by or the wind blowing through tree tops. As children climb a hill and roll down the other side or scramble over a log, they experience distance and depth and learn about their bodies in space. An unexpected rain shower may give them the experience of raindrops on their faces, an impromptu romp in a puddle, and the feel of gooey mud on their hands and feet.

Your attitude about messy activities and waste can encourage or discourage children's sensory exploration. Support children's exploration by providing space that can be used without fear of mess and materials that can be fully explored without concern about waste. Teachers can help children focus on sensory

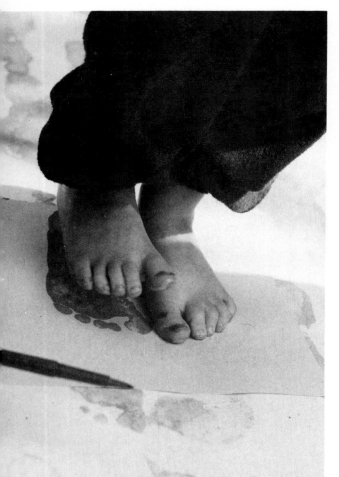

aspects of materials and experiences by the ways they call attention to them. Activities such as sand, mud, water, clay, and finger paints are sometimes rejected by fastidious children, particularly when these activities are available only occasionally for short periods. Reluctant children are much more likely to learn to use and enjoy materials that are available and that are enjoyed by other children. It also helps when the use of materials moves in a sequence over several weeks or even months, from structured and contained to more open and free form. For example, finger paints might be presented first on a cafeteria tray with small paper, small amounts of paint, and protective smocks. Later activities involving a group mural or using finger paints on the tables in the playground with sand and gravel may be added.

You can also provide for sensory activities through games and materials that help children to focus on sensory variables. We appreciate the aesthetic materials for sensory development designed by Maria Montessori, such as cylinders which vary in only one dimension—diameter, circumference, or height—and colored chips which children can arrange by gradations in shade and hue. Teachers can also make games that children can use independently, sometimes called *workjobs,* to develop sensory awareness—sound cylinders, color matching games, and feel boxes are teacher-made materials found in many classrooms.

SMALL MUSCLE CURRICULUM

The small muscle curriculum, learning to coordinate the hands and fingers, begins when babies in their cribs reach out to feel—to grasp, to manipulate and explore. Those initial impulses will eventually lead to the competent use of hands, fingers, and tools. One of the characteristics that marks our common humanity is that we seek out, use, and create devices that extend our abilities for surviving, communicating, creating, and discovering. A spoon, a crayon, a hammer, a needle, and a keyboard are all tools that are manipulated by the hands and fingers. The early childhood small muscle curriculum makes an important contribution to this eventual mastery.

A Framework for Small Muscle Curriculum

All small muscle activities involve control, agility, strength, and coordination. This combination of elements is involved in the multitude of skills that children need to develop. These elements and the related skills provide a useful framework for planning and presenting small muscle experiences to young children.

Small muscle **control** involves knowing what you want your hands and fingers to do for you and being able to direct them to do it. The direction, size, speed, shape, force, and characteristic of hand movements must be controlled in daily living and learning. To be able to pat a cat and beat a drum requires conscious differing of the force, direction, speed, and size of a very similar movement. Time, practice, and many experiences are required to develop this competence.

Agility concerns the ability to move in a precise and intentional way at the speed that is desired. Young children's small muscle agility is limited. However motivated and intelligent they are, they

can only rarely master skills such as touch typing, playing the piano, and knitting. Before children can become agile, they must gain a great deal of control over the direction, shape, force, and speed of other less complicated movements.

Strength concerns the stamina and force that is available to apply to and sustain movement. Children growing up with normal abilities and opportunities to use their hands also develop the strength required to do most small muscle activities. However, you may remember how tiring some small muscle activities can be—to cut the cloth for a heavy garment, or use a screwdriver for a prolonged period of time. As children persist at small muscle activities in the preschool, they develop greater strength and stamina.

Coordination means being able to control the interrelationship of hands, fingers, and other body parts. It involves sensory and muscular interplay—hand-eye coordination, moving hands based on visual data, and coordination of the two hands, based on visual and kinesthetic awareness (sensing where the hands are in space). Clapping hands, moving spoon to mouth, and stringing beads are examples of activities that require coordinated movement.

Some of the skills involving all of these small muscle elements that children learn are:

Grasping and Releasing—whole hand and pincer
Dumping/Pouring/Spooning
Twisting/Turning
Writing/Drawing/Painting
Tapping/Striking
Clapping/Slapping/Patting

Rubbing/Rolling
Folding/Tearing
Cutting
Pulling
Stringing/Sewing
Tying/Buttoning/Zipping
Pointing/Fingering

The equipment, materials, and activities that you present should provide opportunities for all of these skills to develop.

As we created this list, we were astonished by the complexity of the movements involved and by the sheer quantity of small muscle tasks that young children need to develop. We enjoyed figuring out which elements and discrete movements were involved in each task. For example, cutting involves all of the elements (strength, control, agility, and coordination) and consists of grasping, directing, releasing tension but not releasing grasp, and twisting and turning the opposing hand. No wonder it's hard for young children! Simply feeding oneself requires control and coordination and involves grasping, directing, and releasing an object with enough finesse to avoid spills and hunger. The importance of a two year old's grasping and dumping can be more readily appreciated as a learning task when viewed as an important step in the mastery of some very complicated fine motor skills.

Supporting Children in Small Muscle Development

Every classroom for young children needs to have toys and materials that build small muscle skills. Fortunately there are many kinds of materials which do this.

Almost all small toys develop fine motor skill. Most preschools have an area exclusively for construction and manipu-

lative toys such as pegboards, puzzles, and Legos. These need to be sized for the age of the children: younger children need fewer, larger pieces that cannot be swallowed and are easier to manipulate.

Self-help activities are major contributors to small muscle development. As children learn to serve their own food, pour their own beverages, use the water fountain, put on their shoes, and fasten their clothes, they are not only gaining independence but are also practicing important skills. The challenge of opening your own lunchbox and thermos with the payoff of eating without waiting for a teacher's assistance points out the real-life significance of fine motor development. Teachers can add pouring activities and lacing frames to help develop these skills. The materials which are found in the *practical life* area of a Montessori classroom also provide this skill development and can be added to any classroom.

Many curriculum materials contribute to small muscle development. As children cook, use math materials like Cuisenaire rods, build with blocks, probe and investigate science materials, do finger-plays, play instruments, and even as they turn pages in a book, they are practicing fine motor skills.

Art activities are especially well suited for small muscle development. Clay and dough are especially versatile materials through which children develop almost every small muscle skill: grasping, squeezing, folding, tearing, cutting, rolling, rubbing, slapping, poking, twisting, pulling. The tools and materials commonly found in art and writing centers (paper, pencils, pens, crayons, hole punches, staplers, rulers, scissors, stamps, etc.) also develop these skills.

Sufficient time, variety and quantity of materials are needed for children to develop the use of hands and fingers. This time is valuable and children are not *just playing*. Children's obvious delight in fine motor activity is a good indicator of their interest and need for frequent and prolonged practice through play. Daily choice times of at least an hour should include access to manipulative and other materials that support fine motor development.

An essential part of supporting children's fine motor growth is knowledge of developmental sequence and sensitivity to individual differences. You will **observe** children, interpret the meaning of their activity, and present materials and activities that provide optimal challenge.

When a child is clearly frustrated or bored with a material, you have several choices based on what you know about development and your judgment of the child's skill and personal style. A child who is struggling to cut a small slip of tissue paper might experience greater success with a large piece of construction paper. You might offer stiffer paper. Another response would be to note the difficulty, observe how the child copes with this problem and then make an appropriate comment: "Jenna, I see you tore that paper that was so hard to cut; that solved your problem!" You might then decide to stock the shelf with a variety of different weights of paper or more functional scissors. Yet another response would be to intervene verbally and instruct and offer technical assistance, or comment and suggest an alternative: "I like to use construction paper when I'm cutting because it doesn't flop."

Sometimes the developmentally appropriate response to a child's need is even more obvious. A child who hasn't yet mastered scissors needs plenty of grasping, tension/release, coordination, and strength building experiences. Providing dough, clay to build strength, and tools like tongs, hole punches, tweezers, and staplers that require similar motor action would help to build towards this skill.

LARGE MUSCLE CURRICULUM

Human beings come into the world unprepared to deal with gravity, to stand upright and move through space in a coordinated way. Some mastery over the large muscles of our bodies must precede almost any other learning and skill development. The large muscle curriculum—that part of the early childhood program that is concerned with the development of children's skill and strength in arms, legs, and torso—is designed to help children gain and retain physical skills and abilities as they work and play.

The large muscle curriculum contributes to learning and health in the preschool years and throughout life. Attention span and concentration are enhanced as children engage in active, challenging physical activity. Such activity helps to release tension and promotes relaxation. Physical fitness is essential for lifelong

health. The large muscle curriculum is of critical importance because it can develop the skills and attitudes that will enable children to enjoy physical activity throughout life.

A Framework for Large Muscle Curriculum

To become physically competent children must develop kinesthetic awareness, strength and stamina, flexibility, coordination, and agility. These form the basis for the large muscle curriculum.

The large muscle curriculum gives children opportunities to satisfy their need for **kinesthetic** stimulation through activities such as climbing, running, jumping, and rolling. They lead to the ability to balance, to identify one's position

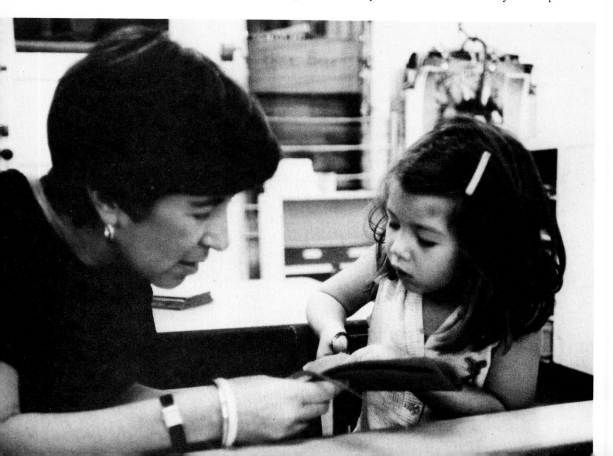

in space, and to control physical motions. Swinging, turning somersaults, walking on a beam, and jumping on a trampoline are skills which are dependent on kinesthetic awareness and control.

Strength is the physical energy available for movement or resistance. **Stamina** or endurance is the capacity for the sustained use of strength or physical energy. Older children generally are stronger and have greater and more predictable endurance. An activity that requires sustained exertion like a hike or walk will point out the difference between a child who has had many experiences that build strength and endurance and one who has had few. The more inexperienced child may find even a short walk very taxing. Strength and stamina increase as children exert energy and effort for prolonged periods of time.

Flexibility concerns the ease and range of movement. Physical suppleness lessens with age as the muscle system develops and becomes less elastic. An infant easily brings toes to mouth, but this flexibility wanes as children get older. One of the goals of the physical development curriculum is to help children to retain flexibility while developing muscular strength. Running, dancing, climbing, wiggling, and stretching maintain flexibility and are the opposite of the confinement to desks that is typical of later schooling. The outcome of a typical sedentary lifestyle is the inflexibility that makes it difficult for many adults to sit comfortably on the floor.

Coordination means being able to move different body parts together in relation to one another. A child pumping a swing moves arms and legs forward and backward in unison. A baby crawling or a young child climbing on a jungle gym moves arms and legs in opposition. Young children learn to coordinate their bodies first by experimenting, imitating, and exploring movement to gain control. Practice then internalizes the new skill. Opportunities to move freely for large periods of time encourage such experimentation. Controlled exercise situations and directed movement cannot substitute for unstructured large muscle play time although they can be enjoyable additions.

Agility means to move with speed, grace, and precision. A child who can stop abruptly and change directions is agile. Agility requires flexibility, strength, coordination, and a well-developed kinesthetic sense. As children gain agility, they feel a sense of mastery. Much of the pleasure children find in large muscle play stems from the enjoyment of growing agility.

Large Muscle Skills and Activities
Movement activities develop some combination of the elements of physical competence. When children engage in a range of large muscle activities, they develop kinesthetic awareness, strength, coordination, flexibility and agililty. The following list provides a framework for the physical development opportunities you should offer in your program. Evaluate the environment and schedule in terms of each of the items. There should be space, time, and equipment for children to develop each skill.

Balancing
Walking/Running/Stopping
Galloping/Skipping
Jumping/Hopping
Pedalling vehicles
Climbing
Pulling/Pushing

Swinging
Swaying/Rocking
Twisting/Turning
Stretching
Rolling
Crawling
Catching
Punting/Striking/Kicking
Throwing
Bouncing/Dribbling

Supporting Children in Large Muscle Development

Children need opportunities to engage in large muscle play for at least an hour in each half day. Through this prolonged play they develop all of the abilities just described. Teachers can provide encouragement, an environment rich in equipment and materials, and enough time and space for exploration.

Motor development opportunities abound in a well-designed play yard for young children. Perhaps the most critical aspect of the environment is whether or not you have space for large muscle activity. The most desirable outdoor space for a group of young children would include a hill for climbing and rolling, large flat even areas for running and galloping, uneven surfaces for walking and developing coordination, paved areas for wheel toys, dirt and sand for digging, and trees for climbing and shade. Frequent trips to parks can substitute for and supplement a less than ideal outdoor environment.

Children need equipment for climbing, swinging, throwing, digging, hammering, balancing, and exploring space with their bodies. The most important and versatile piece of equipment for large muscle development is a well-designed and

constructed climbing structure. Such a structure should have different ways to get up and down: ramps, ladders, stairs, slides, firepoles, and cargo nets or webs of tires. These lead to platforms of different heights on or under which children can rest, pretend, play, and dream. If you don't have such a structure, you can create an alternative with sawhorses, cable spools, tires, logs, boards, heavy rope, and cargo nets. Aluminum climbing equipment that is portable can be rearranged by you and children either indoors or outdoors. Swings, slides, jungle gyms, and other standard pieces of playground equipment contribute to development although these are less versatile. Smaller pieces of equipment should also be a part of the outdoor environment: rocking boats, balance beams, woodworking tables and tools, hollow blocks, small trampolines, balls, wheelbarrows, wagons, digging tools, trikes, scooters, and balance boards.

If the climate dictates that you spend long periods of time indoors, you will need to find ways to provide large muscle development experiences daily. Activities like creative movement, circle games, and physical exercises can give children the chance to use and develop large muscles. Since these group experiences require teacher structure and control, they must usually be of short duration. Children need a great deal more physical activity than these can provide. The portable equipment described above—balance beams, trampolines, hollow blocks, etc.—can be used indoors when outdoor play is not available.

Children develop physical competence from exploration of a well-planned and equipped environment. Teacher-led activities that provide practice in develop-

ing physical competencies also have a valid place in the program. These activities can include simple yoga, creative movement, exercises, and group games like tag, dodgeball, and follow the leader. We prefer games which minimize competition and win/lose situations. It is important to observe individuals, so that you can encourage reticent children to practice skills they lack and so that you provide adequate challenge for more skilled children. It is also important to provide special opportunities for those children who might never choose to practice a particular skill. Children who have definite developmental lags in physical ability may require direct intervention in the form of formal instruction or one-to-one practice. This direct physical training needs to be carried out in spirited, pleasurable play situations so that the child's attitude will be positive, and spontaneous physical activity will become a source of pleasure.

You support safe, productive, physical activity when you make sure that equipment is free of hazards, appropriately placed, and sufficiently challenging. Young children can be inadvertently discouraged from climbing, sliding, and swinging by teachers who are overly concerned about possible injury. Individual teachers' perceptions of danger differ greatly. A useful guideline is that if children are willing to attempt using a piece of equipment, they can usually manage it. If they can get up on a climbing structure, they can generally get down from it on their own. Your role is to watch carefully so that you are aware of their growing skill and so that you are available to offer support, instruction, or help as needed. Occasionally a challenge will be beyond an individual's capabilities, and you must move to provide assistance. If a child climbs onto something and is not able to reverse the process, you can give instruction and encouragement—"I think you can do it. Put your foot on the bar and move your hand down a little bit; now you can step safely"—or even a lift back to the ground, without admonishing the failed attempt, encouraging helplessness, or discouraging future attempts. Children need optimal challenge—equipment, materials, and activities that provide the right degree of difficulty—to develop the skill that is just within their reach.

How you talk can encourage or discourage children's engagement in physical activities. It is best to avoid comments that create comparison and competition between children. Saying, "Look how high Sam can climb. Can anyone else climb as high?" may encourage Sam but more often leads to overconfidence. The remainder of the children may attempt to reach dangerously beyond their current skill level in order to please you, or they may feel inadequate because they cannot achieve the standard you have set. Real encouragement relates only to the individual's accomplishment: "Sam, that's the highest I've ever seen you climb. You're becoming a very strong person." This comment acknowledges effort and new accomplishments and avoids implying everyone else should be able to do the same thing.

Your participation in children's physical development activities is an important part of your teacher role. By playing *with* children, you encourage and support their activity, and you provide a model of an adult who is physically active; this is a powerful demonstration that being active is natural and pleasurable. We've observed many teachers sitting and watching rather than participating during children's outside activities. Children need your active involvement in their play; they need someone to toss a ball to them, to play follow the leader with, to play the guitar and sing as they play *Ring Around the Rosie*, to explain the rules of *What Time is it Mister Wolf?*, to share their triumph as they discover how to scramble *up* the firepole, to draw a hopscotch pattern on the sidewalk, and countless other things.

Making sure that you are providing for sensory, small muscle and large muscle development opportunities is an important part of your role as a teacher. You will want to read further to enlarge your repertoire of activities and skills in this area. We have devised a checklist (see box) to help our students evaluate, plan, and teach for a range of physical development opportunities.

CHECKLIST FOR PHYSICAL DEVELOPMENT CURRICULUM AREAS

Program Structure
☐ Stated goals include support of physical and sensory development
☐ Daily time for outdoor play and exploration provided for an hour in the morning and an hour in the afternoon—at least half an hour of this time is continuous
☐ Daily free choice periods of at least an hour include opportunities to use sensory and manipulative materials

Environment and Materials

sensory:
☐ Dirt, sand, water available in the outdoors
☐ Access to nature
☐ Space where messy materials can be used indoors
☐ A variety of surfaces for sitting and lying—grass, carpet, pillows with different textures

☐ Tubs, troughs, or tables for holding water, sand, dirt, mud, and dry material such as sawdust

☐ Scoops, cups, sponges, tubing, house painting brushes, pitchers, sieves, etc. to use with sand and water

☐ Mild soap for bubble blowing and suds making

☐ Shaving cream or other material for finger painting

☐ Materials for mixing—sawdust, pine needles, dry rice, oatmeal, corn meal, cornstarch mixed with water, etc.

☐ Food color and flavor extracts for coloring and scenting water and dough

☐ Rocking boats, balance boards, or other rocking equipment

☐ Equipment for cooking—measuring utensils, bowls, spoons, hotplate, etc.

☐ An art area with paint, finger paint, paste, clay, and dough

☐ Tools for dough and clay—texture mallets, rollers

☐ A unit block area

☐ Materials designed specifically for sensory development such as ____ sound cannisters, ____ sorting boxes, ____ texture boards, ____ color chips, ____ smelling jars, ____ color wheels, ____ kaleidoscopes

☐ Collections of things to sort by color, shape, size, texture, pattern, smell, taste, weight (seeds, liquids, stones, buttons, food, flowers, leaves, shells, fabric, spices, etc.)

☐ Musical instruments and a record collection

☐ Puzzles, pegboards, etc.

small muscle:

☐ Tables, chairs, and comfortable floor space for children to work with materials

☐ Art and/or writing area with paper for folding and tearing and a variety of tools—paint brushes, crayons, marking pens, pencils, hole punch, stapler, typewriter, etc.

☐ Dough and clay

☐ Musical instruments

☐ Dramatic play area with dress-up clothes, telephones

☐ Scissors that cut easily and well and that can be used in either right or left hand

☐ Pegs and pegboards appropriate to the developmental level of the children

☐ Puzzles that are complete and appropriate to the skills and interests of the children

☐ Several different kinds of manufactured manipulative toys such as ____ lego, ____ bristle blocks, ____ crystal climbers, ____ linking loops, ____ stacking rings, ____ tinker toys, ____ beads and laces, ____ table blocks

☐ Dressing frames or garments that close in different ways (zipping, buttoning, lacing, tying, snapping)

☐ Activities made by teachers such as ___ tongs and things to pick up, ___ pouring activities, ___ spooning activities, ___ jar and lid games

☐ Water and sand toys—pitchers, tubing, funnels, spoons, measuring implements, sieves

☐ Woodworking area

large muscle:

☐ A large open outdoor space for that is fenced, unobstructed, and relatively even for running, galloping, skipping, etc.

☐ Large enough indoor space for movement activities

☐ Variety of outdoor surfaces—pavement, grass, dirt

☐ A climbing structure that offers several ways to get up and down with adequate space for safe sitting and bars for hanging

☐ Something to swing from—sling, rope or tire swings, no more than 18″ off the ground

☐ Large inflated balls that bounce (10-24 inches in diameter)

☐ Trikes or push vehicles that are proportioned to the size of the children and are in good working order

☐ Dirt or sand for digging and tools—spades, shovels, hoes, rakes

☐ A woodworking table with wood, hammers and nails, saws, a clamp or vise, hand drill, screwdriver and screws

☐ A balance beam

☐ A wagon and/or wheel barrow

☐ Large blocks

☐ Planned, enjoyable, teacher-led physical development activities are provided regularly—at least once a week

☐ Trips to parks and/or walks are provided at least once a week if the outside environment is inadequate

FOR FURTHER THOUGHT AND DISCUSSION

1 Think of a sensory experience that you especially enjoy (a hot bath, a walk in the woods, putting up a Christmas tree). Compare your thoughts with someone else's. In what ways are they similar or different? What do you feel or think of as you recall this experience? What makes it important to

you? How could you bring experiences like this into the classroom?

2 Think about your favorite large muscle activity—jogging, hiking, dancing, etc. Reflect on what makes the activity especially enjoyable to you. Compare your favorites and the characteristics that make them enjoyable with other people's. Discuss how you could bring different kinds of large muscle experiences to young children.

3 What talents that involve small muscle skills have you developed particularly well (playing the piano, crafts, cooking, sewing, auto mechanics, calligraphy, typing, drawing, crocheting, etc.)? Think about the kinds of motions that are involved in them. How did you become proficient in your skill? Was it hard or easy to develop? How long did it take? Compare your experience with other people's. What implications might this have for a teacher of young children?

PROJECTS

1 Use the **Checklist for Physical Development Curriculum Areas** from this chapter to observe an early childhood program. Report on the extent to which the program seems to support children's sensory and physical development. Suggest some ways to provide some additional experiences from which children would benefit.

2 Design an ideal environment for the support of physical development of a group of young children. Sketch your ideal and describe what you have provided and why. Share your plan with a teacher, a parent, a child, and an early childhood program administrator, and report on their responses and suggestions.

3 Use the lesson plan outline in Chapter 9 to design and implement a physical development activity for young children. Report on what happened. Describe what you learned about yourself, children, physical development, and teaching.

4 Design a week's plan for a group of children that includes all of the physical development activities. Use one of the weekly planning forms from Chapter 9. Implement part or all of your plan. Report on what happened. Describe what you learned about yourself, children, physical development, and teaching.

RECOMMENDED READING

Barratta-Lorton, Mary. *Workjobs*. Menlo Park, Cal.: Addison-Wesley, 1972.

Bentley, William G. *Learning to Move and Moving to Learn*. New York: Citation Press, 1970.

Curtis, Sandra R. *The Joy of Movement in Early Childhood*. New York: Teachers College Press, 1982.

Hill, Dorothy M. *Mud, Sand, and Water*. Washington, D.C.: National Association for the Education of Young Children, 1977.

Prudden, Bonnie. *How to Keep Your Child Fit from Birth to Six*. New York: The Dial Press, 1964.

Riggs, Maida L. *Jump to Joy: Helping Children Grow Through Active Play*. Englewood Cliffs, N.J.: Prentice-Hall, 1980.

Rowen, Betty. *Learning Through Movement*, 2d ed. New York: Teachers College Press, 1982.

Sinclair, Caroline B. *Movement of the Young Child: Ages Two to Six*. Columbus, O.: Charles E. Merrill, 1973.

Skeen, Patsy; Garner, Anita Payne; and Cartwright, Sally. *Woodworking for Young Children*. Washington, D.C.: National Association for the Education of Young Children, 1984.

Sprung, Barbara. *Non-Sexist Education for Young Children: A Practical Guide*. New York: Citation Press, 1975.

Torbert, Marianne. *Follow Me: A Handbook of Movement Activities for Children*. Englewood Cliffs, N.J.: Prentice-Hall, 1980.

Whitken, Kate, with Philip, Richard. *To Move To Learn*. New York: Schocken Books, 1978.

11

The Creative Curriculum

"Every child is an artist. The problem is how to remain an artist . . . "

Pablo Picasso

*This chapter concerns the arts—music, art, and creative movement—and the development of creativity and the aesthetic sense. In it we discuss children's development in the arts, consider issues in teaching, look at the role of the teacher, provide frameworks for planning creative curricula, and suggest strategies for teaching. A checklist for evaluating this area of curriculum is included. This chapter relates to the CDA areas **Creative** and **Self.***

Although the arts can be a vehicle for many other kinds of learning and while creativity is not confined to the arts, we link the two in this chapter because arts are especially appropriate and powerful ways to express creative ideas. The arts are vital in the development of children who can feel as well as think and who are sensitive and creative. Through the arts, children can come to recognize and express their feelings and responses, communicate their ideas in new forms, and develop their senses. The arts nurture an awareness of aesthetics (the appreciation of beauty) that is often destroyed in the pervasive grayness of factories, freeways, and institutional buildings. When children's unique expressions are acknowledged, they become aware of their value as individuals, and their self-concept is enhanced. For young children, these are the most important aspects of the arts: the development of awareness and skill, and feelings of self-worth. The final product is not nearly as important.

Creativity, or originality, is not confined to artists or people who have great talent or a high I.Q. All people are creative when they put together what they know and build something that is new *to them*: an idea, a process, or product. The arts are a primary avenue for developing the ability to think and act creatively.

Creativity is easy to see in the arts, but it also occurs in children's play and other curriculum activities: as they build with blocks, act out roles, use manipulative toys, explore their environment, write stories and play with words, solve problems and invent games. The creativity of play leaves no lasting product but is important to recognize and acknowledge. Moreover, children are not always being creative when they are involved in the arts. If they are afraid of not being accepted or feel that their work must meet adult standards, they may make stereotypic "acceptable" products or responses in order to receive approval and praise.

A DEVELOPMENTAL PERSPECTIVE

It is essential to understand how young children develop in order to provide a climate that supports creativity. Your knowledge of children's physical, social, emotional, and cognitive growth can guide you as you plan arts activities. Satisfying and successful experiences with the arts occur when you understand what you can reasonably expect of children and when you provide activities that match their needs and abilities.

Young preschoolers are primarily interested in exploring and manipulating materials, movement, sound, and words. They are developing basic motor and language skills. While they enjoy other children's company, they often have difficulty sharing and cooperating. They view the world from their own perspective and have difficulty understanding that the experience of others may be different from their own. Arts are enjoyed as opportunities for exploration; most representation that occurs is an after-thought. Some two and three year olds still display the characteristic behavior of children in the sensorimotor stage of development. They respond to the world as an extension of themselves. They touch, taste, and smell materials and are not amenable to a great deal of adult control. Arts' experiences for these children must be correspondingly safe, sensory, and flexible.

Older preschool and kindergarten age children are more capable of language, rational thought, and cooperative social interaction. Their attention span is longer, and their work is often representational. They spontaneously represent their world in creative expression, but they symbolize aspects of the world that they know and care about rather than attempting to represent it as it is. Sensory experience and exploration continues to be a motivation for involvement in the arts. At this age the easier give-and-take of relationships and eagerness to involve others in their work leads to cooperation with peers.

TEACHER ROLE

Your role in the arts is to provide an environment, materials, experiences, and relationships that support creative development. Neither children nor adults create in a void; creative expression is an outgrowth of other life experiences. You provide experiences that heighten children's awareness of sensations to give data and inspiration for artistic expression. These may be things as simple as the careful examination of an apple, a visit to a new baby, or a trip to the beach. Creative expression is also stimulated by experiences with good art. When children have opportunities to view artwork of many kinds, to listen to serious music, and to attend dance and drama produc-tions, they begin to understand the potential power and joy of the arts.

Creativity involves disclosing private thoughts, feelings, and ways of perceiving. Children can only risk this when they feel safe, valued, and encouraged. You support children's creativity by accepting *all* of their feelings, ideas, and creative expression, whether or not these are *nice* or *pretty* by adult standards. Those things that move children and adults are not always the most pleasant aspects of their lives. Nevertheless, if they have the power to evoke strong feelings, they are impor-tant, and important parts of life are a part of art.

Children's creative expression is supported when you demonstrate your genuine appreciation for effort, innovation, and individuality. When you reserve your appreciation and acknowledgment for work that meets your standards, you demonstrate to children that you are looking for correct rather than creative responses. Indiscriminate or insincere praise, however, is not an appropriate alternative. It suggests to children that your ability to make critical judgments may be impaired and renders your praise meaningless.

Acknowledge children's works by commenting on effort, innovation, or technique: "You worked hard." "You tried it a new way." "You covered the whole paper." "You put lots of bounces in your dance." Refrain from evaluative responses such as *good, bad, ugly, beautiful,* and *messy,* and instead, help children to become their own evaluators: "What do you like best about it?" "When you do it again, what will you do differently?" Children who are encouraged rather than evaluated or demeaned develop skills that help them to create their own standards and meet their own goals.

For some children, a long period of apparent disinterest or observation may precede participation in the arts. They may simply be more interested in different kinds of activities and alternative ways of being creative. They may not want to attempt creative activities because they already feel they cannot measure up to their teacher or parent's expectations. Time, teacher acceptance, and encourage-

ment are needed for them to discover an interest in the arts.

Finally, the physical environment must support children's creative expression. Materials need to be chosen and organized with care and aesthetic awareness. Select arts materials that are good quality and proportionate to the size of the children. Make sure there are enough materials available and that they are stored so that it is easy for children to get them and put them away. If materials are scarce, children may focus on obtaining and hoarding rather than on creative expression. Space should allow for concentration (neither too noisy nor too crowded) and enough time should be allowed for children to thoroughly explore the nature and possibilities of the activity or material. Children who are repeatedly frustrated at having to leave activities just as they are getting involved may become unwilling to invest energy in the arts. A classroom that provides for all of these needs has a *creative climate*: an atmosphere where creative expression is nurtured and where creativity can flourish.

We often hear teachers despair of their ability to make meaningful creative experiences a part of their classrooms because they do not feel they are talented or creative. It is not necessary to be an artist, musician, or dancer in order to help children have good experiences with the arts. Children are not harsh critics and will learn from your participation and enthusiasm. Even if you do not feel that you are talented in the arts, you need to include them in your curriculum. You can develop a receptive attitude toward the creative expression of children and toward the arts in general. Every community has resources—artists, educators, reference materials—that can guide you to good art experiences for children. In the Recommended Reading section, we provide a list of books that will help as you plan a program of creative expression.

ART

Art provides opportunities for children to explore and manipulate materials and express their feelings and understanding of the world. Its sensory and physical nature makes it especially appropriate for young children. The primary purpose of an early childhood art program is to enhance artistic and creative development. This creative process is most important; the value of a final art product is the feelings and awareness that it generates in the child.

The simple, nonrepresentational character of young children's art and the sequence of children's growth as artists is closely related to development. Sophistication of the finished product is limited by strength and motor coordination.

Children's art is also simple because children view the world simply; for example, children often create portraits that consist exclusively of a smiling head—to them the most important feature of a human being. The sensory pleasure of the art experience and the process of exploration are the primary motivation for children's involvement in art. As children mature, they use art to express ideas and to communicate with others, but throughout the early childhood years, they continue to enjoy the satisfaction of "messing about" with materials. Table 11.1 describes stages of development of children's art.

It can be hard for adults, especially parents, to accept the messiness and nonproductive nature of young children's artistic expression. Your essential roles include allowing this messiness and helping parents to understand the importance of their children's artistic process. In their efforts to make parents happy, some teachers resort to "coloring book" and other forms of pattern activities that they call "art." Since creative expression is primarily for the artist, it should be a reflection of the artist's ideas and abilities—not the teacher's. Coloring books and teacher-made patterns to be copied by children have nothing to do with the development of creativity or self expression; in fact, they can be destructive to children's feelings of competence and self-worth. The skills, thus taught, are almost always developmentally inappropriate and usually lead to feelings of failure and dissatisfaction in children. These activities can take up valuable time that children should be using to develop other skills, awareness, and ideas. They are not a part of good early childhood programs.

TABLE 11.1
The development of creative expression in art.

Age	Developmental Stage	Characteristics as an Artist
Birth to two years Infants and toddlers	Sensory-motor stage of development Work in creative expression is sensory and exploratory in nature.	Reacts to sensory experience. Explores media through *all* senses. Draws for the first time from 15–20 months. Begins to follow a universal developmental sequence in "scribbling" (See Figure 11.1).
Two to fours years Young preschoolers	Preoperational stage of development (preconceptual phase) Work in creative expression is manipulative and oriented toward discovery and skill development.	*Manipulative Stage of Art:* Explores and manipulates materials. Experiences art as exploratory play. Tries to discover what can be done—explores color, texture, tools and techniques. Often repeats an action. Begins to name and control symbols. Views final product as unimportant (may not be pleasing to adults). May destroy product during process. Perceives shapes in work.
Four to six years Older preschoolers and kindergartners	Preoperational stage of development (intuitive phase) Work in creative expression becomes more complex and representational.	*Symbolic Stage in Art:* Creates symbols to represent feelings and ideas. Represents what is *known* not what is *seen* (may not be recognizable to adults). Represents important parts of ideas or objects. Gradually begins to create more detailed and realistic work. Creates definite forms and shapes. Often preplans and then implements with great care and deliberation. Relationships exist between aspects of work. Rarely destroys work during process.

Creative art activities reap other educational benefits. As children use art media, they develop motor control and perceptual discrimination. Language is often inspired, and experiences with new vocabulary are provided. Work with art materials develops understanding of the world as children gain concepts about characteristics of these substances.

Confronted with problems in artwork, children develop problem-solving strategies. Working with others, their social skills are enhanced. Developing aesthetic awareness and appreciation for the natural and man-made world in all its diversity is a very direct and important benefit of art experiences. As you explain to parents what their children do and what it means, you are helping them to understand their child's development and your role in supporting it.

A Framework for Organizing Art

The framework for organizing art consists of two parts. The first is art activities which includes both the kinds of media that we provide for children and the techniques that are used. The second part of the framework consists of the elements which make up every work of art. It is essential that we make the media available and give time and encouragement. Teachers who have some understanding of the elements can extend these experiences to help children respond to art with greater sensitivity and create with more awareness.

Art Activities We use five categories to help organize thinking about the creative art experiences offered to children. Each utilizes different materials and develops different skills. All are important and

should be offered frequently—at least once a week.

Painting is the application of a liquid medium to a surface with a tool like a brush or sponge. The paint flows on the paper. When providing paint for young children, it is most important to provide primary colors (red, yellow, and blue) as well as black and white, since these colors can be mixed to create all other colors. There are many types of appropriate painting experiences for young children, but one of the most important is painting at an easel (or similar surface) because such painting involves the large muscles of the arms and shoulders over which children first develop control, as well as the small muscles of hands and fingers. In addition to easel painting, you will want to provide experiences with finger painting, watercolor painting, painting with large brushes and water on a fence or wall, string painting, and other variations. We are especially fond of palette painting (using small containers of red, blue, yellow, black, and white paint to

mix on a tray to create a palette of colors) since this technique allows children to create their own colors and is like the process that artists use as they paint. Nancy Smith's excellent book *Experience and Art* gives a detailed explanation of the palette painting technique.

Drawing is done with tools like crayons, marking pens, chalk, and pencils. Unlike paint, they are nonfluid and need no additional material to mark a surface; thus, they are easy for young children to control. Thick primary crayons provide excellent first drawing experiences. They can be used with greatest facility when they are short and chunky to fit small hands without the encumbering paper wrappers that prevent use of the whole crayon. Felt markers are another good first drawing medium for young children. They require less strength than crayons, and they produce bright appealing colors. Children will also draw with their fingers and sticks in sand, dirt, snow, fogged windows, finger paint, flour dropped on the table during cooking activities, and other media. Every child, throughout the world, follows the same sequence of drawing whether they use sticks in the dirt or the latest form of felt-tipped pen (see Figure 11.1).

Printing involves the use of an object to make an image. Printmaking is an ancient art that is found in every culture: it is one of the oldest ways of creating an image. Prints can be made by applying paint or ink to an object and stamping the imprint on a surface. Anything that will hold the ink or paint can be used—corks, hands, cookie cutters, spools, feet, paper rolls, fruits, vegetables, and many other things will make a print. The other method is sometimes called rubbing. A flat textured object or surface is used beneath a paper or similar material, and the image is impressed usually using crayon, chalk, or charcoal. Leaves, surfaces of sidewalks and rocks, fabrics, boards, coins, inscriptions, and any other interesting surface will make an interesting rubbing. The creative aspect of printing involves the selections children make as they choose what to print with, what colors to use, and how to arrange prints on paper.

Collage and Construction are art activities where materials are attached. Collage involves sticking relatively flat materials together with paste or glue. Tissue paper, magazine pictures, cloth scraps, macaroni, ribbons, yarn, leaves, sticks, and sand are all frequently used. They are commonly glued on sturdy construction paper, cardboard scraps, and similar materials. The skills of cutting, tearing, and folding are often employed in collage. Construction involves three-dimensional materials like paper towel rolls, wood scraps, cardboard boxes, cans, toothpicks, and styrofoam. Sturdy bases are required for glued construction. Woodworking, stitchery, weaving, sculpture, and paper-maché are techniques that we include in this category. These activities can recycle materials that would otherwise be thrown away.

Modeling and Sculpting materials include potter's clay, flour and salt dough (usually called playdough), and oil-based modeling media (sometimes called plasticene). Children form shapes out of these malleable three-dimensional substances. Potter's clay, the most versatile of these, can be used over and over again, can be reconstituted with water, and can be fired (baked in a kiln) for a permanent product. For very young children who do not have adequate

Basic scribbles (often random)

dots   lines   multiple lines   zig-zags   roaming lines   whorls   loops   circles

Combined Scribbles (controlled)

crosses   mandalas   stars   closed shapes

Suns

Sun Faces

Human Figures with Limbs

Human Figures with Torsos

Human Figure with Limbs Used in a Drawing

by a Four-year Old.

FIGURE 11.1
Stages of development in children's drawing.

strength to manipulate potter's clay, homemade dough provides an introduction to modeling. Children should be given plenty of opportunity to work with modeling materials, using only their hands. When they are ready for a more complex experience, blunt knives, rounded sticks, and lengths of dowel for rolling make excellent tools. Cookie cutters and similar pattern shapes do not offer a creative experience since they prescribe and limit.

Variation   Each of the basic art materials and processes can be varied to heighten interest and provide new challenges. Variations should be presented when children have mastered the basic processes and are seeking variation on their own. Opportunities for variation should heighten the creative and aesthetic experience. Variation can be provided by:

1   Changing the *materials and tools* (a new type or shape of paper, the addition of real potter's tools, making homemade paste).
2   Changing the *setting* in which the work is done (painting outside).
3   Providing a *motivating experience* (collecting collage materials on a walk, playing music while children work, setting a vase of flowers on the table).
4   Varying the *technique or task* (showing children how to spatter instead of brush paint, adding a drill to the woodworking materials, instructing children in the use of rolled clay to make coil pots).

Although there is much scope for varying art experiences, children do not require the amount of variety that adults tend to think children need. Children benefit from using the same media over and over and find the same basic activities satisfying over long periods of time. It takes many experiences with the same materials to fully explore their possibilities: clay and paint and crayons, for example, can be available every day.

Art Elements   Every work of art is composed of visual, graphic, and other sensory elements. We experience these elements long before we are consciously aware of them or learn to talk about them. Adults are often eager to push children into representational art because it is easier to identify and understand what children are communicating in a representational work. A smiling face says more to us than a series of lines of different lengths, widths, and direction. Much of the process of art for young children is exploration of the elements of art, as well as of the media and techniques. Realizing this can help you appreciate children's early artwork. As you expand your own awareness, you will find that you are more sensitive to this artistic discovery process and will be better able to support children. The following paragraphs describe some of the elements that children explore in their art.

   Line is a part of every painting, drawing, collage, print, or sculpture. Line can be described by kind or quality: straight, curved, wandering, wiggling, jagged, broken, zigzag, heavy, light, wide, thin. Every linear aspect of a piece of art has length, a beginning and end, and direction (up/down, diagonal, side-to-side). Lines have relationships with one another and other parts of the work. They can be separate, parallel, crossed. When children fill their paintings and drawings with many different kinds of lines, they are exploring this element.

Colors have qualities and can be referred to by name or hue—red, scarlet, turquoise, magenta. These color names add richness to our experience of color. They can be pure—primary colors (red, blue, yellow), white and black—or mixed. Different colors are considered to have temperature—coolness, at the blue end of the spectrum, or warmth at the red end of the spectrum. They have different degrees of intensity or saturation (brightness or dullness) and value (lightness or darkness). Colors change as they are mixed. They are related to one another (orange is a color which is related to red) and look different when placed next to other colors. Children who combine colors in painting or coloring with chalk or crayons are exploring the nature of this element. Discovering color by mixing to attain the colors that are desired takes much experimentation.

Shape or **form** in art is far more than named geometric shapes like circles, squares, and triangles. Children and artists rarely fill their work with regular geometric shapes; instead they combine these regular shapes with irregular shapes. The forms in artwork can be thought of as filled or empty. In relationship to each other they may be separated by space, connected or overlapping, or enclosed within each other. When the boundaries of a shape are completed, the shape is closed; if the boundary is left uncompleted (like *U* or a *C*), the shape is open. Shapes in three-dimensional art may be solid (like a ball) or may use empty space as part of the form (like a tire). In two-dimensional art the shapes

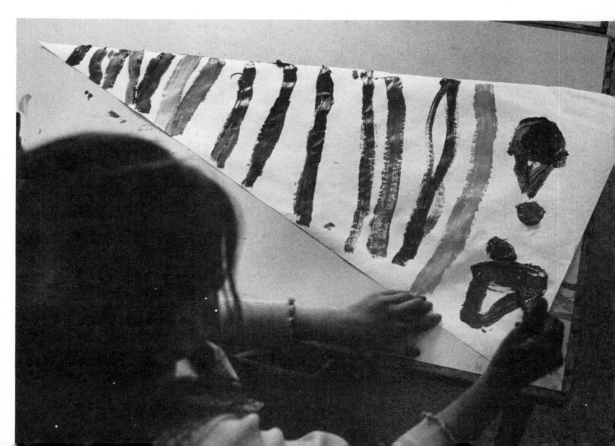

may be filled in or outlined. Shapes are large or small and have a comparative relationship with other shapes in the work (bigger, smaller, rounder, more angular, etc.).

Space refers to the distance within or between aspects of a piece of artwork. The location of a line, shape, or color is part of the work—center, top, bottom, side, left, right. Space can be crowded and full, sparse or empty; these give feelings of freedom or cramped enclosure to the work. The space can have balance with other spaces or forms. Boundaries in a work and ideas like inclusion and exclusion are a part of the spatial qualities of artwork. Space can be solid or permeable.

Design refers to the organization of a piece of work. Children initially work without plan or artistic purpose: art is sensory and exploratory. Nancy Smith refers to children's approach to paper in painting at this stage as a place ". . . to play, a sort of two-dimensional park . . ."(1983 p. 33). As children gain experience, they become aware, and the elements of design enter their work. There is awareness of the unity of the work or of a division of elements. A planned, organized piece of work may have a concept (like a circular shape) repeated or varied. The way color, line, shape and form are placed may give the work an actual texture or the impression of texture. Elements are used with an awareness of their relationship to one another although effects may be unexpected. Symmetry, balance, and alternation are some of the characteristics found in design.

Supporting Children in Art

The work of an artist, child or adult, requires a special kind of environment that supports artistic expression, enabling the artist to work with full concentration on the process of creation. It includes materials and equipment that are appropriate to the task, that are functional, and that inspire use. An environment for artistic expression also involves having sufficient time and space for exploration. For young children, especially, the environment may be a source of motivation.

When designing an art area for children, you may find it useful to use an artist's studio as a model—a place designed by an artist primarily for art. In a studio the amount of external stimulation is controlled; people, objects, and sound are brought in only when desired as models or for motivation. The work area is well lit, usually with natural light. Materials are organized so that they can be found easily. Work tables and easels are the correct size for the artist and the work. Floors, walls, and furnishings are sturdy, washable, and able to bear the brunt of messy procedures. Storage is easily reached, smocks are available to protect clothes, and facilities for cleaning up are nearby. Space is set aside for drying work or storing art that is still in progress. It would be difficult to completely duplicate an artist's studio within a preschool classroom, but it is possible to include many of its important features. Locate art areas near windows, sinks, and on tile or linoleum. Carefully arrange and maintain storage so that all materials and tools are within children's reach. If these are clearly organized and uncrowded, children will be able to put things away. Make sure that furnishings in the art area are the correct size for the children. Use old or secondhand furniture or cover tables and floors so that inevitable paint and glue spills are not tragic.

For child artists, like their adult counterparts, the impulse to create does not occur on a schedule. Art media should be included daily in the free choice of activities in every early childhood program so that children can use media to express creative ideas as they occur. Time to use art materials must be long enough for children to really explore and become involved. Little of creative significance occurs if access to art materials is limited to under an hour a day.

Make basic media (easels, clay, crayons, etc.) available daily, and provide other materials several times a week. The same medium can be presented over several days to enable children to experience it in depth. Great complexity in art materials is not necessary. Children develop creativity as they find new ways to use the familiar.

As a teacher, you help children to develop appreciation for the aesthetic elements of art by what you do and say in your classroom. Careful attention to aesthetics in the choice of materials, the display of artwork, and your comments to children introduces them to a variety of the characteristics of visual art and heightens their aesthetic sensitivity. These are some of the most important goals of art education.

As you look at and talk with children about beauty, remember to discuss color, shape, space, line, form, design, and effect—the elements of art. For example, if a bouquet of flowers has been brought into the classroom, take time with children to arrange them in an attractive container. Comment on the shading of the petals, the scent, the delicate structure. Note the way it makes you feel: "The lavender in the petals of these roses makes me think of the sunset; it makes me feel very peaceful." Similarly, as you and a child

mount and display a piece of artwork you might say, "You must have used hundreds of dots to fill in that big shape; it makes it stand out on your paper." You may want to write down all the words you can think of to describe an element of art; for example, line—jagged, broken, wide, narrow, short, long, curved, flowing, wavy, zigzag, curly, twisted, straight, upright, leaning, turned. These kinds of words give you important things to say with children about their work and make you less dependent on the representational content: "You used several kinds of lines in your work—short narrow ones, wide jagged lines; there are even two wavy lines!"

As children work, it is best, especially at first, to offer only minimal input. Comment on children's effort, innovation, and technique. Avoid asking children *what* they have created. They may have had nothing particular in mind, and the question implies that they should have. Instead you can ask them if they wish to tell you about what they have done, and accept it if they do not. Finished artwork should be mounted carefully and prominently displayed in the classroom to demonstrate to children and their parents your appreciation for the work. Carefully package children's work for the journey home; we recently observed a teacher who used ribbon to tie children's paintings in a neat roll. This conveyed a message to parents and children: this work is valuable.

MUSIC

Children respond to music from the first moments of life; they are soothed by quiet music and respond to a distinct beat with strong rhythmic movement.

Music evokes and describes feelings and provides an emotional outlet. As they grow, children may come to express feelings of joy or sadness with a song or aggressive feelings in a dance to rhythmic or dissonant music. They can come to understand, in simple terms, the elements that make up the discipline of music.

Adults sometimes have difficulty knowing how to present music experiences to young children. Young children's musical responses are strong and very characteristic of the preoperational and sensorimotor stage of development. These responses are physical, individual, and oriented towards personal experience and not the experience of others.

Even from infancy, children are active explorers of music. Many first vocalizations are akin to song and have sometimes been called *lalling* and *trilling*. Physical response to music in infancy is enthusiastic and frequent. Among a baby's first and favorite toys are objects that make sounds: rattles, chimes, bells, and music boxes. By approximately eighteen months, many children begin to sing. From age two, they are responsive listeners. Two year olds sing within a limited range, move to music at their own tempo, and are fascinated by instruments. This development proceeds, and by age four or five, given opportunity, encouragement, and sufficient musical experience, children can sing tunefully, understand basic music concepts, remember elaborate songs, move rhythmically to music, and play simple instruments appropriately. Table 11.2 illustrates children's development in music.

A Framework for Organizing Music

Musical elements such as rhythm, tone, and form are the raw materials out of which every piece of music is made. It is useful for teachers to understand these elements, although they are not meaningful to children if isolated from active music involvement. Children can be helped to respond to the elements in their daily experiences with music. As they participate in music activities, they can come to recognize and label some of the elements of music: "Let's clap to the beat!" "We sang that song faster than we usually do."

Rhythm involves all of the characteristics that relate to the movement and time of

TABLE 11.2
The development of creative expression in music.

Age	Developmental Stage	Characteristics as a Musician
Birth to two years Infants and toddlers	Sensory-motor stage of development Work in creative expression is sensory and exploratory in nature.	Is receptive to music. Responds by listening, singing (vocalizes from approx. 6 months; sings from 18 months) moves, makes sounds with materials—rattles, pots and pans, etc. Enjoys songs and nursery rhymes.
Two to fours years Young preschoolers	Preoperational stage of development (preconceptual phase) Work in creative expression is oriented toward discovery and skill development.	Is interested in and responsive to strongly rhythmic music. Moves and sings to music. Perceives differences in tone color. Sings spontaneously in play. Has a comfortable singing range (D to A above middle C). Does not match pitch when singing with others. May sing only phrases from songs. Enjoys singing the same songs repeatedly. Responds at own tempo. Is interested in musical intruments.
Four to six years Older preschoolers and kindergartners	Preoperational stage of development (intuitive phase) Work in creative expression becomes more complex.	Enjoys group music, musical games, elaborate songs, and singing alone. Can enjoy listening to short musical selections. Has increased singing range (from A below C to the C# an octave above middle C). Is increasingly accurate in matching pitch and tempo when singing in a group. Is able to synchronize movement with rhythm of a piece of music. Can identify and use simple instruments appropriately.

a piece of music. It includes *beat,* the musical pulse that we respond to by tapping our toes, swaying, or clapping. *Melodic rhythm* is the rhythm of the melody or words in a piece of music. When you clap to every syllable of a song as if you were singing it, you are demonstrating the melodic rhythm. Speed in music is called *tempo.* Songs vary in their fastness and slowness, and children can sing songs at different tempos. The points of silence in a piece of music are called *rests.* Children recognize these more easily when they are very distinct, as in the rest that occurs just before the last line of the chorus of "This Land is Your Land" by Woody Guthrie.

Tone concerns the musical notes. It involves *pitch*, which is the highness or lowness of the notes, and *melody,* or *tune,* which is the arrangement of notes into a singable sequence. Tone also involves the way that musical notes sound. *Tone color* or *timbre* (pronounced tamber) refers to the characteristic sounds that musical instruments create. Difference in tone color (for example, between a violin and a flute) is one of the elements that children respond to strongly. Children are also very responsive to the loudness or softness of tones, called *dynamics.*

Form involves the structure of musical pieces. Children learn to respond to an *introduction* when you play several chords or the first part of the tune to establish the pitch and tempo. Structurally, all songs are composed of *phrases*, short but complete musical ideas; for example, the first line of "The Eency Weency Spider." *Repetition* is when identical musical phrases occur in a song, as in the first and last two lines of "Twinkle Twinkle Little Star." When similar phrases occur in a song, as in the first two lines of "Shoo Fly," it is called *variation.* A phrase which is obviously different from the ones that came before provides *contrast*; for example, the third line of "Happy Birthday to You."

Supporting Children in Music

Music experiences in early childhood programs can help children to retain and develop their innate musical expressiveness and learn to enjoy and participate in music. Through these experiences children can come to:

- [ ] Feel good about themselves as musical individuals.
- [ ] Develop the ability to listen sensitively to music.
- [ ] Develop skill and creativity in singing, moving in response to music, and playing simple instruments.
- [ ] Develop beginning understanding of musical elements.
- [ ] Become aware of music from their own and other cultures, times, and places.

Daily experience with music enables children to gradually build and practice a repertoire of skills and songs. These will form the base for individual exploration and appreciation. Schedule group sessions at a regular time each day for ten to twenty minutes. Children will have more successful experiences with groups of less than fifteen. The age appropriateness of your plans, your sensitivity to children's responses, and your awareness that music can be very stimulating will also contribute to positive, easily managed music sessions.

As you plan and participate in musical activities with children, you help them to develop the skills and attitudes of a musician. *Listening* to music involves appreciating and enjoying music, and recognizing, comparing, feeling, imagining, and describing aspects of songs and musical compositions. *Performing* involves singing, moving to music, or playing instruments for others. *Composing* and *improvising* are creative uses of singing, movement, and playing instruments.

Singing offers many opportunities for children to experience music and to develop musical skills. The songs that you teach will contribute to musical growth and will be more successful if they have aesthetic value (beautiful melodies and/or words). Children will have an easier time learning songs if they are relatively short and simple and have a distinct rhythm. An appropriate vocal range for young children is approximately the octave from middle C or slightly lower to C an octave higher; the younger the children, the more narrow the range. Your repertoire of songs should include pieces with a variety of moods, subjects, and tempos, and should reflect a diversity of styles.

Singing in the preschool needs to be primarily a music experience. While songs may teach concepts, that should not be their primary purpose. Children are being cheated if their music has limited value and is really just a drill on color names, the alphabet, or counting. Excessive use of "limited value" songs dilutes the quality of the music experience. Many good songs for young children touch on sensitive subjects, the hard edges of life that teachers sometimes try to eliminate from the classroom: death, loneliness, fear, and anger. Children demonstrate by their obvious interest in such songs that they do not need their music sanitized and cute. However, you should be sensitive to children's responses to songs that have a strong emotional impact. We once observed a child who became very upset when "John Henry" was sung perhaps because of the line "He laid down his hammer and he died." It would have been insensitive and disrespectful had the teacher gone on singing this song in his presence.

Sit with children as you sing. We prefer sitting on the carpet or outside under a tree. Encourage children to choose songs. If you can, accompany the singing with a guitar, autoharp, or ukulele; this will add to the experience. If not, clap your hands, keep time with a drum, or sway as you sing. Piano accompaniment does not

offer the intimacy and accessibility of sitting near children and singing with them and is difficult to manage with groups of young children.

Moving to music is a natural response: our toes tap, our heads nod, and our bodies sway almost without our realizing it. Movement often helps young children to concentrate on a music session. Hand gestures and fingerplays illustrate songs and help children to understand the meaning of the words. Use body movements with songs, and encourage children to think of new ways to move. Instrumental music also often evokes images and ways of moving and contributes to music sessions.

Children are spontaneous music makers. They hum tunes, make up songs, explore sounds, create rhythms, and use music to communicate. You can encourage spontaneous music by acknowledging it and initiating it. If you make up or improvise songs and chants as you work with children, they will follow suit. A music center that includes instruments to explore provides stimulus for music making. Interesting events are often the topics of children's spontaneous songs.

Every classroom needs simple instruments, generally called rhythm instruments. These are used at music time as part of the structured experience. They can also be used in a music center. Good quality instruments have good tone and are satisfying to play. They are a worthwhile investment, but they must be stored and handled carefully like any other piece of equipment. Instruments that are tossed into a box and grabbed out again the next time have a short life span. These instruments must be sturdy enough to take the enthusiastic handling of many young children. It is neither necessary nor desirable for every child to have an instrument at the same time. It tends to amplify noise and chaos. Instead, introduce instruments singly in small groups. Let each child have a turn to play, and give instruction in the care and handling of the instrument. The musical elements provide a useful framework for learning about instruments. Comparing the sound of a triangle and tone block, for example, and using them to accompany different verses of "Froggie Went-a-Courtin' " gives children an experience with timbre.

Listening to music created by others is worthwhile for young children. Recordings can provide children with important experiences with talented musicians, symphonic music, and music from many cultures. Recorded music is so common-place in our society that it has become like audible wallpaper: something children and adults tend to ignore. When you use recorded music with children, make your choices carefully and present them as important. To help children be attentive listeners to recorded music, ask them to listen for a sound, move a part of their body to the beat, or notice what kind of feeling the music creates in them. Short, evocative pieces of music are best able to hold children's attention. Be eclectic in your choices of recorded music, and help children to be aware of musical alternatives. Your responsibility as a teacher is to acquaint children with a range of good music, not merely what is easiest or most familiar to you. Most children have plenty of exposure to *Top Forty, Sesame Street,* and *Muzak,* but may never have heard chamber music, folk music, bluegrass, jazz, Gregorian chants, symphonic music, classical guitar, flute, sitar, or opera. Most public libraries have a selection of different kinds of recorded music available for borrowing, and you can pick up a new record each week as you borrow new books.

Recordings are not a replacement for real people making music. When you play instruments and sing in the classroom, you prove that music comes from people, not mechanical boxes. Have musicians visit your classroom to play short pieces of music for children. They need not be professionals; your next door neighbor's daughter who is studying the clarinet, the high school string quartet, or a parent who plays the banjo will provide a listening experience with live music and real instruments that will impress itself indelibly in the minds of the children you teach. It's best if children are allowed to gently try the instruments themselves after the musician plays.

Your classroom is a place where children are introduced to new experiences. While you may wish to begin with music that is comfortable and familiar, you will also want to present the best you can offer and expand children's musical horizons.

CREATIVE MOVEMENT

Young children are nearly always moving. As they move, they learn. Concepts such as rough, smooth, run, creep, and push must be experienced before they can be understood. Children move to play, to express feelings, and to communicate. Creative movement for young children is the art form in which the entire body is used in expressive ways.

Creative movement activities can be done with children of all ages, but the younger the children, the simpler the activities must be. Activities should match the level of physical and language development of the children. Your observations of the children you teach and the developmental chart presented in Table 11.3 can be helpful in planning appropriate movement activities. Sustained interest is harder to maintain for very young children because of their more limited language and attention span for group activities.

When is movement creative? When ideas and feelings are expressed through movement in individual ways, children are using their bodies as an art medium. This is different from, and not a substitute for, large muscle activity on the playground or games and exercises such as the *Hokey Pokey*. It differs from dance in which the teacher instructs in specific, predetermined ways of moving. In a creative movement activity, children interpret and follow suggestions from the teacher who encourages them to find their own personal, creative, and innovative ways of moving. During these activities, children discover joy and satisfaction in expressing ideas with their bodies and develop a repertoire of movement possibilities. Creative movement offers challenges and new ways to use and practice developing physical skills. As you direct children in movement, encourage

TABLE 11.3
The development of creative expression in movement.

Age	Developmental Stage	Characteristics as a Creative Mover
Birth to two years Infants and toddlers	Sensory-motor stage of development Work in creative expression is sensory and exploratory in nature.	Is developing basic motor skills by age two: walking, running, jumping. Takes pleasure in new skills.
Two to fours years Young preschoolers	Preoperational stage of development (preconceptual phase) Work in creative expression is oriented toward discovery and skill development.	Walks with uniform stride. Walks backwards, sideways, or on tiptoe. Runs well but cannot stop or turn quickly. Gallops. Jumps with two feet. Can hop, by approximately age four. Enjoys repetition of movement activities. Enjoys directed movement activities.
Four to six years Older preschoolers and kindergartners	Preoperational stage of development (intuitive phase) Work in creative expression becomes more complex and representational.	Has well developed skill in walking, running, and jumping. Controls speed, stopping, and turning. Skips well by approximately age six. Follows direction well. Maintains personal space. Understands and can move forward, backwards, sideways, up, down, fast, slow, lightly, heavily. Moves body parts in isolation with practice.

them to make suggestions and express ideas in innovative ways. This supports children's developing imagination and positive self-concept. It is this focus on individual ways of moving that makes it *creative* movement. Social development is enhanced as they learn to move with respect for the group and come to appreciate the creativity of others.

A Framework for Creative Movement

Understanding the different aspects of movement enables you to plan and guide activities that are purposeful. These develop children's awareness and skill and help them to become confident, creative movers—people who can use their bodies in expressive ways and who know a range of ways to express ideas and feelings through body movement.

In order for the body to be an effective medium for expression, children need to develop **body awareness**: where they are in space, the *shapes* they can create, the ways they can travel from one place to another, called *locomotor movement*, and the ways they can move while staying in the same place, or *nonlocomotor movement*. Among the most difficult skills for children to develop is the ability to move one part of the body while keeping the rest still, called *body isolation*.

All movement takes place in **space**, uses **time**, and involves **force**. These are the elements of movement. The space in which we move, includes direction (forward, backward, sideways) and level (high, middle, low). Time concerns the tempo or speed of the movement, and force, the amount of energy used.

Personal space is the space right around you, defined by your presence. *General space* is used by the whole group. Activities can help children to use all of their personal space—up high, down low, to the side, in back—and to learn to share the general space. As you guide creative movement activities, you should include suggestions that encourage children to move at different speeds and levels without touching or bumping anyone else. Boundaries (for example, a chalked circle) can define the space for children to move within and around. Space may be filled in different ways while children stay in one place. Images motivate and encourage children to use space in diverse ways. Invite children to think about moving and filling space like balloons, fish, worms, trees, bubbles, birds, and different animals.

Young children experience tempo, or time, through a contrast of fast and slow movements. They generally find it easier to move quickly since slow movements require greater concentration and body control. Slow movement is sustained while fast movement can be jerky. Speed can be contrasted by moving body parts at different tempos (raise your arms slowly, shake your hands quickly) or moving the body as a whole at different paces (run, creep, trot, slowly unbend, jump). Imagery of animals, plants, and machines can encourage exploration of speed, and the use of a drum beat or music can help children learn to move to a particular tempo.

Some movements, such as stamping heavily or punching into the air, require a lot of force. Others, such as tiptoeing, or jumping lightly, use less. Young children find strong, forceful movements very satisfying, but they also enjoy developing the control needed to move lightly. Activities that involve force may contrast heavy and light movement (stamping and then tiptoeing) and can involve body parts or the whole body while in motion or stationary. Music can evoke heavy or light movements as can images of animals and fantasy creatures (elephants, butterflies, bears, birds, monsters, fairies, giants, ghosts).

Supporting Children in Creative Movement

Your role in creative movement is to provide a safe, encouraging, and stimulating atmosphere within which children may experiment. First you must ensure that the environment is safe for movement and conducive to creativity. Uncluttered open space with clear boundaries is needed. Wood or low-pile carpeted floors provide the best surface. If you use your classroom, push back the furniture to create a safe, open, inviting space.

Basic rules for safety need to be established (no pushing, bumping, and so on), and an attitude of respect for individual interpretations and skill levels is essential. Children should never be forced to participate in a creative movement activity or ridiculed or criticized for the way they move. As children develop confidence and movement skills, they will be able to use movement to express creative ideas with little direction. In the beginning, however, you will need to provide a good deal of guidance.

The ideal group size for creative movement is from five to twelve children. If you must work with larger groups, have the children alternate between moving and being the audience. Regularly scheduled movement activities, at least twice a week, help children develop skill and build on previous experience.

Creative movement activities can be quite structured (as when children move parts of their bodies to the beat of a drum) or more open-ended (as when children are invited to explore all the ways they can move to music with a scarf). Managing movement activities is often difficult for beginning teachers. Children who have had little experience with structured movement activities can become overexcited and uncontrolled,

and this can be difficult to handle. While every group of children is different—some need very specific limits and others need lots of opportunity to explore—it is usually best to begin with short (fifteen minutes or less), simple, well-planned, and fairly structured activities moving on to more open activities later. When you first begin creative movement with a group, establish a signal like a hard drumbeat, which will tell the children to become still immediately. Practice stopping to this signal as a game until they come to understand it as an integral part of every movement activity. This will help you to maintain control of the group and will help children to focus their movement. Alternate vigorous and quiet activities, and begin activities sitting down or standing still before inviting children to move freely around the room. When you have reached a planned or natural ending place, it is best to finish the activity while it is still going well. End sessions in a way that provides a transition to the next activity. "Tiptoe to the playground when I touch you on the shoulder."

If a movement session does go badly, do not blame the children or yourself. Know that in the beginning you will have some successful sessions and others that are less successful. The learning that comes out of these experiences can be valuable for you as a teacher.

Creative Drama

In working with young children creative movement and drama are closely tied to one another. The motivation for movement activities is often the suggestion to act like a character, animal, or object. Children naturally take on roles in their play and dramatize stories and scenes. With very young children, creative drama and movement are often part of the same activities. As you direct children in creative movement, you may alternate between directions that are exclusively related to body movement ("Bounce"), to directions that are related to a dramatic idea ("Bounce like a ball"; "Hop like a rabbit"), to directions that are dramatic ideas, as a part of a story or scenario ("The rabbit is hopping slowly now; he hears something. Quickly hop away and run to your burrow").

Children's literature can offer motivation for creative movement and drama. The rabbit in the above example may become Peter Rabbit fleeing from Mr. MacGregor. Leo Lionni's story *Swimmy*, is another example that intertwines the story of a fish with descriptions of the movements of sea creatures and serves as an excellent outline for a movement/drama session. Creative drama for young children involves their interpretations of story lines and ideas, not memorization of scripts, and should be outgrowths of children's ideas, not production efforts put on by teachers for parents. Some four, five, and six year olds do become entranced by performance, however. With a skillful teacher they can begin to extend their developing skills into a performing arts of dance and drama productions.

Thoughtful planning and periodic reevaluation of your teaching are necessary to provide children with the opportunity to be truly creative. The Creative Curriculum Checklist provided is designed to help you in this process.

CHECKLIST FOR CREATIVE CURRICULUM AREAS

Program Structure

☐ Stated goals include the support of the development of creativity and aesthetic awareness through art, music, and movement

☐ Products and performances are considered secondary parts of the arts program

☐ Daily free choice periods of at least an hour include opportunities to use art materials, blocks, dramatic play, and manipulative toys

☐ Daily group music experiences are provided

☐ Creative movement and drama activities are provided regularly—at least weekly

Environment and Materials

General Environment:

☐ An art center

☐ A dramatic play area

☐ A block area

☐ A manipulative toy area

☐ Adequate space for group movement and music activities without protruding furniture or fixtures

☐ Relatively quiet and uncrowded space when music or movement are in progress

☐ Works of art and beautiful objects from nature displayed, some at child's eye level

☐ Children's artwork carefully and aesthetically mounted and displayed

☐ Materials and supplies aesthetically arranged, stored, and organized

☐ Equipment and materials are stored so that they are easily found and reached, e.g., paper and pens

☐ Fragile or delicate materials are stored to avoid damage, e.g., records and instruments

☐ Equipment and materials are available in sufficient quantity that children have plenty of opportunity to use them

☐ Materials that require supervision are stored out of children's reach and view, e.g., saws and nails

☐ Storage area for children's completed artwork is set up so that children can file and retrieve their own work

Equipment, Materials, and Supplies:

art:

- ☐ Trays or cookie sheets to hold materials and delineate space
- ☐ Airtight containers for storage
- ☐ Scissors that cut well and can be used in either hand
- ☐ Paper in a variety of shapes, weights, colors, and sizes, including cardboard
- ☐ White glue and paste
- ☐ Tempera paint in primary colors (red, yellow, blue), white, and black
- ☐ Finger-paint base (bentonite, laundry starch, etc.)
- ☐ Large format paper for the easel
- ☐ Paint containers that do not tip when brushes are set in them
- ☐ Brushes that are ½″ to 1″ wide for easel painting in a variety of lengths
- ☐ Water color brushes, house painting brushes, feathers, sponges, swabs
- ☐ Materials such as ____ peeled large crayons, ____ felt-tip marking pens (nontoxic in both wide and narrow sizes), ____ colored chalk, ____ oil pastels, ____ pencils, ____ hole punch, ____ ruler and protractor, ____ tape, ____ envelopes, ____ potter's clay, ____ dough, ____ clayboards or mats, ____ dowels or rolling pins, ____ tongue depressors or blunt knives, ____ clayworking tools
- ☐ Found materials such as paper rolls, fabric pieces, yarn scraps, Popsicle sticks, macaroni, rice, rocks, buttons, wood scraps, seeds, shells, etc.
- ☐ Crewel needles
- ☐ Woodworking equipment such as ____ small, light hammers, ____ screwdrivers, ____ short saws, ____ a vise or a C-clamp

music:

- ☐ A sturdy record player
- ☐ A tape recorder
- ☐ Recordings representing a number of areas and styles such as, ____ folk music from different cultures, ____ instrumental good quality records designed for children, ____ meditation music
- ☐ A variety of good quality instruments such as ____ tambourine, ____ hand drum, ____ claves and rhythm sticks, ____ triangle, ____ tone blocks, ____ maracas, ____ cymbals, ____ a harmony instrument (e.g., guitar, autoharp, ukulele)

movement:
- ☐ A good quality tunable tambourine or hand drum
- ☐ Supplies such as ____ chiffon scarves, ____ streamers, ____ Chinese jump ropes, ____ hoops, ____ bean bags

furniture:
- ☐ Small low tables and chairs or tables low enough for children to sit on the floor
- ☐ A small table for one child to work alone or with a partner
- ☐ Low, open storage shelves for art supplies located near the art area
- ☐ An easel low enough that the smallest child can reach the top of the painting surface comfortably
- ☐ A drying rack or shelf
- ☐ A small heavyweight table for woodworking

FOR FURTHER THOUGHT AND DISCUSSION

1 Think of a place that is beautiful to you, that refreshes you. What kinds of things do you find there? What makes it special to you? Compare your ideas to those of other people— what is similar, what is different about your visions? How could elements of this beauty be a part of a classroom? What would need to happen to make this a reality?

2 What kind of experiences did you have in school with art, music, and movement? Did your teachers support or discourage creativity and individuality? In what ways did they support it? In what ways did they discourage it? How have these experiences affected your feelings about your present-day creativity and ability in art, music, or dance?

3 Reflect on programs that you have observed. Compare how these provided creative and aesthetic experiences for children. Was time for art, music, and movement scheduled? Was the environment arranged for children's independent creative expression? Was artwork displayed in the classroom? How did teachers talk to children about their creative efforts? What were the characteristics of the programs you liked best? How did these differ from the programs you liked least?

PROJECTS

1 Use the **Checklist for Creative Curriculum Areas** in this chapter to observe an early childhood program. Report on the extent to which the program seems to support children's creative expression and aesthetic sensitivity.

2 Design an art area for an early childhood classroom. Make sure all the tools and materials that a child would need for each of the different kinds of art activities are available for independent use. Put your design into effect in a classroom. Take pictures of the results of your efforts showing both before and after, or draw a floor and shelf plan showing what you did. Report on what you did and the effect on children's creative work.

3 Use the lesson plan form in Chapter 9 to design and implement an art activity for children. Report on what happened. Describe what you learned about yourself, children, art, and teaching.

4 Use the lesson plan form in Chapter 9 to design and implement a music or creative movement/drama activity for children. Report on what happened. Describe what you learned about yourself, children, music or movement, and teaching.

5 Design a week's plans for young children that includes all of the arts. Use one of the weekly planning forms in Chapter 9. Implement part or all of your plan. Report on what happened. Describe what you learned about yourself, children, creativity, and planning.

RECOMMENDED READING

Barlin, Anne Lief. *Teaching Your Wings to Fly*. Santa Monica, Cal.: Goodyear Publishing Co., 1979.

Brittain, W. Lambert. *Creativity, Art, and the Young Child*. New York: Macmillan Publishing Co., Inc., 1979.

Burton, Leon. *Musicplay*. Menlo Park, Cal.: Addison-Wesley Publishing Co., 1980.

Burton, Leon, and Kuroda, Kathy. *Artsplay: Creative Activities in Dance, Drama, Art, and Music for Young Children*. Menlo Park, Cal.: Addison-Wesley Publishing Co., 1981.

Chenfeld, Mimi Brodsky. *Creative Activities for Young Children.* New York: Harcourt Brace Jovanovich, 1983.

Cherry, Claire. *Creative Movement for the Developing Child: A Nursery School Handbook for Non-Musicians.* Rev. ed. Belmont, Cal.: Fearon Publishers, 1971.

Curtis, Sandra R. *The Joy of Movement in Early Childhood.* New York: Teachers College Press, 1982.

Greenberg, Marvin. *Your Children Need Music.* Englewood Cliffs, N.J.: Prentice-Hall, 1979.

Jenkins, Peggy Davison. *Art for the Fun of It.* Englewood Cliffs, N.J.: Prentice-Hall, 1980.

Kellogg, Rhoda. *Analyzing Children's Art.* Palo Alto, Cal.: Mayfield Publishing Co., 1982.

Lasky, Lila, and Mukerji, Rose. *Art: Basic for Young Children.* Washington, D.C.: National Association for the Education of Young Children, 1980.

MacDonald, Dorothy T. *Music in Our Lives: The Early Years.* Washington, D.C.: National Association for the Education of Young Children, 1979.

Rowen, Betty. *Learning Through Movement: Activities for the Preschool and Elementary School Grades.* 2d ed. New York: Teachers College Press, 1982.

Seeger, Ruth Crawford, *American Folksongs for Children.* Garden City, N.Y.: Doubleday and Company, Inc., 1945.

Sinclair, Caroline B. *Movement of the Young Child: Age Two to Six.* Columbus, O.: Charles E. Merrill, 1973.

Smith, Nancy. *Experience and Art: Teaching Children to Paint.* New York: Teachers College Press, 1983.

Sullivan, Molly. *Feeling Strong, Feeling Free: Movement Exploration for Young Children.* Washington D.C.: National Association for the Education of Young Children, 1982.

Whitken, Kate, with Philip, Richard. *To Move To Learn.* New York: Schocken Books, 1978.

Zeitlin, Patty. *A Song Is a Rainbow.* Glenview, Ill.: Scott, Foresman and Company, 1982.

12

The Language and Literacy Curriculum

"Experience needs language to give it form. Language needs experience to give it content."

Walter Loban

This chapter examines the role of the early childhood teacher and program in the development of language, literacy, and in the appreciation of literature. It is related to the CDA areas Communication, Cognitive, Self, and Learning Environment.

In order to understand the world and function in it, we need to be competent in communicating with others. The strong desire to do this is one of the characteristics that unites human beings in a common bond. People communicate through language, systematic and symbolic forms which represent human thinking. Reading and writing are tools that have been devised to extend this ability over distance and time. Literature is the art form that uses language. Within this curriculum cluster (often referred to as **language arts**) oral language is primary; reading, writing, and literature are dependent upon it.

Classrooms can be designed to foster children's natural desire, ability, and pleasure in communicating with others. The goals of the language and literacy curriculum areas are to help children become enthusiastic, competent communicators who use and enjoy spoken and written language.

A DEVELOPMENTAL PERSPECTIVE

Language development, the basis of the language and literacy curriculum, is like physical development in that it follows a predictable sequence and is related, but not tied to, chronological age. Children need experiences with oral and written language that are appropriate to their developmental abilities. For younger and less mature children meaningful social,

physical, and sensory activity is an important underpinning for talking. As children mature, they are more interested in and able to understand complex language, and they use more language in their relationships with others. Within any group of young children of a similar age, there is a wide variety of differences in language facility, in individual style, and in interest in using spoken and written language.

Language uses a shared system of symbols that has structure, rules, and meaning that are accepted and unconsciously known by those who use it. The symbols can be combined, organized, and enlarged to convey an infinite variety and complexity of messages. Except for a few routine phrases like "Have a nice day," language is creative. Most utterances have not been spoken or written before. Children learn the complex structure, rules, and meanings of language and develop the ability to create their own speech and read and write their own words through processes that are still not completely understood.

Language Development

Although individuals may vary in the speed of language acquisition and in how much they speak, the language learning process is universal. Psychologists and linguists have long theorized about how children learn to speak. The previously influential behaviorist view that language is gradually built up through imitation and reinforcement is now seen as inadequate to explain the creative nature of speech.

Linguist Noam Chomsky, as described in Bruner (1983), proposed that humans must have an innate ability to process language, which he referred to as a *language acquisition device* (LAD). The existence of this innate ability explains why children are able to produce word forms and sentences they have never heard. Chomsky's work sparked an interest to find out what young children naturally understand about the structure of language when they start to talk—for example, identifying similarities in the ways all young children combine words or use grammatical forms. While this research helped us learn the formal features of language, *what* children do, it did little to explain *how* young children learn to speak.

We know that language and thought go hand in hand; however, the exact nature of the relationship is not clear. Piaget suggested that language develops as cognitive ability matures; that is, children become capable of acquiring and using language as they begin to understand concepts. Vygotsky argues that language is primary: as children learn language, they gain a tool that permits them to understand and organize their experiences in human terms. There is general agreement that a strong relationship exists between thinking and language, between concepts and the words used to express them. There is also agreement that development of language is part of an active mental process. It involves constructing intuitive rules that guide behavior. Both experiences with the physical world *and* experiences using

language for communicating with others are vital in its development.

As children learn language, they master a complex task which involves a system of speech sounds (**phonology**), grammatical forms and relationships (**syntax**), meaning (**semantics**), and socially based customs for language use (**pragmatics**). Experimentation with all of these elements, exposure to everyday speech, and a desire to interact socially all contribute to children's construction of their own understanding of language principles. By the age of five or six, most children have mastered the basics in all of these areas in their native tongue; they have "learned language."

Language learning begins with children's experiences with their caregivers in the first months of life. During the first year, before speaking, children make and respond to many sounds. Crying, gurgling, babbling, and cooing are important parts of the language learning process. Caregivers respond to the sounds that infants make, and some important language abilities are established. Current theories of language development proposed by Jerome Bruner, Gordon Wells, and others follow Vygotsky's view that early social experiences form the basis for language development. Bruner (1983) proposes that these experiences form a *language acquisition support system* (LASS) to assist Chomsky's LAD.

Since the communication between infant and caregiver is important, examining what takes place during this process helps us understand how children learn to talk. Routine events in the everyday life of an infant are the major context for language learning: games like peek-a-boo, pointing at and naming objects, picture book reading and nonverbal play. Adults act as informal guides to support and foster language learning through these interactions.

By the end of their first year, children generally speak their first word. It is important to note that children enter language stages at different ages; the speed of language learning does not correlate to intelligence. A significant delay in speech development, however, can be a signal for assessing a child for possible developmental problems.

The first stage of spoken language involves single words or syllables called *holophrases* which stand for whole sentences or phrases. Holophrases have different meanings in different situations. For example, "Car" said while looking out the window may mean, "Look at the car outside," while "Car" said while standing next to the toy box may mean, "I want my toy car." A vocabulary of holophrases is developed that enables children to communicate with parents and other familiar people. Before the next stage, children use successive holophrases to increase their communicative power: "Car" pause "Go" to indicate "I want to go for a ride." Two word sentences often appear between eighteen and twenty months of age. These express ideas concerning relationships: "Mommy sock" (possessor-possession), "Cat sleeping" (actor-action), "Drink milk" (action-object), and so on. Children next use short simple sentences made up of groups of words that each convey meaning: "Where Daddy go?" "Me push truck." These are called *telegraphic* because they omit the function words and endings that do not contribute greatly to meaning, similar to a telegram. Bruner suggests that caregivers provide a temporary framework or *scaffold* for language by assuming that young children

intend to communicate, by listening carefully, and by assisting only as much as needed. In early conversations caregivers provide some of the child's responses. As the ability to participate is demonstrated, the adult adjusts, gradually permitting the child to take over on his or her own.

As language development proceeds, children learn to join related sentences logically and express ideas concerning time and spatial relationships. They come to understand social expectations for language use and begin to use adult forms of language. Vocabularies expand rapidly, the ability to use words increases, and children intuitively acquire many of the rules of language. While this is happening, they often overgeneralize and speak in ways that follow a rule accurately but are inconsistent with common usage—for example, "I comed home" for "I came home." The correct form is temporarily replaced as the child internalizes and generalizes the rule. Overgeneralizations are natural parts of children's active language development and have added to understanding the language learning process. They have helped linguists realize that children analyze and construct language rather than merely imitate adults or respond to adult instruction. As children formulate ideas about language, they try them out and listen to adult language models. This process of exploration is not affected by instruction or correction, but by speaking and listening.

Literacy Development

Our view of how literacy develops in young children is changing based on research that shows children's early awareness of written language. Young children learn to speak at an early age, a complex and difficult task. Many contemporary researchers think that children draw on these same capabilities in learning to read and write. It is becoming clear that the foundations for making sense of written language start with early social uses of print long before reading begins.

Much current research has its basis in Vygotsky's suggestion that we look for what happens before writing and reading and how these are supported in children's social interactions. Children do not wait for formal lessons to begin to formulate ideas about written language. Some children even begin to read and write without instruction, although careful investigation shows that they usually live in homes where many experiences with written language are available, and they have much adult support. Jerome Harste (1984) and others found that many young children from all socio-economic backgrounds in the United States already "read" print as it appears in their environment; for example, they read the McDonald's sign and understand the purpose of the red, white, and blue U.S. Mail symbol.

Young children's interpretation of storybooks provides additional evidence of their early knowledge of written language. They come to understand how books work, that is, to start at the front cover and go through page by page. They develop understanding of basic story structure by retelling familiar stories and pretending to read books to themselves or others using language forms which sound more like "book language" than talk. Understanding of the purposes and characteristics of books, and the ability to

understand and find personal meaning in story reading are essential underpinnings for later reading success. Gordon Wells (1981) found that how well young children understood the conventions of print used in books was the best way to predict later success in reading.

As children begin to recognize the connection between speech and print, they construct rules to explain this relationship. For example, a child who knows a few alphabet letter names may begin to write "words" by matching letter names with sounds in speech, e.g., they print the *M* to stand for mommy. Research has led to the recognition that some young children independently produce readable written messages, using *invented spelling*, before they receive formal instruction in writing; for example, a child we know wrote "hp vltn" on a valentine.

All these studies point out that children gradually develop rules and generalizations about written language for themselves, often proceeding through stages where they hold inaccurate or partially accurate concepts as they attempt to sort out how written language works. Current research also emphasizes that social interaction about print (between adult and child and between children) plays a role in helping children understand written language.

TEACHER ROLE

Children's school experiences with the language and literacy are highly dependent on you, the teacher. Your job is to provide relationships that are supportive, caring, and filled with language in all its forms. As you speak to children honestly and respectfully and listen to them attentively and patiently, you are encouraging language use. As you use language to mediate problems, communicate information, and share feelings and ideas, you are demonstrating the usefulness and value of oral language.

In a similar way, the value of written language is demonstrated to children as you use it in your daily activities. When you write a note to a child or parent, a grocery list, or a thank-you letter, or read a recipe, story, poem, or book, you model the importance of writing and reading. When children see that significant adults in their lives use reading and writing, it provides a powerful incentive to begin learning these useful skills.

An environment that is rich in language, writing, good books, and other reading experiences is vital. You must provide ample opportunities for each child to use language and written words for a variety of purposes. As a teacher, you should provide lots of experiences with talk and print. Good literature will come to be appreciated as children are introduced to many well-written books.

Just as it would be inappropriate to expect every child to master the same physical challenges, so is it inappropriate to expect every child to be able to follow the same verbal directions, enjoy the same books, or have the same interest in written words. A single group of young children may include a range from nonverbal to beginning readers. Culture, as well as developmental differences, effects language use. School customs can be quite different from those of home and may require a greater adjustment for children from some social and cultural groups than for others. As a teacher of young children, you will need to be aware of and sensitive to the social customs for talking that children have learned. Children from some cultures learn to show respect for adults by remaining silent and looking away, while those from another cultural background learn to maintain eye contact and speak up. Anthropologists, such as Shirley Brice Heath (1983), have found that children from different cultural backgrounds learn different ways of talking about and expressing the meaning of events. Ways of telling stories, looking at picture books, and asking or answering questions may also be affected by cultural differences.

ORAL LANGUAGE

Learning to understand and use language is one of the most significant accomplishments of early childhood. Almost all children acquire language without any formal teaching before they enter school; it is a skill that appears to be "caught, not taught." As they forge their language, children develop an inseparable part of themselves, as well as a tool for communication, expression, and learning.

Young children learn the customs for language that are familiar in their own homes and communities. They learn to select speech appropriate to the setting; different speech is used in the classroom than on the playground. The purpose for speaking and the particular people being addressed will come to be associated with different kinds of language. Children learn very early to include such nonverbal social features as gestures, facial expressions, body position, and intonation in their style of speaking. They come to understand the expectations and signals for turn-taking in conversations.

There are variations in the way individuals speak. Some are personal, relating to word and phrase preferences and individual characteristics such as voice quality. Other variations relate to the language that is used, valued, and taught in a particular locale. In the United States, Canada, Australia, and Great Britian, for example, English is spoken as the primary language, but there are regional differences. When the differences are distinct, these are called **dialects**. Dialects vary from the dominant language in vocabulary, pronunciation, and grammatical rules. Often they have different rules for forming plurals, negatives, and past tenses (e.g., "ain't" for "isn't").

In the United States, there are variations of English that have roots in other languages. These variations use English words, but are sufficiently different from standard English to be considered separate languages. These are called the *Creole*

languages, *Gullah* in South Carolina and Georgia, and *Pidgin* in Hawaii. They use some non-English words, substantially different grammar, and are quite difficult for most standard English speakers to understand.

Black English, which is spoken among the black population of urban ghettos in the northern United States and throughout the South, uses elements of southern dialects and words and structure that reflect a Creole language. Although it has greater differences from standard English than most dialects, it is not considered a separate language.

Language differences have deeper implications, however, than simple grammatical or pronunciation variations. Because language is intimately connected to the way that we live, a language expresses a particular culture's unique perception of the world. Certain African cultures, for example, have fewer names for colors than English; hence, the colors themselves are probably perceived differently. The Inuit culture of the Arctic, to point to another example, has many different words to describe snow. Language, then, is more than written and spoken communication. It is an intrinsic part of our culture and reflects a distinctive vision of the world.

In order for children to become confident, effective communicators, they must first feel good about themselves and their language, and they must feel comfortable speaking. Whatever language they speak, it is *vital* that you accept and respect it. While dialects have often been characterized as inferior, they are in fact, simply different. Like standard English, they are flexible, capable of expansion, rule-governed, and expressive. Dialect speakers communicate effectively in day-to-day interactions in their own communities. Standard English (sometimes called the school dialect) has no inherent superiority for communicating or for thinking. It is, however, widely used and understood as the language of education, literature, business, and technology. Because of this, teachers are generally expected to provide a model of Standard English. Programs aimed at changing oral language through drill and practice separate talk from meaning. They are likely to be ineffective, and may have a negative effect on children's self-concepts by demeaning their natural expression.

In our diverse society you may have children in your class whose first language is not English. At one time these children were considered disadvantaged, and the job of the teacher was to develop the child's skill in English while decreasing the use of the native tongue. Knowledge of two languages is now generally viewed as advantageous and continued development in *both* languages is the goal.

To support bilingualism teachers need to visibly and actively value the child's first language and culture. Janet Gonzales-Mena (1981) suggests that the basis for teaching young children whose first language is not English must be relationships within a program for total development, ideally involving teachers who speak both languages. This view of second language learning is consistent with knowledge of language development, but it is not always possible. Indeed, we have experienced classrooms in Hawaii where children came from eight different language backgrounds. A United Nations translator would have been the only solution. Creative monolingual teachers can successfully work with the non-English speaking children in their classes by using the resources available to them. They learn key words and phrases in the child's language; have children use their first language to teach the group words, songs, and games; and encourage bilingual family and community members to participate in the classroom. Most important, they build strong relationships with the children and their families and help them feel comfortable sharing their language and culture in the school.

Reading, home visits, and discussions with the parents will help you develop understanding of children whose backgrounds are different from your own. Your goal is to help children find ways to use and show what they already know while extending their experiences and helping them to find new ways of using language.

A Framework for Thinking About Oral Language

Oral language is used for a variety of purposes. It can be used to get people to do something, to express needs and direct one's own behavior, to establish and maintain relationships with others, or to call attention to oneself. We also use language to ask for and give information and interpret our experiences, to play, and to create imaginary scenes or think about events that are not happening in the present. Most young children have ample experience using language for directing behavior and other interpersonal purposes. When they first come to school, some children may have had little opportunity to use language to describe and explain their experiences, or to talk about things beyond the "here and now" of immediate events. Differences will reflect the wide range of possible

ways language was used by individual caregivers and social groups. If you become familiar with the different uses of language, you will be able to see where children's usual purposes for talking might be extended and to ensure that a range of language opportunities are encouraged in your classroom.

Informative Language   Informative language is used to share facts and opinions with others. In classrooms children, as well as teachers, need opportunities to practice using language to exchange information. You may need to provide a model of this kind of talk and a great deal of encouragement. You must be a careful and respectful listener. Children who learn that you will listen to them and take them seriously will come to feel pride and delight in their own

abilities. These children may be the ones that often say, "Did you know that. . .?" "My mommy says. . ." "I saw. . ."

Descriptive Language   As you work and talk with young children, there are many chances to descibe experiences in words. Many parents and teachers naturally model the use of descriptive language, particularly with very young children. They talk about what is happening, giving a running commentary as they go through an activity: "Dylan sure seems to be enjoying himself on the trampoline. He's bouncing up and down and smiling. Look how his hair flops up and down as he jumps." Skillful teachers doing this make sure that ample time is left for children to contribute. Children may need your help to become more specific in their talk. For example, if a child says, "I got the stuff," you can expand by saying, "Oh good; you brought the sawdust and scraper. Now we can clean the mouse cage." Expanding on the child's language in this way must be done naturally without being distracting or seeming like correction.

Reasoning Language   One of the kinds of language that children may experience for the first time in the early childhood program is the language of cause and effect. It helps them to understand the relationships between actions: "If we go out now while it's raining, we'll get wet"; and relationships between people: "If you invite him over he may play with you." Young children need your help as they learn to use language for reasoning and solving problems. In social problem-solving situations some children may need to know specific words or phrases to give in place of physical action. For example, teachers often instruct children to substitute, "Stop it" for pushing or hitting another child. They suggest alternative ways to express problems: "Tell him you want him to stop taking your blocks"; and model problem-solving language: "Please don't put that bucket on my lap; it's getting me wet." Children then try out the new language in their play situations.

The Language of Imagination and Recall Children first talk about objects and activities in the immediate present, the here and now. Eventually they begin to use language for talking about things they remember, things that happened outside of school or in the past. Some children learn quite early to use language to build imaginary scenarios for their play; others have little experience with

this kind of talk. If children are not familiar with this kind of language use, they will need adult support. Talking about your memories or personal experiences outside of school may help children to use talk to create or recall things not present.

Language Play   Young children often use language in playful ways. They invent silly words, use "naughty" language, state things they know to be incorrect as a joke (teacher: pointing to a new hat the child is wearing, "What's that?"; child: (giggling), "A watermelon!"), experiment with sounds, and make up rhymes (child swinging and chanting: "Swinging, ringing, pringing, flinging, minging"). Such language play may help children begin to develop a conscious awareness of language itself, the kind of thinking about language they will need as they learn to read. Thinking and talking about language requires a different focus than using language to communicate. Since playing with language may help children to develop this important awareness, you will want to encourage and initiate verbal exploration. Nonsense words, rhymes, jokes, tongue twisters, and "silly talk" in literature and conversation will foster language play.

Supporting Children's Language Development

Since most children learn language so well at home in their interactions with family members, we can draw on this natural environment as a model for a classroom which supports language development. In such a natural environment, people communicate about meaningful events; real people use real talk about the real things they are doing. Children participate in dialogues with their parents. The classroom language environment is very different because of the high adult-child ratio (a low classroom ratio of l:8 would be a very high ratio for a home), so there may be fewer opportunities for children to talk with adults. To support language development in school, teachers need to make time and create an environment where conversations between adults and children and among children are encouraged.

The overall organization of your program will influence children's talk. You set the stage for language development by preparing a language-rich environment filled with interesting things to do, see, and talk about. Plan classroom activities that will enable children to see connections with similar experiences outside of school (for example: cooking, gardening, caring for pets), and they will have much to talk about. Arrange space into small areas, and provide enough time for children to come together and converse as they work and play. Value the buzz of conversation, and do not demand silence as an indication of order. Let the children know that talking to each other is worthwhile and something that you want them to do. Engage in conversations with children that are dialogues, not teacher monologues. Use classroom volunteers such as parents or students to increase the opportunites for extended conversations between children and adults.

The kinds of language described in the framework above can be used as a guide to ensure that you are using language for a number of different purposes. Use variety and specificity in the words you choose **to direct** or describe:

"It's on the top shelf next to the striped basket." Ask open-ended questions (those that do not require a particular answer) and expand children's language. Trust that all children (unless handicapped in some way) have language facility that you can nurture. Hesitant or shy children may require a longer time to speak or answer questions, and it is important to be patient and give them enough time. While you must plan for language, you also must take advantage of the unplanned moments when language can occur.

You will not actually instruct children in a subject called language (a discipline studied by linguists and other scholars). Instead you will help children develop language by using it. As children act out roles in block and dramatic play areas, they develop variety and complexity in their language. As they work together on group projects, they use language to plan, compare, and describe. Comfortable areas to talk in and materials like picture books, puppet theaters, dramatic play props, language games, flannelboards, and art projects, motivate language. When children take trips, they share experiences that they will enjoy talking about.

Routines and daily activities also provide opportunities for language development. Lunch and snack and transitions are also conversation times. Daily music, movement, meetings, art, and storytimes involve language.

How you talk with children is important. Children need to have a chance to express their ideas, to tell about the things they know and that are important to them, to be able to make sense of their experiences. In conversations you can help children by allowing them to take the lead and then following their topics, showing interest and encouraging them to continue the discussion. A child's thinking about a topic may be broadened as he or she draws different ideas into the talk. It is not necessary to plan specific questions to use when you have conversations with children. Questioning by adults may seem like a test, and some children will focus on finding the answer expected by the adult, rather than on doing their own thinking.

Children who are learning English or who speak nonstandard English also learn best through an activity-based, natural language approach. As you learn more about these children through observation, home visits, and discussions with their parents, you will be able to provide special experiences for them within the activities that you are already providing.

LITERACY

Reading and writing are facets of communication, tools to unlock ideas, adventures, and relationships. They are much more than skills to be mastered for their own sake. Before children learn to read, they need experience in the world to give them a basis for understanding, and they need skill in comprehending and using oral language.

For the last thirty years, a lively debate has gone on over the teaching of reading. Traditional views usually present reading and writing as requiring instruction in a set of skills which cannot be taught until children have demonstrated certain "readiness" behaviors, for example: large and small muscle skills, visual and auditory discrimination, sequencing ability, and the ability to follow a left-to-

right orientation. More current theories suggest that while demonstrating such "readiness" behaviors may be an indication of the child's growing abilities in several areas, it is likely that children develop concepts about written language along with these other abilities, rather than waiting until they have been declared officially "ready." Children who live in our print-filled world gradually develop concepts about written language from a very early age. Everyday experiences and the presence of adults who interpret and call attention to print give children opportunities to actively explore and think about written language. They construct rules or models which help children make sense of experiences with print.

There are many different ways children show a developing awareness of written language. Teachers need to recognize these signs in order to be responsive to natural interest. Some children begin to take an interest in writing or reading as familiar or favorite storybooks are read to them. As they hear and see the same words over and over, they read along and point to the print. Others recognize or discuss the meanings of signs or labels frequently encountered. Children's first interest is often in their own names, which they recognize and wish to write, or they may print their initial, saying, "That's my J." Some children will pretend to write and read messages in their play. Familiar books may be "read" to a group by a child who pretends to be the "teacher." Others show interest in the print of books by asking questions. All of these are evidence that print has been noticed and is being explored. In most programs for four and five year olds, some children will be actively interested in learning about written language, while others will display little interest. Interest in print sometimes occurs in very young children; we recently observed a two-and-a-half year old laboriously writing "names" on the paintings of all of the children in her group.

Marie Clay (1975) and others have found that children begin to grasp principles of how print works as they explore and attempt to create graphic forms that resemble letters. In their early concepts of writing children rarely look for connections between spoken words and their written forms. They explore the graphic features of print, finding that it follows certain rules such as linearity, repetition of individual elements, directionality, variation of symbols, arrangement and spacing of letters on a page. Children make guesses or assumptions about how print works as they explore; for example, one study found that most young children believe that a certain number of characters (at least three or four) must be written before a message or "word" can be read. These early concepts must be revised as the child's thinking progresses, to accommodate new information. In this way meaning is "constructed" by each child.

Motivation and thinking about literacy must arise from within the child. Adult-conceived reading tasks, such as matching upper case to lower case letters, frequently do not match child concepts about written language. Reading and writing require conceptual development that resists direct teaching. Instead, knowledge construction depends on experiences which are within a child's understanding.

A Framework for Thinking About Literacy

Adults and young children do many things together that involve written language and contribute to children's ideas about writing and reading. Many of

these come naturally to teachers and parents. The different ways that adults interact with children with regard to print can be used as a framework for thinking about the kinds of experiences that you can provide in your classroom.

Reading Books   Children who are read to often and who spend time with books during their early years usually become successful readers. Today researchers are looking more specifically at what concepts children gain in this way and at the kinds of supportive adult interactions that take place as children learn to read. Children develop appreciation of books when being "read to" is a positive experience, when there is physical closeness, individual attention, and a responsive adult. They become familiar with print, match spoken to written word, and relate the illustrations to the content. Children begin to see that what is read must make sense, and they begin to be able to make connections between their own experiences and books. Hearing stories read gives children

familiarity with the elements of a story and with "book language" which is different and more formal than day-to-day speech.

Reading Signs   Most children are exposed to symbols, signs, and printed messages all around them in the form of traffic signs, logos for products on packages, and in television advertising. Adults often make use of and refer to these forms of printed messages and discuss them with children. This exposure to printed material sensitizes children and helps them to feel like they are reading—as indeed they are. Teachers can support these early reading experiences by creating signs and symbols for their classrooms, for example, by having a name label on the rabbit's cage or by labelling containers with pictures of the contents.

Observing and Creating Graphic Forms
Children are exposed to the graphic elements of writing in signs and symbols and in alphabet books, toys, and decora-

296

tions. They naturally incorporate these in their art as they begin to notice print. Teachers can display alphabet charts, and provide other materials and decorations that heighten this awareness. Children can experiment with letter forms using writing and art materials.

Experiencing Language Written Down

Another way to help children see that reading is speech written down and to assist them in beginning reading, is to have them dictate stories to you. As a group or as individuals, children can create stories based on such experiences as trips, activities, or home life. These can be illustrated by the children and hung on charts or bound in books for the classroom library. This technique is called *language experience*. It helps children understand the connection between written and spoken language, and we have seen it used successfully in many preschool and kindergarten classes. Key vocabulary is another technique that uses the words of the child to develop reading skills. It is described by Sylvia Ashton-Warner in her book *Teacher*. It involves having children dictate and keep a file of words that have special meaning to them, such as *Mommy, Daddy, kiss,* and *rocket*.

Observing Adults Who Read and Write

Adults who enjoy and use reading and writing for themselves provide a powerful model for children. Instead of restricting adult writing and reading to preparation or personal time, teachers can do some writing and reading in the classroom. Notes to teachers and families, signs for the parent bulletin board, and planning notes can be written in the children's presence. Teachers can also comment on their use of books as resources: "I wonder what ingredients we'll need for the lasagna; I'm going to look it up here in my cookbook." Some teachers have a short quiet time set aside when everyone, teachers included, takes out a book and reads.

Writing to Communicate

Children who experience adults writing and then talking with them about that writing will soon come to write their own "messages." At first these are collections of graphic forms which may have no connection to any meaning; when asked to "read" the message the child may have nothing to say. Later children may attach meaning to the message although there is no connection between what is printed and what is said. Older children begin to use the words they know (their names and words like love), and they "invent" spelling. Children's invented spelling often uses the sounds of the letter name. For example, engine might be spelled NJN and dress might be GS. Classrooms where writing supplies are available to children and where there are words to copy encourage children to write to communicate.

Supporting Children in Becoming Literate

Each child learns to read and write as an individual, putting together ideas in ways that make personal sense. Part of your job is to observe what each child in your class currently understands and how he or she approaches learning about the written word. They need opportunities to explore and use materials and receive responsive, supportive adult interaction. Take advantage of every opportunity to use print in the natural, ongoing activities of your classroom; encourage the children's interest, allow them to explore print and writing on their own, and provide follow-up activities.

Literature stimulates children's interest in words and in reading. Your appreciation of children's literature and your visible enjoyment of reading demonstrate that it is a worthwhile and pleasurable experience. Books of all kinds, magazines and newspapers can be kept as reference material throughout the classroom, as well as in the library area. Be sure children understand that they, and not just adults, have permission to explore the books. Include books that adults use—encyclopedias, dictionaries, some books with few or no pictures, as well as those specifically written for children—so children will have a broader exposure to what "reading" means. Children come to school with wide differences in their exposure to books. You will need to find books and experiences with print that will reach the interests of all the children, particularly those who do not seem "turned on" to books.

Read to children every day. When you read to individual children, you will have more opportunity to talk about the books and print at the level of each child's interest and understanding and will be able to assess their progress. The box below suggests some things to do as you read with one or two children at a time to help them build concepts about print.

Young children have the ability to make sense of written language just as they do oral language. It is important to understand how each individual is putting together ideas about the relationship between print and meaning. Feedback that has personal meaning seems to be the most effective way to help children begin to develop concepts of literacy. For a child who expects adults to be able to read anything printlike, specific feedback such as reading phonetically "ppptttppp" or responding that "This doesn't look like any word I know" provides new information

READING TO CHILDREN TO DEVELOP CONCEPTS ABOUT PRINT

- ☐ Make books an important part of your classroom and use them frequently.
- ☐ Reread favorite stories many times.
- ☐ Read so that the child can see the print.
- ☐ Let the child turn the page as you read.
- ☐ Sometimes point out words.
- ☐ Keep favorite books in the classroom over time.
- ☐ Talk with the child about the story, about its meaning, and the child's own experience.
- ☐ Refer to books after you have read them, making connections to life.
- ☐ Try to find other adults to read one-to-one with children (parents, volunteers, nonteaching staff, students, siblings).

which conflicts with the child's expectations. Such conflicts require the child to adjust his or her thinking to make sense of this new information.

As an adult who knows how to write, you will need to model the process of writing and talk about this with children. Write in front of children, so they can see what you are doing. Talk informally about letters or words in the context of other tasks that children are doing and demonstrate writing: for example, writing the child's name and saying the letters as you write, pointing out words or letters in messages as you write, taking dictation, making charts, or recording stories composed by groups of children. Write what the child says, using his or her natural form of expression, when you are recording the child's language. You might also create simple stories for the children, and talk about your thinking as you write. Show your writing to children when they express interest, tell them what you are doing, and answer their questions so they will begin to understand adult purposes for writing. Recently, while one of us was writing an observation of a teacher, a child questioned, "What are you doing?" This led to a discussion: "I'm writing about the things that children and teachers are doing in your school. Then I can remember it and talk with your teacher later about the things that she can do to help you learn." The child asked about specific words and later in the day brought her own written "message" to share.

The best guide to introducing activities is to observe what children can do and provide a wide range of experiences, including individual assistance, that will help them take the appropriate next step. Base the help you provide on a child's requests and immediate needs within

299

self-selected writing or reading tasks. Respond to children's thinking and questions as they are pursuing their own ideas about written language. For example, a child who is trying to find a friend's name on a list may read "Sam" as "Steven" because he is looking only at the first letters. You could point out what the child knows: "You're right! There's an 'S' in both names"; and also call attention to the differences: "But Steven's name is a lot longer than Sam's." The atmosphere of your classroom must encourage risk taking with an emphasis on what children *can do* rather than on the mistakes they make. Focus on the process, on what children are doing and how they are doing it, and on the *ideas* children are trying to express.

With older preschoolers and kindergarten aged children use print throughout your classroom for purposes that will make sense to them. Have name cards to read, copy, and use in activities; label games, materials, shelves, belongings, and children's work. Use charts and lists that include children's names. Put up signs and labels for various areas of the classroom; refer to the signs when talking to children. Use charts that include both print and pictures: recipe charts, stories, alphabet charts, words to songs, poems. Read everything to the children.

Let children play games or do workjobs that use letters and print. Some of these materials should be open-ended: examples of this would be a set of large, sturdy plastic alphabet letters that can be spread out on the floor and used for active games, or a basket of wooden letters for tracing and coloring. Have a "name hunt" or "letter hunt" to look for print in the classroom. More specific tasks might include workjobs where small items are

sorted by beginning sounds, or matching of upper and lower case alphabet letters; such activities should be child-selected. Teacher-planned "readiness" lessons rarely have the kind of personal "fit" needed by young children. Use of structured materials and planned lessons are not recommended. Avoid lessons which present isolated language tasks out of context of real language situations and the context of children's real life experiences.

Make materials readily available so children can try producing written language on their own. You will need a variety of unstructured materials, including different types and sizes of paper (include envelopes, note cards, paper to be made into little "books," notepads), and different writing tools (pencils, erasers, markers of various widths, crayons). Other materials might include sets of small plastic letters (both upper and lower case) for constructing words and sentences, three- or four-inch wooden letters for tracing, a letter stamp set for printing, a typewriter or a computer with simple word processing programs designed for children. Children can use these materials for producing messages, free exploration, artwork, or self-selected practice.

Encourage and value children's attempts to produce writing and explore reading. Let them do "free" writing, including scribble writing and pretend writing. Help them write their own name when they show interest in doing this. Encourage them by telling them: "Try to write it all by yourself" or "Pretend you can write it." Suggest that they write labels, lists, signs, or whatever fits the situation as they play. Allow children to copy (or even trace) any print that is of interest, if the

copying is a self-initiated activity. For example, the four-year-old daughter of a friend decided one day to copy the titles of all the books in her personal library.

To help children understand reading, encourage them to read back messages they pretend to write and to "read" dictation you have written for them. Often children will be able to convey the sense of what has been said. Let them "read" familiar picture books to you and to classmates. Some children enjoy trying to match print to known message; for example, reading along with the words of familiar songs, rhymes, poems, or pattern stories. Storytelling, puppets, flannel board stories, and dramatizations of books are other ways to help children begin to understand books and experiment with creating stories.

Children also learn about reading and writing from each other. Provide opportunities for them to work together while they are "writing," and encourage them to talk about what they are doing. Often children will understand that written messages are "gifts" for their friends or families before they are able to actually write, and you can encourage this. Display children's writing, and include child-made "books" in the classroom library or book area.

As children begin to understand more about written language, you can support their efforts to learn to read and write. Encourage them to write with "invented" spelling. Help them acquire a set of their own "sight" words based on Sylvia Ashton-Warner's idea of a *key vocabulary*. Assist children who are beginning to write on their own by answering questions and providing specific information or help. For example, one boy of our acquaintance could hear and write the *Z* pronounced in the name of a favorite superhero but needed help with the other letters. Accept efforts and errors, and focus comments on what the child can do. Your most essential contribution is to encourage children to try to write. Attempts should arise from the child's interests and choices.

LITERATURE

Children who have many positive experiences with literature come to love books. Children who love books come to love reading. There are good books for children about almost every subject. Through them, children experience both language and art and learn about the world and human relationships. Literature can motivate exploration, creativity, a concern for others, and a love of reading.

Not all books are literature, and not all children's books contribute to development. Literature has permanent value: the poetry, stories, and other writing that we will continue to use despite the passage of time. Most children's literature is relatively new. The classics are a mere generation or two old. Picture books are even newer: the great bulk were written in the last fifteen or twenty years. Time has not yet defined those that will endure. Books based on momentary fads or commercial products written without care or artistry are not good literature and do not belong in classrooms.

Good literature for young children has the qualities that we look for in good literature for adults. It shows respect for the reader; does not stereotype, preach, or moralize; has integrity (that is, honesty and truthfulness within the context of the

story); uses aesthetic language; and in some way, helps the reader to understand and feel more deeply. Good literature teaches by example. *The Story of Ferdinand*'s message about peace and nonviolence is positive and not overstated. Illustrations are essential in children's books and should enhance and enlarge the experience of the words. They should be executed beautifully, with care and craftsmanship, in a medium that is appropriate to the content of the book.

Children generally do not choose books for themselves, so it is up to adults to present a range of quality literature from which children can make choices. Since many parents are not acquainted with the qualities that characterize good literature for children, the task of providing guidance often falls to teachers.

The best, most honest, and most beautiful children's book may not be best for every child. It is important to select books that are appropriate for the developmental level of the children. Very young preschoolers have not yet developed the fine motor skills necessary for turning pages carefully, have an attention span that is relatively short for seated activities, are limited in experience and vocabulary, and are primarily interested in their own experience of the world. For these children, books should be durable with heavy pages and hard covers (board and cloth books for toddlers), relatively short, and concerned with experiences that the child knows or can relate to. For example, *The Runaway Bunny* by Margaret Wise Brown deals with feelings of anger, love, and security that all children have experienced. It is best if books for young preschoolers are written in a straightforward manner with easy to interpret words and illustrations.

If you work with older preschoolers or kindergarten children, you can include stories that deal with events and characters that are beyond their realm of experience, and longer stories with more complex words and plots and more intricate and subtle illustrations. Older children will also have more distinctive personal likes and interests. While a book like *Where the Wild Things Are* by Maurice Sendak seems to have almost universal appeal because of its illustrations and subject matter (monsters, feelings, and reassurance), other books appeal to some individuals more than others. Some children are moved and entranced by the moody poetry of *Dawn* by Uri Shulevitz, others enjoy the rhythmic silliness of Beatrice Shenck De Regnier's *May I Bring a Friend?* and still others enjoy a well-told tale like William Steig's *Sylvester and the Magic Pebble.* Knowing children, their interests, their developmental level, their attention span, and the day-to-day events in their lives will help you to pick books that are appropriate and meaningful.

A Framework for Organizing Literature Choices

Every classroom library should have a variety of books. Each serves a different purpose and appeals to different children at different times, supporting the existing interests of children and helping to build new ones.

Fiction   In choosing which works of fiction to present to children, you should first evaluate the idea behind the story. The author's intention should be to illustrate life, enchant children, instill a love of literature, entertain, and evoke feeling. This must be done with respect

for childhood, and children's lives. Stories that preach or devalue children's experience are not good literature.

Second, you will want to evaluate the style of writing. The author's ability to communicate in ways that create memorable, believable characters, and the illusion of reality in time and place (even in a fantasy) should enhance an understanding of life's experience. The point of the story should not be belabored, and the plot should be more than a mere recounting of events. A plot should also encourage children to understand the reasons behind events. Fiction can be fanciful (real people doing fantastic things and fantastic characters doing real things) or realistic. Both are important, and neither is an adequate substitute for the other.

Informational Books   Informational books for young children should be written in understandable, direct language; be aesthetically worded and illustrated; and relate to the experience of children. They *must* be factually accurate, not overgeneralized or filled with half-truths. In order to enhance interest and not bore, they should not be too fact-filled or lecture-like in their presentation or concepts. Illustrations should help to convey more than the words alone can.

Mood or Concept Books   Mood and concept books sensitize children to ideas and feelings. They help to expand the realm of an individual's experience. Into this category we place books that use organizing frameworks like the alphabet, aesthetic experiences, elements of design, colors, shapes, and numbers. Wordless books are generally a part of this category. They encourage children to think and use language. These books are most valuable when they provide a sense of joy and wonder in the world and are not used to drill children on concepts.

Poetry   Many books for young children are written in poetry. Poetry that is sometimes, but not always, rhythmic and rhymed presents mood and melody in language in a natural and unforced manner. Good poetry helps to enhance children's understanding of the world and develops their sensitivity to language.

Supporting Children's Appreciation of Literature

Presenting literature to young children involves choosing books thoughtfully, designing space for group reading and independent exploration of books, reading with skill and responsiveness, and designing experiences to expand on literature. Make sure that the books represent diverse ethnicities, lifestyles, cultures, appearances, races, ages and activities. Mothers should not be cast solely in the role of nurturers. Families should include single parents and only children. Minorities should appear in many professions and activities. Girls as well as boys should be adventurous and outgoing, and creative. Grandparents should sometimes be attractive and active as well as aged and infirm.

A comfortable, reasonably quiet, well-stocked library area in the classroom enhances children's experience with books. A low shelf designed to display the front covers of books enables children themselves to select and replace books. Soft pillows, artwork, a rocking chair, and an adult lap to sit on attract children to a library corner. For reading to groups, a quiet area of the classroom with adequate lighting and comfortable seating enables children to hear the words and see the pictures, setting the stage for positive literature experiences.

There are different ways of reading to children depending on your purpose and the type of book you are reading. When you are reading to children, it is important to read the words the author has written. This gives children the experience of rich language, one of the most important parts of literature. Children who are beginning to attend to reading will also develop understanding of the constancy of print. It is usually best to read the text continuously without interruption. This helps children to develop the sense of the story, the flow of the book's language, and helps groups of children to remain attentive.

More dialogue is possible when you read to one or two children at a time. These are the times when you build relationships with children. When reading a book with one or two children, comments and questions can help develop understanding of the story experience by enlarging on events in the books: "I wonder what the Gunniwolf wants. The little girl seems to be going deeper into the jungle. Why do you think the Gunniwolf talks like that?" Such interaction can help you to become better attuned to children's feelings and interests. Questions and comments can also serve as a bridge between the child's life and the book: "Little Sal is filling her bucket with blueberries just the way we filled our buckets with crabapples when we went to the farm." One of your most important goals in presenting literature to children is to help them to develop understanding and love of books. They should never feel

pressured by questions about books; if they feel that storytime is quiz time (and failure time), they may learn to avoid reading.

Group book times should occur daily and can last from ten to twenty minutes depending on the interest and developmental level of the children. While books can be read to quite large groups, smaller groups will have more positive and longer book times. In order for children to fully benefit from being read to, they must first be interested. Bored, uncomfortable, hungry, or overtired children will not be able to lend their full attention to books.

Reading a story to a group requires skill and practice. You prepare by being well-acquainted with the story and with the children. It is important to make frequent eye contact while reading to keep you in touch with children's responses. Children will be more attentive if you speak in a clear, audible voice and if your expression relates to the content of the story. Your natural conversational tone contains distinct differences and nuances that you can use as you read.

Variations and Expansions on Literature

Literature is enhanced when it is not isolated from other classroom experiences. It can be a launching point for many other kinds of activities. For example, a memorable phrase such as "Cats here, cats there, cats and kittens everywhere, hundreds of cats, thousands of cats, millions and billions and trillions of cats" (in *Millions of Cats,* by Wanda Gag) may be the perfect response to a squirming litter of kittens if children know and love the book.

Books and poems have tremendous potential for motivating children in creative drama and movement. It is a rare group of young children, for example, that does not spontaneously begin to take on the role of the monkeys in Slobodkinas' *The Peddler and His Caps* after hearing it one or two times. With the addition of a few props and some teacher direction you can introduce a new dimension to children's innate sense of drama. Flannel-boards and puppets are effective ways to present literature to very young children. They also contribute to the experience of older children who appreciate props that can be manipulated and who enjoy using the materials for their own storytelling.

Some recorded stories and poems for children add an extra dimension to a familiar book. We are especially fond of recordings of authors reading their own work. It is vital to remember that no recording, however good, is a substitute for daily reading time with a teacher. Many recordings are made without

aesthetic awareness or respect for children and are not appropriate classroom materials. These often have been designed to be sold in grocery stores and seem to be the literary equivalent of the candy and junk food displayed at checkout stands.

One of the important things a teacher can do is to help parents use and choose good books for their children. Few parents have spent time learning about good literature for young children. Their own early experiences and the books that are marketed by department stores may be their primary sources. A simple and effective way to help parents is to make good classroom books available for overnight borrowing. Your careful explanation of how important reading is to children and how special the books are to you will help ensure that they are returned undamaged. Special book borrowing envelopes can be used to record the titles of the books borrowed and to protect them as they travel to children's homes and back to school again in the morning. The establishment of this routine will help children later on when they begin to use public libraries. You can also prepare children by taking field trips to the local library and by encouraging parents to take regular trips to the library with their children to borrow books and to attend story hours.

CHECKLIST FOR LANGUAGE AND LITERACY CURRICULUM AREAS

Program Structure
- ☐ Stated goals include support of language and literacy development
- ☐ Daily free choice periods of at least an hour include opportunities for children to talk to one another and adults, explore printed material, use writing equipment, and look at books
- ☐ Daily schedule includes planned story times
- ☐ Trips are a regular feature of the program

Environment and Materials
- ☐ Well-equipped centers designed so that small groups of children can work and talk together, such as ____ a block center, ____ a dramatic play area, ____ an art area, ____ a writing center, ____ a library area, ____ a science area, ____ a manipulative toy area, ____ a listening center
- ☐ Comfortable outside space for playing, sitting and talking; for example, benches in the shade, a water table, a climbing structure with space for sitting, and a sandbox

☐ Interesting activities in the yard, such as gardening, digging, animal homes, bird feeders

☐ Printed materials, charts, and signs displayed in the classroom

☐ Shelves and cubbies labeled with words and pictures

☐ A parent bulletin board and parent message pockets

☐ Samples of children's graphic productions and beginning writing displayed in the room and reproduced in a newsletter*

☐ Children's books kept in parent area to encourage parents to read to children

☐ Interesting objects, pictures, and photographs that children can talk about displayed in the classroom at child eye level

☐ Books and reading materials found in relevant interest centers; for example, newspapers or magazines in the dramatic play area, and illustrated science books in the science center

☐ Language related workjobs and learning games*

☐ At least two puppets

☐ At least two toy or disconnected telephones for children's use in dramatic play

writing center:

☐ Tables and chairs proportioned to the children

☐ Marking pens in narrow and broad widths, pencils, and crayons

☐ Standard size paper and notecards

☐ Letter stamp set*

☐ Recycled envelopes to hold messages

☐ An alphabet poster*

☐ Stapler, hole punch, tape, yarn to tie books together

☐ Typewriter*

☐ Name cards and/or key vocabulary collections*

☐ Word cards*

☐ Wooden letters for tracing—lower case and upper case*

☐ A folder to hold each child's writing*

☐ An illustrated children's dictionary*

library center:

☐ A selection of books appropriate to the developmental level of the children which show characters of diverse race, culture, age, and social class without moralizing or stereotyping by gender or other characteristics:

_____ realistic fiction, _____ fanciful fiction, _____ wordless books, _____ poetry, _____ mood and concept books, _____ informational books, _____ child and teacher authored books

- ☐ Photograph albums with photos of children from the class and their families on trips, at work, at play, at school, and at home
- ☐ Beautifully illustrated books that include different styles of artwork—photographs, prints, drawing, painting, collage, etc.
- ☐ A shelf displaying children's books with covers visible
- ☐ Book jackets and posters for decoration
- ☐ Comfortable clean carpeting and pillows to rest on
- ☐ Good lighting—neither too harsh nor too soft
- ☐ A flannelboard with pieces that can be used by children

---

* Items most appropriate for older preschoolers and not generally necessary in a classroom for 2 and young 3 year olds

FOR FURTHER THOUGHT AND DISCUSSION

1 Think of yourself as an adult reader and writer. Think of the things you read and write (novels, newspapers, reports, grocery lists, weekly plans, papers for school). Do you do a lot of reading and writing? How much is for work; how much for pleasure? How do you feel about literature and about the other reading and writing you do? How do you think your feelings are effected by your experiences as a child in school? Compare your thoughts with someone else's. In what ways are they similar or different?

2 Think of the ways you use oral language (talking to a friend, giving a presentation, talking to children, ordering in a restaurant, etc.). Do you think of yourself as a competent, skillful talker? In what circumstances are you most comfortable? Do any situations make you uncomfortable? Why? Compare your feelings with another person. Does this have any implications for your work with young children?

3 Think of the books you loved as a child. What did you love about them? Why were they important to you? How did you discover those books? What books would you like to share with children? Does this have any implications for your work with young children?

PROJECTS

1 Use the **Checklist for Language and Literacy Curriculum Areas** from this chapter to observe an early childhood classroom. Report on the extent to which the program seems to support children's language and literacy development. Suggest some ways to provide some additional experiences from which children would benefit.

2 Design an ideal early childhood environment for the support of language and literacy development. Describe your plan including what you have provided and why. Share your plan with a teacher and a parent, and include their response and suggestions.

3 Use the lesson plan form in Chapter 9 to design and implement an activity for young children that would support language, literature, or literacy development. Report on what happened. Describe what you learned about yourself, children, language, literacy or literature development, and teaching.

4 Design a week's plan for a group of children that includes oral language, literature, and literacy activities. Use one of the weekly planning forms from Chapter 9. Implement part or all of your plan. Report on what happened. Describe what you learned about yourself, children, language, literature, and literacy development, and teaching.

RECOMMENDED READING

Ashton-Warner, Sylvia. *Teacher.* Touchstone ed. New York: Simon and Schuster, 1985.

Barratta-Lorton, Mary. *Workjobs.* Menlo Park, Cal.: Addison-Wesley, 1972.

Bissex, Glenda. *Gnys at Wrk: A Child Learns to Write and Read.* Cambridge, Mass.: Harvard University Press, 1980.

Cazden, Courtney B., ed. *Language in Early Childhood Education.* Rev. ed. Washington, D.C.: National Association for the Education of Young Children, 1981.

Clay, Marie. *What Did I Write? Beginning Writing Behavior.* Portsmouth, N.H.: Heinemann, 1975.

Cochran-Smith, Marilyn. *The Making of a Reader.* Norwood, N.J.: Ablex, 1984.

Genishi, Celia, and Dyson, Anne Haas. *Language Assessment in the Early Years.* Norwood, N.J.: Ablex, 1984.

Graves, Donald H. *Writing: Teachers and Children At Work.* Portsmouth, N.H.: Heinemann, 1982.

Hall, MaryAnne. *Teaching Reading as a Language Experience.* 3d. ed. Columbus, O.: Charles E. Merrill, 1981.

Jacobs, Leland B., ed. *Using Literature With Young Children.* New York: Teachers College Press, 1965.

Palewicz-Rousseau, Pam, and Madaras, Lynda. *The Alphabet Connection.* New York: Schocken, 1979.

Paley, Vivian G. *Wally's Stories.* Cambridge, Mass.: Harvard University Press, 1981.

Schickedanz, Judith. *More Than ABC's.* Washington, D.C.: National Association for the Education of Young Children, 1981.

Tough, Joan. *Talking and Learning: A Guide to Fostering Communication Skills in Nursery and Infant Schools.* Portsmouth, N.H.: Heinemann, 1977.

13

The Inquiry
Curriculum

"The universe is the child's curriculum."

Maria Montessori

"It is little short of a miracle that modern methods of instruction have not already completely strangled the holy curiosity of inquiry, because what this delicate little plant needs most, apart from initial stimulation, is freedom; without that it is surely destroyed."

Albert Einstein

*In this chapter we look at curriculum areas that deal with the physical and social aspects of the world and that focus most directly on thinking and problem solving in Math, Science, Social Studies, and Nutrition. A framework for each of the subject areas is provided as well as suggestions for presenting each topic in early childhood programs. We also consider the qualities that determine whether concepts are knowable and worth knowing for young children and describe inquiry processes. This chapter relates to the CDA areas **Cognitive, Learning Environment, Self, Social,** and **Health.***

I nquiry is the active process of seeking understanding. It produces the new ideas, which contribute to building human civilization. Every person has the potential to create new ideas, and the process of inquiry is both an individual and interpersonal adventure. Children are naturally curious and eagerly seek to understand the world around them, the essence of inquiry. It is your task as a teacher to create the climate in which each child can discover the power of ideas and generate concepts about the world.

Experiences in mathematics, science, social studies, and nutrition are fertile ground for the development of inquiry skills and concepts and are the primary focus of this chapter. Children also inquire and develop concepts as they participate in other curriculum areas.

A DEVELOPMENTAL PERSPECTIVE

For the young child inquiry involves learning through exploration and investigation. The inquiring child uses sight, sound, taste, smell, touch, and the kinesthetic sense to gain general and specific information that will help form

concepts—categories for making sense of experiences and seeing connections between them. Concepts cannot be taught directly but grow out of inquiry experiences. Each individual constructs his or her own concepts in a unique and personal way. While curriculum specialists identify between ten and fifteen distinct inquiry processes, we find those in the box on page 315 the most appropriate for use with young children who learn from concrete experience.

The development of thinking is a fascinating area of child development. The work of Jean Piaget is most useful to early childhood educators because of his careful observations of the characteristic ways that children develop concepts through direct sensory experiences. A child repeatedly experiences the characteristics of an object, animal, person, or event and mentally combines and organizes these to form a concept. For example, an infant may have constructed the concept *door* based on many repeated experiences: a slam, mother returning through this spot, the way to get where you want to go, pinched fingers, a light source at night, and the barrier to what is desired. Concepts are generalized as children recognize the common attributes

INQUIRY PROCESSES USED BY YOUNG CHILDREN

- ☐ *Exploring*: using the senses to observe, investigate, and manipulate.
- ☐ *Identifying*: naming and describing what is experienced.
- ☐ *Classifying*: grouping objects or experiences by their common characteristics.
- ☐ *Comparing and Contrasting*: observing similarities and differences between objects or experiences.
- ☐ *Hypothesizing*: using the data from experiences to make guesses (hypotheses) about what might happen.
- ☐ *Generalizing*: applying previous experience to new situations.

of objects, people, ideas, and experiences. In the door example the initial concept of door may only refer to the door of the bedroom. As many doors are experienced, the concept is generalized and different doors are recognized: the door of the family car, of grandma's house; the automatic door at the supermarket; and, finally, doors in general. Although the doors differ greatly, the common characteristics are recognized, and the concept is established.

A child's ability to understand and develop a concept is dependent on cognitive maturation and the availability of relevant experiences. Whether or not a concept is developmentally appropriate and likely to be understood by a young child depends on the extent to which it is concrete and its level of complexity.

Concepts can be thought of as existing on a continuum from concrete to abstract. The **concreteness** of a concept refers to whether or not it can be directly experienced or observed. Children can understand concrete concepts. These can be experienced through the senses—seen, heard, held, felt, touched, tasted. Concepts

that depend on information outside of direct experience are abstract and cannot be completely understood by a young child regardless of how hard adults try to provide the missing experience through language. This makes a Thanksgiving unit on Pilgrims and Indians mostly meaningless to preschool age children. Such a unit may be fun but will not develop understanding of historical events or the concepts of cooperation and celebration that teachers may be trying to convey. In a unit on Pilgrims and Indians, the concepts remain abstract. Children will learn better about sharing, gratitude, and celebration by focusing on their own Thanksgiving experiences at home and at school.

The **complexity** of a concept is the second quality that effects a young child's ability to understand. To be adequately understood by a young child a concept needs to be quite simple and have only a few interdependent ideas. Some concepts are available to children through direct experience but involve many interrelated ideas. These cannot be understood since young children's capacity for creating and retaining connections between such ideas has not yet developed. The concept of wind is both relatively simple and concrete, defined primarily by the experience of air moving against the skin and its ability to move objects about. The concept of weather, however, is complex and requires the grasp of numerous other supporting concepts including evaporation, wind patterns, cloud formation, low- and high-pressure areas, and precipitation. Young children will not really understand the phenomena of weather because it requires attending to a variety of attributes simultaneously which they are not able to do.

TEACHER ROLE

We group the curriculum areas of math, science, social studies, and nutrition together because they can be approached in similar ways and require similar teacher role and techniques. In order for inquiry and concept development in each of the areas to take place, you must provide a physical environment that is stimulating and also reasonably ordered. There must be space, interesting equipment and materials, and lots of time to explore how things work and to develop and test ideas. Activities that stimulate inquiry and lead to concept development need to be planned for and provided. When you design inquiry experiences, you will want to take into account the developmental appropriateness of the concepts and inquiry processes.

Children approach the world with a sense of wonder and an almost infinite curiosity. Your attitudes toward exploration can significantly influence how they pursue this curiosity. It is important to be responsive to children and share and support their interest in many aspects of life. Because adults have a great deal more experience, skill, and information than young children, it is tempting to provide them with answers, but pronouncing facts may deprive children of the opportunity to learn through discovery. A child we knew found a praying mantis and asked his teacher what it ate so that it could be fed. The teacher readily admitted that she did not know but asked, "How can we find out?" This resourceful four year old questioned other adults and finally looked through a book about insects in the science area and found a photograph of a praying mantis. He took it to his teacher, and she read to the group about the dining habits of this insect. Had the teacher simply said, "It eats bugs," an important lesson in the use of resources would not have taken place.

Talking with children when they are exploring and discovering is one of the most important things you will do in the inquiry areas of your program. In order to do this effectively you need to be a good observer. Skilled teachers gauge children's responses and target their comments, questions, and activities to make optimal use of the natural curiosity of children. Questions help children to notice detail, make comparisons, and come to conclusions. For example, if a group of children are exploring what happens when they narrow a faucet with a finger, making the water spray out, you might comment: "You found a way to change the water flow. Can you make it come out slower? faster? What do you have to do to change it? I wonder why that happens? What do you think?"

Many children are taught that some subjects and experiences are taboo or somehow undesirable or "not nice." These vary according to culture, place, and time. In our culture children often learn to be disgusted by defecation and decay, to be horrified by death, and uncomfortable with difference. They do not learn these biases until they experience other people's responses. We observed a group of children and a teacher who were fascinated by an animal skeleton they had found along the side of the road. They took the bones back to the classroom for further exploration. Another teacher responded to their find with repulsion which implied that exploration of this nature was not acceptable. Fortunately, the first teacher was not deterred, and they spent several days examining, reassembling the skeleton, counting the bones and teeth, and figuring out that it had been a dog. The teacher's openness to the experience led to important learning in math and science.

Teachers express a sense of curiosity about and appreciation of the world in statements like, "I wonder why the clouds are moving so quickly." "Look at how different each shell is." "The baskets all nest together, the little ones inside the big ones." "I wonder why cats purr—I wish I could." "The mother bear is looking after her cubs—every mother seems to do that." "I can feel the rabbit's heart is beating quickly and hard—I wonder how she's feeling." Statements like these model an inquiring mind. They help children to form concepts but do not hand them preformed ideas.

Questions can encourage children to explore. There are open questions and closed questions. Open questions facilitate inquiry. They say to the child, "Tell me more." Questions are open when they can be answered in a number of different ways and have more than one correct answer. You can develop skill in asking open questions by practicing until you can ask them with comfort. The following are the beginning phrases of some open questions.

What do you see? (hear, feel, smell)

How are these the same? (different)

What do you think about . . . ?

How do you know . . . ?

What do you think would happen if . . . ?

How do you think we could find out . . . ?

A closed question has only one correct or acceptable answer, for example, "What color is this bead?" "Is this a circle?" Closed questions are often useful for learning whether children have acquired a concept or piece of information, but they do not stimulate inquiry. In most classrooms, teachers use a mixture of open and closed questions. The kind of mix is influenced by values, objectives, and the nature of the particular situation. Awareness of the purpose of each type of question can help you to make conscious choices about which to use. When you wish to stimulate children to inquire, you will want to ask many open-ended questions.

The silence that a teacher allows between statements or questions is also an important factor in how children respond. Researchers have found that three to five seconds is the average amount of silence that occurs between teacher questions and the child's response or a follow-up comment from the teacher. They found that if the teacher waits only one or two seconds, one word responses are most frequent. If the wait lasts for several seconds, children respond with whole sentences and complex thoughts that represent more creativity and increased speculativeness (Costa, 1974).

MATHEMATICS

Mathematics is a way to structure experience to form ideas and concepts about quantitative, logical, and spatial relationships. During the early childhood years young children come to think of themselves as part of a community of people who use numbers to order and communicate about their world; in the same way that young children will pretend to write and read, they will label

distance and ages with numbers (my doll is twenteen—it's thirty–fifty miles—I don't have to go to bed till eighty o'clock—not for five twenty minutes). The development of mathematical thinking is a long process that consists of far more than simply knowing how to count and manipulate numbers in computations. Math experiences for young children should lead toward the ability to think logically and to creatively solve problems found in daily life.

Adults make assumptions about what children know, and about what they need to know based on adult understanding of practical skills like using money, balancing a checkbook, and reading a clock. Children's thinking, needs and development, however, are different. The conceptual underpinnings of practical skills are based on many years of concrete experiences that may not seem to relate to mathematics. Concepts such as more and fewer, far and near, similar and different, short and tall, now and later, first and last, over and under, precede later mastery of complex mathematical concepts.

The work of Piaget and others has led to an investigation of the kinds of math concepts children are capable of grasping and the ways they best acquire them. Young children are developing concepts of classification, space, number, measurement, ordering (seriation), patterning, and time. New understanding of what young children can learn has led to a rethinking of the traditional content of math curriculum. Counting and shape and numeral recognition are no longer considered sufficient content for a preschool or kindergarten math program.

Counting is a rote activity unless the child has a concept of number (oneness, twoness, threeness, and so on). Only then does the child understand that the name represents a specific quantity. A child who "knows" numbers up to twenty is not able to point out a stack of six blocks until she or he understands the concept of "sixness."

Numerals are symbols representing numbers, and their recognition is a visual perceptual task that is unrelated to the concept they represent. Until children develop the number concept (oneness, twoness, etc.) and understand that the word only represents the concept, they are not able to understand the meaning of the symbol. Although young children may appear to be reading numerals, a closer look at their understanding will usually demonstrate that they are naming the shape of the numeral rather than understanding the number concept. Children who are beginning to identify numerals and letters, for example, often add these to their paintings and drawings because they enjoy their new-found ability to identify and make these forms; the forms become design elements rather than symbols for quantity or sound.

Children learn about shape and space as they experience position, distance, boundaries, and shapes in relation to their world. The practice of memorizing shape names (triangle, circle, square, etc.) is a sensory-perceptual and labeling task that is a minor part of helping children develop understanding about the relation-ships between physical objects in the world. Because memorization of shape names is such a limited task and is generally taught without connection to the larger world of mathematics, it is not helpful to children in gaining the concepts that are needed for later mathematical and logical thought.

A Framework for Organizing the Math Curriculum

If learning to count, recognize numerals, and name shapes are not enough, what are the math concepts that young children need to develop to help them to make sense of the physical and social world?

Classification   Classification is one of the important math skills that children need

to learn. When they understand that they can group things together, based on the ways they are alike, and exclude them, based on the ways that they are different (negation, or "not like"), they have developed the basic concept of classification. Objects that are grouped together are considered to be part of a set. As children become more sophisticated and flexible in the categories they use, they are developing more profound understanding of classification. They are learning to group things according to their common attributes when they hang dresses up, place all the dishes in the cupboard, put all the large beads in a basket and all the small beads in a can, and sort buttons by size, shape, color, number of holes, or type of shank.

Space   Space involves the way one object or set of objects relates to others based on position, direction, and distance. Children develop concepts about space as they notice the relationship of their bodies to other people and objects. The concept of position may be developed in day-to-day activities such as putting away the blocks, the long on the bottom shelf and the short on the top shelf. The concept of direction may be discovered as a child first drives a tricycle forward and then backward, and distance explored when a child kicks a ball to a nearby child and then to a child who is further away.

Number   Number is the term that is used to refer to ideas that concern the quantity and order of objects. Sets of objects are recognized as a certain quantity that is unchanging and unrelated to the physical act of touching and

naming (1–2–3). Children only gradually come to understand number despite rather easily learning to count using number names in the correct order. We recently heard a five year old counting the bricks in a building as she walked along. She counted perfectly to thirty-nine at which point she was asked, "What if we took one brick away; how many would there be then?" Without hesitation she answered, "seventy-nine" and returned to counting the rest of the bricks. Children cannot use counting as a reliable tool until underlying number concepts are in place—usually around the age of seven. During the early childhood years other number concepts are being developed. Children can learn to compare quantity to determine more, less, fewer, or the same amounts; to comprehend position (first, second, third, etc.); and to match objects one for one—*one-to-one correspondence* (for example, a napkin for each person).

Measurement   Measurement is the process of comparing size, volume, weight, or quantity to a standard. Adults use numerically expressed standards such as meters, ounces, or dollars. Children discover the concept of measurement when they experiment to find how many unit blocks equal the width of the carpet, count how many cups of water fill a large container at the water table, or compare their height to the heights of their friends and teachers.

Seriation   Seriation takes place when objects are ordered in a sequence based on a difference in the degree of some quality such as size, weight, texture, or shading. Children gain experience in seriating when they arrange things in their environment; for example, themselves from shortest to tallest, balls from smallest to largest, or a set of color chips from palest to darkest.

Patterning   Patterning is another form of ordering based on repetition. When children create bead necklaces with alternating colors, arrange parquetry blocks, or sing the chorus after every verse of a song, they are experiencing patterns.

Time   Time concepts develop as children notice the sequence of events in their daily lives; for example, lunch is always followed by rest time, and a story about zoo animals is read before a visit to the zoo. *Duration* is another time-related concept. Children begin to understand as they notice such things as outdoor play lasting a long time in comparison to booktime which lasts for a short period.

Supporting Children's Learning in Mathematics

Children are discovering math concepts in the course of the ordinary activities and routines of classroom living. You can help them by providing a math-rich environment in which each child has the raw materials needed for understanding important mathematical concepts and relationships. You may also plan specific activities to give children a broad range of math experiences.

A math area equipped with carefully chosen equipment and materials can encourage children to experiment and thus discover many math concepts. Purchased equipment like attribute blocks (regular shapes which vary in size, thickness, and color), Cuisenaire rods (small colored blocks which are numerically related), colored cubes, pegboards,

measuring tools, and seriation toys like stacking cups are designed to enhance math learning. Unit blocks provide excellent experiences for the development of number, spatial, seriation, and classification concepts. Some computer software can provide math experiences appropriate for young children. Some of these allow children to program and others provide experience with patterning, seriation, and number. Computers can be very motivating. If the software is thoughtfully and appropriately designed, it can supplement, but not substitute for, an experience based math program for young children.

Math learning opportunities abound throughout the program day. Materials that relate to math are found in manipulative games, in water play with measuring cups and containers, in dramatic play areas, and outdoors where spatial concepts like on/off, top/bottom, to/from, in/out, up/down are experienced.

Teacher-made games like button sorting, lotto games, and matching activities foster math learning. We have found Mary Baratta-Lorton's books *Workjobs* and *Mathematics Their Way* good sources for ideas for teacher-made math games. You may also wish to use a developmentally appropriate packaged curriculum program, such as those developed by Celia Stendler Lavatelli and the High/Scope Foundation.

Children learn about math through the routines and activities of the school day. When each child has one cracker and rests on one mat, one-to-one correspondence is experienced. Sequencing is learned through observing the daily schedule. You can help children begin to be aware of math concepts by using math ideas in your conversations: "Would you like your cracker whole or in two pieces?"

"Which beads do you think belong together? Why?" "Can you find me a doll that is smaller than this one but larger than this one?" "Can you cover this mat with blocks?" "How many cubes do you think we'll need to measure the length of the box?" These are only a sample of the potential of the total school environment for exploring math concepts. Look closely at how your classroom supports math learning so you can better evaluate what you might do to expand and enrich the existing possibilities.

The world, the classroom, and our daily lives are filled with math concepts. Children can become math conscious. Talking about time, dates, ages, amounts, quantity, money, and other math ideas is both natural and a necessary preparation for later understanding. Children who have a background with the concrete

experiences upon which math is based come to see themselves as individuals who use number and measurement as important tools in daily life.

SCIENCE

Young children have a compelling curiosity to figure out why and how the world works. From their earliest months they observe and identify phenomena, discover relationships, search for answers, and communicate their discoveries. Your main teaching role in science is to make it an active process that preserves and encourages the natural curiosity of children.

Teachers who have maintained their own interest and enthusiasm for science view it as a process through which they and children find out about the world together. Children's questions provide them with opportunities to model the qualities and behaviors of the scientist: curiosity, experimentation, willingness to explore and solve problems. These teachers help children to learn the answers to questions through their own observation, research, and experimentation.

In early childhood programs science is the process of exploring the universe, the earth and the creatures that live within it, in ways that young children can understand. It is not, as some teachers fear, a scary, mysterious field involving complex concepts that they don't know and equipment that they don't have— a hard and fast collection of facts associated with biology assignments and a lab manual. Neither is it a body of information which adults know and which must be told to children.

A Framework for Organizing the Science Curriculum

While it is not necessary to be a scientist or to know a great deal of scientific information in order to offer science experiences in your classroom, you do need to know the kind of subject matter suitable for young children. Like other curriculum for young children, science is not isolated nor clearly divided into separate subject areas. It can be much more than a fish tank and a rock collection in a corner of the classroom. Science for young children can be divided into two broad categories: **life science** and **physical science**.

Life Science   Children are naturally curious about living things: what they are, how they survive, their life cycles. Their

movement and change makes them even more intriguing. Many concepts basic to the fields of biology, physiology, and ecology can be explored, discovered, and validated by young children in their daily lives.

We call the study of plants and animals, their structure, origin, growth, and reproduction **Biology**. The young child is filled with wonder about where the butterfly came from, how a bean grew into a plant, how the bulging mother mouse got the babies inside her, and why the dog has four legs and the spider has eight. The raw materials for the study of biology are an integral part of every young child's life and can abound in and around the classroom. As you work with children, you will help them to observe, compare and contrast living things, and to ask questions about what they see. As children observe the transformation of a caterpillar into a butterfly, the seed into a plant, and the pregnant mouse into a mouse family, they are having concrete experiences which will lead to understanding the concepts of reproduction, growth, and change.

Physiology is the biological science dealing with the processes and functions of living organisms. Starting with their own bodies, young children can notice functions such as breath, movement, sensation, and digestion. Interest in their own growth and developing skill can lead children to explore and learn about physiological structures such as bone and muscle systems. Children's fascination with their own bodies can be used as the springboard to further physiological discovery.

The branch of biological science dealing with interactions between organisms and their environment is called **Ecology**.

When, during your regular walk near school, you pass an empty lot filled with trees, birds, bugs, weeds, mice, and wild flowers that is bulldozed and then filled with a parking lot, children have the opportunity to observe the impact of human beings on their environment. Through this kind of experience children see ecology in action and learn about their own potential impact on their environment.

Physical Science   Physical science involves the study of matter, form, and change. Children explore and observe the properties of the earth, the sky, and solid and liquid matter. Concepts basic to physics, geology, and chemistry are experienced and explored in the course of daily activity. Like all other inquiry areas, children's curiosity is aroused by these subjects when they have personal impact.

Physics is the study of matter, energy, motion, and force. When children explore speed, leverage, balance, gravity, and mechanical systems, they are experiencing physics. Children first become aware of the physical properties of the world through exploratory play. A toy is dropped and falls to the floor, an unbalanced pile of blocks collapses, a rock dropped into a puddle makes rings of ripples. It takes many repeated experiences such as these for children to grasp that these are predictable phenomena which can be generalized. These are children's first physics experiments.

Chemistry deals with the composition, properties, and transformations of substances. For young children, it is not unrelated to daily living; it can focus on the exploration of daily experiences that are commonplace for adults. Children are experiencing chemistry as they watch

and discuss their playdough disintegrating in the water play table, oil separating from the rest of the salad dressing, and the interaction of vinegar and baking soda. Cooking provides opportunities to observe chemical transformation through the use of heat, moisture, and the combination of substances.

Geology deals with the formation of the earth—its layers, forms, and substances. Children observe and discuss and can visit firsthand common features of the earth such as mountains, lakes, beaches, oceans, rocks, and fossils. They ask questions like "How does the sand get on the beach?" "What makes a beach?" "Why did all the dirt wash away in the rainstorm?" Young children's concepts of geology are limited to what they have experienced repeatedly. For example, one young child from Hawaii on a trip to the mainland had a great deal of difficulty understanding that the land on the opposite side of a lake was not another island. A child from the mainland visiting Hawaii had similar difficulty comprehending the vastness of the Pacific ocean, which could not be driven around or crossed by a bridge.

Astronomy is the science that has to do with the universe beyond the earth's atmosphere—the sun, moon, planets, and stars. Although young children cannot have a "hands-on" experience of astronomy, they can observe the cycle of day and night, the heat of the sun, the waxing and waning of the moon, and the stars in the sky. They are regularly exposed to media concerning space through television, movies, and books. Fantasy and fact are intertwined and are difficult for children to separate in this age of space exploration and satellite use. Children will be curious about these things and in school can have a place to talk and read about astronomy and the exploration of space.

Supporting Children's Learning in Science

Children's natural curiosity is the beginning place for your science curriculum, but it is not the end. You support science learning by encouraging children's innate interest in science and by planning an environment and activities that stimulate and expand those interests. Children should have experience with both biological and physical science in planned and informal ways. The areas of science curriculum described above provide a framework for evaluating the experiences that you provide.

The environment of the school affects the scope and variety of the science curriculum. An outdoor play area with trees, grass, sand, dirt, water, bugs, and other creatures provides a laboratory for science experiences. Earthworms dug from the ground, insects discovered beneath the overturned rock, seedlings growing after a rain are ideal starting places for exploring living things. Children on a seesaw may discover concepts about balance and leverage. The frozen water puddle in the early morning that melts by noon and is miraculously gone as children leave for home provides a chemistry lesson. If you look and listen to children as they interact in the outdoor environment, they will provide you with many ideas for science experiences that you can explore together.

A science area in the classroom can be a laboratory for teacher initiated activities and child discoveries. If an earthworm is brought into the area, a science problem is posed: what does this creature need to survive? Together, children and teachers may solve the problem based on their observations or by referring to books or resource people. Tools and materials for exploration can be stored in a science area: magnifying glasses, magnets, dissection equipment, trays, bug boxes,

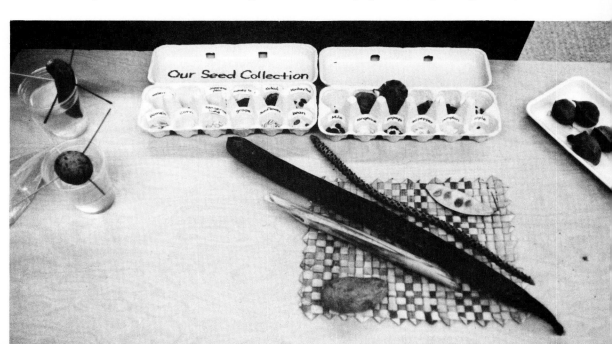

animal cages, tools for manipulating and taking apart a clock or radio, and measuring equipment like scales and rulers. The area can include ongoing projects such as aquariums, terrariums, animal families, and plants. Learning materials, such as a sink and float game, and picture collections for sorting and describing, may be stored and used in the science area. The area can also contain reference books about science topics.

Some appropriate and worthwhile science experiences require moving beyond the school setting. Science learning trips can be as simple as a nature walk in the neighborhood or can involve more elaborate trips to places like the zoo, aquarium, farm, museum of natural science, forest, or seashore. Whether your trips are nearby and spontaneous or more distant and carefully planned, they will promote more science learning if there is enough time for children to learn by discovery. This is facilitated by allowing small, unrushed groups of children to visit sites where they can explore, observe, manipulate, and discuss experiences as they occur.

You can plan specific activities on subjects that are of interest to children. We have observed teachers and children conducting experiments on the needs of seedlings (What happens if one is kept in the dark?); the effect of time on a carrot; keeping track of the progress of monarch caterpillars; and attempting to manufacture dirt from pulverized rocks. One creative teacher we know used her own pregnancy, a subject of much interest to her class of children, as an opportunity to talk about birth and the life cycle.

Whenever science inquiry opportunities occur, in planned or spontaneous activities, you can guide children's curiosity through questioning. Ask children questions like "Why do you suppose . . . ?" "What do you think would happen if . . . ?" and "How do you think we can find out?" to encourage thinking and concept development. Another part of your role is to find just the right resource (a person or a book or object) to expand their knowledge. As you provide experiences and model an inquiring and respectful attitude toward the world, you help children learn to observe and think like scientists. Science, rather than being scary, or mysterious, is accessible, infinitely interesting, and definitely worth knowing.

SOCIAL STUDIES

Social studies concerns relationships among people and between people and their environment. It is an umbrella term for social science fields including geography, history, sociology, anthropology, political science, economics, psychology, and ecology. It can be approached in many different ways and requires careful thought and planning to make these topics meaningful to young children.

Most adults' early memories of social studies consist of recollections of rote learning of dates, state capitols, imports and exports, and the names of presidents. A few songs, dances, and odd customs of faraway places comprise the more positive, if disconnected, remainder of their social studies memories.

For young children social studies can be an exploration of some of the most interesting aspects of life. It concerns their own feelings, family, community, locale, and personal history. It is not a subject to be studied in isolation, but a part of their lives, an exploration of who they are.

A Framework for Organizing the Social Studies Curriculum

We use a framework for social studies that is organized around exploration of the most basic question in a child's life, *Who am I?* (Feeney, 1976). This general theme is divided into six subthemes, each related to one or more social science fields and each with an organizing question. The activities based on these questions help children to gain self-awareness and acquire beginning social studies concepts. Through them adults can see the relevance of classroom social studies activities to children's lives. The six questions and the related social sciences are:

Who am I as a person with feelings?—
  psychology

Who am I as a member of a family?—
  anthropology and *sociology*

Who am I as a member of a community?—
  economics, political science, sociology

Who am I as a person from a culture?—
  anthropology

Who am I as a person in a place?—
  geography and *ecology*

Who am I as a person in time?—*history*

Who Am I as a Person with Feelings?

Teachers can help young children to understand concepts about feelings and to accept and deal with feelings in constructive ways. Children can learn that all people have feelings, that there are many different feelings both pleasant and unpleasant, and that while we all experience negative feelings, it is important to learn to talk about them rather than act on them or keep them inside. Children can come to accept feelings, both their own and those of other people.

Who Am I as a Member of a Family?

Children learn about themselves and their families and the families of others. They discover that most people live in a family, there are similarities and differences in families and the ways they live, there are different ways of meeting family needs, all families share the common goal of caring for their members, and each person has a special role in a family.

Who Am I as a Member of a Community?

Communities are made up of diverse people who do different kinds of work. In this area of social studies children learn about the people in communities, what they do, how they get the goods and services they need, and how and why rules are made to protect them. Children can come to understand what helps the community to function and that each person can contribute to it in a variety of ways.

Who Am I as a Person from a Culture?

Cultural background is something that enhances who we are. Young children can easily see that cultural heritage is defined by differences: different foods, dwellings, clothes, languages, beliefs, music, and dances. With guidance they can also learn about very important similarities. We share a common humanity: members of all cultures have language, rituals, and celebrations and concern themselves with providing their members with food, shelter, protection, and clothing. Children can become aware of and develop pride in their own cultural heritage while learning that differences between cultures contribute to a society that is rich and interesting.

Who Am I as a Person in a Place? In early childhood programs teachers can help children gain awareness of how their lives are connected to the natural features of the environment. All people are dependent on the resources of the earth for survival, and, consequently, have responsibility for the quality of the environment. Children can gain knowledge of the features of their immediate environment, that they can directly experience hill, ravine, harbor, mountain, stream, and ocean. This area of social studies overlaps the science area of ecology but differs in the social studies' focus on the relationship of people to the environment.

Who Am I as a Person in Time? Time for young children involves the duration and sequence of events in daily life. They may know that after they wake up in the morning they eat breakfast and go to school or that booktime precedes rest time in the daily routine. Children experience the duration of time as they wait for bread to come out of the oven. They can begin to recognize that the past influences the present and that time creates change. A weekly trip past a garden or a construction site gives clear evidence of the changes that take place over time. Looking at their own baby pictures lends dramatic credence to the idea that time affects them.

You can use this organizing framework to provide many social studies experiences based on events in the lives of the children in your classroom. In order to do this you will need to know something about children and their families, their ethnic and cultural backgrounds, their community, and their interests and concerns. You will also have the opportu-

nity to share aspects of your heritage and background and things you are interested in and care about.

Supporting Children's Learning in Social Studies

Social studies is a diverse field and can be introduced in many ways. Like the other inquiry subjects it requires a prepared environment; for this area, one which includes blocks, dramatic play materials, books, and writing materials (the tools of the social scientist for reading and recording information). To bring social studies to young children we need to bring them into contact with the people and activities about which they are learning. Most important, it requires you, the teacher, to be awake to the social studies learning possibilities inherent in the children, families, and community. As with math and science, you need to have the ability to ask questions that stimulate inquiry and must share the children's curiosity and talk with them about their interests.

Because social studies is such a broad area and can be approached in so many different ways, it is an excellent tool for organizing and integrating curriculum. Food preparation, visits from resource people, songs, dances, artifacts (from a family, culture, or place), books, and trips all contribute to concept development in the social sciences. Follow-up activities can occur in every area of the curriculum. Children gain deeper understanding when they recreate and reexperience concepts in dramatic play, art work, writing books, block play, songs and games.

In our work with young children, we have used the "Who Am I?" questions and

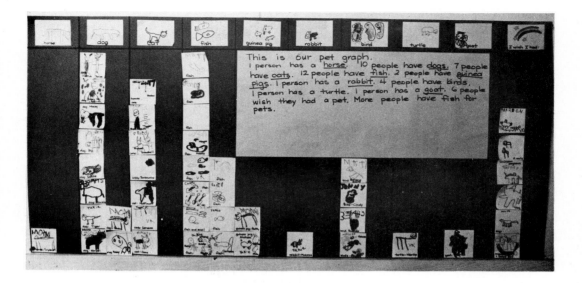

This is our pet graph.
I person has a horse. 10 people have dogs. 7 people have cats. 12 people have fish. 2 people have guinea pigs. I person has a rabbit. 4 people have birds. I person has a turtle. I person has a goat. 6 people wish they had a pet. More people have fish for pets.

accompanying experiences as an organizing framework for the entire school year. One year, while teaching a group of three year olds, we discovered the power of the family theme for this group of children. While reading a story about a baby who thought her mother didn't love her, we found that the children were extremely concerned with the issue of parental love and care. We realized that the stress of separation was high, and we wanted to help them become more comfortable with the dramatic transition from home to school. We used the question "Who am I as a member of a family?" to help the children connect their experiences at school with their lives as family members. As other members of our teaching team joined us, a flurry of creative planning ensued. Together we discovered, created, and used many different activities and projects to connect school and family life. Trips were made to each family's home and parents' workplaces. Children and teachers made books

that recorded the trip experiences. A wall collage was created of photographs of every child's family members. Children visited each other's homes. Although each family was different, they shared similarities: all of the children (and teachers) had families, each family was made up of a different combination of people and pets, each family cared for its members in similar but special ways. A family graph was made to help children more systematically compare the different families. This led to discussions of how families were similar and different, the members of a family, and what families do to take care of one another.

Because this group of children represented much cultural diversity—Americans of Asian, African, European, and Pacific Island origins—we eventually linked the study of families to the question "Who am I as a person from a culture?" Families participated by teaching us about their cultures, sharing items of clothing and other special artifacts, as well as teaching us songs, dances, language, and recipes. The children illustrated a cookbook that included all the recipes and gave it as their holiday gift to their families. Children were able to experience that while there were differences between the cultures in the ways that things were done, basic needs were the same: a futon and a bed were both comfortable places to sleep; chopsticks, forks, and fingers were all good tools for getting food to the mouth; a kilt, a kimono, and a lava-lava all covered bodies and were fun to dress up in. As children's parents participated by sharing information, artifacts, and skills, children began to understand this special part of their identities and that culture enriched us all.

NUTRITION

In an early childhood program you have an opportunity to interest children in nutrition, a subject that will be important to them throughout their lives. Little else will be with them for so long or will have as important an effect on their well-being. All people need knowledge to help them choose foods that contribute to good health, yet nutrition tends to be overlooked in preschool and primary education. If your nutrition education was boring lecture and repetitive drill, you may feel that nutrition is an inappropriate subject in the early childhood years. But if it is introduced in a lively and relevant way, foundations of nutrition understanding can be formed.

As food is prepared and eaten, many kinds of learning occur. Physical and sensory aspects of the food are experienced and motor skills are developed. Foods can be categorized and compared and

processes of change are observed. Mealtimes are often a social experience; friends sit together and share food and conversation. Food may be an aesthetic experience that heightens children's awareness of natural beauty, structure, shape, color, texture, and aroma. We recently observed a class of kindergarten children who became curious about *Apple Pandowdy*, a dessert mentioned in a story. Their teacher researched the dish and cooked it with them. The children illustrated the recipe, wrote about their process, and learned a song that mentioned it. Social studies, science, math, reading, literature, language, physical development, and creative expression were all integrated with this food experience.

We have placed nutrition with inquiry subjects, but clearly it is part of other curriculum areas as well. It is a subject that connects physical, cognitive, social, and creative development. Because it can be used so well to teach other subjects, nutrition content often gets lost. We believe that nutrition in itself is an important part of the curriculum, something worthwhile for young children to know about.

A Framework for Thinking About the Nutrition Curriculum

During the early childhood years, teachers can help children to understand that their health is affected by food, that they can make food choices that will help them to grow and be healthy, that there are a variety of different foods that are worth trying, and that they can develop food preparation skills. Information, attitudes, and skills can be used as a framework for thinking about your teaching in this subject area.

Information   Many teachers do not feel that they have adequate training to provide nutrition education to young children, but a few simple concepts can form the base of early childhood nutrition education. These do not involve memorizing lists of vitamins and minerals or the four basic food groups. Instead, they involve an awareness of food and the value of good nutrition, and the realization that food affects feelings, behavior, and development. Even young preschoolers can understand some very basic nutrition concepts, although they may not be able to verbalize them.

With experience young children will learn that all people need food to grow, live, stay healthy, and have energy for work and play. As you talk during food experiences you can help children understand that different foods have

different substances that are needed for health and growth. Older preschool children can learn that these nutrients are called protein, vitamins, minerals, carbohydrates, and fat. Nutritional needs vary, and as children observe the different eating patterns of others they come to realize that all people need to eat a variety of foods to get all of the needed nutrients and that they need different amounts depending on their age, size, sex, state of health, and the amount of activity they are involved in. Caring adults who talk with children about their food choices help them to see that there are many different kinds of foods that can provide the different nutrients. The way that food is grown, processed, stored, and prepared influences its nutritional value, and the way that you handle and discuss food in the classroom teaches this. Some foods provide many nutrients; some provide very few. For example, soft drinks provide only calories, while fruit juice provides vitamins, minerals, and carbohydrates as well.

Attitudes   People's health is linked to their diets. As more and more information is gained, nutritionists are coming to realize that the typical American diet is not as healthful as was once thought. We can help children to appreciate the value of high fiber and low fat foods that have often been neglected in our diets. By expanding children's food horizons, we offer a range of alternatives and help them to develop competence in making wise food choices. Much of what adults experience as children's reluctance to try healthful foods is the product of their own expectations and biases. In our teaching we found that children usually enjoyed

fruits, vegetables, brown rice, whole wheat bread, and such exotic dishes as borscht, sushi, and ratatouille if they participated in cooking and if they knew that they would not be required to eat the food if they didn't like it. Teachers need to model honest appreciation for healthful foods and give children time and a number of opportunities to try any new or unusual food.

Skills   A range of skills is necessary for children to be competent and independent in choosing and handling food. In school they can begin to learn skills surrounding food choice and preparation including selection, planning, following recipes, stirring, pouring, measuring, and serving. Becoming competent at these skills also fosters feelings of self-confidence and positive attitudes toward nutritious foods and cooking. We have been delighted at the competence of experienced cooks

aged three and four and surprised at the lack of confidence and skill in first and second graders who had not been given cooking opportunities.

Supporting Children in Nutrition Education

You can best teach nutrition through providing children with direct experiences that help them to develop skills and concepts. Effective teaching involves modeling behavior and attitudes that encourage health supporting habits and talking with children when day-to-day experiences touch on nutrition.

Cooking, tasting, eating, shopping for food, gardening, raising animals, and observing food being prepared or grown are all experiences that relate to nutrition. As you design your environment you will want to ensure that the necessary facilities,

equipment, and materials for each of these experiences are available.

An appropriate, nutritious food preparation experience should be offered at least once a week. Cooking activities that are well planned will be most successful. It's a good idea to try the recipe before using it with children. Choose activities where children can do most of the work and remember that in cooking everything from set-up to clean-up is important. Reduce tasks to small child-sized activities so that children have a successful experience. Use good tools; knives that don't cut, eggbeaters that stick, and graters that don't grate properly are frustrating and more dangerous than tools that work. You can extend the learning by using the interests and questions that the children generate in a follow-up to the cooking experience. In food preparation, it is best to work with small groups of children. The younger the children are, the smaller the group should be.

Tasting experiences can introduce a cooking activity, isolate or compare food attributes (sour, sweet, crunchy, creamy, and so on), provide experience with foods that are rich in a particular nutrient, or help children learn to accept and enjoy new or unusual foods. Through tasting children learn about their individual taste preferences.

Cooking activities allow children to feel responsible, independent, and successful. Cooking in the classroom (which need not involve heat) is a very important vehicle for teaching about nutrition. Concepts are taught as you take note of the nutrient contributions of the foods that are being prepared: "The raisins in the trail mix will help to give us energy on our hike"; as you help children to notice differences in tastes: "Some of us like the

carrots best; other people prefer the celery"; and as you work with food to preserve the nutrients and enhance flavor and appearance.

Children can be regular contributors to the daily process of snack and meal preparation. Simple snacks make rewarding "cooking" experiences for young children. For example, spreading peanut butter on a slice of celery is not usually thought of as a cooking activity, but it involves food preparation skills that young children need to practice to master. Allowing children to become actively involved instead of remaining the passive recipients helps them begin to develop the skills and attitudes they will need to take care of themselves.

Nutrition is a part of the daily early childhood program experience. If children see adults making food choices that help maintain growth, health, and energy, and avoiding nonnutritious foods, they will be gaining nutrition awareness. When adults prepare and handle food with care, children begin to understand that this is an important thing to do. Poor habits can also be taught by modeling. For this reason most schools restrict smoking to teachers' lounges. You should restrict poor food habits (eating junk food, soft drinks, candy, and so forth) to times when you will not be with children, or better yet, take your nutrition knowledge to heart and work to eliminate these habits.

The times that children are actively involved with food and cooking activities are the most appropriate for talking about nutrition. These opportunities may occur during meals and snacks and their preparation, while shopping, gardening, caring for animals, or visiting a home or farm. It is interesting to children to talk about where food comes from and how it helps their bodies to grow. Children will often introduce the subject of nutrition by echoing the information that they have heard. For example, many children have been told that milk makes them strong or big. When a child repeats a statement like this, you can help to develop the concept by adding a short informative statement like, "Yes, milk has protein in it to help you grow and calcium to make your bones strong."

As children cook and eat, they gain an awareness of the importance of good nutrition; they become aware of the properties of food and how it contributes to their lives. And when they experience the food of other cultures, they enhance their awareness and appreciation of all people.

CHECKLIST FOR INQUIRY CURRICULUM AREAS

Program Structure
- [ ] Stated goals include support of play, discovery learning, inquiry and problem-solving skills
- [ ] Time for independent play and exploration in at least one hour time blocks
- [ ] Planned small group activities are provided daily
- [ ] Cooking is a planned activity at least weekly
- [ ] Children participate in snack preparation
- [ ] Trips related to science, math, social studies, and/or nutrition taken at least bi-weekly
- [ ] Visitors who share information and skills regarding inquiry topics
- [ ] Planned science, math, social studies, and nutrition curriculum activities

Environment and Materials
- [ ] Small low tables and chairs at which children can work individually and in small groups
- [ ] A science center and a math center (or a combination of the two)
- [ ] A unit block center
- [ ] A dramatic play center
- [ ] An art center
- [ ] Space for using mud, sand, dough and water
- [ ] An outdoor environment with dirt, plants, insects, birds, and playground equipment
- [ ] Space and equipment for gardening
- [ ] Water table for classroom use by children
- [ ] Access to kitchen equipment

☐ Collections of objects, both natural and manmade, for children to sort and classify in different ways

☐ Useful throw-away materials such as jar lids, corks, cotton, etc.

☐ Plants and animals that are cared for by children

☐ A chart stand and paper

math:

☐ Attribute blocks or beads

☐ Partitioned trays for sorting (e.g., ice cube trays or egg cartons)

☐ Seriation games and toys (e.g., nesting cups, sound cannisters, texture games, color chips)

☐ Puzzles

☐ Colored cubes

☐ Cuisenaire rods

☐ Shape-sorting boxes

☐ Measuring implements: rulers, cups, spoons, tapes, yardsticks, etc.

☐ Coins and play money for the dramatic play area

☐ A balance

☐ Purchased games such as lotto games, number games, and card games

☐ Teacher-made games

☐ Parquetry pieces

☐ Beads for stringing

☐ Pegboards

☐ A working clock at child's eye level

science:

☐ An aquarium to use for fish, plants, etc.

☐ Magnifying glasses

☐ Probes, tweezers, tongs, and scissors

☐ Jars for specimens (e.g., baby food jars)

☐ Sponges, eye droppers, tubing

☐ Machines to examine and dissemble and reassemble

☐ Screwdrivers (flat and phillip's), pliers, wrenches, and hammers

☐ Thermometers for observing temperature variation in water and air

☐ Screen cages for temporarily housing insects, lizards, mice, etc.

☐ Factual books about science topics: books written for children, well-illustrated reference books for adults, child-made books, teacher-made books

☐ Picture collections of animals, plants, geographic and astronomic features, machines, etc.

social studies:
- ☐ Children's books and child-authored books about feelings, families, community, culture, place, and time kept for reading in the class library
- ☐ Picture and poster collections of people from your area and from other places, times and cultures working, playing, interacting, caring for home and family, displaying emotion, celebrating, shopping, etc.
- ☐ Record collections that include music from various ethnic and cultural backgrounds and represent different moods and feelings
- ☐ Dramatic play clothes and props representing different roles, ages, and cultural groups
- ☐ Materials for creating books: paper, pens
- ☐ Teacher-made games that illustrate social studies concepts (e.g., sorting photograph cards into happy and not happy, or arranging pictures in the sequence of a family's day)
- ☐ People and animal figures to supplement block play

nutrition:
- ☐ Unbreakable cooking equipment exclusively for children's use which includes ____ a set of nesting bowls, ____ 4–6 individual portion bowls, ____ measuring cups and spoons, ____ stirring spoons, ____ rubber scrapers, ____ turners, ____ bread knives, ____ sharp paring knives, ____ 4–6 small plastic cutting boards, ____ a good can opener
- ☐ Illustrated cookbooks with simple nutritious recipes
- ☐ Books for children concerning nutrition
- ☐ Teacher-made large illustrated recipe charts
- ☐ A hot plate or electric frying pan
- ☐ A toaster oven
- ☐ Basic ingredients: flour, salt, baking soda and powder, oil, vinegar, milk, etc.
- ☐ Facilities and equipment for hygenic clean-up and food storage: air-tight plastic containers, sink with hot water, a refrigerator, a dishpan, drain board, sponges, dishwashing soap, etc.
- ☐ Picture collections of foods and food production

FOR FURTHER THOUGHT AND DISCUSSION

1 Reflect on science, math, social studies, and nutrition classes from your own school experiences. What stands out for you? Did you enjoy them? If so why; if not why not? What implications does this have for your own teaching of young children?

2 Reflect on programs for young children that you have observed. Compare how these have provided inquiry experiences. Was time for math, science, social studies, and nutrition scheduled? Did teachers plan for these areas? How did the environment support inquiry in these areas? What kinds of questioning did you observe? How did these support or discourage learning?

3 What inquiry subject area do you most look forward to presenting to young children? About which do you feel most apprehensive? Why? What resources or experiences might help you feel more prepared?

4 Think of a time when you were really curious and excited about learning something. What made it interesting? What did you do to find out more about it? Do you still remember what you learned and how you used it?

PROJECTS

1 Use the **Checklist for Inquiry Curriculum Areas** from this chapter to observe an early childhood program. Report on the extent to which the program seems to support children's development of discovery, thinking, and problem solving in the areas of math, science, social studies, and nutrition. Suggest some additional experiences from which children would benefit.

2 Design a math or science area for an early childhood classroom, including all the tools and materials that children would need for independent use. Write and illustrate your plan, and if possible, put it into effect in a classroom. Report on your design and, if implemented, on the effect on children's inquiry and problem solving. If you were unable to put your design into effect, share it with a teacher and include his/her response and suggestions in your report.

3 Use the lesson plan form in Chapter 9 to design and implement a math, science, social studies or nutrition activity for children. Present the lesson to a group of children and report on what happened. Describe what you learned about yourself, children, inquiry, and teaching.

4 Design a week's plans for young children that includes all of the inquiry areas. Use one of the weekly planning forms in Chapter 9. Implement part or all of your plan. Report on what happened and what you learned about yourself, children, inquiry, and planning.

RECOMMENDED READING

Baratta-Lorton, Mary. *Workjobs*. Menlo Park, Cal.: Addison-Wesley, 1972.

————. *Mathematics Their Way*. Menlo Park, Cal.: Addison-Wesley, 1976.

Barron, Linda. *Mathematics Experiences for the Early Childhood Years*. Columbus, O.: Charles E. Merrill, 1979.

Carlsson-Paige, Nancy, and Levin, Diane. *Helping Young Children Understand Peace, War, and the Nuclear Threat*. Washington, D.C.: National Association for the Education of Young Children, 1985.

Goodwin, Mary T., and Pollen, Gerry. *Creative Food Experiences for Children*. Washington D.C.: Center for Science in the Public Interest, 1980.

Harlan, Jean. *Science Experiences for the Early Childhood Years*. 3d ed. Columbus, O.: Charles E. Merrill, 1984.

Harms, Thelma, and Veitch, Bev. *Cook and Learn*. Menlo Park, Cal.: Addison-Wesley, 1980.

Hill, Dorothy M. *Mud, Sand, and Water*. Washington, D.C.: National Association for the Education of Young Children, 1977.

Hirsch, Elisabeth. *The Block Book*. Washington, D.C.: National Association for the Education of Young Children, 1984.

Holt, Bess-Gene. *Science with Young Children*. Washington, D.C.: National Association for the Education of Young Children, 1977.

Kamii, Constance. *Number in Preschool and Kindergarten: Educational Implications of Piaget's Theory*. Washington, D.C.: National Association for the Education of Young Children, 1982.

Kendall, Frances E. *Diversity in the Classroom: A Multi-cultural Approach to the Education of Young Children*. New York: Teachers College Press, 1983.

Nuffield Mathematics Project. *I Do and I Understand*. New York: Wiley, 1967.

Parents Nursery School. *Kids Are Natural Cooks*. Boston: Houghton Mifflin Company, 1972.

Saracho, Olivia N., and Bernard Spodek. *Understanding the Multicultural Experience in Early Childhood Education*. Washington, D.C.: National Association for the Education of Young Children, 1983.

Seefeldt, Carol. *Social Studies for the Preschool-Primary Child*. Columbus O.: Charles E. Merrill, 1984.

Wanamaker, Nancy, et al. *More Than Graham Crackers*. Washington, D.C.: National Association for the Education of Young Children, 1979.

14

Children with
Special Needs

Do what you can with what you have.

Theodore Roosevelt

*In this chapter we help you to prepare to work with children who have physical or psychological conditions which require special attention. We will look at the ways in which you may find yourself with such a child in your classroom, describe some characteristics of disabling conditions including child abuse and neglect, and discuss the preparation, planning and teaching strategies required to provide an optimal learning environment for children with special needs. This chapter relates to the CDA areas **Program Management, Self, Social, Families,** and **Learning Environment.***

All children have special needs. As we thought about the children we have known and taught, we realized that there are many ways to have special needs. From the very active child to the very quiet or exceptionally sensitive one each had aspects which required special teaching. Children from different cultures or who speak different dialects or languages, a child who learns like a six year old but has the feelings of a three year old, a child who wears glasses, a child from a single parent family, a child with a lisp, all have special needs. In every early childhood classroom there are at least as many special needs as there are children. All require special planning and teaching.

Some of the children you work with will be more challenging than others. Their needs will be harder to meet because they will be sufficiently different to require you to modify teaching methods. They may be called disabled or handicapped because they have significant impairment or delay in some area of growth and learning. They may be called gifted because they learn more, and more rapidly, than other young children; they too require individual attention in order to

be stimulated and challenged in school. While it is difficult to test for *giftedness* in very young children, you will be aware of very bright children and will want to be sensitive to their needs for more stimulating intellectual activities. This chapter was originally researched and written under a grant from the Bureau of Education for the Handicapped, so its focus is on those conditions that impair normal functioning in young chidren.

The presence of a special needs child in your classroom will affect your relationship with other children, co-workers, and parents as well as the ways you choose to use time, space, and materials. You will need to assess your feelings, your perceptions of your role, and your values for children and yourself. That is not so different from what you, as a teacher of young children, usually do. Your training will have prepared you to view each child as unique with different skills, interests and needs. You will have learned to design curriculum and environments that support individual differences. The presence of a child with a disability in a regular early childhood classroom requires that you learn specific techniques, but you can apply what you already know about meeting the needs of normal children to meeting the needs of special children.

Our primary purpose in including this chapter is to help you, as the teacher in a regular early childhood classroom, teach not only those children who have already been identified as having disabling conditions, but also those children whom you may be the first to identify as requiring special attention and those who fall in the gray area between *normal* and *disabled*. Keep in mind that all children have special needs, and all children are more alike than they are different.

IDENTIFYING CHILDREN WITH SPECIAL NEEDS

Fifteen eager four year olds are eating morning snack. It is now the middle of the school year, and they have all learned the ropes of making snack a pleasant time, except Jeremy. Jeremy cruises the edges of the room, stopping briefly to dump a puzzle from a shelf and run his hands through the pieces, only to be distracted by the morning's paintings drying nearby. As he passes a table of children, his attention is again deflected. He tries to squeeze his body onto a chair occupied by another child. The result is a struggle in which Jeremy quickly loses interest. This has disrupted snack for the other children, and Jeremy himself has been unable to participate appropriately in an important classroom activity.

Jeremy's behavior is usually like this. His actions consistently precipitate conflicts with other children and adults. He seems unable to engage for any length of time in meaningful activity. As his

teacher, you might feel irritated and frustrated. You know from your training and experience that many young children are easily distractible at age four. Jeremy's case seems extreme. You suspect that Jeremy has an emotional or learning problem.

For many early childhood teachers, a situation similar to this one becomes their first experience in working with a special needs child—a child who has not yet been formally identified as having a problem and who is not receiving any treatment. This is probably the most common way a special needs child appears in a regular early childhood classroom. You may also find yourself with a special needs child by formal mainstreaming or by what we call informal mainstreaming (which we will describe later in this chapter).

A child like Jeremy will most likely appear in your classroom as just another child entering school. It is important to be sensitive to subtle clues that may indicate that a child has a serious problem and needs to be referred for outside help. A friend of ours told us about a child in her classroom who seemed to daydream and who didn't seem to be making the kind of progress that other children were making. Our friend was patient and understanding and calmed parental fears. To her regret it was later determined that the child suffered from a form of epilepsy, that her daydreaming episodes were really *petit mal* seizures, and that the developmental lags were at least the partial result of this overlooked condition.

In situations such as these you will be instrumental in identifying children who need special attention and special services. Almost always you will also remain that child's teacher for the better part of a year while an evaluation and assessment process is completed and a plan of action is developed.

What can you do when you believe that a child in your classroom has a condition—perhaps a disabling condition—that requires special help? The first step is to observe the child in some systematic way so that you can begin to pinpoint the areas in which his or her behavior differs significantly from other children. This will help you view the child's problems more objectively and will also help you decide whether step two—getting help—is necessary.

Sharing your concerns with a co-worker, head teacher, or director will be helpful. They may be able to give support while you sort and organize your thoughts and feelings, or provide useful insights from a more objective point of view.

At some point, you will need to talk with the child's family about your concerns. Probably the best time to do this is after you have collected observational data and researched the community resources that are available to help the child. When you can share your observations and their possible implications with the parents, you can suggest ways in which both of you can work together to get help for the child. If they, too, have been concerned and not known where to turn for help, the parents may be relieved. They may be willing to initiate or support your efforts to initiate a referral for evaluation. Other parents may be unable to accept the possibility that something could be "wrong" with their child. If so, you will need to explore other avenues for getting help and classroom support.

You may need to be very persistent. The child is in your classroom, and it is your responsibility to find out what can be done. Do not assume that you can handle the situation alone. Your director or head teacher may be supportive and be able to provide the resources you will need. Both public and private agencies can provide screening, evaluation, and consultation for children with suspected handicaps. Your own school may be able to provide such services. Outside your school, a good place to begin looking for help is your state, county, or local Department of Health or Department of Education. If they cannot provide the services you require, they can probably direct you to the appropriate agency. Private agencies such as the Association for Children With Learning Disabilities or children's hospitals may also be able to help.

DISABLING CONDITIONS

Awareness of the characteristics of disabling conditions will help you identify and understand special needs children in your classroom. A disabling condition is one that impairs or limits rather than simply changes a child's daily functioning. Children who have disabling conditions have difficulty learning and may develop more slowly in some areas because of a physical, sensory, intellectual, or behavioral problem. These conditions are long-term and not the result of a temporary incapacity due to illness, injury or short-term stress. Such children require special kinds of learning experiences and/or professional treatment to adapt to or overcome their condition and to achieve their fullest potential.

Disabling conditions fall along a continuum: Children can be mildly disabled (require a brace on one leg, for example), moderately disabled (have a hearing loss that affects speech-language development), or severely disabled (such as profound retardation). Children can also have multiple disabilities. The severity of the problem determines to what degree special techniques, equipment, or materials are needed to help the child learn. In general, mildly and sometimes moderately disabled children will be included in regular programs.

Some Shared Characteristics

All disabilities have the potential to inhibit children's social-emotional growth and the development of positive self-concept. Disabled children may have fewer chances to be in social situations because their mobility is limited, or they may have trouble making others understand them. Unsuccessful social experiences, whether the result of the disability or of others' response to it, can lead to feelings of inadequacy and failure that contribute to a negative self-concept.

Four general areas of functioning may be limited by specific disabling conditions:

mobility, communication, information acquisition, and information processing. Children may be affected in more than one of these areas.

Mobility   Children who have difficulty controlling their physical movements cannot fully explore the world nor easily maintain interactions with people or materials. Children with physical and visual handicaps are most likely to have impaired mobility.

Communication   Children who have difficulty communicating may also be slower to develop cognitive skills that help them understand and organize their thoughts. They may be ignored or rejected by other children because they have difficulty making themselves understood. Handicapping conditions that can affect speech and communications include hearing impairments, speech/language disorders, retardation, and some emotional disturbances.

Information Acquisition Many handicapping conditions restrict the amount and the quality of information children can extract from the environment. The major impact is on cognitive development. Social development may also be affected when children are unable to respond appropriately in social interactions because they don't have adequate information. For example, a vision-impaired child may not be able to play a game because he or she cannot see game pieces well enough. Physical disabilities, vision and hearing impairments, retardation, and learning disabilities limit information acquisition.

Information Processing Some conditions make it difficult for children to appropriately organize and understand information. This restricts the development of cognitive skills. Social skills are slow to develop when children are unable to interact with others because they don't understand social situations. Information processing can be inhibited by hearing problems,

speech/language disorders, learning disabilities and retardation. This kind of problem may provide you with the first clue of a suspected disability in a child who has not been identified.

Characteristics of Disabling Conditions

Each specific disabling condition results in some common characteristics of learning and behavior. Awareness of these characteristics can help you collect data and assist you in developing appropriate classroom strategies. It is important to remember that although children with the same disability share these characteristics, they are unlike each other in many other ways. Each child, whether disabled or not has an individual temperament, personality, and social environment which shapes his or her other responses to the world.

Physical Disabilities (Orthopedic or Neurological Impairments) In *neurological impairments,* the brain, spinal cord, or

---

SOME CHARACTERISTICS OF CHILDREN WITH PHYSICAL DISABILITIES

Mildly or moderately physically impaired children may:
- ☐ Be clumsy, walking or bumping into things often.
- ☐ Have difficulty with motor activities involving large muscles, such as crawling, climbing stairs, or riding a tricycle.
- ☐ Have difficulty with activities involving eye-hand coordination, such as stringing beads, building a tower of blocks, cutting or drawing (also a sign of possible visual impairment).
- ☐ Have poor speech due to inability to control their breathing and the muscles needed in articulation.
- ☐ Have difficulty chewing or swallowing.
- ☐ Show a lack of stamina and overall weakness.

nerves have been damaged. The term *orthopedic* indicates injury to the bones, joints and/or muscles. Physical disabilities can be associated with congential abnormalities (problems existing at or dating from birth), accidents or diseases. Neurological impairments can affect intelligence, the senses, speech and other areas as well; their severity depends upon how much damage has occurred in the brain and which areas the damaged part of the brain controls.

Visual Impairments Children are visually impaired if their ability to see interferes with their ability to learn even after the best medical treatment. Partially sighted children may have a *visual acuity* problem which is correctable with glasses. They may have a limited field of vision or uncoordinated eye movements and focusing difficulty resulting from faulty muscle action. Those who have been blind from birth are often developmentally delayed. The development of children whose blindness occurred after birth may be similar to sighted children,

depending on when the vision loss occurred.

Physical development may be delayed for visually impaired children. For example, motor development depends on the ability to explore the environment. Many large and small muscle activities are learned through visual imitation: children watch, then do. Learning to move one's body through space requires a feeling of safety that visually impaired children may not have. Social and cognitive development may also be affected. Visually impaired children often prefer talking to people, especially adults, to playing with toys or playing group games with other children. They usually rely on their other senses, especially hearing, to compensate. They may develop speech and language skills faster than other children and have good listening and memory skills. In general, visually impaired children need encouragement and assistance to achieve more balanced development through a wider range of activities than they might choose for themselves.

SOME CHARACTERISTICS OF CHILDREN WITH VISUAL IMPAIRMENTS

Children with vision problems may:
- ☐ Rub their eyes excessively, squint, or frown.
- ☐ Shut or cover eyes, tilt or thrust their heads forward.
- ☐ Hold objects close to their eyes and show difficulty with tasks requiring close use of eyes.
- ☐ Stumble over objects.
- ☐ Be unable to see distant things clearly.
- ☐ Be irritable or blink frequently when doing close work.
- ☐ Have inflammation or other eye problems such as swelling or styes.

SOME CHARACTERISTICS OF CHILDREN WITH HEARING IMPAIRMENTS

Children with hearing impairments may:
- ☐ Have trouble paying attention, especially in group activities.
- ☐ Not answer when called.
- ☐ Get confused about directions or not understand them at all.
- ☐ Frequently give the wrong answers to questions.
- ☐ Often say "What?" or look confused by questions, statements, or directions.
- ☐ Have poor speech, substitute sounds, omit sounds, or have poor voice quality.
- ☐ Avoid people, prefer to play alone.
- ☐ Get tired early in the day.
- ☐ Turn one side of the head towards sounds, indicating a hearing loss in one ear.

Hearing Impairments Hearing loss may be due to damage to the outer or middle ear (*conductive loss*) or to the inner ear or the nerves that carry sound to the brain (*sensorineural loss*). Both types of loss can occur before or after birth. Conductive losses, frequently caused by infection, are less severe than sensorineural losses and can be treated. Sensorineural losses are permanent. They can be caused by diseases, heredity, physical damage to the head or ear, or by excessive, intense noise.

Children with hearing impairments may have problems perceiving the volume or clarity of sound. They have difficulty learning to speak because they cannot hear a language model. Because these children cannot monitor their own voices, hearing loss also greatly affects the ability to develop clear and understandable speech. Certain speech sounds may be omitted (wa-uh for water) or distorted (tsoe for shoe). Voice quality may be unusually high- or low-pitched, nasal, gutteral, soft, or loud. Speech rhythm might also be abnormal, slow, unsteady, or stressed in the wrong places. Social-emotional development can be delayed when it is difficult for children to express feelings or needs or to have others understand and respond. Age-appropriate cognitive skills may be slower to develop if hearing loss has resulted in a language delay.

Speech-Language Impairment *Receptive language* problems may be the result of hearing loss; they result in children not understanding the meaning of words or the way words are put together. Directions may confuse them. They may need visual cues or gestures to understand. They also have difficulty learning to talk.

If there is no hearing loss, there may be an *auditory processing* problem: sounds are not understood. Children with this difficulty may not be able to tell the difference between speech sounds (auditory discrimination), may not be able to pick out the important sounds from a background of noises, may have trouble remembering what is heard, may confuse the correct order of a series of sounds, or may have trouble developing concepts.

Children with *expressive language* problems have trouble verbalizing ideas. They may have a limited vocabulary, have trouble using the right word, put words together in the wrong order, or use incorrect grammatical structures.

Children with *speech* problems may have trouble articulating or clearly producing speech sounds. Many articulation errors in preschool children, however, are a normal part of developing language, for example, substituting an "f" sound for "th." When these articulation difficulties

persist beyond the age of five, children should be evaluated for possible speech problems. Chronic voice disorders are another type of speech problem typified by unusual pitch, volume, or voice quality.

The primary challenge for a child with an expressive language problem is to learn to communicate with others. Those with receptive difficulty may have more complex problems: they do not fully understand language. Language differences due to variations based on culture or dialect should not be confused with speech-language impairments.

Mental Retardation   Although all children learn at different rates, those who are retarded have a significantly slower pace of learning and development. They appear much younger than their

---

SOME CHARACTERISTICS OF CHILDREN WITH SPEECH-LANGUAGE IMPAIRMENT

Speech-language difficulties may be indicated if a child:
- ☐ Is not talking by age two.
- ☐ Does not use two or three word sentences by age three.
- ☐ Is still very difficult to understand after age three (relying mostly on vowel sounds and omitting the beginnings and endings of words).
- ☐ Uses poor sentence structure after age five, such as, "Me school go."
- ☐ Stutters after age five.
- ☐ Has poor voice quality.
- ☐ Has difficulty hearing speech sounds.
- ☐ Has difficulty understanding what is said.
- ☐ Appears shy and embarrassed by his or her speech.
- ☐ Has trouble following directions, describing things, using correct parts of speech, or putting words into sentences compared with other children.

SOME CHARACTERISTICS OF MENTALLY RETARDED CHILDREN

Children who are mildly to moderately retarded may:
- ☐ Be unable to follow directions that contain more than one or two steps.
- ☐ Not be able to independently choose an activity.
- ☐ Have a tendency to imitate rather than create.
- ☐ Have poor eye-hand coordination.
- ☐ Be slow to learn simple games or classroom routines.
- ☐ Be very slow in learning language.

chronological age. During the preschool years they have difficulty learning skills and developing concepts. They may be unable to remember what they've learned and unable to use information to solve problems in new or unfamiliar situations. They have trouble developing and using language, playing cooperatively, initiating activities or interactions, and learning to function independently. Mental retardation can occur before, during, or after birth.

Mildly retarded children may seem little different than the youngest children in their age group. Moderately retarded children will have greater difficulties in self-help skills, motor development, social skills, and language development. In general, they tend to behave like children

about half their age. Severely retarded children have so many areas of dysfunction that they are rarely integrated into a regular program.

Learning Disabilities   Children with learning disabilities tend to be extremely uneven in their development. For example, a child may have average to above average motor skills, but considerable delay in language. Because of these inconsistencies, learning disabled children are often accused of not trying hard enough or of being lazy, uncontrollable, or stubborn. During early childhood years, learning disabilities are difficult to identify. Your knowledge of the normal developmental range of behaviors and skills may help you assess whether a child should be evaluated for a possible learning disability.

Many children with learning disabilities exhibit an inability to attend. They may show impulsive behavior beyond what seems developmentally appropriate. In the past these learning disabled children have been called hyperkinetic or hyperactive or have been said to have mininal brain dysfunction. These symptoms are

SOME CHARACTERISTICS OF CHILDREN WITH ATTENTION DEFICIT DISORDERS

Behaviors characteristic of children with attention deficit may include:

- ☐ Impulsivity: acting quickly without thinking about the consequences; recklessness.
- ☐ Short attention span: inability to concentrate on one task or activity long enough to complete it; constant switching from activity to activity without seeming to gain satisfaction.
- ☐ Difficulty organizing and completing work: lack of goal direction, haphazardness.
- ☐ Distractibility: trouble paying attention to the task at hand; easily drawn to irrelevant sights and sounds; unable to redirect attention to original task once distracted.
- ☐ Hyperactivity: constant motion even when surroundings are quiet; excessive movement—child seems to be running like a motor; constant restlessness and fidgeting.

now commonly referred to as *attention deficit disorder*. The problem occurs more frequently in boys and tends to appear by age three. Children with an attention deficit disorder are easily excitable, have trouble waiting for explanations or taking turns, and can seldom pause long enough to relax, watch, or listen to what's going on. Consequently, they often rush into situations without purpose and without anticipating outcomes. Many cannot tolerate physical restriction. Jeremy, the child in the example at the beginning of this chapter, may be suffering from this disorder. Do not assume that every extremely active young child has an attention deficit disorder. Children with this problem are generally identifiable because of the extremeness of their behavior.

Emotional Disturbance   Emotional difficulties can result from a number of causes including inadequate nurturing, physical injury, or biochemical imbalance. Emotional disturbance (sometimes called *behavior disorder*) interferes with the development and maintenance of meaningful relationships with others and in the development of a positive and accurate sense of self.

In mild and moderate cases, these children tend to be more aggressive, unhappy, anxious or withdrawn than their peers. Severely emotionally disturbed children are much more extreme in their reactions and usually require care in specialized settings. They are not just delayed in development but have severe qualitative abnormalities in functioning. They may be either hypersensitive or insensitive to their environment and avoid or be unable to communicate with others. They may display unusual behaviors such as rocking, running with arms flapping, walking on tiptoes or gliding about the room. If you have such a child in your group, it will be important to share your concerns with the family and to seek help. Less severe emotional disturbance may develop while a child is in your group or may have been unde- tected by the family and previous teachers. Several types of behavior characterize children who are mildly or moderately emotionally disturbed.

Withdrawal Children who do not interact with others, but react by moving away when someone gets too close are withdrawn. These children appear disin- terested in and unaware of what goes on in the classroom. They seem to have few interests and frequently seek comfort in thumbsucking or rocking. Most withdrawn children learn primarily from watching others. Although their cognitive, motor and speech-language skills may be age-appropriate, they tend to be infrequently used. Their self-concept may be poor and social skills limited because they do not attempt to interact or participate in activities.

Anxiety Anxious children are fearful and their ability to learn and perform normally is limited. They can display aggressive, hyperactive, or withdrawn behaviors in a rapid and confusing succession. Signs of anxiety include crying easily and often, constant stomachaches or headaches, fear of new people and situations, fear of emotionally laden situations, heavy reliance on order and routine, overcau- tiousness, or impulsiveness. Anxious children generally understand how to use materials because they learn by watching others, but their reluctance to try new things may delay their mastery of skills. Their anxiety can cause body movements to appear tense and awkward. Speech and

language skills, on the other hand, may be well developed, although what these children say may be confusing and difficult to understand. When feeling less anxious, they may play fairly well with others. Usually, however, they will watch from a safe distance. If other children come too close, they might become verbally or physically aggressive. With adults they may be overly dependent and seek reassurance constantly or withdraw entirely.

Aggression Aggressive children typically react to others by forceful and uncontrolled physical or verbal hostility and abusive- ness with or without provocation. They may be quite destructive of materials, demanding or impatient in their interac- tions with other children, and disruptive in group activities. It is often difficult to determine what provokes aggressive behavior in these children because almost anything appears to set them off. Many aggressive children think poorly of themselves, are frightened by their own uncontrolled behavior, and fear aggression from others.

Some Cautions About Emotional Dis- turbance Emotional problems may be especially difficult for teachers to handle not only because the children are so intense, but also because there is so much disagreement among experts about the causes, classification, and treatment of these conditions. You will probably want someone to help you understand and work with a disturbed child, but you may find that everyone you talk to has a different opinion and gives you contradic- tory advice about what you should do. We believe that a variety of approaches can contribute to understanding and working with disturbed children, but we are

concerned about experts who think that any one single approach can be applied in every situation.

Many children exhibit symptoms of emotional disturbance in response to highly stressful situations. Children whose parents are divorcing, for example, often become extremely anxious over their perception of the loss of one or both parents. The death of a beloved grandparent or other close relative or friend also can temporarily upset a child's emotional equilibrium. These children may require some sort of short-term treatment and should not be labeled as emotionally disturbed.

Abuse and Neglect

Children who are abused or neglected have another kind of special need that you need to learn to identify and respond to as part of your role as a teacher of young children. Symptoms of emotional disturbance may sometimes be an

indication of child abuse or neglect. If you suspect this is the case, you will need to watch the child carefully for unusual physical injuries. Fantasy play may also provide clues. If the themes of such play are often violent or sexually explicit with the child or an alter ego as a passive or powerless victim, it is possible that the child is experiencing some type of abuse. In the case of neglect, a child may demonstrate unusual competence in self-help skills and assume adult responsibilities yet have difficulty playing cooperatively with other children or be unable to handle a change in the daily routine. This type of behavior often indicates that a child has had to learn certain survival skills such as dressing and feeding without assistance because a nurturing adult has not been available. As much as we value independence in children, it is not developmentally appropriate for a three year old to prepare breakfast every morning or to walk to school alone each day.

SOME CHARACTERISTICS OF ABUSED OR NEGLECTED CHILDREN

☐ Overcompliance, passivity, extreme avoidance of confrontation both with children and adults.

☐ Extremely demanding, aggressive and rage-filled behavior.

☐ Premature competence, e.g., preparing meals, taking the bus alone, caring for younger siblings when it is neither developmentally nor culturally appropriate to do so.

☐ Extreme dependent behavior.

☐ Developmental delays, especially in combination with any of the above.

There is a continuum between parental discipline and child abuse. This makes it difficult sometimes to discern whether there is simply a difference in values or abuse to the child. In general, if a physical injury or a child's behavior concerns you, watch for repetition of similar injuries or behaviors. You should be concerned if the child comes to school with physical evidence of abuse including bruises, belt marks, burns, welts, and difficulty in movement. Another signal for concern is when a child shows precocious sexual awareness in play or talk. This may be the outward evidence of sexual abuse such as being made to observe adult sexual behavior. A consistent lack of emotional support and attention on the part of parents or strong verbal attacks on the child through name-calling or profanity can also alert you to abuse.

While the listed behaviors in the box above are occasionally displayed by almost all children, if any of them are frequently or consistently repeated, further investigation is warranted.

In some states teachers are mandated by law to report suspected cases of child abuse or neglect. Whether or not that is true in your state, it is your responsibility as a teacher and an advocate for children to be aware of the indicators of abuse and neglect and to be prepared to report suspected cases to the appropriate agency so that the child and family can receive the help they need as soon as possible. The program where you teach should have procedures for reporting suspected cases. If it does not, you will need to urge the administration to develop some immediately.

A critical issue in reporting abuse or neglect will be when to tell the parents that you are making a report. All parents should be informed of the reporting procedures as part of their orientation to the program. Your relationship with the parents and your assessment of the possible consequences to the child will determine whether you inform them when you make a report or later. You may choose to delay if you think there is a possibility of retaliation to the child or you fear that the family might leave the center. There are no easy answers to handling problems of child abuse and neglect. We urge you to seek the support of trained specialists. With the recent public attention focused on reported cases of child abuse and neglect, especially sexual abuse, many communities have created special task forces or expanded services to deal with the problem. Be sure you know what is available in your community.

WORKING WITH CHILDREN WITH SPECIAL NEEDS

You will need some special preparation and skills to work with disabled children. Your role is to observe and understand the problem as fully as you can, to read about different approaches to working with the child, to seek consultation to help you in the classroom, and to support parents in dealing with the child and in seeking treatment.

Mainstreaming

Mainstreaming is a term coined to emphasize the importance of educating special needs children in the *mainstream of society* rather than at home, in

institutions, or in special segregated classes. In mainstreaming it is assumed that since all children differ in abilities, interests and needs, classrooms can be designed to provide learning experiences for both disabled and nondisabled children.

More and more children with special needs are being mainstreamed into public schools as a result of federal law (94–142) that requires that all disabled children have access to a "free, appropriate public education, in the least restrictive environment." The law requires an individualized education plan (IEP) for each child identified as handicapped. Since that law includes children as young as three years, disabled children are being mainstreamed into preschool settings as well as elementary schools. You may be asked to accept a handicapped child in your classroom. If a child who is already in your classroom is identified as handicapped, you may be asked to allow him or her to remain there. In either case, you will be part of the team designing the IEP since you will have responsibility for carrying out or coordinating a substantial

RECOMMENDATIONS FOR PREPARING YOURSELF FOR MAINSTREAMING

☐ Learn about the specific disability by talking with the child's parents, doctor, therapists, or others who have worked with the child.

☐ Find out what services will be available to support your work.

☐ Ask specific questions such as, "How can I make group time relevant to this child and also meet the needs of the other children?"

☐ Brainstorm with the experts and consultants available to you.

☐ Be flexible and easy on yourself; you can learn from your experience.

GUIDELINES FOR WRITING AN INDIVIDUALIZED EDUCATION PLAN

An IEP should include:
- ☐ A description of the present educational performance of the child.
- ☐ The annual goals set for the child, including a statement of short-term instructional objectives.
- ☐ A statement of specific special education and related services to be provided and the extent to which the child will be able to participate in the regular educational program.
- ☐ The projected initiation date and duration of special services.
- ☐ An evaluation scheme including appropriate objectives, evaluation procedures, and schedules for determining the achievement of short-term objectives.

part of the program. All handicapped children, whether or not they are in federally funded programs, may benefit from planning that follows IEP guidelines.

The IEP is based on a professional diagnostic evaluation of the child. It must be developed and revised by a team that includes the professional diagnostician (such as a medical doctor, a speech pathologist, etc.), a representative of the public agency (such as the school director or principal), the child's teacher, the child's parents, and the child (when appropriate). Arrangements must be made for an interpreter if the parents are deaf or do not speak English.

Informal mainstreaming occurs when a child is referred to your program by a school, agency, or individual because your program is perceived as one which will better meet the needs of that child. These children may fall into that grey area in which it is difficult to identify specific problems, but where it is clear that certain environments will be more

beneficial than others; for example, a highly distractible child who will cope more easily in a smaller, more tranquil environment or a child who is aggressive or emotionally vulnerable who may feel more accepted in a program where special attention is paid to children's social and emotional development. These children may or may not later be identified as having disabling conditions. With rare exceptions, even though your program is suitable for them, they will be difficult to teach at least some of the time, and you will need to think carefully about ways to reach them.

Preparing Yourself and Children

As you work with a special needs child on a day-to-day basis, you may find yourself confronting thoughts and feelings that are new or difficult to understand. The relationship with that child's parents may differ in some ways from those you have with other parents. You will also need to help other children understand and accept the special child as a fully participating member of the classroom group.

One way to prepare yourself to work with the special needs child is to ask yourself, "Who is this child as a whole person: likes, dislikes, learning style, friends, personal qualities?" Remember that a disability is only one part. As you focus on the whole child, begin to think about other children you know. Ask yourself the same questions about them. You will soon see that the disabled child is basically a child like any other. You may need to do this exercise frequently at first, especially if you did not know the child well before the disability was identified. Eventually it will become automatic to respond to the child as an individual first and as a person with a disability only when it is appropriate to do so. For example, when Amanda, who wears a brace on one leg, sits on the floor to work a puzzle or stands at an easel to paint, your first response will be to her competence at working the puzzle or the beauty of her painting, *not* to the brace on her leg. When she is on the playground and cannot run or climb like the other children, you will need to help her find alternatives. Your focus will be on what she can do, not on what she cannot do because she wears a brace.

You may find yourself encountering feelings about a special needs child that you are not "supposed" to have. For example, if you were Jeremy's teacher, you might find yourself overwhelmed and exhausted, and it might be difficult to keep from reacting negatively to such an unfocused, perpetually moving child. Yet it will be important to do your best to remain positive and supportive, for we

know that attention deficit children often develop low self-esteem, become negative, do very badly in school, and may develop symptoms of emotional disturbance when they are in nonsupportive environments. We cannot say often enough that when you feel yourself becoming less able to help a child with any disability, get help for yourself—from your director, head teacher, co-worker, or an agency. It is also important to remember that you must balance the special needs of each individual child with those of the entire group. If a disabled child demands so much of your time that the experience for the other children in your group suffers, then it is your responsibility to find a solution to the problem. One preschool we know has made arrangements with the special education department of the state university to provide student volunteers to assist disabled children in their setting. Even if your school is not located near a college or university, you may be able to find volunteers through a public service agency or club.

In another case, a friend of ours told us about Kevin, a child with a neurological impairment who drooled continuously. Our friend, an excellent preschool teacher, was surprised to find herself feeling repulsed by Kevin's drooling. It brought up childhood memories of another youngster who had been teased and tormented by other children, including herself, as the neighborhood "dummy." She knew the prejudice was irrational, but somehow that did little to lessen her feeling of repulsion. Such feelings are normal and should be accepted, not judged as right or wrong. Our friend took care to spend extra time with Kevin, made an effort to see him as a whole child, and eventually found that she not only forgot about her response to his drooling, but also deeply treasured this child's sense of humor and his affection toward her. She also worked hard to help the other children in her class accept Kevin.

Preparing other children for the presence of a special needs child is an important part of your work and requires sensitivity on your part. A simple explanation of the disability with some examples which can be related to from their experience is probably the best method. You might say about a child with an expressive language problem, for example, "Mark has trouble saying what he wants to say sometimes. Do you ever want to tell someone something and the words come out all mixed up?"

Making a special child appear to be too different is not wise. Other children may be excessively helpful and overprotective, or they may exclude the child, believing he or she is not capable of participating. Both children and adults in the classroom should avoid overprotection.

By trying things on their own, handicapped children have a better chance to acquire skills and competencies. Show children specific ways to include a special needs child in their play. For example, with a visually impaired child, you might encourage others to help the child feel the shape of an elaborate block structure after giving verbal guidance so that the child can place blocks in the structure.

Answer other children's questions about handicaps as honestly and directly as you can. Help them understand any differences they may observe in the special child. You could say, "Rose wears a hearing aid so that she can hear us when we talk to her." With the child's permission, other children may want to try the hearing aid.

Or you may be able to ask a speech therapist to bring some hearing aids for children to try and to explain how they work.

Be ready to assure other children that the disabling condition isn't "catching." Older children may initially laugh at or ridicule a handicapped child. Remember that this response is fueled by their own embarrassment. It provides you with an opportunity to talk about the wide range of differences among people and the value of helpful and respectful relationships. Teachers who have had special needs children in their classrooms report time and again that the caring relationships developed among the children are an overwhelmingly positive outcome. Your warm, accepting attitude will provide a powerful model for the development of these relationships.

Working with Parents

A disabled child in your classroom will affect your relationships not only with the child's parents but also with the parents of the other children. With formal and informal mainstreaming you will usually have a chance to talk with parents before the child enters your group. If you are the person who initially identifies the child, however, you will be faced with changes in ongoing relationships. In both cases you will need to have a clear idea of how to proceed.

We know that parents who learn that their child is disabled often go though a grieving process much as if the child had died. Indeed they have suffered a loss, the loss of some of their dreams, hopes, and expectations for that child. They will experience denial, anger, despair and, finally, acceptance. You may encounter parents at any point in this process, and it is important for you to understand and accept their feelings as appropriate. It may be hard for you to feel as if you've reached parents if they are somewhere in the first three stages. Keep in mind that if properly supported, the process resolves itself in acceptance, in the sense that although they would not have wished their child to be disabled, they are able to view it as a fact of their lives with which they must deal. Your role is to be patient and understanding in the early stages of the process and to demonstrate the ways in which you can help their child learn to cope with and compensate for the disability.

While you should not be "on call" to parents twenty-four hours a day, you will want to be sure that the parents of a

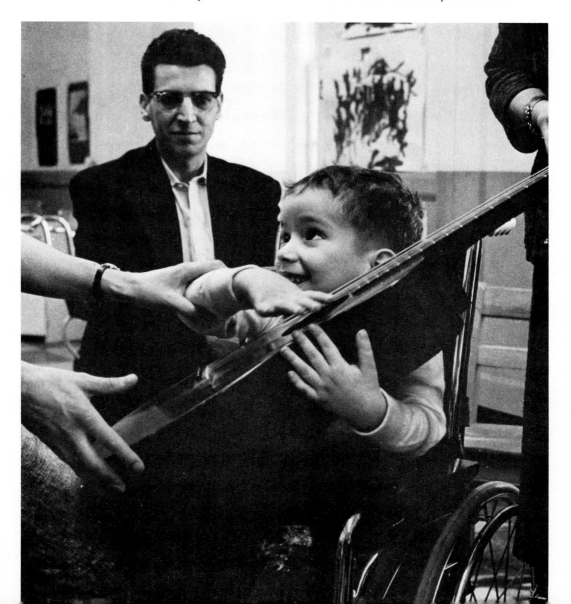

special needs child have access to you in several different ways. Conferences should feel "safe" to parents so that they can hear information about their child without feeling it is prejudiced or judgmental. It will be important to keep good notes on the special needs child's development, both as a record of progress and as the basis for dialogue with his or her parents. Sometimes it will be easier for the parents to share their concerns indirectly in writing than to speak to you directly.

Parents must be involved in decisions about and give their consent to any treatment their child receives other than the usual classroom routine. You may be the bridge for parents to therapists or other professionals who will work with their child. Your role will be to ensure that communication is clear among home, school, and other professional helpers.

Just as it is important to avoid making a special needs child appear too different, so it is necessary to help the parents feel a welcome part of the ongoing life of the school. If the family is new to your school, be sure they meet other families at school functions or when they drop off or pick up their child. You might say, "Mrs. Brown, I'd like you to meet Mrs. Nishimoto. Her daughter Lisa was Nicole's partner on our field trip today." Don't hesitate to ask the parents of a disabled child to help at a work day or provide field trip transportation just as you would any other parent. As a matter of fact, the more regular parent involvement you have in your program, the more likely parents of a disabled child will feel comfortable and accepted.

If the family has been in your program for a while before their child is identified as disabled, you may need to increase the frequency of parent communication around getting help for the child, but also make a special effort to keep those parents involved in ordinary events as well. Even if they can't participate much while they are adjusting to this new dimension of their lives, later they will appreciate being kept informed and treated as old friends.

Confidentiality is one of the issues you will face whether the family is new or ongoing. How much is appropriate to reveal to other parents about a child's disability? Other parents will have questions you must be prepared to answer. Like children they may need to be reassured that the disability or the behaviors of the disabled child are not "catching."

They need to know that children who have many rich learning opportunities are more motivated to learn new skills and behaviors than they are to adopt the behaviors of the disabled child. It is important to keep private specific details about the disability or the family from the other parents. To a pointed question you might reply, "Anna needs extra help in some areas. If you'd like to know more about it, you might want to ask her parents." You will need to offer general reassurance, emphasizing the benefits of learning to accept differences and to be caring and respectful in relationships. You should also encourage other families to help the parents of the disabled child feel welcome. Your own attitude will provide a positive model.

Modifying the Program

Play is the primary vehicle for learning for all young children. Spontaneous play activities develop physical and perceptual skills, provide opportunities for language development, are the medium for social relationships, and sharpen thinking skills. Sometimes teachers of children with special needs get so concerned with remedial tasks that they forget that these children need the same opportunities for play that all children do. Play is particularly important for disabled children because it is through play that they can experience the feelings of mastery, resourcefulness, and competence that are crucial for development of a positive self-concept. In addition, spontaneous play experiences allow them the freedom to learn through their own interaction with materials and people.

You will need to provide special needs children with support and guidance in dealing with unfamiliar situations. You may need to allow them additional time to develop comfort and competence in play situations and assist them in learning specific play skills.

Some special needs children require more structure for certain program activities and tasks. You may need to include more time for structured teaching and take a more active role in helping these children strengthen newly developing skills. Your classroom environment probably will not need to be changed much to accommodate a disabled child unless there is a physical handicap or visual impairment. For these children you will want to be especially careful about safety and providing clearly demarcated centers. Children with learning disabilities will do better if they have a work space with few distractions—perhaps a special table in a quiet, partially enclosed place.

Disabled children, like other children, need opportunities to engage with a variety of both open-ended and specific

purpose materials. Clay, paint, and blocks stimulate exploration and creative play. More defined activities such as lotto, puzzles, and pegboards provide experiences in developing and strengthening specific skills and problem-solving strategies.Some materials may be adapted. Yarn or masking tape wrapped around pencils and marking pens makes them easier to hold and use. Puzzles with knobs are less difficult to manipulate. Scissors that can be used with either hand make cutting activities easier. Visually impaired and learning disabled children may have difficulty discerning details, so large, colorful materials may be most effective. Variety in textures, sounds or motion will help maintain interest and attention in the materials for visually impaired children.

A daily routine which includes a variety of learning experiences is just as important to a special needs child as it is to other children. Free play and teacher-directed times, child- and teacher-chosen activities, large as well as small groups all provide opportunities for learning.

You may want to plan individual sessions with disabled children several times a week or on a daily basis. The focused attention of an adult helps the child to concentrate on tasks and respond without the distraction of other children. It also allows you to concentrate on the child's particular interests and needs. You may need to enlist help from volunteers or support from your co-workers to allow you to schedule this individual time.

Planning Your knowledge of what is developmentally appropriate for young children in general will guide your planning as you decide what materials and activities to use with special needs

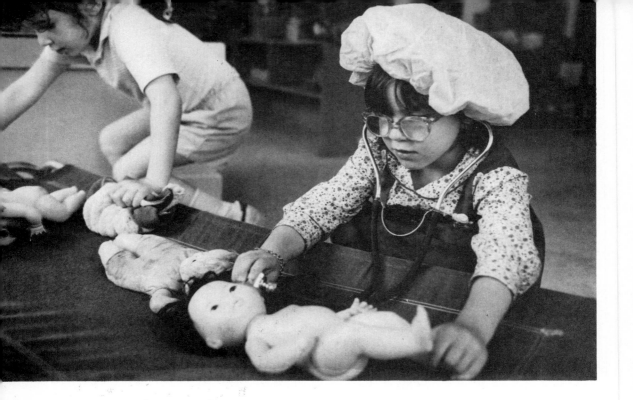

children, how to introduce these activities, and what responses you will expect. Some of these children may benefit from using a *task analysis* approach in planning. This involves breaking down tasks or skills into their component parts and teaching them separately as a series of subskills. Think for a moment about the task of opening a door; you have to know where the door is, be able to get to it, know which way the door opens, turn the knob and work the latch, and push or pull to get it open. You may need to break down such tasks as putting on clothes, and going to the bathroom. Some children may need to practice each subskill for a period of time before they can succeed with the overall activity. You may wish to attend a special education class or workshop to learn about task analysis.

Classroom observations supplemented by data from assessment instruments will be very helpful in planning. These will enable you to identify disabled children's strengths and weaknesses and will help you to discover the conditions under which they perform best and the kinds of teaching strategies that suit them. You can then understand where children experience difficulty and will be able to set objectives and design activities that will help you meet their needs. Co-workers or volunteers may be needed to free you to take the time necessary to do systematic observation.

Teaching Strategies Many children with special needs have difficulty controlling their attention. Understanding spoken language, verbal expression, and generalizing concepts from one context to another can also be problematic. Specific strategies can be used in dealing with these difficulties.

To help children focus on the task at hand use attention-getting words such as *look*, *listen*, or *watch me*. Allow children to touch and manipulate materials. Require active responses by asking questions about the activity.

Disabled children are often highly distractible. Control the amount of stimulation by simplifying the task by presenting only one part at a time. Keep transitions short between activities. Be sure that all procedures are planned and materials organized so that long lapses can be avoided. Include many opportunities for individual and small group activities. Large group activities may be overstimulating and require more waiting than some special needs children can tolerate.

Be especially careful to pay attention to children's efforts at communication whenever and wherever they occur. If the child has difficulty with expressive language, listen closely in order to decipher communication. Ask to make sure you have understood what was meant: "You have a bunny like that at your house?" If receptive language is difficult, you may need to simplify your speech somewhat. Encourage children to talk about feelings during times of stress, frustration, or excitement. Encourage talking among children. When a child shares with you or calls your attention to something, acknowledge this and sometimes redirect the communication to another child: "Tell Willie what you told me."

When introducing a new concept, it usually works best to focus on contrast by giving lots of positive and negative instances. For example, if you are helping children to develop the concept of a circle, present contrasting shapes so children can see "circle" versus "not circle," and present many real-life examples such as a bracelet, saucer, hula hoop, and so on. Present examples of the concept throughout the day: join hands to make a circle at group time, eat round crackers for snack; make circular vegetable prints during art. In general, teach much the same way you would with other children, but keep in mind that you may need to spend a longer period of time with some special needs children.

A FINAL NOTE

Almost every chapter in this book contains information that will help you work with all kinds of children—children who differ in the color of their skin, hair and eyes, physical size, language spoken in the home, in their skills and abilities to understand and operate in the world. That same information is valid for working with disabled children. You may need to adapt some of your usual teaching practices and to find an extra measure of patience and acceptance within yourself. You will also need the help and support of parents, co-workers, your director, health specialists, and perhaps, volunteers. While at first this may sound like a monumental task, it has the potential to be an unprecedented learning experience in your own development as a teacher. You will learn about different kinds of children and develop interpersonal skills as you work with families and agencies. And you will gain new insight into the meaning of our shared humanity within the wide spectrum of individual differences.

FOR FURTHER THOUGHT AND DISCUSSION

1 Think about your own abilities and disabilities. How have they affected your life? How did they influence your childhood experiences? What do you wish your teachers had known or felt?

2 Think about the ways that disabled children were a part of your early school experiences. How do you think your teachers felt about these children? How did you feel? What implications does this have for your teaching?

3 Recall a relationship or an interaction that you have had as an adult with a disabled individual. How did you feel? Did this change your ideas about disabled people? How?

4 Explore your thoughts and feelings about working with special needs children. Are you comfortable? Why or why not? What implications does this have for you as a teacher?

PROJECTS

1 Observe an early childhood classroom that mainstreams a special needs child. Report on how the teacher attempts to meet the child's needs. Describe your impressions of the teacher's attitudes and values regarding this work? Reflect and then comment on the effect this has on all of the children in the class.

2 Interview a teacher of mainstreamed children to find out what procedures were followed in identifying and planning for his or her educational experience. Describe this process and your feelings about it.

3 For at least an hour observe and "put yourself in the shoes of" a child who you suspect has a disability. Try to experience the program as the child might. Describe what you think the child's experience may be. Based on this experience suggest how the program might be structured to meet this child's needs.

4 Observe a special needs child in a regular preschool setting. Report on what you would do if you were going to have a conference with the child's parents. What would you tell them? What questions would you ask? How would you create a climate of safety and trust within the conference?

5 Find out what services your local Departments of Education and Health and/or Social Services (and other agencies) offer to handicapped children under the age of five. Write a pamphlet, including phone numbers and names, of contact persons for teachers that explains this information.

RECOMMENDED READING

Allen, K. Eileen. *Mainstreaming in Early Childhood Education.* Albany, N.Y.: Delmar, 1980.

Braun, Samuel J., and Lasher, Miriam G. *Are You Ready to Mainstream? Helping Preschoolers with Learning and Behavior Problems.* Columbus, O.: Charles E. Merrill, 1978.

Cartwright, G. Philip; Cartwright, Carol A.; and Ward, Marjorie E. *Educating Special Learners.* Belmont, Cal.: Wadsworth, 1981.

Featherstone, Helen. *A Difference in the Family: Life With a Disabled Child.* New York: Basic Books, 1980.

Jordon, June; Dayden, Alice; Karnes, Merle; and Wood, Mary, eds. *Early Childhood Education for Exceptional Children.* Reston, Va.: Council for Exceptional Children, 1977.

Mainstreaming Preschoolers. Washington, D.C.: U.S. Department of Health, Education, and Welfare. Administration for Children, Youth, and Families, Head Start Bureau, 1978.
   a. *Orthopedic Handicaps*
   b. *Learning Disabilities*
   c. *Visual Impairments*
   d. *Speech/Language Impairments*
   e. *Hearing Impairments*
   f. *Emotional Handicaps*
   g. *Mental Retardation*

Meisels, Samuel J. *Developmental Screening in Early Childhood Education.* Washington, D.C.: National Association for the Education of Young Children, 1978.

Piazza, Robert, and Rothman, Roz. *Preschool Education for the Handicapped.* Guilford, Conn.: Special Learning Corporation, 1979.

Research for Better Schools. *Clarification of P. L. 94–142 for the Classroom Teacher.* Philadelphia: Research for Better Schools, 1978.

Smith, Sally L. *No Easy Answers.* Cambridge, Mass.: Winthrop, 1979.

Souweine, Judith; Crimmins, Sheila; and Mazel, Carolyn. *Mainstreaming: Ideas for Teaching Young Children.* Washington, D.C.: National Association for the Education of Young Children, 1981.

15

Families
and Teachers
Together

Just keep in mind, though it seems hard I
know, most parents were children long
ago—incredible.

H. Rome

*This chapter focuses on the importance of children's families in early childhood programs. In it we discuss the knowledge and skills you need to work with families including knowledge of child development and early childhood curriculum, skill in building relationships, understanding of parenting, and the ability to help families find resources. We explore a variety of important ways that programs can involve family members. These include information sharing with families, education, and participation in the program. This chapter relates to the CDA area **Families.***

C hildren come to school wrapped in the values, attitudes, and behaviors of their families. While the first challenge of teaching is to create learning experiences that support children's development, you need to see and support each child as a part of a unique family whose members are also important teachers. Families today take a variety of forms which sometimes include adults other than parents (step-parents, siblings, grandparents, and other relatives or friends) who assume parental roles in the lives of children. To simplify the wording of this chapter we will speak of both parents and families and in so doing are speaking of the entire cast of adults who play an intimate and significant role in a child's life. When we speak of parenting, we are discussing the nurturing done by these important adults.

You probably chose to become a teacher because of your interest in and allegiance to children, and you may not yet see working with parents as an important part of your job. The needs of children cannot be adequately met, however, if you do not also take families into consideration. The relationships that you build with parents will bring about collaboration between home and school to enhance children's development.

Contemporary research suggests that the most effective programs for young children are those which involve their families.

Interacting with families can be gratifying. Parents who recognize the importance of their children's early years appreciate your effort and skill as few others can. Since parents know their children best, they will be the first to notice when your work has had an impact. As you enrich their children's lives and help them with the task of parenting, you can develop warm relationships that may even blossom into friendships. Learning that you have made a positive difference to a family is among the most rewarding experiences that a teacher can have.

Relating to parents has its own unique challenges and demands. The awareness and sensitivity that you have developed in your work with children are important as you work with adults. Adults, like children, need to feel safe and respected in their relationships. While they differ in their needs, interests, awareness, knowledge and skill, there are similarities among them. Parents are concerned for the welfare of their children. They want the best for them, and want to be kept informed of the important events in their children's lives away from home. The basis for your relationships with parents is your commitment to a joint venture of providing good experiences for children. Your acceptance and awareness of diversity can help make you and the family an effective team working for the child.

It is not necessary to become intimate friends with parents, nor do you need to be the ultimate authority on child rearing to be effective in working with them. You have yourself to offer, a knowledgeable professional who is able to relate to and engage with family members to support their child's growth.

There are times when working with families may be difficult. As a teacher trained to work with young children you may feel frustrated because you have fewer skills in working with adults than children. The results of this work with families are not always easy to observe. Unlike their young children, parents cannot always live in the moment, the attention that they have to give their child's teacher is limited by their concerns for other, possibly more critical aspects of their lives. If you are a young beginning teacher with no children of your own, you may feel that you are viewed as inexperienced or incapable. Working with adults may seem more threatening than working with children because adults are more likely to make negative judgments. Indeed, there will be times when parental concerns over seeming trivialities voiced at a time when you are tired and trying to work with a group of active children may seem inconsequential and even irritating. It is important at such times to remember that the values which parents are expressing are important to them and that you have a responsibility to respond in a way

which acknowledges their right to their concerns.

Just as you looked at your values and attitudes about working with children, you will want to examine your values and attitudes regarding your involvement with parents. You will also want to explore your attitudes about child rearing to see if you can allow for a variety of approaches that reflect differences in values, cultures, and lifestyles. You will encounter differences in values about education and about child rearing with some of the parents with whom you work and you will want to be prepared to deal with these differences in constructive ways—acknowledging parental knowledge and sharing your own without assuming the role of "expert," expressing concern and responsibility without blaming, accusing, or putting down. It may be difficult to accept parents whose goals for children are very different from yours. Because of your commitment to children, it may be hard to deal with parents who appear uncaring or who seem to treat their children in harsh or inappropriate ways. It may sometimes be difficult to decide which behaviors simply reflect differences in values, beliefs, and skills and which are abuse, where you have a legal and ethical obligation to intervene. You need to keep in mind that parenting *is* difficult, that there are few resources available, and that the great majority of families *are* trying to do the best they can given their circumstances, beliefs, and values.

WHAT YOU NEED TO KNOW TO WORK WITH FAMILIES

The knowledge and skills that you developed to work with children will serve you well as you work with families. There are additional knowledge and skills that you will need that relate specifically to this part of your work. You will need to:

- [ ] Know how to communicate information to adults.
- [ ] Understand what parenting is like.
- [ ] Understand how relationships are built.
- [ ] Know how to support families in stress.

How to Communicate Information to Adults

Your knowledge of child development influences your relationships with children and serves as a basis for the kind of program you plan for them. You need to

be able to clearly communicate your understanding of this theory in order to enhance parents' understanding of their children and the program.

Clearly communicating specialized information means translating the sometimes puzzling professional terms that you use with your colleagues into words that have meaning to the uninitiated. Simply saying that you provide opportunities for motor development is not as valuable as letting parents know that creative movement, swinging, sliding, trike riding, and climbing all help their child to develop skill, strength, and coordination in the the arms, legs, and torso and that using pegboards, the easel, puzzles, and beads help develop the hands and fingers. Additionally, all of this may not be nearly as meaningful as letting parents know that physical competence contributes to social and academic success.

Both parents and teachers have information that contributes to the child's well-being and that allows them to meet each other on equal ground. Parents bring knowledge and experience of their child as a unique human being, and you bring your theoretical knowledge of children in general. Both types of information are vital if you are to create the best possible educational experience for each child.

You will be comfortable with what you are doing and better able to explain your program choices and rationale when your decisions are based on knowledge of children and curriculum and on clear value choices. As you explain what you do and why, it is important to separate and communicate your *preferences* in teaching and child management from your *knowledge* about what constitutes appropriate, desirable practice in teaching and relating to children. Your clarity about methods and their implications as well as your awareness of alternatives will be communicated to parents. As they observe your approach to curriculum and classroom management and learn why you have made these choices, parents will learn more about development and will have a broader understanding of their choices. For example, you can tell parents that you have chosen not to provide workbook experiences for young children because you know that they learn concepts through real experiences. You might then show parents a sorting activity where children make discriminations similar to a workbook task and share some ways that similar activities (such as sorting and putting away the silverware) might be provided at home.

Learning how to provide families with information meaningfully, respectfully, and usefully is a skill that you will develop with time and experience. Share what you know, and be willing to admit what you may need to find out. Remember that you have much to offer in this area as do family members and that neither of you is infallible. You are the professional in these situations, however, and while you want to be respectful of parents, it is important for you to act on your best professional judgment. If the requests of parents violate what you know to be best in the field of early childhood education, you have a responsibility to explain and maintain appropriate practice.

What Parenting Is Like

Your work with families will be enhanced by your awareness of the many aspects of parenting—the joys, as well as the needs and problems. Being sympathetic is easier when you realize that it is not an easy task. The stresses of parenting can sometimes overshadow its pleasures. You can help parents renew their appreciation for their child and the process of parenting.

The purpose of the family has enlarged from the performance of specific survival functions such as providing food, shelter, clothing, and supervision to ensure children's physical well-being (Fargo and Pickarts, 1971). It now includes the more abstract tasks of providing psychological security and skills in dealing with an increasingly complex and dangerous world. Society's view of family roles has changed over the last several decades. Today we are aware of the importance of the early years, and parents are told that they need specialized skills to aid in their child's development. Some families today also feel a greatly increased pressure to hurry their children into the activities that are supposed to ensure success: lessons in physical skills, early academics, and achieving entrance into the best preschool in order to assure entrance into the best primary schools later.

Methods of child rearing have changed since today's parents were children. Strict discipline versus total permissiveness has given way to a number of different and often contradictory approaches. Learning about these approaches and choosing those that are consistent with personal values and style and the temperament of the child is a complex process. As an accessible professional with knowledge of a range of choices and the implications of those choices, you may find yourself being asked for advice or may feel a strong desire to offer it when you are not asked. We have found that it works better to offer such advice in a tentative fashion (e.g., "You might try bringing a small nutritious snack with you for Johnny to eat as you leave school. All of the children seem to get cranky when they're hungry and it's close to supper").

The very structure of the family has also been changing. Families are more precarious today. Single parents and step-parents have become commonplace, and you can expect that many of the children in your care will come from such families. Newly "blended" families that include a step-parent's children, the children of a parent's new marriage, and related and unrelated aunts, grandparents, and other adults are also common. The process of changing family structure necessarily takes energy and effort and is usually stressful even if positive and wanted. Both parents are often part of today's work force and families in which two parents are working must deal with multiple roles and the resulting time and energy constraints. Moreover there is a dramatic increase in one-parent families (most frequently mothers) who are operating under severe financial constraints (Children's Defense Fund, 1986).

Changes in the nature of child rearing require new skills and responses that many adults are not prepared for and that may be difficult to acquire if they lead stressful lives or if they are struggling to survive financially. They may be forced to rely on social agencies, including schools, to perform many of the roles that were once the responsibility of the extended family. Part of the reason that your job includes working with parents is that a good relationship helps them to feel easier about sharing some of the responsibility for their child with you, and about turning to you and the school for assistance.

How Relationships Are Built

In order to work effectively with families you need to focus on building relationships with adults as well as with children. While this need not be difficult or time consuming, it does require thoughtfulness and attention. Good relationships with families do not develop simply because you have good intentions.

Relationships begin with the attitudes that you hold and express. All people are more trusting and open in an atmosphere of concern, respect, acceptance, and individual attention. The things that you do to build such an atmosphere for families in your program are usually small, easy to overlook, and as simple as the courtesies you extend to colleagues and friends in your private life.

In good relationships individuals feel welcomed. This can be accomplished if you know names, remember to greet individuals daily, and provide space for parents in or near your classroom. Since all relationships are based on sharing and trust, you can begin by learning about family members and telling them about you. Take time regularly to find out what families are interested in, what they do, and what they care about. Help parents to get to know you by sharing this same kind of information about yourself—remember though, it is not appropriate to share your personal problems. Acknowledge events and transitions in the child's life at school and in the family's life at home. Recognize and share a family's joys and sorrows. Be scrupulous about maintaining confidentiality; nothing destroys trust faster than idle gossip and broken confidences.

You will want to convey to parents that you are committed to hearing their concerns and that you will face problems rather than avoid issues or insist on your own solutions. Skills in active listening, giving *I-messages*, and avoiding *roadblocks* will help. Although you may sometimes feel that listening to families' concerns is extra work, remember that what you are doing may ultimately contribute to the relationship and to the child's well-being at home and in school.

How to Support Families in Stress

While it is not your role to be a counselor, you will need to have information and strategies for supporting families in stress.

As a teacher of young children, you may be the first professional to identify problems that may have an impact on children. These may range from things as simple as a change in schedule that is causing a child to have difficulty staying awake to a serious case of child abuse or neglect.

Family Changes   Families often need assistance when there is a change in family structure such as a new baby, death, divorce, or remarriage. You will want to have knowledge of programs such as child guidance and divorce clinics, mental health and family counseling services, and family mediation agencies, as well as resources available at the local public school and church.

As a person who works closely with a family in today's society, it is almost inevitable that you will find yourself being asked to play a supportive role for one or both parents in divorce or child custody conflicts. Such conflicts can be traumatic. Policies and procedures need to be established prior to problems to help parents understand that the welfare of the child is your primary concern. These will also help families to understand that such problems are by no means unique or a sign of parental failure. When a divorce or custody battle does take place, it can be tempting to express a preference for one or another parent. You may have developed a feeling of loyalty if one parent seems to have abandoned or neglected their obligations. Keep in mind that you serve a child better by maintaining neutrality, unless the child appears endangered.

Abuse and Neglect   You have an ethical and, in many states, a legal obligation to report suspected cases of neglect and physical, sexual, or psychological abuse. It is part of your professional responsibility to learn to identify and report child abuse and neglect. The Child Protective Unit of your local Department of Health or Social Services may be able to provide this training and may be the agency through which you will report suspected cases. Such training will include how to distinguish normal childhood bumps and bruises from signs of possible battering or sexual abuse, what behaviors of children and parents may indicate abuse or neglect, and the steps involved in documenting your observations prior to reporting. It is important to remember that problems of abuse and neglect occur in all communities and throughout all strata of society; no school, regardless of clientele, can be considered immune. Stress, one of the greatest causes of abuse and neglect, can occur in any family.

While sexual abuse most often occurs in the context of the family, it is by no means unheard of for a child to be sexually abused by others with whom they have contact such as neighbors, friends, and—in some of the most tragic and publicized cases—their school staff members. Children and families can be given information that will help children to protect themselves from molestation. Schools can take steps to ensure security by having stringent staff screening policies, rigorous sign-in and sign-out procedures that all staff are aware of, by taking special care to secure entrances and playgrounds, and by maintaining low ratios even in the late afternoon hours. Perhaps most important is that families and teachers learn to take seriously children's reports of abuse and that children learn how to report

incidents to caring adults without fear of repercussions for themselves or their loved ones.

You, as a teacher, have an obligation to intervene on behalf of children, whatever the source of the abuse. Regardless of the severity of the problem, it is important that you work with families with sensitivity and respect. You may confer with the family, and attempt to develop mutually acceptable strategies; point parents to resources when they require outside help. If family members are hostile and unwilling to self-report, you must seek outside authority to intervene on behalf of the child.

WHAT YOU DO TO INVOLVE FAMILIES

Family involvement in an early childhood program can range from rare talks only when there is a problem to frequent and regular participation. In ideal situations parents and teachers work closely in a variety of ways. They confer and plan together to meet the developmental needs of the child. Parents participate in classroom activities. They plan and attend parent education programs. They sit on policy-setting groups and contribute to the growth and development of the program through work on facilities, fundraising, and lobbying in the community.

Family involvement begins when you provide parents with information about the kinds of involvement available to them. It is important to find out some things about the family members: what they want and need, their level of interest in the program, their time constraints, and the kinds of activities in which they might enjoy participating.

Sharing Information

You help parents to understand and support what you are trying to do by sharing information with them. It helps them to make contributions to the program and to be better equipped to work with their children at home in activities that support learning when they know what you are doing and why.

The first opportunity to share information with a family will occur when they visit your program to learn about it and to decide if it is the right one for them. Staff members aid parents in their decision making by openly exchanging information. If you participate in this process you must provide an explanation of what is done in the program and why. You will also want to encourage parents to tell you what their child is like and what kind of program they are looking for. During your discussion you can share, in an unbiased way, what you know about other program alternatives in your community. This is especially important if you suspect that what is desired by the family is different from what your program offers. Such an open sharing of information sets the stage for a truly collaborative effort between staff and family members. It also increases the likelihood that the family will become committed to the school and find meaningful, fulfilling ways to become involved in the school community.

Once the family has chosen your program, there are other avenues for continuing and expanding this new relationship. At the beginning of a school year or when there are a number of

new families, you may wish to have an orientation meeting. Such group meetings tend to work best when they combine information sharing with an opportunity for socializing. A particularly good format begins at the end of a school day when families arrive to pick up their children. The meeting will be more successful if you make provisions for child care. Start with a very brief, structured introduction such as a family/staff circle time at which everyone gathers to introduce themselves and their children. If this is followed quickly by a light meal, families and staff can engage in informal mealtime conversation and learn more about each other. After the meal parents and staff can meet for an information sharing time while children participate in familiar activities in their classrooms. During this portion of the meeting you can learn about the interests and concerns of families and let them know more about the program and your expectations of them. The initial visit and a good orientation meeting are useful in setting the climate for teacher-parent interactions and family involvement; however, they are only the beginning of an ongoing process of communication.

Daily information sharing with parents is one of the most important aspects of your work. The basis for your relationship with parents is your knowledge of and commitment to their child. Because of previous experiences with schools and teachers, parents may not feel comfortable in their initial contacts with you. In the beginning, you will need to take the lead and assume the bulk of the responsibility for building the relationship. You can accomplish this by frequent and positive sharing of information about the school's activities and your experiences with and observations of their child. Sharing the small joys and sorrows of the child's life creates a bond between you.

Good daily communication with families requires flexible and creative planning. No one method will be effective for every family, teacher, or program.

As you observe children, you can keep both mental and written notes to share at the end of the day: "Christopher worked really hard in the block area today. He was very persistent and figured out how to make his tower as tall as the shelf. His face shone with delight when he was finally able to make his tower strong enough not to topple." Sharing like this is best face to face, but you can also make a phone call or leave a note.

Keeping in contact with busy working parents involves a special effort. Responsibility for greeting these parents at early arrival or late departure may need to be assigned to one staff member since you may not get to talk to them during your normal work hours. A message center where each family has a mailbox or message pocket helps to make communication easier. In some programs this is also where journals in which teachers and parents share written information about the child are kept.

Families can be informed of the activities of the program by reading a week's plans posted near the sign-in area daily or sent home each week. Bulletin boards, notes, and newsletters offer opportunities to explain aspects of the program in greater detail, to solicit

aid from families, and to provide information about child development and other topics of interest. These techniques are most successful if they are very visible, attractive, *short and to the point*, and easy to read. If reading them is built into some other routine, such as sign-in, they are far more likely to get attention.

Yet another way to communicate to families that they are valued parts of the program is to create a parent corner near the entrance to the school or classroom. This area might have a comfortable adult chair or couch, reading material, coffee and tea, pictures of the children at play, or even a slide/tape presentation about the program. Parents may enjoy talking to one another in this area, or a child and parent might spend a quiet moment there together.

Addressing Special Concerns

Because of the sensitive and personal nature of parenting, it is inevitable that concerns and questions about the child's development and the program will surface. Very predictably, parents have concerns about their child's health and safety in the program, about the care of their child's possessions and clothing, and about the purpose of play and the child's academic progress. Teachers are concerned about similar issues: the child's well-being, use of materials, and developmental progress. Despite a good relationship, addressing these concerns can be worrisome and sometimes threatening to either parent or teacher. It is important that parents feel heard, that their concerns be addressed and their efforts and judgment respected. If you consistently display this kind of sensitivity, it is more likely (though not certain) to be

reciprocated. In order to be prepared, you need to be able to broach and respond to questions and concerns in ways that keep the lines of communication open and without being devastated by negative reactions.

A family's questions and concerns may arise from the nature and philosophy of the program. Young children's programs are very different from other kinds of educational settings. The materials and experiences provided seem to bear little relationship to conventional learning. Parents may wonder why their children play so much, why they're not learning "academic" skills, why they come home so dirty, and why you let them do things that appear dangerous.

The concerns that parents have about play often reflect a lack of understanding of how young children learn. They may relax as you help them to understand that children learn in significantly different ways from adults and that the development of motor and perceptual skills form the base of later, more abstract learning. Since the formal educational experiences of most adults have usually been abstract, they may have lost touch with the learning that goes on in active, hands-on experiences. Remind them of the things that they have learned by doing—cooking, driving a car, bathing a baby, using a computer—and that *doing* is an important way of learning, too. Explain the sequence of development in very concrete terms: "Children first have to learn to tell the difference between more obvious things like blue round beads and square purple ones before they can tell the difference between more subtle things like numbers and letters." This will help adults to see the purpose of the activities that you provide for children. You might also give information about the sequence of skill development (for example in drawing, writing, or skipping) to help parents understand and share your enthusiasm for their child's efforts.

The messes inherent in the sensory development, art, and science curricula can be disturbing to adults. Knowing the purpose of these activities makes it easier for parents to appreciate them. Discomfort may be eased if the activities are known about in advance, if children are sent to school in play clothes, and if you provide smocks to protect clothing from damage.

Many parents will be astonished and alarmed by the physical challenges that children undertake in the school setting. They may never have allowed their children to climb to the top of the jungle gym, or to use functional saws, scissors, or cooking equipment, and they may not understand why you do. Families often cannot provide independent or adventurous physical activities and thus may not be aware of what young children can safely do with close supervision. People vary greatly in their judgment of what is or is not dangerous or foolish. Parents may judge an activity or piece of equipment based on their own experience. It is important to listen thoughtfully to these fears since they reflect genuine concerns. You can let parents and children know that you won't allow or encourage children to attempt activities that are clearly beyond their capacities, but that your situation safely provides opportunities for exploration that contribute to development.

Parent-Teacher Conferences

A conference provides you and parents an opportunity for in-depth and personal dialogue that is not possible in other ways. During conferences, you may explore issues relating to the child at home and at school. This is a time when personal or family problems may become known to you. You can then help parents express and clarify their feelings and values, provide information, and help them develop their skills and resources. Routine conferences support your work and build parent-teacher relationships. If conferences are held rarely or only in the event of a problem, they will be more stressful and less productive.

The goal of your conference is to form an alliance with parents to help the child become competent and confident. This requires acceptance, understanding, and a belief that solutions to problems can be found. When there is a problem, you can use conference time to agree on goals, to develop a plan of action for home and school, and to decide when you will meet again to evaluate what you have done and to begin the process anew.

Planning will help you to spend conference time effectively. You will need to first plan for quiet, undisturbed space and sufficient time. This ensures that the conference can be unpressured and productive. Scheduling ten parent conferences for twenty minutes each on one day is neither an effective nor pleasant way to plan for this important part of your teaching.

You can prepare for the conference by looking over your observations, anecdotal records, photographs, assessments, samples of work, and records on the child. You might write a summary of these to use as a complement to what you show parents. Many teachers complete a checklist to use as a conference guideline.

Parents may be apprehensive if they do not understand the conference purpose. You will want to begin by explaining that you are both there to share information and to get to know one another better. Assure them that you welcome their ideas, concerns, and questions, that the conference is a joint process. As you share your perceptions of the child in school, try to describe what the child *does* rather than saying what he or she *is* ("Matthew usually watches the others use a new piece of equipment before he tries it. He seems to like to have a quiet space and a long period of time," not "Matthew is very slow"). In positive conferences the child's areas of strength are discussed and other areas are looked at in terms of growth and direction for parents and teacher.

It is natural and necessary for parents to be intense, emotional, and partial to their child. Teachers play a different role. They must be less intense and more objective. In approaching conferences assume that parents have good intentions and that they will share as honestly as you do. You may disagree with one another because of your different experiences in life and with the child, but you are ultimately on the same side—the child's.

Family Education

Family education is any planned activity in your program that contributes to the functioning of the family unit. Family education activities can take a variety of forms including such things as how to pack a nutritious lunch, how to select appropriate medical care, and where to find community resources such as recreation programs and an appropriate elementary school for the preschool graduate.

Traditionally, many programs for young children and their families have included parent education activities. Parent education can involve helping parents understand that they have a tremendously important role in their child's development and that they are their child's first and most important teacher. As they come to know and trust you, some parents will seek advice about problematic areas in their relationship with their child. When you find commonly shared areas of concern among parents, you can structure opportunities for them to clarify their values and goals for their children and provide them with information about child

development, early childhood education, and parenting skills that are consistent with their values and goals.

Parent education can take many forms. You may act as a direct provider of education, or you may help find others to serve as resources. Informally, you may model behavior that contributes to the development of children. You can talk with parents about child rearing in the course of your daily contact. Such informal parent education can be very powerful. Formally, newsletters, workshops, parent discussion groups, and parenting courses can be provided. We have worked with programs that have offered many educational services to parents including weekly newsletters with a "Help Your Child Learn at Home" feature; workshops on subjects such as making and choosing toys, preparing children for kindergarten, language and reading, and nutrition; courses on a subject that parents were interested in, such as Parent Effectiveness Training (P.E.T.); and parent-coordinated support groups.

Family education can encompass many topics. The only limits are the imaginations of the families and staff members involved in your program. Obviously, many of the topics will be beyond the skills and expertise you gain in your preparation to become a teacher of young children. However, you need only be aware of the special skills and interests of the families and community members who are and have been involved in your program, and you are likely to have a vast store of resources for a very dynamic family education program. Family members who understand the goals of the program will often be willing to share their special skills and knowledge and even invite their friends to contribute.

Like many things you do in a program for children, a family education program requires some careful planning. Probably the single most important step in planning is to survey the parents to learn what they wish to learn about. It is very disconcerting to invite an expert on child development to speak to a group of parents and present your speaker with a nearly empty house. If you seek the reason for a low turnout for such an event, you will probably discover that the topic was a staff idea and the parents might have been anxious to attend another kind of meeting.

Assessing the interests and needs of parents can be accomplished in a variety of ways. It is quite simple to have small groups of parents get together and brainstorm everything they would like to learn about how to make family life easier. Even if the representation is small, the initial list of topics can be distributed to the rest of the families for additions, comments, and prioritization. In subsequent years, after a list of topics has been generated, you can distribute the list with space for parents to indicate topics they would like to know more about and those in which they have special knowledge and skill that they would be willing to share.

When you have a list of topics relevant to the families, a good idea of some likely presenters, or knowledge of other sources of the desired information (films, videos, printed materials), it is time to attend to the quality of presentation. Printed materials can be made available to families in the special area you provide for them in your facility. Films and videos can be screened in a family lounge or area of the school if you have the appropriate equipment. Presenters of workshops, courses, and lectures need to be scheduled at a time that is convenient for families. If the program makes provisions for child care, a meal, and a comfortable location, participation will be greater. Finally, it is essential that someone from the program communicate to presenters about the skill and knowledge level of the families and check that the type of presentation will be lively and well delivered. We have found that the best learning experiences for adults almost always include an opportunity for active participation as well as the presentation of information.

Classroom Involvement

You play an important role in encouraging and supporting parent participation in your program. Active concerned parents can function as members of the teaching team, providing enriching experiences for the children and working with individual children, or freeing you to do so. They support children's school experience when they join you in the classroom and accompany you as you take children on trips.

When parents function as part of the teaching team, everyone benefits—the parents, the teachers, and the children.

As *parents* participate in the program they:

☐ Have an opportunity to learn about the teacher's way of guiding growth and development.
☐ Gain firsthand insight into the meaning of the curriculum that they may be able to apply at home.
☐ Gain a sense of competence and a feeling of being needed as they contribute to the program.

As parents participate in school *children*:

☐ Have a chance to see their parents in a different role.
☐ Become acquainted with adults who have different skills, feelings, and ways of relating.
☐ Have more individualized attention available to them.
☐ Experience a richer curriculum.

When parents participate *teachers*:

☐ Have a chance to expand their program because of the improved ratios.
☐ Can learn from the knowledge and expertise parents bring and share.
☐ Have an opportunity to observe the relationship between parent and child.
☐ Have a chance to develop a more meaningful relationship with individual parents.
☐ Can contribute to the competence of parents.

Involving parents in the daily program takes some additional planning and can be somewhat complicated, especially at the beginning, but the results are well worth it. You may want to start it in easy stages until it becomes comfortable for both you and the parents.

It is relatively easy to invite parents to visit the program and observe their child in the classroom. With just a little additional planning and work, parents can be invited to come for special occasions such as a birthday party or a child-prepared luncheon. More thought and preparation are required when parents work with you and the children in the educational program. To ensure a successful first experience for the parent, it is wise to have them begin with a simple task such as reading a story to two or three children or assisting as you set up activities. You will need to make an effort to ensure that fathers as well as mothers participate, since they may feel that the early childhood program is not their natural province and may not be certain that they have anything to contribute. In fact, most fathers will be perfectly comfortable doing the activities suggested above, but may require a special invitation from you to feel assured that they are welcome in your classroom. It is important to allow parents to participate in ways that feel comfortable and natural to them and to offer them support in developing skills. As they gain skill, parents can take a more active part in the classroom by planning with you and possibly sharing special abilities and knowledge.

When parents and teachers cooperatively plan activities to do with groups of children, it does a great deal to set the stage for a satisfying classroom experience for everyone involved. An orientation to learn routines and procedures will help parents to feel prepared. A card file containing information about activities and jobs that need to be done is useful for letting parents know what kind of participation is needed and will be welcomed. Posting written statements in each area of the classroom describing the purpose of the activities and how adults can interact with children is another good technique for supporting participation. An opportunity for parents and teachers to meet together and discuss the day's events allows them to share experiences and give each other feedback.

Other Ways to Involve Families

Family members who lack the time or who are uncomfortable participating in the classroom regularly may be involved in a variety of other ways. Some may enjoy making educational materials at home. If people express an interest in this, you might help them get started by organizing a workshop on how to create learning games. Involve them in identifying what specific learning games would help round out the curriculum in their child's classroom. This workshop should include ideas for useful junk to save and materials one must purchase.

As families become involved and committed to the program, they may recognize that you operate on a shoestring budget and that staff members spend a great deal of time doing things that could more efficiently be accomplished if there were more financial resources available. Parents who become aware of the constraints of the program may have special expertise and be willing to spearhead or participate in fundraising events or grant writing projects. Others may be willing to join together with the staff to do renovation, repair, or clean-up projects. Many programs hold special workdays periodically at which families and staff work together on school related projects. Workdays are better attended if parents have had some say in what needs doing and can choose their jobs based on skill and interest. To ensure a successful workday someone must identify the work to be accomplished, gather the required equipment and materials, arrange for childcare and food, and make sure that the jobs can be done in the designated time. If participants can end the workday with a feeling of accomplishment, they are more likely to volunteer for similar projects again.

Parents can also be involved in advisory and policy-making groups. This form of involvement can help your program more accurately reflect the interests and needs of the families you serve. Parents who participate in policy making feel that the program truly belongs to them and their children. They are willing to expend more of their energy and resources because of their greater commitment. The program thus gains valuable parental advocacy and skill.

As a classroom teacher, you may have a little or a lot to do with the planning, evaluation, and decision-making aspects of the program. Regardless of your circumstance, you are the person most likely to know the special interests, concerns, and talents of the parents of the children with whom you work. Parents, children, and the program benefit when you invite families to participate in your classroom or to attend special events and when you direct them to additional avenues for involvement.

FOR FURTHER THOUGHT AND DISCUSSION

1 Share all the ways you recall your own family participating in your early educational experiences. What do you believe the attitudes were regarding the role of the family in school? How did you feel about having your family participate or fail to participate? How do you think they felt about it?

2 Choose an early childhood program you have observed. Share some of your perceptions of the values and attitudes concerning family involvement. What kinds of participation did you observe?

3 What are your feelings regarding the role of families in programs for young children? What understandings and skills do you feel are essential for effectiveness in this area? What do you see as your potential strengths in this area? What additional skills do you feel you will need?

4 What kind of families might you feel most comfortable working with? Are there families you would find it difficult to work with? Talk about some different options for handling these feelings.

PROJECTS

1 Observe an early childhood program for evidence of family involvement. Describe your impressions of the amount and kinds of parent-teacher communication, family education, and parent participation in the classroom and in school decision making. What seems to be the staff and administration's attitudes and values regarding work with families? Do you feel they are committed to a close home-school relationship? Describe what you observed and the impressions you gathered. How does this seem to affect the quality of the program? Of the things that you saw what would you like to be able to implement in your own classroom? What might you wish to change?

2 Observe a situation in which family members and teachers are interacting (an informal drop-off or pick-up, a conference, a school social function, a parent-teacher meeting). Describe your impressions of the nature of the teacher-parent relationships (Open or closed? Formal or informal? Collaborative or antagonistic? Do parents and teachers appear to be peers or does one seem to take a more dominant role?). What kind of information was exchanged about the children and the program? Do you think the relationship was strengthened, weakened or unchanged by the interaction? Describe what you saw and thought, and its implications for you as a teacher.

3 Write an article for a school newsletter that explains an activity commonly found in an early childhood program. Using lay terms, describe how it contributes to the child's development, and give suggestions for ways that this experience can be built on at home. Share it with a parent and a teacher, and get their reactions. Compare their responses and discuss how these might be helpful in similar ventures in the future.

4 Explore your thoughts and feelings about working with families. Do you feel as comfortable working with parents as you do with children? Why or why not? Investigate the

available resources in your community that might help you to feel more comfortable with this aspect of your chosen career, and describe what you discovered.

5 Create an imaginary dialogue between a teacher and a parent concerning one of the following situations or another that you have encountered:
□ The parent is concerned because the child is reluctant to come to school.
□ The parent is uncomfortable with the messy activities that you are providing.
□ The child has been biting other children recently.
□ The parent is resentful of an ex-spouse's failure to cooperate in parenting.

6 Explore your community's resources for training teachers to identify and report child abuse and neglect. Investigate your legal obligation in your state. Find out what agencies handle reporting and training and what the procedures for reporting are. Create a pamphlet for other teachers to tell them what you've learned.

RECOMMENDED READING

Coletta, Anthony J. *Working Together: A Guide to Parent Involvement.* Atlanta, Ga.: Humanics Limited, 1982.

Croft, Doreen J. *Parents and Teachers: Resources for Home, School, and Community.* Belmont, Cal.: Wadsworth, 1979.

Elkind, David *The Hurried Child: Growing Up Too Fast, Too Soon.* Reading, Mass.: Addison-Wesley, 1981.

Galinsky, Ellen. *Between Generations: The Six Stages of Parenthood.* New York: Times Books, 1981.

Galvin, Kathleen M., and Brommel, Bernard J., *Family Communication: Cohesion and Change.* Glenview, Ill.: Scott-Foresman, 1982.

Gordon,Thomas. *Parent Effectiveness Training.* New York: David McKay Co., 1974.

Honig, Alice. *Parent Involvement in Early Childhood Education.* Rev. ed. Washington, D.C.: National Association for the Education of Young Children, 1979.

Lawrence, Gerda, and Hunter, Madeline. *Parent-Teacher Conferencing.* El Segundo, Cal.: Theory Into Practice Publications (TIP), 1978.

Lightfoot, Sarah Lawrence. *Worlds Apart: Relationships Between Families and Schools.* New York: Basic Books, 1978.

Nedler, Shari E., and MacAfee, Oralie. *Working With Parents: Guidelines for Early Childhood and Elementary Teachers.* Belmont, Cal.: Wadsworth, 1979.

Rappoport, Rhona, and Strelitz, Robert and Ziona. *Fathers, Mothers, and Society: Perspectives on Parenting.* New York: Vintage Books, 1980.

Ricci, Isolina. *Mom's House/Dad's House.* New York: Collier Books, 1980.

Stevens, J., and Matthews, M., eds. *Mother/Child, Father/Child Relationships.* Washington, D.C.: National Association for the Education of Young Children, 1979.

Taylor, Katherine. *Parents and Children Learn Together.* 3d. ed. New York: Teachers College Press, 1981.

Wilson, Gary. *Parents and Teachers: Humanistic Educational Techniques to Facilitate Communication Between Parents and Staff of Educational Programs.* Atlanta, Ga.: Humanics Limited, 1974.

Postscript

We hope that this book has helped you to reflect on yourself as a teacher or prospective teacher of young children. If you are a student in a college program, you have probably had opportunities to interact with children from a variety of backgrounds in a number of different settings. Through these experiences you may have learned about your needs and the kinds of situations that suit you best, your strengths in working with children and adults, and the areas in which you need to work harder. You may also have discovered whether you really want to be a teacher of young children.

People concerned with the education and welfare of young children can work in many different ways, and each person has to find the area that best reflects his or her interests, talents and style. Some of our students discover that teaching young children is just right for them. Others have told us apologetically that they have decided not to become teachers, but that they would rather go into preschool administration or a field like social work or psychology where they can work with children individually. Still others have decided that they did not wish to work in early childhood education at all. Even if you decide that teaching is not for you, you may find that knowledge of child development and early education will have positive effects on your family and friends. Moreover, you might find yourself at some time in your life working as an advocate for young children outside of the field. What is most important is that you learn about yourself and make the right personal decision.

Training in early childhood education provides a valuable perspective on child development and experience that can serve in a number of other kinds of careers. In addition to teaching, these may include positions that involve program support and administration (center directors, curriculum specialists, education directors); research and training; and services for children, families, and schools (child psychologists, pediatricians and nurses, dietitians, social workers, parent education specialists, day care licensing workers). Newer professional roles involve advocacy for children's rights and services. Career decisions are not set in concrete and don't have to last forever. As we grow and change, so do our needs for professional fulfillment; there are many kinds of work where we can act upon our commitment to children. Judith Seaver's book, *Careers with Young Children: Making Your Decision* (NAEYC, 1979), provides an excellent resource for exploring alternatives and clarifying individual interests and concerns.

If you have decided that the classroom is for you and you are looking forward to your first teaching position, there are some things you should be aware of. We have found that no training program, no matter how good, can truly prepare you for the real world of teaching. The first year is often the hardest and most stressful, partly because everything is new, but also because beginning teachers tend to have unrealistically high expectations of themselves. Indeed, if you have read this whole book, you may be overwhelmed by what is expected of you. Remember that we wrote what we feel is best for children and focused on the ideal early childhood program. We have no expectation that a first (or even fifth) year teacher can do all of it perfectly. In the first year it is important that you set realistic goals for yourself, that you find your strengths and build from them, and that you acknowledge your mistakes and learn from them. It helps to find a friend you can share your joys and sorrows with, and to pay special attention to your physical health. It is important at this stage to remember that you, like the children you teach, are a person in the process of development. If you apply the same developmental perspective to yourself that you do to them, you may be able to appreciate yourself in terms of how much you have grown and not in terms of what you perceive as failures or shortcomings.

If you are now teaching, we hope that you will take this opportunity to examine your feelings and reactions and consider whether what you are doing is best for you and best for the children. Your growing ability to observe yourself and your awareness of your own temperament and personality will help you become more aware of the best kinds of teaching situations for you and more sensitive to the impact of your behavior on others. Becoming a teacher is the first goal. After several years of classroom experience, you may want to set new objectives for yourself.

"Who am I?" and "Who am I in the lives of children?" are questions that need to be asked over and over again in the career of a teacher. Going back to these questions will help you to reflect on the very basis of what you do and why you do it. The answers will become clearer, deeper, and more meaningful as you gain new awareness and understanding through your experiences with children. We are convinced that the most important characteristic of a good teacher is the ability to *be with* children and not what one does to or for them. This means respecting the child as a person and being attentive to the individual and the relationship.

It is also very important that you learn to use feedback constructively. When people share their responses to you and your work (both positively and negatively), it gives you valuable insight into how they perceive and react to you. Negative feedback need not be construed as criticism, and it is not productive to react to it defensively. Rather, you can use the information to learn about yourself and how to do your job better.

There are three things that we have stressed in this book that we hope you will take with you into teaching: first, that you will be flexible and remain open to new ideas and experiences; second, that you will really listen to the adults and children with whom you work; and finally, that you will weigh new information and make teaching choices in terms of the long-range positive effects on the children. Teaching, like living, is a process of constant growth and change. If you keep this in mind, you will continue to become a more fulfilled person and a better experience for children.

JOURNALS

Child Care Information Exchange. C-44, Redmond, Washington 98073.

Childhood Education. Association for Childhood Education International, 11141 Georgia Ave. #200, Wheaton, Md. 20902.

Daycare and Early Education. Human Sciences Press, 72 Fifth Ave. New York. N.Y. 10011.

Young Children. National Association for the Education of Young Children, 1834 Connecticut Ave. N.W., Washington, D.C. 20009.

PROFESSIONAL ORGANIZATIONS

Association for Childhood Education International (ACEI), 11141 Georgia Ave. #200, Wheaton, Md. 20902.

Children's Defense Fund, 122 C Street. N.W. Washington, D.C. 20001.

National Association for the Education of Young Children (NAEYC), 1834 Connecticut Ave. N.W., Washington, D.C. 20009.

Organization Mondiale pour L' Éducation Prescholaire (OMEP), and the U.S. National Committee for Early Childhood Education, 24000 Lahser Rd., Southfield, Mich. 48034.

References

**CHAPTER 1
The Field
of Early
Childhood
Education**

Aries, Philippe. *Centuries of Childhood.* New York: Vintage Books, 1962.

Auleta, Michael S. *Foundations of Early Childhood Education.* New York: Random House, 1969.

Braun, Samuel J., and Edwards, Esther P. *History and Theory of Early Childhood Education.* Belmont, Cal.: Wadsworth, 1972.

Cartwright, G. Philip; Cartwright, Carol A.; and Ward, Marjorie E. *Educating Special Learners.* Belmont, Cal.: Wadsworth, 1981.

Clarke-Stewart , Alison, *Childcare in the Family: A Review of Research and Some Propositions for Policy.* New York: Academic Press, 1977.

Clegg, Sir Alex. *Revolution in the British Primary Schools.* Washington D.C.: National Education Association, 1971.

Combs, Arthur W., et al. *The Professional Education of Teachers.* 2d ed. Boston: Allyn and Bacon, 1974.

Dewey, John. *Experience and Education.* New York: Collier Books, 1972.

Dittman, Laura L. "Project Head Start Becomes a Long-Distance Runner." *Young Children* 35, (September 1980).

Featherstone, Joseph. *Schools Where Children Learn.* New York: Liveright, 1971.

Frost, Joe L., and Kissinger, Joan B. *The Young Child and the Educative Process.* New York: Holt, Rinehart and Winston, 1976.

Gearheart, Bill R., and Weishahn, Mel W. *The Handicapped Child in the Regular Classroom.* St. Louis: C.V. Mosby Co., 1976.

Hymes, James L. Jr. *Early Childhood Education: An Introduction to the Profession.* 2d ed. Washington, D.C.: National Assocation for the Education of Young Children, 1977.

——————. *Teaching the Child Under Six.* 3d ed. Columbus, O.: Charles E. Merrill, 1981.

Klein, Jenni W. "Making or Breaking It: The Teacher's Role in Model (Curriculum) Implementation." *Young Children* 28 (August 1973).

Lazar, Irving, and Darlington, Richard. *Lasting Effects after Preschool: Summary Report.* Washington, D.C.: U.S. Department of Health and Human Services, Administration of Children, Youth and Families, October 1979.

Maccoby, Eleanor E., and Zellner, Miriam. *Experiments in Primary Education: Aspects of Project Follow-Through.* New York: Harcourt Brace Jovanovich, 1970.

MacDonald, James B. "Introduction." In *A New Look at Progressive Education,* edited by James R. Squire. Washington, D.C.: Association for Supervision and Curriculum Development, 1972.

Montessori, Maria. *Dr. Montessori's Own Handbook.* New York: Schocken Books, 1965.

————. *The Absorbent Mind.* New York: Holt, Rinehart and Winston, 1967.

Osborn, D. Keith. *Early Childhood Education in Historical Perspective.* Athens, Ga.: Education Associates, 1980.

Read, Katherine. *The Nursery School: A Human Relations Laboratory.* 6th ed. Philadelphia: Saunders, 1976.

Reynolds, Maynard C., and Birch, Jack W. *Teaching Exceptional Children in All America's Schools.* Reston, Va.: Council for Exceptional Children, 1977.

Schweinhart, L.J., and Weikart D.P. *Young Children Grow Up: The Effects of the Perry Preschool Program on Youths through Age 15.* Monograph #7. Ypsilanti, Mich.: High/Scope Foundation, 1980.

Seaver, Judith W., et al. *Careers with Young Children: Making Your Decision.* Washington, D.C.: National Assocation for the Education of Young Children, 1979.

Silberman, Charles E. *Crisis in the Classroom.* New York: Random House, 1970.

Spodek, Bernard, *Early Childhood Education.* Englewood Cliffs, N.J.: Prentice-Hall, 1973.

Standing, E.M. *Maria Montessori: Her Life and Work.* Fresno, Cal.: Academy Library Guild, 1959.

Steiner, Gilbert Y. *The Children's Cause.* Washington, D.C.: The Brookings Institute, 1976.

Steinfels, Margaret O. *Who's Minding the Children?* New York: Simon and Schuster, 1973.

Weber, Evelyn. *The Kindergarten: Its Encounter with Educational Thought in America.* New York: Teachers College Press, 1969.

Weber, Lillian. *The English Infant School and Informal Education.* Englewood Cliffs, N.J.: Prentice-Hall, 1971.

Zigler, Edward, and Hunsinger, Susan. "Bringing Up Daycare." *American Psychological Monitor* 7 (March 1977).

——————, and Valentine, Jeanette. *Project Head Start: A Legacy of the War On Poverty.* New York: Free Press, 1979.

CHAPTER 2 The Teacher of Young Children

Ade, W. "Professionalism and Its Implications for the Field of Early Childhood Education." *Young Children* 28 (March 1982).

Buhler, June H.; Roebuck, Flora; and Brookshire, William. "The Relationship Between the Physical Fitness of the Selected Sample of Student Teachers and Their Performances on Flanders Interaction Analysis Categories." In *Physical Health for Educators,* edited by June H. Buhler and David N. Aspy. Denton, Tex: North Texas State University, 1975.

Burks, Jayne, and Rubenstein, Melvin. *Temperament Styles in Adult Interaction.* New York: Brunner/Mazel, 1979.

Buscaglia, Leo. *Love.* Thorofare, N.J.: Charles B. Slack, 1972.

Combs, Arthur W.; Avila, Donald L.; and Purkey, William W. *Helping Relationships.* 2d ed. Boston: Allyn and Bacon, 1978.

Dennison, George. *The Lives of Children.* New York: Vintage Books, 1969.

Jersild, Arthur. *When Teachers Face Themselves.* New York: Teachers College Press, 1955.

Jordan, Daniel C., and Streets, Donald T. "The ANISA Model: A New Basis for Educational Planning." *Young Children* 28 (June 1973).

Katz, Lilian. "Developmental Stages of Preschool Teachers." *The Elementary School Journal* 23:1 (1972).

——————. "Mothering and Teaching—Some Significant Distinctions." In *Current Topics in Early Childhood Education,* vol. 3. Norwood, N.J.: Ablex Publishing Co., 1980.

——————, and Ward, Evangeline. *Ethical Behavior in Early Childhood Education.* Washington, D.C.: National Association for the Education of Young Children, 1978.

——————. *The Nature of Professions: Where is Early Childhood Education?* Paper presented to the ECHO Conference, Bristol Polytechnic, Bristol, England, September 1985.

Keirsey, C., and Bates, M. *Please Understand Me: Character and Temperament Types.* Del Mar, Cal.: Prometheus Memesis Books, 1978.

Kipnis, Kenneth. "Professional Responsibility and the Responsibility of Professions. In *Profits and Professions: Essays in Business and Professional Ethics,* edited by Michael S. Pritchard and Joseph Ellin. Clifton, N.J.: Humana Press, 1978.

Kohl, Herbert. *Growing Minds: On Becoming a Teacher.* New York: Harper and Row, 1984.

Maslow, Abraham. *Toward a Psychology of Being.* 2d ed. New York: Van Nostrand Reinhold, 1968.

McCaulley, M.H., and Natter, F.L. *Psychological Type Differences in Education.* Gainesville, Fla.: Center for Application of Psychological Type (CAPT), 1980.

Neugebauer, Roger. "Staff Selection: Choosing the One from the Many." Child Care Information Exchange (Summer 1978).

Rogers, Carl. *Freedom to Learn.* Columbus, O.: Charles E. Merrill, 1982.

Rosen, J. L. "Personality and First Year Teachers' Relationships with Children." *The School Review.* 76:3 (September 1968).

——————. "Matching Teachers with Children." *The School Review* 80:3 (May 1972).

——————. *Perceptions of the Childhood Self and Teacher-Child Relationships.* Final Report, National Institute of Education. New York: Bank Street College Research Division, August 1975.

Silin, J.G. "Authority as Knowledge: A Problem of Professionalization." *Young Children* 40:3 (March 1985).

Souper, Patrick. *About to Teach.* London and Boston: Routedge, Kegan and Paul, 1976.

Thomas, Alexander, and Chess, Stella. *Temperament and Development.* New York: Brunner/Mazel, 1977.

Trubitt, Anita. *A Study of the Relationship of Temperament of Preschool Childen and Their Teachers.* Unpublished Master's Thesis. Honolulu, Hawaii: University of Hawaii School of Social Work, 1981.

Whitebook, Marcy, et al. "Who's Minding the Child Care Workers? A Look At Staff Burnout." Berkeley, Cal.: Child Care Staff Education Project, 1980.

Williams, Roger J. *You Are Extraordinary.* New York: Pyramid Books, 1971.

**CHAPTER 3
Values and
Ethics in Early
Childhood
Education**

Biber, Barbara. *Challenges Ahead for Early Childhood Education.* Washington, D.C.: National Association for the Education of Young Children, 1969.

Butler, Annie L. "Humanistic Early Childhood Education: A Challenge Now and in the Future." *Viewpoints in Teaching and Learning* 55 (Summer 1979).

Feeney, Stephanie, and Kipnis, Kenneth. "Professional Ethics in Early Childhood Education. *Young Children* 40 (March 1985).

——————; Phelps, Carol; and Stanfield, Doris. "Values Examination: A Crucial Issue in Early Childhood Education." In *Early Childhood Education: It's an Art? It's a Science?,* edited by J.D. Andrews. Washington, D.C.: National Assocation for the Education of Young Children, 1976.

Good, Thomas, and Brophy, Jere. *Looking at Classrooms.* New York: Harper and Row, 1973.

Hedges, William D., and Martinello, Marian L. "What the Schools Might Do: Some Alternatives for Here and Now." In *Feeling, Valuing and the Art of Growing,* edited by Louise M. Berman and Jessie A. Roderick. Washington, D.C.: Association for Supervision and Curriculum Development, 1977.

Jackson, Phillip. *Life in Classrooms.* New York: Holt, Rinehart and Winston, 1968.

Karpius, Dewayne. "Developing Teacher Competencies." In *Developing Teacher Competencies,* edited by James Weigand. Englewood Cliffs, N.J.: Prentice-Hall, 1971.

Katz, Lilian, and Ward, Evangeline. *Ethical Behavior in Early Childhood Education.* Washington, D.C.: National Association for the Education of Young Children, 1978.

Kipnis, Kenneth. "Professional Responsibility and the Responsibility of Professions." In *Profits and Professions: Essays in Business and Professional Ethics,* edited by Michael S. Pritchard and Joseph Ellin. Clifton, N.J.: Humana Press, 1978.

Patterson, Cecil H. "Insights About Persons: Psychological Foundations of Humanistic and Affective Education." In *Feeling, Valuing and the Art of Growing,* edited by Louise M. Berman and Jessie A. Roderick. Washington, D.C.: Association for Supervision and Curriculum Development, 1977.

Pickarts, Evelyn, and Fargo, Jean. *Parent Education: Toward Parental Competence.* New York: Appleton-Century-Crofts, 1971.

Raths, Louis, and Simon, Sidney. *Values and Teaching.* Columbus, O.: Charles E. Merrill, 1966.

Riley, Sue Spayth. *How to Generate Values in Young Children.* Washington, D.C.: National Association for the Education of Young Children, 1984.

Rogers, Carl. *Freedom to Learn.* Columbus, O.: Charles E. Merrill, 1982.

Rokeach, Milton. *Beliefs, Attitudes and Values.* San Francisco: Jossey-Bass, 1967.

Saiwin, Enoch. *Evaluation and the Work of the Teacher.* Belmont, Cal.: Wadsworth, 1969.

**CHAPTER 4
Child
Development**

Athey, Irene. "Contributions of Play to Development." In *Child's Play: Development and Applied,* edited by Thomas Yawkey and Anthony D. Pellegrini. Hillsdale, N.J.: Lawrence Erlbaum Associates, 1984.

Baldwin, A.L. *Theories of Child Development.* New York: John Wiley & Sons, 1967.

Berger, Kathleen S. *The Developing Person.* New York: Worth Publishers, 1980.

Biber, Barbara. "A Learning-Teaching Paradigm Integrating Intellectual and Affective Processes." In *Behavioral Science Frontiers in Education,* edited by Eli M. Bower and William G. Hollister. New York: John Wiley and Sons, 1967.

——————, and Franklin, Margery B. "The Relevance of Developmental and Psychodynamic Concepts to the Education of the Preschool Child." *Journal of the American Academy of Child Psychiatry* 6 (January 1967).

Bloom, Benjamin J. *Stability and Change in Human Characteristics.* New York: John Wiley and Sons, 1964.

Bowlby, John. *Attachment and Loss.* New York: Basic Books, 1969.

Brophy, Jere E. *Child Development and Socialization.* Chicago: Science Research Associates, 1977.

Bruner, Jerome S.; Genova, Paul; and Sylva, Kathy. "The Role of Play in the Problem Solving of Children 3–5 Years Old." In J.S. Bruner et al., *Play and Its Role in Development and Evolution.* New York: Basic Books, 1976.

Caplan, F., and Caplan, T. *The Power of Play.* New York: Anchor Press/Doubleday, 1973.

Combs, Arthur W.; Richards, Anne Cohen; and Richards, Fred. *Perceptual Psychology.* New York: Harper and Row, 1976.

Cooper, Arnold M. "Narcissistic Disorders Within Psychoanalytic Theory." In *Psychiatry Annual Review,* Part V. Washington, D.C.: American Psychiatric Press, 1982.

Cowles, Millie. "Four Views of Learning and Development." *Educational Leadership* 28 (May 1971).

De Vries, Rheta. "Theory in Educational Practice." In *Preschool Education: A Handbook for the Training of Early Childhood Educators,* edited by Ralph W. Colvin and Esther M. Zaffiro. New York: Springer Publishing, 1974.

Donaldson, Margaret C. *Children's Minds.* New York: Norton, 1978.

Elkind, David. *A Sympathetic Understanding of the Child: Birth to Sixteen.* Boston: Allyn and Bacon, 1974.

——————. *Child Development and Education: A Piagetian Perspective.* New York: Oxford University Press, 1976.

——————. *The Hurried Child: Growing Up Too Fast Too Soon.* Reading, Mass.: Addison-Wesley, 1981.

Epstein, Herman T. "Growth Spurts During Brain Development: Implications for Educational Policy and Practice." In *Education and the Brain, the Seventy-Seventh Yearbook of the National Society for the Study of Education,* Part II, edited by Jeanne S. Chall and Allan F. Mirsky. Chicago: The University of Chicago Press, 1978.

Erikson, Erik. *Childhood and Society.* New York: Norton, 1950.

Flavell, John H. *Cognitive Development.* 2d ed. Englewood Cliffs, N.J.: Prentice-Hall, 1985.

Gardner, Howard. *Developmental Psychology.* Boston: Little, Brown and Co., 1978.

Garvey, Catherine. *Play.* Cambridge, Mass.: Harvard University Press, 1977.

Gessell, Arnold, et al. *The First Five Years of Life: A Guide to the Study of the Preschool Child.* New York: Harper and Row, 1940.

Ginsberg, Herbert, and Opper, Sylvia. *Piaget's Theory of Intellectual Development*. Englewood Cliffs, N.J.: Prentice-Hall, 1969.

Hamachek, Don E. *Behavior Dynamics in Teaching, Learning, and Growth*. Boston: Allyn and Bacon, 1975.

Hart, Leslie A. "The Three-Brain Concept and the Classroom." *Phi Delta Kappan* 62 (1981).

Horowitz, Frances D. "The First Two Years of Life: Factors Related to Thriving." In *The Young Child: Reviews of Research,* vol. 3, edited by Shirley G. Moore and Catherine Cooper. Washington, D.C.: National Association for the Education of Young Children, 1982.

Huizinga, Johan. *Homo Ludens: A Study of the Play Element in Culture*. Boston: Beacon Press, 1964.

Hunt, J. McVicker. *Intelligence and Experience*. New York: Ronald Press Co., 1961.

Kagan, Jerome. "Do the First Two Years Matter? A Conversation with Jerome Kagan." *Saturday Review of Education* (April 1973).

—————. *The Nature of the Child*. New York: Basic Books, 1984.

Kaluger, George, and Kaluger, Mereim Fair. *Human Development: The Span of Life*. St. Louis: C.V. Mosby Co., 1974.

Kamii, Constance, and DeVries, Rheta. *Group Games in Early Childhood Education: Implications of Piaget's Theory*. Washington, D.C.: National Association for the Education of Young Children, 1980.

Klaus, Marshall H., and Kennell, John H. *Maternal-Infant Bonding*. St. Louis: C.V. Mosby Co., 1976.

Langer, Jonas. *Theories of Development*. New York: Holt, Rinehart and Winston, 1969.

Languis, Marlin; Sanders, Tobie; and Tibbs, Steven. *Brain and Learning*. Washington, D.C.: National Assocation for the Education of Young Children, 1980.

Lazar, Irving, and Darlington, Richard. *Lasting Effects after Preschool: Summary Report*. Washington D.C.: U.S. Department of Health and Human Services, Administration of Children, Youth and Families, October, 1979.

Levy, Joseph. *Play Behavior*. New York: John Wiley and Sons, 1978.

Lieberman, J. Nina. *Playfulness: Its Relationship to Imagination and Creativity*. New York: Academic Press, 1977.

Lugo, James O., and Hershey, Gerald L. *Human Development*. 3d ed. New York: Macmillan, 1981.

Mahler, Margaret S. *The Psychological Birth of the Human Infant: Symbiosis and Individuation*. New York: Basic Books, 1975.

Maslow, Abraham. *Toward a Psychology of Being*. 2d ed. New York: Van Nostrand Reinhold, 1968.

Ornstein, Robert E. *The Psychology of Consciousness*. San Francisco: W.H. Freeman and Co., 1972.

Papalia, Diane E., and Olds, Sally Wendkos. *A Child's World*. 3d ed. New York: McGraw-Hill, 1982.

Piaget, Jean. *The Origins of Intelligence in Children*. 2d ed. Translated by Margaret Cook. New York: International Universities Press, 1966.

Postman, Neil. *The Disappearance of Childhood*. New York: Delacorte Press, 1982.

Rogers, Carl R. *Freedom to Learn*. Columbus, O.: Charles E. Merrill, 1982.

Rubin, K.H., and Pepler, D.S. *The Play of Children: Current Theory and Research*. Switzerland: S. Karger, 1982.

Smilansky, Sara. *The Effects of Sociodramatic Play on Disadvantaged Preschool Children*. New York: John Wiley and Sons, 1968.

Sutton-Smith, Brian, and Kelly-Byrne, Diana. "The Phenomenon of Bipolarity in Play Theories." In *Child's Play: Development and Applied,* edited by Thomas Yawkey and Anthony D. Pellegrini. Hillsdale, N.J.: Lawrence Erlbaum Associates, 1984.

Thomas, Alexander, and Chess, Stella. *Temperament and Development*. New York: Brunner/Mazel, 1977.

Vygotsky, L.S. *Thought and Language*. Cambridge, Mass.: MIT Press, 1962.

Wadsworth, Barry J. *Processes of Cognitive Development*. 3d ed. New York: Longman, 1984.

Wittrock, M.C., et al. *The Human Brain*. Englewood Cliffs, N.J.: Prentice-Hall, 1977.

**CHAPTER 5
Observation
and Evaluation**

Almy, Millie, and Genishi, Celia. *Ways of Studying Children*. rev. ed. New York: Teachers College Press, 1979.

Bailie, Laura; Bender, Sarah; Jackson, Christine; Watada, Carolyn; and Zane, Joanna. *A Manual to Identify and Serve Children with Specific Learning Disabilities: Ages 3–5*. Honolulu: Department of Education, University of Hawaii, 1980.

Blume, Susan, et al. *Portage Guide to Early Education*. Portage, Wis.: Cooperative Educational Service Agency, 1976.

Boehm, Ann E., and Weinberg, Richard A. *The Classroom Observer: A Guide for Developing Observation Skills*. New York: Teachers College Press, 1977.

Boyer, E. Gil, ed. *Measures of Maturation: An Anthology of Observation Instruments*. Philadelphia: Research for Better Schools, 1973.

Brophy, Jere E., et. al. *Teaching in the Preschool*. New York: Harper and Row, 1975.

Cartwright, C., and Cartwright, P. *Developing Observation Skills*. New York: McGraw-Hill, 1974.

Cohen, Dorothy H., and Stern, Virginia. *Observing and Recording the Behavior of Young Children*. New York: Teachers College Press, 1958.

Lindberg, Lucile, and Swerdlow, Rita. *Early Childhood Education: A Guide for Observation and Participation*. Boston: Allyn and Bacon, 1976.

Medinnus, Gene R. *Child Study and Observation Guide.* New York: John Wiley and Sons, 1976.

Meisels, Samuel, *Developmental Screening in Early Childhood Education.* Washington, D.C.: National Association for the Education of Young Children, 1978.

Nyberg, David. *Tough and Tender Learning.* Palo Alto, Cal.: National Press Books, 1971.

Phinney, Jean S. "Observing Children: Ideas for Teachers." *Young Children* 37 (July 1982).

Read, Katherine, and Patterson, June. *The Nursery School and Kindergarten: Human Relationships and Learning.* 7th ed. New York: Holt, Rinehart and Winston, 1980.

Rowen, Betty. *The Children We See: An Observational Approach to Child Study.* New York: Holt, Rinehart and Winston, 1973.

Sommer, Steve E., and Churton, Margaret. *Screening, Assessment and Educational Programming Preschool Handicapped Children: A Primer.* Ironton, O.: Ironton Lawrence Co., 1978.

Stallings, Jane A. *Learning to Look, A Handbook on Classroom Observations and Teaching Models.* Belmont, Cal.: Wadsworth, 1977.

Szasz, Susanne. *The Unspoken Language of Children.* New York: W.W. Norton and Co., 1978.

**CHAPTER 6
The Child in
School**

Abt Associates. *Final Report of the National Day Care Study: Children At the Center.* Cambridge, Mass.: Contract No. HEW-10507401100., 1979.

Berger, Allen S. "Anxiety in Young Children." *Young Children* 26 (October 1971).

Berk, Laura E. "How Well Do Classroom Practices Reflect Teacher Goals?" *Young Children* 33 (November 1978).

Bowlby, John. *Attachment and Loss.* London: The Hogarth Press and the Institute of Psycho-Analysis, 1973.

Galinsky, Ellen. "School Beginnings: The First Day." Sound filmstrip, Bank Street College of Education, 1971.

——————. "School Beginnings: The First Weeks." Sound filmstrip, Bank Street College of Education, 1971.

Gross, Dorothy W. "On Separation and School Entrance." *Childhood Education* (February 1970).

Harms, Thelma, and Clifford, Richard. *Early Childhood Environment Rating Scale.* New York: Teachers College Press, 1980.

Hirsch, Elisabeth. *Transition Periods: Stumbling Blocks of Education.* New York: Early Childhood Education Council of New York, n.d.

Janis, Marjorie Graham. *A Two Year Old Goes to Nursery School: A Case Study of Separation Reaction.* Washington, D.C.: National Association for the Education of Young Children, 1965.

Kaplan, Louise J. *Oneness and Separation: From Infant to Individual*. New York: Simon and Schuster, 1978.

Katz, Lilian. "Education or Excitement ?" In *Talks with Teachers*, edited by Lilian Katz. Washington, D.C.: National Association for the Education of Young Children, 1977.

Lazar, Irving, and Darlington, Richard. *Lasting Effects After Preschool: Summary Report*. Washington, D.C.: U.S. Department of Health and Human Services, Administrator of Children, Youth and Families, October, 1979.

National Academy of Early Childhood Programs. *Accreditation Criteria & Procedures*. Washington, D.C.: National Association for the Education of Young Children, 1984.

Read, Katherine B., and Patterson, June. *The Nursery School and Kindergarten: Human Relationships and Learning*. 7th ed. New York: Holt, Rinehart and Winston, 1980.

Steinfels, Margaret O. *Who's Minding the Children?* New York: Simon and Schuster, 1973.

Stevens, Joseph H., and Matthews, Marilyn. *Mother/Child, Father/Child Relationships*. Washington D.C.: National Assocation for the Education of Young Children, 1978.

**CHAPTER 7
The Learning
Environment**

CDA National Credentialing Program. *Preschool Caregivers in Center-Based Programs: Child Development Associate Assessment System and Competency Standards*. Washington, D.C.: CDA National Credentialing Program, 1986.

Feeney, Stephanie, and Magarick, Marion. "Choosing Good Toys for Young Children." *Young Children* 40 (November 1984).

Gandini, Leila. "Not Just Anywhere: Making Child Care Centers Into Particular Places." *Beginnings*, (Summer, 1984).

Gordon, Thomas. *T.E.T.: Teacher Effectiveness Training*. New York: David McKay Co., 1974.

Harms, Thelma. "Evaluating Settings for Learning." In *Ideas that Work with Young Children*, edited by Katherine Read Baker. Washington, D.C.: National Association for the Education of Young Children, 1972.

——————, and Clifford, Richard. *Early Childhood Environment Rating Scale*. New York: Teachers College Press, 1980.

Jones, Elizabeth. *Dimensions of Teaching-Learning Environments: Handbook for Teachers*. Pasadena, Cal.: Pacific Oaks, 1977.

Kritchevsky, Sybil, and Prescott, Elizabeth, with Lee Walling. *Physical Space: Planning Environments for Young Children*. Washington, D.C.: National Assocation for the Education of Young Children, 1969.

National Academy of Early Childhood Programs. *Accreditation Criteria & Procedures*. Washington, D.C.: National Association for the Education of Young Children, 1984.

Prescott, Elizabeth. "Approaches to Quality in Early Childhood Programs." *Childhood Education* 50 (1974).

——————. "Is Day Care as Good as a Good Home?" *Young Children* 33 (1978).

Rauscher, Shirley R., and Young, Teresa. *Sexism: Teachers and Young Children*. New York: Early Childhood Education Council of New York City, 1974.

Sommer, Robert. *Tight Spaces*. Englewood Cliffs, N.J.: Prentice-Hall, 1974.

——————. *Personal Space: The Behavioral Basis for Design*. Englewood Cliffs, N.J.: Prentice-Hall, 1969.

Sprung, Barbara. *Non-Sexist Education for Young Children: A Practical Guide*. New York: Citation Press, 1975.

**CHAPTER 8
Relationships
and Classroom
Management**

Bettelheim, Bruno. *Love Is Not Enough*. New York: Free Press, 1950.

Carkhuff, Robert R. *The Art of Helping*. Amherst: Human Resources Development, 1972.

Charles, C.M. *Building Classroom Discipline*. 2d ed. New York: Longman, 1985.

Combs, Arthur W.; Richards, Anne Cohen; and Richards, Fred. *Perceptual Psychology*. New York: Harper and Row, 1976.

Dillon, J.T. *Personal Teaching*. Columbus O.: Charles E. Merrill, 1971.

Dinkmeyer, Don; McKay, Gary; Dinkmeyer, Don Jr. *Systematic Training for Effective Parenting*. Kit with leaders' manual. Circle Pines, Minn.: American Guidance Service, 1980.

Dreikurs, Rudolf. *Psychology in the Classroom*. New York: Harper and Row, 1969.

Elmers, Robert, and Aitchson, Robert. *Effective Parents, Responsible Children*. New York: McGraw-Hill, 1977.

Erikson, Erik H. *Childhood and Society*. New York: Norton, 1963.

Faber, Adele, and Mazlish, Elizabeth. *How to Talk so Kids will Listen and Listen So Kids Will Talk*. New York: Avon Books, 1980.

Fargo, Jean M. *Education for Parenthood in the Community College*. Ph.D. diss., Seattle: University of Washington, 1974.

Gazda, George M. *Human Relations Development*. Boston: Allyn and Bacon, 1975.

Ginott, Haim. *Teacher and Child*. New York: Macmillan, 1972.

Glasser, William. *Schools Without Failure*. New York: Harper and Row, 1961.

Gordon, Thomas. *T. E. T.: Teacher Effectiveness Training*. New York: David McKay Co., 1974.

Hamachek, Don E. *Encounters with the Self*. New York: Holt, Rinehart and Winston, 1971.

Jones, Elizabeth, ed. *Joys and Risks in Teaching Young Children*. Pasadena, Cal.: Pacific Oaks, 1978.

Katz, Lilian. "Condition with Caution: Think Thrice Before Conditioning." *Preschool Education Newsletter* (February 1971).

LaBenne, Wallace D., and Greene, Bert D. *Educational Implications of Self Concept Theory*. Pacific Palisades, Cal.: Goodyear Publishing, 1969.

Maslow, Abraham. *Toward a Psychology of Being*. 2d. ed. New York: Van Nostrand Reinhold, 1968.

Read, Katherine B., and Patterson, June. *The Nursery School: Human Relationships and Learning*. 7th ed. New York: Holt, Rinehart and Winston, 1980.

Rogers, Carl. *Freedom to Learn*. Columbus, O.: Charles E. Merrill, 1982.

Samuels, Shirley C. *Enhancing Self-Concept in Early Childhood*. New York: Human Science Press, 1977.

Yamamoto, Kaoru, ed. *The Child and His Image*. Boston: Houghton Mifflin Co., 1972.

**CHAPTER 9
Curriculum
Development**

Brown, Janet F., ed. *Curriculum Planning for Young Children*. Washington, D.C.: National Association for the Education of Young Children, 1982.

Bruner, Jerome. "The Role of Play in the Problem-solving of Children Three to Five Years Old." In *Play and Its Role in Development and Growth*, edited by Jerome Bruner, Paul Genova, and Kathy Sylva. New York: Basic Books, 1976.

Dittman, Laura L., ed. *Curriculum is What Happens: Planning is the Key*. Washington, D.C.: National Association for the Education of Young Children, 1977.

Hartley, Ruth E. *Understanding Children's Play*. New York: Columbia University Press, 1952.

Jones, Elizabeth. *Dimensions of Teaching-Learning Environments*. Pasadena, Cal.: Pacific Oaks, 1977.

Joyce, Bruce R. *Selecting Learning Experiences: Linking Theory and Practice*. Washington, D.C.: Association for Supervision and Curriculum Development, 1978.

Mager, Robert F. *Preparing Instructional Objectives*. Belmont, Cal.: Fearon Publishers, 1963.

Seefeldt, Carol. *Teaching Young Children*. Englewood Cliffs, N.J.: Prentice-Hall, 1980.

Streets, Donald, and Jordan, Daniel. *Guiding the Process of Becoming: The Anisa Theories of Curriculum and Teaching*. Wilmette, Ill.: World Order, 1973.

Strom, Robert D., ed. *Growing Through Play: Readings for Parents and Teachers*. Monterey, Cal.: Brooks/Cole Publishing Co.,1981.

Spodek, Bernard, ed. *Play: The Child Strives Toward Self-Actualization.* Washington, D.C.: National Association for the Education of Young Children, 1971.

——————. "What Are the Sources of Early Childhood Curriculum?" *Young Children* 25 (October 1970).

Sponseller, Doris, ed. *Play as a Learning Medium.* Washington, D.C.: National Association for the Education of Young Children, 1974.

**CHAPTER 10
The Physical
Development
Curriculum**

Berger, Kathleen S. *The Developing Person.* New York: Worth Publishers, 1980.

Curtis, Sandra R. *The Joy of Movement in Early Childhood.* New York: Teachers College Press, 1982.

Gesell, Arnold, et. al. *The First Five Years of Life: A Guide to the Study of the Preschool Child.* New York: Harper and Row, 1940.

Hendrick, Joanne. *The Whole Child: Early Education for the Eighties.* St. Louis: Times Mirror/Mosby Company, 1984.

Montague, Ashley. *Touching: The Human Significance of the Skin.* New York: Harper and Row, 1972.

Papalia, Diane E., and Olds, Sally Wendkos. *A Child's World: Infancy Through Adolescence.* 3d ed. New York: McGraw-Hill, 1982.

Prudden, Bonnie. *How to Keep Your Child Fit from Birth to Six.* New York: The Dial Press, 1964.

Riggs, Maida L. *Jump to Joy: Helping Children Grow Through Active Play.* Englewood Cliffs, N.J.: Prentice-Hall, 1980.

Rowen, Betty. *Learning Through Movement.* 2d ed. New York: Teachers College Press, 1982.

Sprung, Barbara. *Non-Sexist Education for Young Children: A Practical Guide.* New York: Citation Press, 1975.

Torbert, Marianne. *Follow Me: A Handbook of Movement Activities for Children.* Englewood Cliffs, N.J.: Prentice-Hall, 1980.

**CHAPTER 11
The Creative
Curriculum**

Bland, Jane Cooper. *Art of the Young Child: Understanding and Encouraging Creative Growth in Children Three to Five.* New York: The Museum of Modern Art, 1968.

Chenfeld, Mimi Brodsky. *Creative Activities for Young Children.* New York: Harcourt Brace Jovanovich, 1983.

Cohen, Elaine Pear, and Gainer, Ruth Straus. *Art: Another Language for Learning.* New York: Citation Press, 1976.

Gardner, Howard. *Artful Scribbles: The Significance of Children's Drawings.* New York: Basic Books, 1980.

Greenberg, Marvin. *Your Children Need Music.* Englewood Cliffs, N.J.: Prentice-Hall, 1979.

Haines, B. Joan E.; and Gerber, Linda L. *Leading Young Children to Music*. 2d. ed. Columbus, O.: Charles E. Merrill, 1984.

Jenkins, Peggy Davison. *Art for the Fun of It*. Englewood Cliffs, N.J.: Prentice-Hall, 1980.

Kellogg, Rhoda. *Analyzing Children's Art*. Palo Alto, Cal.: Mayfield Publishing, 1970.

Lasky, Lila, and Mukerji, Rose. *Art: Basic for Young Children*. Washington, D.C.: National Association for the Education of Young Children, 1980.

Lowenfeld, Viktor, and Brittain, W. Lambert. *Creative and Mental Growth*. New York: Macmillan, 1970.

MacDonald, Dorothy T. *Music in Our Lives: The Early Years*. Washington, D.C.: National Assocation for the Education of Young Children, 1979.

Magarick, Marion. *Child Development Associate Module: Creative Movement*. Honolulu, Hi.: Curriculum Research and Development Group, 1975.

Montgomery, Chandler. *What Difference Does Art Make in Young Children's Learning?* New York: Early Childhood Education Council of New York, 1976.

Rockefeller, David Jr. (Chairperson), The Arts, Education and Americans Panel. *Coming to Our Senses: The Significance of the Arts for American Education*. New York: McGraw-Hill, 1977.

Ross, Malcolm. *The Aesthetic Imperative: Relevance and Responsibility in Art Education*. Oxford: Pergamon Press, 1981.

Sullivan, Molly. *Feeling Strong, Feeling Free: Movement Exploration for Young Children*. Washington, D.C.: National Association for the Education of Young Children, 1982.

Smith, Nancy. *Experience and Art: Teaching Children to Paint*. New York: Teachers College Press, 1983.

Trubitt, Anita. "Music." In *Early Childhood Curriculum Modules*, edited by Stephanie Feeney. Honolulu: University of Hawaii, 1977.

Zeitlin, Patty. *A Song Is A Rainbow*. Glenville, Ill.: Scott, Foresman and Co., 1982.

**CHAPTER 12
The Language
and Literacy
Curriculum**

Ashton-Warner, Sylvia. *Teacher*. New York: Simon and Schuster, 1963.

Bissex, Glenda. *Gnys at Wrk: A Child Learns to Write and Read*. Cambridge, Mass.: Harvard University Press, 1980.

Bruner, Jerome. *Child's Talk: Learning to Use Language*. New York: W.W. Norton, 1983.

Bryen, Diane Nelson. *Inquiries into Child Language*. Boston: Allyn and Bacon, 1971.

Cazden, Courtney B., ed. *Language in Early Childhood Education*, rev. ed. Washington, D.C.: National Association for the Education of Young Children, 1981.

————————. "Play with Language and Metalinguistic Awareness." In *Dimensions of Language Experience*, edited by C. B. Winsor. New York: Agathom Publications, 1975.

Chomsky, Carol. "Write Now, Read Later." *Childhood Education* 47 (1971).

Clay, Marie M. *What Did I Write? Beginning Writing Behavior*. Portsmouth, N.H. : Heinemann, 1975.

Cochran-Smith, Marilyn. *The Making of A Reader*. Norwood, N.J.: Ablex, 1984.

Durkin, Dolores. "Is Kindergarten Reading Instruction Really Desirable?" *Ferguson Lectures in Education, 1980: Lecture Symposium of the 1979–1980 Series*. Evanston, Ill.: National College of Education, 1980.

Feeney, Stephanie. "A Learner-Centered Approach to Early Reading Experiences for Young Children." In *Claremont Reading Conference 40th Yearbook*, edited by Malcolm P. Douglas. Claremont, Cal.: Claremont Reading Conference, 1976.

Ferreiro, Emilia, and Tebrosky, Ana. *Literacy Before Schooling*. Translated by Karen G. Castro. Portsmouth, N.H.: Heinemann, 1979.

Genishi, Celia, and Dyson, Anne Haas. *Language Assessment in the Early Years*. Norwood, N.J.: Ablex, 1984.

Gonzales-Mena, Janet. "English as Second Language for Preschool Children." In *Language in Early Childhood*, rev. ed., edited by Courtney B. Cazden. Washington, D.C.: National Association for the Education of Young Children, 1981.

Graves, Donald H. *Writing: Teachers and Children at Work*. Portsmouth, N.H. : Heinemann, 1982.

Harste, Jerome; Woodward, Virginia; and Burke, Carolyn. *Language Stories and Literacy Lessons*. Portsmouth, N.H. : Heinemann, 1984.

Heath, Shirley Brice. *Ways With Words: Language, Life and Work in Communities and Classrooms*. New York: Cambridge University Press, 1983.

Hymes, James L. Jr. *Before the Child Reads*. Evanston, Ill.: Row, Peterson and Co., 1958.

Jacobs, Leland B., ed. *Using Literature with Young Children*. New York: Teachers College Press, 1965.

Liebergott, Jacqueline, et al. *Mainstreaming Preschoolers: Children with Speech and Language Impairments*. HEW publication no. (OHDS) 78-31113. Washington, D.C.: U.S. Department of Health, Education and Welfare, Administration for Children, Youth and Families, Head Start Bureau.

Moskowitz, Arlene B. "The Acquisition of Language." *Scientific American* 5 (November 1979).

Parker, Robert P., and Davis, Francis A., eds. *Developing Literacy: Young Children's Use of Language*. Newark, Del.: International Reading Association, 1983.

Pflaum-Conner, Susanna. *The Development of Language and Reading in Young Children*. 2d ed. Columbus, O.: Charles E. Merrill, 1978.

Read, Charles. "Preschool Children's Knowledge of English Phonology." *Harvard Educational Review* 41:1 (1971).

Schickedanz, Judith A. "Please Read that Story Again! Exploring Relationships Between Story Reading and Learning to Read." *Young Children* 33 (July 1978).

Tough, Joan. *The Development of Meaning.* Boston: Allen and Unwin, 1977.

——————. *Talking and Learning: A Guide to Fostering Communication Skills in Nursery and Infant Schools.* Portsmouth, N.H. : Heinemann, 1977.

Vygotsky, L.S. *Mind in Society: The Development of Higher Psychological Process.* Cambridge, Mass.: Harvard University Press, 1978.

——————. *Thought and Learning.* Cambridge, Mass.: MIT Press, 1962.

Wells, Gordon. *Learning Through Interaction: The Study of Language Development.* New York: Cambridge University Press, 1981.

Wilkinson, Andrew. *The Foundations of Language.* London: Oxford University Press, 1971.

CHAPTER 13
The Inquiry
Curriculum

Camaren, Marjorie. "An Application of a Curriculum Model in Multicultural Education." Paper presented at the SPATE Conference, Adelaide, Australia, 1981.

Carr, Albert. "Science in the Elementary School: A Humanistic Approach." *Educational Perspectives* 10 (1971).

Costa, Arthur. *Basic Teaching Behaviors.* San Anselmo, Cal.: Search Models Unlimited, 1974.

Elkind, David. *Children and Adolescents: Interpretive Essays on Jean Piaget.* 2d ed. New York: Oxford University Press, 1974.

Feeney, Stephanie. *Child Development Associate Module: Social Studies.* Honolulu, Hi.: Curriculum Research and Development Group, 1976.

Flavell, John H. *Cognitive Development.* Englewood Cliffs, N.J.: Prentice-Hall, 1977.

Forman, George, and Kushchner, David S. *The Child's Construction of Knowledge.* Monterey, Cal.: Brooks/Cole Publishing Co., 1977.

Goodwin, Mary T., and Pollen, Gerry. *Creative Food Experiences for Children.* rev. ed. Washington, D.C.: Center for Science in the Public Interest, 1980.

Goya, Mary E. "Identifying and Expanding Science Interests: For Preschool Teachers and Children." Master's project, Dept. of Curriculum and Instruction, University of Hawaii, Honolulu, Hi., 1979.

Harlan, Jean. *Science Experiences for the Early Childhood Years.* 3d ed. Columbus, O.: Charles E. Merrill, 1984.

Herrera, Sharon, and Their, Herbert D. *Beginnings.* Teacher's Guide (SCIS). Chicago: Rand McNally, 1974.

Hill, Mary M. *Nutrition Program News, November-December, 1964.* Washington, D.C.: U.S. Dept. of Agriculture, 1964.

Holt, Bess-Gene. *Science with Young Children*. Washington, D.C.: National Association for the Education of Young Children, 1977.

Kamii, Constance. *Number in Preschool and Kindergarten: Educational Implications of Piaget's Theory*. Washington D.C. National Association for the Education of Young Children, 1982.

Kendall, Frances. *Diversity in the Classroom: A Multi-Cultural Approach to the Education of Young Children*. New York: Teachers College Press, 1983.

Kowataluk, Helen. *Discovering Nutrition*. Peoria, Ill.: Charles A. Bennett, 1980.

Moravcik, Eva. "Good Snacks for Hawaii's Young Children." Master's project, Dept. of Curriculum and Instruction, University of Hawaii, Honolulu, Hi., 1981.

Phelps, Erin. "A Toddler's Two." In *Beginnings* 2:4 (Winter 1985).

Picard, Anthony J. "Mathematics." In *Early Childhood Curriculum Modules*, edited by Stephanie Feeney. Honolulu: University of Hawaii, 1977.

Seefeldt, Carol. *Social Studies for the Preschool-Primary Child*. Columbus, O.: Charles E. Merrill, 1984.

Smith, Robert F. "Early Childhood Science Education—A Piagetian Perspective." *Young Children* (January 1981).

Spodek, Bernard. *Teaching in the Early Years*. 3d ed. Englewood Cliffs, N.J.: Prentice-Hall, 1985.

Vander Zaag, Carla. "A Social Studies Resource Guide for Teacher's of Hawaii's Young Children." Masters project, Dept. of Curriculum and Instruction, University of Hawaii, Honolulu, 1977.

Wanamaker, Nancy, et al. *More Than Graham Crackers*. Washington, D.C.: National Association for the Education of Young Children, 1979.

CHAPTER 14 Children with Special Needs

Allen, K. Eileen. *Mainstreaming in Early Childhood Education*. Albany, N.Y.: Delmar, 1980.

————; Rieke, Jane; Dmitriev, Valentine; and Hayden, Alice H. "Early Warning: Observation as a Tool for Recognizing Potential Handicaps in Young Children." *Young Children* (May 1979).

American Association of Psychiatric Services for Children, Inc. *Developmental Review in the Early and Periodic Screening, Diagnosis and Treatment Program*. Washington, D.C.: U.S. Department of Health, Education, and Welfare, 1977.

American Psychiatric Association. *Diagnostic and Statistical Manual of Mental Disorders* (DSM III). 3d ed. Washington, D.C.: American Psychiatric Association, 1980.

Bailie, Laura; Bender, Sarah; Jackson, Chris; Watada, Carolyn; Zane, Joanna. *A Manual to Identify and Serve Children with Specific Learning Disabilities: Ages 3–5*. Honolulu, Hi.: Department of Education, University of Hawaii, 1980.

Ballard, Joseph. *Public Law 94–142 and Section 504—Understanding What They Are and Are Not*. Reston, Va.: Council of Exceptional Children, 1977.

Braun, Samuel J., and Lasher, Miriam G. *Are You Really Ready to Mainstream? Helping Preschoolers with Learning and Behavior Problems*. Columbus, O.: Charles E. Merrill, 1978.

Cartwright, G. Philip; Cartwright, Carol A.; and Ward, Majorie E. *Educating Special Learners*. Belmont, Cal.: Wadsworth, 1981.

Chamberlain, Harrie R. "Hyperactivity: Still a Maze of Questions." *Journal of Developmental and Behavioral Pediatrics* 3 (September 1980).

Cohen, Shirley; Semmes, Marilyn; and Guralnick, Michael. "Public Law 94–142 and the Education of Preschool Handicapped Children." *Exceptional Children* (January 1979).

Featherstone, Helen. *A Difference in the Family: Life with a Disabled Child*. New York: Basic Books, 1980.

Gearheart, B.R., and Weishahn, M.W. *The Handicapped Child in the Regular Classroom*. St. Louis: C.V. Mosby, 1976.

Jordan, June; Dayden, Alice; Karnes, Merle; and Wood, Mary, eds. *Early Childhood Education for Exceptional Children*. Reston, Va.: Council for Exceptional Children, 1977.

Lipton, Morris A.; Nemeroff, Charles M.; and Mailman, Richard B. "Hyperkinesis and Food Additives." In *Nutrition and the Brain*, edited by R.J. Wurtman and J.J. Wurtman. New York: Raven Press, 1979.

Lundesteen, Sarah W., and Tarrow, Norma B., *Guiding Young Children's Learning*. New York: McGraw-Hill, 1981.

Mainstreaming Preschoolers. Washington, D.C.: U.S. Department of Health, Education, and Welfare, Administration for Children, Youth and Families, Head Start Bureau, 1978.
  a. *Orthopedic Handicaps* (Kieran, S; Conner, F,; Saaz von Hippel, C.; Jones, S.)
  b. *Learning Disabilities* (Hayden, A.; Smith R.; Saaz von Hippel, C.; Baer, S.)
  c. *Visual Impairments* (Alonso, L.; Moor, P.; Raynor, S.; Saaz von Hippel, C.; Baer, S.)
  d. Speech/Language Impairments (Leibergott, J.; Favors, A.; Saaz von Hippel, C; Needleman, H.)
  e. *Hearing Impairments* (La Porta, R.; McGee, D.; Simmons-Martin, A.; Vorce, E.; Saaz von Hippel, C.; Donavan, J.)
  f. *Emotional Handicaps* (Lasher, M.; Mattick, I.; Perkins, F.; Saaz von Hippel, C.; Hailey, L.)
  g. *Mental Retardation* (Lynch, E.; Simms, B.; Saaz von Hippel, C.; Shuchat, J.; Mayer, Colleen A.)

Mayer, Coleen A., *Sunshine Series: Basic Development and Developmental Disabilities*. Alaska: Alaska Special Services Resource Access Project, 1978.

a. *Motor Disabilities (#6)*
b. *Intellectual Disabilities (#7)*
c. *Visual Disabilities (#8)*
d. *Learning Disabilities (#9)*
e. *Hearing Disabilities (#10)*
f. *Language Disabilities (#ll)*
g. *Emotional and Behavioral Disabilities (#12)*
h. *The Handicapped Child in the Normal Class (#13)*

Meisels, Samuel. *Developmental Screening in Early Childhood Education.* Washington, D.C.: National Association for the Education of Young Children, 1978.

Murray, Michael E. "Behavioral Management of the Hyperactive Child." *Journal of Developmental and Behavioral Pediatrics* 3 (September 1980).

Neisworth, John T.; Willoughby-Herb, Sara J.; Bagnato, Stephen J.; Cartwright, Carol A.; and Laub, Karen W. *Individualized Education for Preschool Exceptional Children.* Germantown, Md.: Aspen Systems Corp., 1980.

Piazza, Robert, and Rothman, Roz. *Preschool Education for the Handicapped.* Guilford, Conn.: Special Learning Corporation, 1979.

Raman, S.P., and Jordan, Daniel C. *Minimal Brain Dysfunction Syndrome: An ANISA Perspective on Its Treatment and the Use of Stimulant Drugs.* Escondido, Cal.: ANISA Publications, 1979.

Research for Better Schools. *Clarification of P.L. 94–142 for The Classroom Teacher.* Philadelphia: Research for Better Schools, Inc., 1978.

Reynolds, Maynard C., and Birch, Jack W. *Teaching Exceptional Children in All America's Schools.* Reston, Va: Council for Exceptional Children, 1977.

Satterfield, James H.; Schell, Anne M.; and Barb, Susan D. "Potential Risk of Prolonged Administration of Stimulant Medication for Hyperactive Children." *Journal of Developmental and Behavioral Pediatrics* 3 (September 1980).

Sitko, Merrill C.; Fink, Albert H.; and Gillespie, Patricia H. "Utilizing Systematic Observation for Decision Making in School Psychology." *School Psychology Monographs,* 1977.

Smith, Sally L. *No Easy Answers.* Cambridge, Mass.: Winthrop, 1979.

Souweine, Judith; Crimmins, Sheila; and Mazel, Carolyn. *Mainstreaming: Ideas for Teaching Young Children.* Washington, D.C.: National Association for the Education of Young Children, 1981.

**CHAPTER 15
Families and
Teachers
Together**

Adair, Thelma, and Eckstein, Esther. *Parents and the Day Care Center.* New York: Federation of Protestant Welfare Agencies, Inc., 1969.

Bromberg, Susan. "A Beginning Teacher Works With Parents." *Young Children* 24 (December 1968).

Coletta, Anthony. *Working Together: A Guide to Parental Involvement.* Atlanta, Ga.: Humanics Limited, 1977.

Children's Defense Fund. *A Children's Defense Budget.* Washington, D.C.: Children's Defense Fund, 1986.

Elkind, David. *The Hurried Child: Growing Up Too Fast, Too Soon.* Reading, Mass.: Addison-Wesley, 1981.

Galinsky, Ellen. *Between Generations: The Six Stages of Parenthood.* New York: Times Books, 1981.

Hetznecker, William; Arnold, L. Eugene; and Phillipps, Arlene. "Teachers, Principals, and Parents: Guidance by Educators." In *Helping Parents Help Their Children*, edited by L. Eugene Arnold. New York: Bruner/Mazel, 1980.

Honig, Alice. *Parent Involvement in Early Childhood Education.* rev. ed. Washington, D.C.: National Association for the Education of Young Children, 1979.

Katz, Lilian. "Mother and Teaching—Some Significant Distinctions." In *Current Topics in Early Childhood Education*, vol. 3, edited by Lilian Katz. Norwood N.J.: Ablex Publishing Corporation, 1980.

Lawrence, Gerda, and Hunter, Madeline. *Parent-Teacher Conferencing.* El Segunda, Cal. : Theory Into Practice Publications (TIP), 1978.

Lightfoot, Sarah Lawrence. *Worlds Apart: Relationships Between Families and Schools.* New York: Basic Books, 1978.

Nedler, Shari. "Working with Parents on the Run." *Childhood Education* (January 1977).

Pickarts, Evelyn, and Fargo, Jean. *Parent Education: Toward Parental Competence.* New York: Appleton-Century-Crofts, 1971.

Rappoport, Rhona, and Strelitz, Robert and Ziona. *Fathers, Mothers and Society*: Perspectives on Parenting. New York: Vintage Books, 1980.

Ricci, Isolina. *Mom's House/Dad's House.* New York: Collier Books, 1980.

Simmons-Martin, Audrey. "Facilitating Parent-Child Interactions through the Education of Parents." *Journal of Research and Development in Education* (Winter 1975).

Stevens, J., and Matthews M., eds. *Mother/Child, Father/Child Relationships.* Washington, D.C.: National Association for the Education of Young Children, 1979.

——————, and King, Edith. *Administering Early Childhood Programs.* Boston: Little, Brown and Co., 1976.

Wilson, Gary. *Parents and Teachers: Humanistic Education Techniques to Facilitate Communication Between Parents and Staff of Educational Programs.* Atlanta, Ga.: Humanics Limited, 1974.

Name Index

Subject Index